THEATRE

PRODUCING THEATRE

A Comprehensive Legal and Business Guide

By Donald C. Farber

Third Revised Edition

LIMELIGHT EDITIONS

Limelight Editions
512 Newark Pompton Turnpike
Pompton Plains, New Jersey 07444

Copyright © 1981, 1997, 2006 by Donald C. Farber

Originally published in 1981 by Drama Book Publishers
Third revised edition published in 2006 by Limelight Editions

Printed in the United States of America

Library of Congress Cataloging-in-Publication Data

Farber, Donald C.
     Producing theatre.
     1. Theater---Production and direction---Law and legislation---United States.
     2. Theater---United States---Production and direction. I. Title
KF4296.F37 1987
343.73'078792   86-27312
                                                            CIP

ISBN 0-87910-317-5

www.limelighteditions.com

For My Dear Grandchildren,
Miranda and Justin,
with love, affection, and thanks for
making me the monkey in the middle
about 96% of the time
and
for making sure that I was Marco,
also about 96% of the time,
when playing Marco Polo.

It sure was good exercise and it helped
to take my mind off the writing.

Contents

Acknowledgments

THIS BOOK IS DEDICATED to my dear grandchildren, Miranda and Justin, but not only by me. My darling Annie joins me in the dedication, just as she has joined me in almost everything I do. I wrote the book with all her support and love. So, when it comes to thanking people, I thank Annie first. She has been such an important part of my personal and professional life that there is really no way to express my appreciation, love, and devotion.

My dear daughter, Pat, deserves special praise. She is without doubt not only the best daughter around, she is also the best fourth grade teacher in the City. Don't ask me, just ask the mothers and the kids. Her classes are filled with students that love her and love being in school.

My son, Seth, writes books too. In fact he is a genuine "author" and a much better writer than I am. I thank him for his unbelievable knowledge, his perseverance and his remarkable talent.

Thanks to my reliable assistant, Lillian Gallardo, who always finds those lost papers on my desk that I wrongfully accuse her of losing in the first place.

Justin and Miranda, my grand kids have been an inspiration and when Lillian decides to take a vacation, whether she needs it or not, they both have helped with the office chores. I appreciate that Neftali Martinez, the father of Justin and Miranda, is always there for them and Pat's husband, Sal Russo, has been a great help in so many ways for which I thank him.

Peter A. Cross who works with me at Jacobs Medinger and Finnegan LLP has been a tremendous help with everything that happens with the Entertainment Department at the firm, and he is not only a superb lawyer but a good friend for which I thank him. The guys in the mailroom at the firm, Nigel Rafferty, Roberto Martinez, Donald Culhane and Jonathan Rafferty deserve my special thanks and appreciation for all of their most helpful support in so many ways, and for always smiling when I go sailing on by their domain.

Preface

I have this problem. It plagued me when I just rewrote my first book From Option to Opening for a fifth edition and I find in working on this it's even plaguing me here. When I started in this business, Off-Broadway was just getting started to become a force that must be recognized and Broadway had established a good body of precedents to rely on. So writing in a simple fashion about "The Business" was easier because life was simple and the business was more "simple."

So here's the problem, I can't dumb down! The business is no longer that simple for me and I am no longer that unsophisticated. Sure, I know enough to know what I don't know in the business, but explaining some of the "show biz" changes just isn't easy.

I will give you just one example. The concept of a First-Class Production has been changing, is still changing and the very future existence of the actor's union, Actors' Equity Association, Inc. is threatened by this changing concept. That's pretty heavy stuff. This is covered in "Chapter Four First-Class Productions" but don't look for a clearly defined definition of First-Class Productions. As explained there, the term always was a bit of a muddle, but at least we knew what it meant, most of the time.

Now it may not even be pertinent to define a First-Class Production except we have to continue to act like it still has the same meaning since there are so many other things are related to the concept. For example, the Approved Production Contract of the Dramatists Guild Inc., negotiated with the League of American Theatres applies to what we all know to be a First-Class Production (with a capital "F," a capital "C," and a capital "P"). Everything else is a different contract that I label as other than First-Class, like an Off-Broadway option, a regional option, etc. If we don't at least act like the term First-Class Production has the same meaning, or a meaning we can define, we really don't know what we are doing. So for now we just pretend it means what it used to mean.

The previous revised edition of this book took care of the Limited Liability Law that was an important improvement in organizing an entity to produce a play. The National Securities Market Improvements Act of 1996, which took jurisdiction away from the states in securities offerings, if done in a certain fashion, at least clarified how to satisfy the securities laws in a fashion that was understandable and doable is explained in this revision.

All editions up to now have attempted to digest the union contracts necessary to produce a play on Broadway. I realize now that is pretty silly, since they are changing constantly, being renegotiated and the changes becoming effective at different times. It makes sense to do this with the 10 Volumes of Entertainment Industry Contracts that I write and edit for Lexis/Nexis because the volumes are updated three times a year. But this book is a "bound" book and by time it goes to press some of the contracts will already be obsolete. So when you get to that spot in the book, you will find a description of what each union does and how to communicate with that Union to get the then current contract you need. You can expect that everything costs more now than it did when the previous edition of this book was published.

But in one way the legal side of theatre has not changed at all. I have always complained that many lawyers find words more important than people. And, in fact, I continue to see attorneys argue and win points by using language that enhances the positions of their clients at the cost of ruining their clients' plays. The reason for a contract, the reason for the words, is to further a cause, not to destroy it.

It's true that there are other businesses where ego, personal relationships, paranoia, unbelievable insecurities, and severe hardships are built into the job, but these are especially inherent in the theatre. We should accept that and should acknowledge it in our dealings. We have to treat different people in different ways in order to have a continuing, successful relationship with them. We should not make a deal good for one party unless it's good for both. I don't know how you can take advantage of a "Star" in the contract and prevent the unhappy "Star" from singing flat for you every night—that is, if he or she shows up to perform at all.

I do hope that this book helps you understand the business of "Show Biz." It's fun and it's rewarding, but never ever forget the fact that it is a business. It's a team operation in which all parties make their contribution. But remember that it starts with the investors, for without them, there is no show. Treat them right. I love to quote that legendary stand-up comedian, Joe E. Lewis, who said, "What good's happiness; it can't buy money." Break a leg and enjoy the trip!

PRODUCING THEATRE

CHAPTER 1

Obtaining a Property

A N ORIGINAL WORK OF AUTHORSHIP, regardless of when it was created, is protected either by common law or by statutory copyright unless the work has fallen into the public domain. Copyright protection generally means that no one may use the work in any manner whatsoever without first securing the permission of the copyright owner or the person who acquired ownership of those rights through purchase, assignment, inheritance, or otherwise. Failure to acquire permission can result in a lawsuit to collect the damages caused by the infringement, and can also give rise to an injunction to stop the unauthorized use. In order to avoid potential liability, and also to be fair to the owner of the work, a person interested in producing a copyrighted play in any manner—whether it be a Broadway production, an amateur production with free admission, or anything in between—should proceed first to acquire the performance rights. In so doing, the prospective producer must, among other things, determine if the rights are available and, if so, at what price and upon what conditions.

Finding the Owner of the Property

In determining if the rights are available, the producer must find the person who has authority to deal with the property. If the author is alive, this can be done simply by contacting the author directly or by contacting his attorney or other representative. The names, addresses, and phone numbers of these persons can be obtained from either the Dramatists Guild, if the author has had a play previously produced; the publisher of the play or music; the Writers Guild; or the Register of Copyrights in Washington, D.C.

If the play is an original play that has never been produced, a copyright search may be unnecessary, but if it is a play based on a film, or other basic work and has been around for awhile, a copyright search may be necessary in any event. There may have been multiple owners and the copyright search is one of the better ways to ascertain ownership of record.

If the play was previously produced in New York and was relatively successful, chances are good that one of the play-licensing companies has the work in its catalogue (i.e., Music Theatre International, Samuel French, Inc., Dramatist's Play Service, Tams Witmark Music Library, or the Rodgers and Hammerstein Library). In this instance, a producer could contact the appropriate company rather than the author, his agent, or attorney.

You should be cautious in dealing with a play-licensing company. They deal mostly in stock and amateur rights and very often do not control the First-Class Performance rights. This may not prevent them from suggesting that they control the first-class rights, when they don't, and then going to the owner of those rights to get the rights to deal with you. This may be expeditious in some cases, that is, you may find it easier to deal with a licensing agent than with several estates, if the authors are dead, or with several difficult author's representatives if they are alive. But sometimes you may end up better off going to the source for these rights.

In all of the above cases, the process of finding who owns or controls the rights is usually quite easy; however, when the author is either deceased, foreign, or deceased and foreign, complications can be encountered.

A deceased author's works are most often controlled by his estate through a literary executor who may be the author's spouse, child, or other relative. The literary executor could also be the author's attorney, agent, or bank if the works are held in trust. Tracking down the right person can be very time consuming, especially if the author has been dead for many years. The spouse may have died also, transferring the work to someone else; children may have married or remarried and taken different surnames; the trust may have terminated—the difficulties in tracing the rights owner(s) are too numerous to mention. If the deceased author's play was previously produced, however, there is the possibility that a licensing company will be handling the rights on behalf of the estate, thus simplifying the procedure.

A foreign author is, in most instances represented by a foreign agent, and sometimes the agent has a United States representative. The problems of distance and language differences oftentimes present obstacles in determining the identity of the person who controls the rights. At the very least, trying to contact the proper person in a foreign country will usually require more time.

Needless to say, if an author is both foreign and deceased, it's likely that nothing short of perseverance and steadfastness of purpose will bring forth the identity of the owner of the work. And even then there can be little assurance that the person found is indeed the true owner of the desired rights. For this reason (as well as others that will be discussed later in Chapter 2), the producer's representative should always insist that the contract for the rights to the play include language to the effect that the person granting the rights (a) warrants and represents that he is the owner of the copyright in the work, and (b) that he has full right and authority to grant the rights he is granting.

In addition to the problems sometimes encountered in finding the owner of the needed rights, the acquisition of performing rights in music and lyrics presents yet another obstacle. The person to contact in order to acquire these rights depends primarily on whether the producer needs "grand" or "small" performing rights, and the determination to be made as to which of these rights is needed in a given situation depends on a number of intertwining factors.

Grand rights are those needed to perform the music in a dramatic fashion, while only small performing rights are required for nondramatic performances. The determination of what is dramatic and what is nondramatic is usually the essence of the problem, and in attempting a definition it becomes apparent that although the extremes are clear, the dividing line is not. If there exists a story connecting the songs together, the performance is considered a musical play and dramatic, thus requiring grand rights. If there is no story but just improvised patter connecting the songs, the performance may be more like a nondramatic nightclub act, requiring only small rights. But the kind of dialogue between songs is not the only basis on which to decide if a story line exists. Sets, costumes, and props could, with the music and lyrics create a dramatic sequence conveying a story, especially if one or all of those elements are similar to the sets, costumes, and props used in a play from which the songs were originally performed. Thus, although television, radio, nightclub, and concert performances of songs usually require only small performing rights, if a story is conveyed through any of the elements of dialogue, sets, costumes, and props, grand rights may be required. In certain instances grand rights are necessary if all the songs from a musical play are used in concert in the same sequence in which they were originally performed, even if none of the above elements are present. There are no definite rules that apply in order to determine whether a story is being told or not. However, if a producer has any question of which rights to acquire, it's always safer to get the grand rights, if possible, to avoid any lawsuits or injunctions for copyright infringement.

If the producer receives assurances from the apparent owner of the rights that the owner controls those rights that the producer needs, without specifying whether those rights are grand or small, the producer needing grand rights may be lulled into a false sense of security. The producer may be made to believe either that the owner has the grand rights when in fact he controls just the small rights, or that the grand rights are not needed for the production, when in fact they are. Therefore, the producer should always try to have the person or company granting the small rights give him a warranty and indemnity on any losses he may sustain due to their granting the rights, in the event the grand rights are in fact required. The indemnity should not be limited to the amount of money paid by the producer to the grantor of the rights for the use of the music. The amounts paid may be so small as to be of little value to the producer in the event of a lawsuit for infringement. It's the producer's obligation to make certain he or she has in fact acquired the grand rights if they are needed.

Small performing rights are usually licensed by either one of three major companies: ASCAP, BMI, or SESAC. Payment of either a designated fee per song or a blanket payment covering all the songs in the company's catalogue will authorize the use of the music. Although grand rights are safer to have, they are usually more expensive and sometimes more difficult to acquire than small performing rights.

The composer and lyricist of the songs will usually hold the grand rights to their compositions, but there are times when the music publishing company will be the owner. Songs written for the movies is another example of such ownership. These songs are usually considered works for hire (i.e., the film companies paid the composers and lyricists as employees to write the songs), and under the copyright law, the employer enjoys complete ownership of the works. Since many of the major film companies have publishing companies as subsidiaries, a producer wishing to acquire the grand rights to such songs would have to contact either the film company or the music publishers rather than the composers and lyricists.

Another example of complete ownership of a song by a publishing company is the situation where a young, unknown writer will sign an exclusive songwriter's contract with a publishing company that gives the writer a meaningful advance payment against future royalties. In exchange, the company owns all of the writer's musical output for the duration of the contract.

In any event, whomever the owner may be, the cost for the grand rights for the music and lyrics will vary, as discussed later in this book.

It should be noted that the procedure of separately acquiring the grand performing rights to songs is only necessary when a producer intends to present on stage, and in a dramatic fashion, songs that were never part of a play, that were part of a play but did not merge with the play when presented, or that did merge with the play but have been released by permission. The rights to the book, music, and lyrics of a musical play—either old or new—are usually acquired simultaneously.

Determining How and Where to Present the Property

Before obtaining the property—in fact, even before determining who the owner of the rights is—the producer should have a clear idea of how and where he or she intends to produce the play (i.e., Broadway, Off- Broadway, stock, a First-Class Production or second-class production tour, regional or amateur theatre). This will be one of the factors determining whether the producer will acquire an exclusive option to produce the play, which should include the right to earn certain production rights and subsidiary rights income, or merely a nonexclusive license to present the play for a specified number of performances. In most cases, stock, second-class tours, and all amateur theatres acquire only a simple license. Broadway, Off-Broadway, and pre-Broadway tours, First-Class Production tours, and some regional theatres will usually get options with the amount of additional and subsidiary rights varying greatly (this will be discussed in more detail in the next chapter).

The reason for granting an option rather than a license is based in part on the potential contribution the production will make to the play. If a producer intends to mount a First-Class Production to open on Broadway, the play will receive a great deal of exposure both by the number of people attending and the press coverage. This increases the future subsidiary market for the play in the stock, touring, and amateur circuit; and, in addition, can be the catalyst for the making of a movie, television series or miniseries, and cast album. If the play is produced Off Broadway, a future market is also created to a somewhat lesser degree since the play's exposure may be less.

The contribution made by the production to the value of the subsidiary uses would not be possible without the large contribution of money made by investors to produce the play. Since investors generally want to see their investment returned, they have learned to expect that the production company producing the play will participate in future profits derived from sales of the play to subsidiary markets. The investors' reason for this is simple: If they and the producer took an unknown property and made it into a successful play, which in turn caused it to make even more money by subsidiary uses, they should share in the author's receipts from those other sources. This advantage is achieved by the producer entering into an option agreement with the author, who will be willing to give up a share of his future earnings from the play since he knows that his play would have little future without a successful commercial production.

Generally, the more remote the production is from a First-Class Production, the less the author will be inclined to share the future earnings, since the chance of that production being the cause of future earnings becomes proportionately less. There are, of course, exceptions to this general rule for other than First-Class Productions, which are performed in major theatres in major cities in the United States; however, Broadway and other First-Class Productions still reign supreme.

It should be added here that a simple license is almost always granted to a producer provided he agrees to pay the license fee. A license, however, may not be available if an agreement exists granting the exclusive production rights to another. This usually occurs when a producer holds the exclusive option to present the play, or when a play has been produced while under an option agreement, whereby the producer acquires additional exclusive rights to continue to produce the play. There are occasions when a producer who holds these exclusive rights will release them for use by another producer for a stock or amateur presentation, provided that such a production will not be within a competitive radius of one of the former's productions of the play.

In contrast to the often ready availability of a license, an option may sometimes be impossible to acquire even if the property is available and even if the producer is willing to pay an exorbitant price. The reason for this is that an author is sometimes more interested in having his or her work produced, directed, and acted by certain persons at certain times. If these persons are not interested or available at the right time, the author may lose interest and the play becomes unavailable. This situation will often be found with the estate of a famous deceased author, where the trustees or executors of the estate sometimes become overzealous in protecting the integrity of the author's works.

Methods of Acquiring Rights to a Property

A person wishing to produce a play can acquire the rights by one of several methods discussed below.

Produce a Play in the Public Domain

As mentioned earlier, all original works of authorship are protected either by common law or statutory copyright unless the work has fallen into the public domain. A work in the public domain is available to be used in any manner imaginable without the need to acquire or pay for rights. In order to understand how a work gets into the public domain, a basic understanding of the copyright law (both old and new) is necessary.

Under the old copyright law, prior to 1978, once a play was written it automatically enjoyed the protection of a common law copyright. If anyone misappropriates the work, the author can sue the wrongdoer in a court of law. This common law copyright can exist forever, provided the author does not "publish" his or her creation by distributing it to the general public. If such publication occurs, in order to have statutory copyright protection the author must comply with the provisions of the copyright law, providing that a "copyright notice" be prominently displayed on the work—i.e., (or copyright) 1977 John Doe. Failure to affix this notice upon publication will usually cause the work to fall into the public domain. There are some rare exceptions to this rule which are written into the copyright law. For example, an inadvertent failure to affix the notice may not be fatal in certain instances.

Once the work was published with the copyright notice affixed, the common law copyright terminated and the work was then protected by statutory copyright under the old federal copyright law. Although the common law copyright was perpetual, the statutory right under the old law granted protection for only a certain number of years. Prior to January 1, 1978, the copyright term was twenty-eight years, with the opportunity of renewing the protection for an additional period of twenty-eight years, thereby bringing the total to fifty-six years. Since under the old law the federal copyright became activated when the work was published with a notice of copyright, the term of fifty-six years is measured from the date of publication. After the period of fifty-six years, the work falls into the public domain. Furthermore, if the copyright was not renewed before the first twenty-eight-year term expired, the work would similarly become part of the public domain.

The new copyright law—effective January 1, 1978, for works created on or after that date—changed the term for the duration of copyright to the life of the author plus fifty years with no renewal term. The term begins from the date the work was created (if on or after January 1, 1978) and is not therefore measured from the publication date as under the old law. Furthermore, there is no longer any common law copyright since the new federal law preempted the area by providing statutory copyright protection upon creation of the work. Consequently, works created on or after January 1, 1978, no longer have a perpetual common law copyright until first publication. As under the old law, failure to publish with a copyright notice affixed will invalidate the copyright except under certain specific circumstances.

Although it may appear that determining if a work is in the public domain is simply a matter of adding fifty-six to the date of publication for a work created prior to 1978, such is not the case. The new copyright law provides many exceptions to the general rules mentioned above, and only a careful reading by a person familiar with the law will give an accurate answer. One such example of where the general rules do not apply (and where a producer intending to present a play in the public domain should proceed with caution) is with works whose renewal term (second twenty-eight years) was in existence in 1962, when Congress began to write the new law. Since Congress quickly realized it was going to take a considerable amount of time to revise the old law—and that it would be unfair to penalize authors whose copyrights would expire by the time the new law became effective, thus depriving them of the benefits of its provisions—Congress enacted legislation beginning in 1962 that extended the copyright of those works for a period of two years. Similar enactments (extending the copyright for one- or two-year periods) were made eight times more during the course of the revisions, extending those copyrights up until the date of effectiveness of the new law, January 1, 1978, which again extended all copyrights then in their renewal term to seventy-five years from the date the original copyright was secured. The effect of all these extensions is that works copyrighted anytime after September 18, 1906, whose copyright was duly renewed, now enjoy copyright protection for seventy-five years. Therefore, a less than fully informed person attempting to determine whether such work first published in late 1906 was in the public domain would add fifty-six to 1906, come up with 1962 as the last year of copyright protection, and incorrectly conclude that the work would be in the public domain and thus free to use.

The copyright office, for a nominal fee, will make a copyright search to determine if and when a work in question was copyrighted and if and when the renewal registration was filed. The office will not, however, render a legal opinion as to whether a work has fallen into the public domain.

Although great care must be taken in determining if a work is actually in the public domain, a producer can save a great deal of money by producing such a play. There are no royalties to be paid, and no negotiations for an option. One of the drawbacks is that there is also no exclusivity. Anyone else can produce the same play in the theatre next door, and the producer will find himself in competition with the play he is producing. The chances of this happening, however, are somewhat remote, since the other producer would find himself similarly situated. Another drawback is that the producer and his investors will receive no income from the distribution of the subsidiary rights, since the work no longer enjoys the protection of a copyright, neither the author (if he is still alive) nor his estate have any rights to distribute. The work is free to be used by anyone anywhere in any media without charge.

Commission an Adaptation of a Public Domain Work

The work in the public domain that attracts a producer's interest need not be restricted to a play. A novel, short story, or epic poem, for example, can be adapted into a stage play. Although the underlying work (i.e., the novel) may be free to use, the person commissioned to do the adaptation would usually hold the copyright on the dramatized version. In a rare instance, a producer may "hire" an adaptor as an employee. In such a case, the producer would be the owner of the copyright, since it would be considered a "work for hire." The procedure is for the producer and author (as well as composer and lyricist, if it's to be a musical adaptation) to enter into a Dramatist Guild Approved Production Contract (or other option agreement for the rights) if mounting a

First-Class Production is intended. If it is to be other than a First-Class (such as an Off-Broadway presentation), an option agreement drawn by the producer's attorney will be used with similar provisions.

Even if the producer's intention is to present the play as a second-class production in a remote location, the producer will still, in most instances, acquire some form of option rather than merely a license. This is so because the producer is offering to pay the author to write the adaptation, and if the producer does not get what he or she wants in return, regarding a future interest in the play, the producer will simply not commission that author. Of course, the protection normally afforded to a producer by entering into an option (wherein he or she receives the exclusive rights to present the play) does not strictly apply in this case. Although the producer will have the exclusive right to produce the adaptation, the underlying work is in the public domain, and anyone else can come along and present a different adaptation thus creating the competitive situation mentioned before. But, once again, while the chances of this happening are somewhat remote, it does sometimes happen.

A problem which can arise, however, whenever anyone uses a public domain work, is that if the production is successful, other producers around the country (or even the world) can produce a similar show and cut into the producer's potential stock, amateur, and other subsidiary markets. Furthermore, if a movie company thinks that adapting the work is a good idea for a film, it may not bother to negotiate a film deal for the producer's adaptation if it can do its own for a fraction of the cost. It is important to note in this context that although the idea for the adaptation may have been uniquely and originally that of the producer, an idea is not copyrightable. Therefore, others can use the same idea, provided they do not copy the producer's newly created version. In some circumstances, they can even use the same title, since titles—like ideas—do not enjoy copyright protection.

Commission the Translation of a Public Domain Work

If the work in the public domain is a foreign-written play, and there is no need for a dramatic adaptation, commissioning a translation would be appropriate. What was said in the preceding section concerning adapting a public domain work is equally applicable here. In this area, a producer may find it easier to hire a translator as an employee and thereby retain complete copyright ownership. This is, of course, a matter of negotiation and depends to a large extent on the reputation of the translator. Because a translation can be done by a person with little knowledge of the theatre, the final product may be awkward and unplayable, and the producer may own the copyright of a relatively useless translation. Paying more for a well-written translation by a talented translator will increase the chances of producing a good play.

Acquire the Rights to the Adaptation or Translation of a Public Domain Work

The previous two sections dealt with a producer hiring or commissioning an author, composer, lyricist, or translator. However, if a producer finds a previous adaptation or translation that he or she feels has chances for success, the producer can produce that version without commissioning a new version. The fact that the underlying work may be in the public domain does not mean that the adaptation or translation is also free to use. As stated before, any new versions are themselves protected by a copyright unless, that is, they have also fallen into the public domain.

The same problems of competition attendant to producing other public domain works apply here.

If the producer intends to present the play as a First-Class Production, he or she would ordinarily negotiate and enter into a Dramatists Guild contract (or a contract with similar terms) with the translator or adaptor. For other-than-First-Class productions, there is no standard option agreement that is generally used. The producer's attorney will usually draft the contract.

Acquire the Rights to an Original Copyrighted Work

In contrast to public domain works, which are free to use without permission, are original works of authorship that enjoy full copyright protection. These works could be completely new and unproduced or could be old standards that have been on the boards many times. In either case, if the producer has in mind a Broadway or other First-Class Production, he will enter into a Dramatists Guild contract (or a contract with similar terms). If other than First-Class, the option to be signed will vary as previously indicated. These options usually provide that the producer has the exclusive right to present the play, thereby eliminating the possibility of a competing production. Bear in mind that an idea cannot be copyrighted, therefore another author could write a different play based on the same idea.

Depending on the reputation of the author, a producer may not be able to option the rights to produce a play unless he or she plans to put the play on Broadway, Off Broadway, or in a major theatre in a major city in the United States. Since the author wants the production of his or her play to be the best possible if the producer is going to share in the author's future earnings from the play, the producer will usually grant only a simple license to smaller theatre companies and producers.

Acquire the Rights to an Adaptation or Translation of an Original Copyrighted Work

Just as a work in the public domain may be adapted or translated, so may an original copyrighted work. A producer desiring to present such a play would enter into the appropriate option agreement with the author of the translation or adaptation. Part of the option agreement should provide not only that the new version of the work is original with the author, but also that the author has full right and authority to grant the rights. This would include a warranty that the author had acquired the rights from the owner of the basic work to do the adaptation or translation, and a clause holding the producer harmless in the event the author breaches the warranty. In the event the producer is sued because he or she produced an unauthorized version of the basic work, the producer could in turn sue the author for breach of contract and recover any losses sustained as a result of the author's misrepresentation.

Acquire the Rights to Adapt or Translate an Original Copyrighted Work

Unlike a work in the public domain, a producer cannot legally commission an author to adapt or translate a copyrighted work and produce it without first obtaining the rights from the owner of the basic work. Provided the rights are available, the basic works such as novels, short stories, poems, plays, motion pictures, radio and television shows, and even comic strips can be translated, adapted, dramatized, or made into musicals. Usually the owner of the basic work will enter into an option agreement that will provide that the producer will own the rights in the basic work to adapt it for the stage in accordance with the terms of the literary purchase agreement.

It is important that the agreement with the author of the basic work provides that the producer has the exclusive right to do the adaptation and that the owner will not, during the term of the agreement, grant similar rights to anyone else. If the owner can no longer grant those rights to others, he or she will want to make sure of getting the best possible production in the best possible location. For this reason, the owner of the basic work will not usually grant adaptation or translation rights to a producer who does not intend eventually to have a New York or other First-Class Production.

Commission an Original Work to be Copyrighted

A producer who has a unique idea can commission a playwright (preferably one with a reputation) to transform that idea into a play.

The terms of the contracts entered into between the producer and author will vary depending on the type of production, as previously stated. The contract will almost invariably be an option with additional rights rather than merely a license, since the producer is taking some risk in producing an unknown property and will want to provide investors with an added incentive to part with their money.

A possible area of interest in the commissioning of new plays is that of dramatizing the lives of famous people or certain interesting or unusual events in the news concerning people known or unknown. A producer desiring to commission the writing of such a play should first acquire good legal counsel, since such a production could give rise to a lawsuit under the right-of-privacy laws that virtually every state now has either by statute or court decision. The privacy statute in New York is found in the Civil Rights Law, Sections 50 and 51. Section 50 states: "A person, firm or corporation that uses for advertising purposes or for purposes of trade, the name, portrait or picture of any living person without having first obtained the written consent of such person, or if a minor, of his or her parent or guardian, is guilty of a misdemeanor." Section 51 states that the person so wronged can sue for an injunction and for money damages. The question of what is "for purposes of trade" is vague and has often come into conflict with the First Amendment guarantees of freedom of speech.

The statute has been further defined and refined by numerous court cases. The results of each case depend on the particular facts. Suffice it to say that if a producer intends to produce a play about a living person, he would be well advised to consult a knowledgeable lawyer.

Write or Adapt a Play to Produce

Since we are enumerating the ways to acquire a play to produce, we must not overlook the fact that the producer could, of course, write or adapt a play, or compose music and lyrics, or do any or all of these things. If a producer does any or all of these things, it would, perhaps, be prudent to find someone else to produce. If no one else wants to produce the work, one might observe that the producer is less than unbiased toward the writer's work, and the producer's objectivity and business judgment should be carefully considered. Perhaps there are people who can write well, compose well, direct well, and then also produce well. There just aren't many. Most people would do well to handle any one of these jobs with a degree of professionalism.

CHAPTER 2

The Option for Other Than a First-Class Production

A FTER THE PRODUCER decides to acquire the rights to a property, determines who controls the rights and where, and how he or she intends to produce the play, the producer must then negotiate the terms of the agreement to acquire the rights. If the producer is acquiring a license with no additional or subsidiary rights, the negotiation process and the terms will be relatively one-sided in favor of the author. The amounts due the author for a license are usually fixed at a percentage of the gross box office receipts or a flat fee, and the only variable is how much of an advance against royalties the producer must pay.

If, on the other hand, the producer is acquiring what is referred to as an "option," he or she should know what terms an option agreement can contain. This chapter will explain the most common terms found in option agreements, their purpose, and how they vary, depending on the bargaining power of the parties.

The Dramatists Guild, Inc. (the "Guild"), Minimum Basic Production Contract for an Off-Broadway show is almost never used. In fact if it is used, it is by someone who does not know the business and does not understand what they are doing. The Guild contract for Off-Broadway was never fully negotiated. When the negotiations between the Guild and the League of Off-Broadway Theatre Owners broke down in the middle of negotiations, early in the seventies, the Guild decided to publish its own version in the hope that it would be accepted as a viable contract. It has never been used by knowledgeable attorneys and agents working in theatre, although some agents representing play authors have tried to force it on producers. The Off-Broadway contract the Guild would like to use is so unfairly pro-author that it would be difficult, if not impossible, to find financing for any play that the production rights are acquired by a producer pursuant to its terms.

After the reader has acquired a basic understanding of an option for other than a First-Class Performance as discussed in this chapter, the Approved Production Contract (which is a form of option sometimes used for First-Class Performances) will be discussed in Chapter 4.

A sample option agreement appears in Appendix G.

Usual Contract Provisions

Warranties of Author or Owner as to
Ownership and Originality of Property

In Chapter 1, we discussed the necessity of the producer acquiring the rights to produce the play to avoid a lawsuit. The language in the contract should serve to guarantee that the producer is, in fact, making a valid acquisition after finding the person who seems to be the owner of the property. The author or owner warrants and represents that the work (a) is original and does not violate anyone's copyright (i.e., the author did not copy from another author); (b) does not violate any other rights of any person (this would include such areas as the right of privacy, defamation of character, libel, slander, and unfair competition); (c) is unencumbered by any claim made by someone against the author that adversely affects the play or the copyright (someone may be claiming a prior grant of the same rights being conveyed; this would be a claim that adversely affects the play); (d) is solely owned by the author, or owner, and that he or she has the right and power to enter into this agreement and to deal with the rights granted in the option. Producers want to option potential hits, not lawsuits.

The author or owner also agrees to "indemnify" (pay) the producer for any losses the producer may suffer due to a "material" (substantial) breach of any of the above warranties. What is material may be a question for the court or an arbitrator to determine. If the court or an arbitrator finds the breach is material, the author must pay the producer's legal fees in addition to other damages, such as lost profits and any payments owing under contractual obligations that the producer undertook (i.e., fees for actors, designers, theatre, etc.) and that the producer cannot fulfill due to the inability to open or continue the play. The author also agrees to hold the producer "harmless" from any claims, demands, lawsuits, etcetera. This means that if the producer is sued by a third party, such as a real or a bogus owner of the play, the author must assume the responsibility so that the producer is not harmed by the claim.

If these provisions seem harsh and unfair to the author, one should realize that a producer spends great amounts of time and money to produce a play, and the investors would like to be assured that the already risky business of investing in plays is not made more hazardous by producing a play that infringes on someone else's rights, not to mention the fact that the author is, in reality, the one person who ought to know whether the material is stolen or whether it is original — and he should be willing to guarantee such facts. The contract will also provide that the producer will similarly indemnify the author with respect to any material that the producer, director, stage manager, or whoever, puts into the play, for which the author suffers damages.

Although the author warrants that the play is original and owned by him or her, this warranty does not extend to the title of the play, since — as previously mentioned — a title cannot be copyrighted. Because the use of a title similar to one that has established a secondary meaning can be considered unfair competition, a producer may suggest that the author change the title to avoid trouble. If the author refuses, the producer will want to add a clause to the above provisions whereby the author warrants that the title will not infringe on anyone's rights.

Author's Grant of Rights

The producer purchases from the author or owner the right to produce the play within a specified period of time in a specified place. This is, in fact, the option, and if he or she does so produce, the rest of the agreement becomes effective. If the producer does not present the play within the option period, the agreement terminates and all rights revert to the author.

The amount the producer pays for the option will vary greatly, depending on numerous factors — including, among other things, the fame of the author and the amount of competition to produce the play. It is not unusual for a one year option for an Off-Broadway production to cost between $500 and $1,500 and the agreement may contain a provision for an automatic extension for an additional year upon payment of an additional $1,000 to $1,500 more or less, prior to the expiration of the first option period. No matter what the option costs, the payments are most usually considered as advances against the royalty payments due to the author once the play opens.

Producers should try to negotiate the option terms so that they pay a smaller amount for the initial term and a larger amount for the extension. After the first term, the producer should be in a better position to know if he will get the play financed and the cast he wants. If the show is close to coming together, the larger second payment can be money well spent and, in most cases, will also be an advance against the royalties due the author when the show opens. If, however, the producer finds that the show cannot be produced, his exposure will be limited to the smaller initial option payment.

A producer will always try to keep the option payment as small as possible, because if the play does not open, the option money belongs to the author and need not be returned to the producer. The option payment purchases the exclusive right to produce the work for a given period of time, during which time the author cannot sell the rights to another producer.

The producer will acquire the rights to produce the play in a definite location — i.e., New York City (on, or off, Broadway, or in a middle theatre), a specific theatre, such as the Kennedy Center in Washington, D.C., or a specific kind of theatre (such as a stock or resident theatre). The author will want this specified in order to know what kind of production it will be. Since the author is also under certain circumstances and conditions granting additional and subsidiary rights, he or she will want to make certain that the play will be presented in a manner that will create a future market. In order to help get a good production, the author may also grant the producer the right to present the play as a tour prior to its presentation at the designated location.

Bear in mind that the author may grant more than one extension and that the extensions may be more or less than a year. An original one-year option with a one-year extension is probably most common for New York productions, whether on, or off, Broadway. An author will rarely grant a producer an option and extensions that will add up to more than three years. If the producer cannot get the play on in three years, he or she probably cannot get it on at all, so the author will want to give it to another producer who can.

Noncompetition Clause

Although the producer is acquiring the sole and exclusive rights to present the play in a certain location or a specific theatre or kind of theatre, it does not specify whether the author can grant the production rights in the play to another producer in another location. It is usual to provide that the rights granted to the producer are the sole and exclusive rights to produce the play throughout the United States and Canada.

The author will agree that he or she will not grant anyone the rights to do a movie version of the play that would be released either during the option period, the run of the play, or any period in which the producer may have any rights to produce the play in the United States, Canada, or the British Isles. A movie released during these periods would possibly directly compete with the play and could cause the play to lose business. This contract protects the producer from such competition; however, it may permit the author to dispose of the movie rights provided the producer grants prior written approval, which will not be unreasonably withheld.

The author may agree to not grant anyone the rights to perform the play in any media (except movies) in the United States, Canada, or the British Isles during the period the producer retains any rights or options to produce the play anywhere in the United States, Canada or the British Isles.

Payments to the Author

In addition to the option payments received by the author, the producer also agrees to pay the author a percentage of the gross weekly box office receipts received from the sale of tickets. As mentioned earlier, the option payments are usually advances against these royalties and are therefore deducted from the first royalties earned by the author.

The difficulty in raising money for theatrical productions has resulted in all kinds of "royalty pool formulas." The most common royalty structure at the present time will always have some element of a royalty pool formula, so that the investors may recoup their investment before the royalty participants make a killing. See the more detailed discussion of royalty pool formulas in Chapter 4.

If a royalty pool is not used, the royalty to the author is usually a minimum of 5 percent of the gross weekly box office receipts, although this figure can and does vary. Some regional theatres have paid as little as 4 percent and some even get by with a flat fee of $100 or $125 per performance.

If the play is by a famous author, or if it is a play that more than one producer wants to option, the royalty may go above 6 percent of the gross weekly box office receipts but usually not over 10 percent. The royalties for a First-Class Production are set forth in Chapter 4, in the discussion of the Approved Production Contract (APC).

If the producer is presenting a musical, a 6 percent royalty is not unusual. It is usually divided 2 percent to the bookwriter, 2 percent to the lyricist, and 2 percent to the composer. Of course, if one of the collaborators is more famous than the other, or if his or her contribution is greater, that person may receive more than half of the gross weekly box office receipts.

The simplest, easiest, and most practical formula for an Off-Broadway or a middle theatre production, although not a pool, is a waiver of half of the royalties by all royalty recipients until recoupment or 150 percent recoupment of the total production costs of the play, and adding an additional 1/2 percent, or 1 percent, of the gross weekly box office receipts to what the royalty would otherwise be, after recoupment.

For example, if the royalty is 5 percent of the gross going to 6 percent after recoupment, under such formula, it would be 5 percent of the gross until recoupment and 6 1/2 or 7 percent thereafter. A musical might be 6 percent of the gross going to 7 percent after recoupment, and under the formula, it would be 6 percent of the gross going to 7 1/2 percent after recoupment.

If you are a producer, don't let the author or the author's agent convince you to defer the royalty until recoupment. Waiver is necessary. A deferral doesn't help you with the major problem of getting investors.

It goes without saying that the same option agreement granting the producer the production rights should have an affirmative statement that the producer does hereby waive half of his or her producer's fee, until recoupment. This means that the fee, which is usually 2 percent of the gross, is 1 percent until recoupment and could go to 2 1/2 percent after recoupment. The producer will now often share in the royalty pool at two or three points in lieu of a percentage of the gross for the producer's fee.

Another compromise is for the producer to give the author some percentage of the producer's profits. Since profits are relatively rare in producing plays, an author will usually opt for more concrete remuneration.

If the producer is presenting a musical adaptation of a copyrighted basic work, in addition to the share of the royalty pool or paying a percentage of gross box office receipts to the authors of the adaptation, he will most usually have to pay the owner of the basic work 1, 1 1/2, or 2 percent of the gross weekly box office receipts. The payment for the right to adapt a basic work will include an option payment, which will usually range between $1,000 and $10,000 for each of two one-year options (and can be more or less). In the contract for the acquisition of the adaptation rights, the owner of such basic work will, in return for this sum, grant the producer (or whoever acquires the rights) a fixed period of time in which to complete the adaptation (usually one year) and an additional fixed period of time in which to produce the play (again, usually one year). The up-front option payment (or some part thereof) is generally considered as an advance against the 1, 1 1/2, or 2 percent royalty earned by the owner when the play opens. If a royalty pool is used, the owner of the basic work will share in the pool usually receiving two points, more or less, in lieu of the gross box office receipts.

In addition, the owner of the basic work will want, and will be entitled to, an interest in the play's subsidiary rights. Usually, the owner of the basic work will receive that proportionate part of the author's share of receipts received from all subsidiary uses of the play that his royalty bears to the total aggregate royalties payable to all of the creators of the new work, the adaptors (bookwriter, composer, lyricist), including in this total the payment to the owner of the basic work. The owner of the basic work should want a limit placed on the aggregate royalties for the purpose of this computation. The limit may be between 10 and 18 percent (the larger amount would be for a musical) or a comparable ratio if a royalty pool is used, so that the producer is not able to dilute the interest of the owner of the basic work.

The producer might hire a talented director and choreographer whose work is so unique that their contributions qualify them as creators. The director and choreographer would, as part of their contract with the producer, receive a percentage of the gross as an "author's" royalty, and would want to share in the subsidiary income as well. As the total aggregate royalty to the creative personnel increases, the percentage of subsidiary rights income payable to the owner of the basic work decreases. Therefore, the limit of between 10 and 18 percent will at least guarantee a limit on the dilution of the share of the owner of the basic work.

The proportionate share of subsidiary rights income of the owner of the basic work would be computed as follows: If the owner of the basic work were paid a royalty of 1 percent and all the creative personnel (bookwriter, composer, and lyricist) jointly receive 6 percent, then the owner of the basic work would share in receipts from subsidiary income by receiving one-seventh of the share of such receipts, since 7 percent is the total aggregate royalties. If there is a 14 percent limitation written into the contract and the owner of the basic work receives a royalty of 1 percent, then the owner cannot receive less than one-fourteenth of such subsidiary receipts even if the total aggregate royalties payable to the adaptors and owner of the basic work exceeds 14 percent of the gross weekly box office receipts.

The term "gross weekly box office receipts" has been frequently referred to. The contract defines it as all receipts at the box office from the sale of tickets, less: theatre party commissions, discount and cut-rate sales, all admission taxes presently or to be levied, Ticketron charges or the cost of any other automated ticket distributor, those sums equivalent to the former 5 percent New York amusement tax (the net proceeds of which are now set aside in pension and welfare funds of the theatrical unions and ultimately paid to said funds), any subscription fees, and Actors' Fund benefits.

The contract will provide that the royalties for each week must be paid to the author usually by the Wednesday following that week's performances. The producer must enclose with the payment a signed copy of the box office statement. The author has the right to examine the books of the producer at any time during regular business hours upon giving the producer reasonable notice. To avoid unnecessary harassment, the producer will attempt to limit such inspections to not more than semiannually.

The contract will provide a waiver clause that is intended to assist the play to stay alive at critical times. In an effort to help keep the show alive, the author may agree to waive his or her royalty, but will want to waive only so much of it, if paid, as would cause the play to operate at a loss. An author may agree with such a waiver only if the producer agrees to waive the producer's fee, and all other royalty recipients, similarly, waive.

Producer's Subsidiary Rights

As previously mentioned, the producer is acquiring only the rights to present the play with live actors on the stage. The producer's production will make a contribution to the value of the play for use in other media if it runs for a certain length of time.

In consideration of the contribution the producer makes to the play, the author agrees to share with the producer a percentage of the net receipts received by the author from the future exploitation of the work in other media.

A Broadway production probably contributes most to the value of a play in other media.

The receipts from subsidiary rights in which the producer shares are usually from the following sources: (a) worldwide — motion picture rights; (b) the continental United States and Canada — any of the following rights: radio and television; touring, stock, Broadway, Off-Broadway, amateur, and foreign-language performances; condensed tabloid and concert-tour versions; commercial uses; original cast album, tapes, cassettes, records, and video cassettes.

Although the producer shares in the receipts from all the above uses, he or she does not control the disposition of the rights. The author is the owner and controls the rights. The producer is a third party beneficiary and shares in what the author receives.

In the case of the original cast album for a musical production, the producer as well as the bookwriter, composer, and lyricist will negotiate and enter into the agreement. The fact that the producer is part of this agreement is not because of an acquired interest in subsidiary rights, but rather because the original cast album will be made using the original cast — i.e. members of the show who are employed and furnished by the producer.

Even though authors control the future uses of their property, they must deal in good faith in disposing of those rights. Authors may not make a deal sacrificing any of the properties they have written in which the producer shares, so that they might make a better deal on another property in which no one shares. For instance, an author may have a play that a movie producer is anxious to make into a film and for which the author has been offered $100,000. In the event a producer previously produced the play and acquired an interest in subsidiary rights, the author should not be able to offer the movie producer the right to do the film for $75,000 on the condition that the movie producer will at the same time purchase another of the author's works worth $100,000 for $150,000.

The number of performances the play has to run in order for the producer to share in the proceeds from the subsidiary rights is often computed in the following manner: 10 percent if the play has run for at least twenty-one consecutive paid performances; 20 percent for forty-two consecutive performances; 30 percent for fifty-six; and 40 percent for sixty-five consecutive paid performances. It is not usual for a producer to receive more than 40 percent. The percentage is calculated on the author's net receipts earned from the disposition of subsidiary rights (less the agent's commission) if the contract for the disposition of such rights is entered into during a fixed period (usually seven, ten, or twelve years after the opening or closing of the original production), even though the receipts may be received after the fixed period expires. All the performances must be consecutive (without a lapse between performances) and must be for paid admission attended by the public.

Preview performances are paid public performances, but since they are prior to the critics' reviews, their contribution to the value of the property may be less. If the play officially opens, up to seven paid preview performances may be counted by the producer in making this computation.

As noted above, the producer's participation in the author's receipts from subsidiaries is for a limited number of years after the last performance of the play in New York City (or more usually after the first performance). The producer will continue to participate in all receipts earned from any disposition of subsidiary rights for as long as those receipts are earned by the author, provided that the contract for the disposition was entered into within the agreed-upon number of years after the last or first performance. It is usually between seven and eighteen years, the extremes being three years or for the duration of the copyright in the play (fifty-six years, under the old copyright law, or the life of the author plus fifty years, under the new law). As a practical matter, the period is usually set on either side of ten years.

An example of this is as follows: The option agreement states that the producer would share in the author's net receipts from any subsidiaries disposed of before the expiration of ten years from the date of the last public performance in New York City. The play opened on January 1, 1980, and ran consecutively until June 15, 1986. The author sold movie rights in July 1990 for $200,000. The producer would receive $80,000 or 40 percent. Although more than ten years transpired from the time the play opened, if the period is measured from the close of the play, then only four years and one month would have elapsed. If the author did not receive another payment from the movie company until July 2000, the producer would still get 40 percent of the new payment. Although the payment in the year 2000 comes more than ten years after 1986, the movie contract was entered into within the ten-year limitation period. It is for this reason that the contract contains the parenthetical phrase that the producer shall receive the percentage of net receipts (regardless of when paid). The date of the contract, not the payment, is usually the controlling factor. The receipts of any contract entered into after the specified period (i.e., June 16, 1996, in the above example) will not have to be shared with the producer; however, all receipts from contracts entered into prior to that date continue to be shared.

The negotiations for subsidiary rights can be very important. If the play is a flop, the fight over subsidiaries may have been in vain. However, since few people—including producers—can predict with accuracy which play will be successful and which will flop, every producer enters into negotiations with the thought in mind that the play will be a hit. The producer, the author, and, most importantly, the investors know the value of subsidiary rights. If a producer does not get a fair deal on the subsidiaries from the author, the author could have a hollow victory. Investors may not invest, and without their money neither the producer nor the author have a show.

The breakdown of percentages per the number of performances (10 percent for twenty-one, 20 percent for forty-two, 30 percent for fifty-six, and 40 percent for sixty-five) is one of the common arrangements for an Off-Broadway production. The APC, which is the contract negotiated by the Dramatists Guild, Inc., and the League of American Theatres and Producers for a First-Class Performance, provides for the sharing of subsidiary rights income in a more complicated manner. This is set forth in detail in Chapter 4.

Elsewhere the numbers may vary. A New York City production can negotiate a better subsidiary rights deal than a Kansas production. The outcome of any such negotiations depends on various factors, probably the most important of which includes the theatre, its location and size, the prestige of the producer or producing company, the total cost of the production, the eagerness of the producer, the stature of the author, the availability of financing, and the sophistication of the investors.

An author will usually not object to granting an interest in the subsidiary rights if it is for an important enough production. If an Off-Broadway show is having a pre-New York tour, it may make sense to count part of the pre-New York performances toward subsidiaries. The parties, for example, may agree to count up to twenty-five out-of-town performances. Thus, if sixty-five performances in New York City would result in the producer getting a 40-percent interest, if the play ran twenty-five or more performances in Boston or elsewhere, only forty additional New York performances would be needed to get that 40 percent.

In selecting a property to produce, the producer may find that the play was previously produced and that another producer has acquired and continues to retain an interest in the author's subsidiaries. Since the author does not want to give away another 40 percent of his or her interest, and since the new producer will have difficulty in financing the play without giving the investors an interest in subsidiary rights, a compromise must be reached.

One method of resolving this problem is to convince the producer of the first production to assign some part of his or her subsidiary rights interest to the new producer if the new production runs for a required number of performances. The original producer may not be unwilling to do this in view of the fact that a successful new production could increase the value of the subsidiary rights for all concerned. In such a situation, the author may also part with some of his or her subsidiary interest as well in order to assist the new production. If the original producer—who had earned a 40 percent interest in subsidiaries—gives up one-half (a 20-percent interest), and the author—who has the other 60 percent—gives up a 10 percent interest, the new producer would have a potential 30-percent interest in the author's receipts from the disposition of subsidiary rights. The original producer would retain 20 percent and the author would still have 50 percent. See Chapter 4 for a discussion of how the APC deals with this problem.

House-Seat Allocation

One of the areas of an option agreement which generates less controversy is that of house-seat allocation (house seats are usually the best and most expensive seats in the theatre). The producer will usually offer the author a pair of house seats for all performances and ten pair for the night of the official opening. The reason for the absence of controversy is that house seats are not free, but they are valuable and the important persons involved in the play get some. The tickets are held at the box office only until 6:00 p.m. of the day before or two days before each evening performance and 12:00 noon of the day before or two days before each matinee. If the author or his designee does not pay for and pick up the tickets by those times, the tickets become available for sale to the general public.

The attorney general of the state of New York has set forth rules and regulations concerning the use of house seats, and the author must agree to keep accurate records in accordance with the law.

Billing Credits

One area of sharp negotiations is that of billing credits. Everyone agrees that the author should receive credit, but where it should appear and how big it should be is open to negotiation. The author usually gets credit in all advertisements (except ABC and teaser ads [an ABC ad is an ad in the alphabetical listings which appear in the *New York Times* and the New York *Post*. A teaser ad is one in which only the name of the play (and sometimes the star) is mentioned together with the name of the theatre]) programs, billboards, and houseboards wherever the name of the play appears. Sometimes the author will want to place a condition on the provision that he need not receive credit in ABC, and teaser ads; that condition being that his name need not appear provided no other name appears.

Depending on the bargaining power of the author, the size of his or her name will vary anywhere from one-third to 100 percent of the size of the title. If the author is famous, the producer will not raise much of an argument on the size of the author's name, since this will be what sells tickets.

Authors will usually want their names to be the biggest with only the title of the play being bigger. The producer may want to hire a director or star of prominence who, as part of their contract, will insist that their names be the largest. An author will often have to accept a clause that provides that no names will be larger than the author's except those of a star or director of prominence.

In negotiating billing, in addition to the size of type used for the author's name, the style, boldness, and prominence of type is established in relation to other names. Placement is also important. Authors usually insist that their names appear on a separate line beneath the title of the play.

When there are multiple authors, as in a musical, the names are usually listed as bookwriter, composer, and lyricist, in that order.

Producer's Additional Rights

If the play is produced in accordance with the terms of the option agreement, and if certain conditions are met—such as the play running twenty-one performances, or opening before a paid audience, or running for any number of performances that may be arbitrarily decided upon—then certain additional rights accrue to the producer.

The rights to tour the play, to produce the play in England, and to produce subsequent productions in different parts of the country are usually options that the producer acquires. These options must be exercised within a certain period of time after the opening or closing of the original production. It is not unusual that the rights must be exercised within six months after the first production of the play before a paying audience. In each instance, to exercise the option the producer must give notice and send an option payment to the author.

The agreement will usually provide that the option to produce the play for a tour of the United States, or in England, or for other productions must be exercised by sending the author notice and a payment of $500 or $750 or $1,000 for each of the rights to open the play in any of these areas, within one year after the giving of the notice. Since it requires more time to set up a tour, it is wise to provide that the tour must be commenced within fifteen or eighteen months instead of a year. For each city in which the producer desires to produce the play other than a tour, he must make a payment of $500, $750, or $1,000. The agreement will provide that the royalties in each instance will be in an amount the same as the royalties provided in the original option agreement.

The agreement will probably provide that the producer may move the play to Broadway at any time during the run of the play, or within six months (or one year) after the close of the original production of the play, by entering into a contract on the terms and conditions set forth.

Approval of Directors, Actors, and Designers

It is usual for the author to have approval of the director, actors, and designers, or some of them. The producer's representative will try to qualify the approvals to provide that they will not be unreasonably withheld by the author. Without such a provision, the author may be as arbitrary as he or she wishes with respect to the approvals. The provision that approvals will not be unreasonably withheld creates a litigatable or arbitratable issue that can be resolved by someone other than the author. A producer could then go ahead and hire the director even without approval, and at a later date, a court or arbitrator would determine whether the author was being unreasonable in withholding the approval. Without such a provision, the author could arbitrarily withhold approval of anyone for whatever whimsical reason he or she wanted.

Duration of Right to Produce the Play

The agreement will provide that the producer can produce the play during the continuous run of the play. The continuous run will usually be defined to mean that the run continues so long as there are no more than two, three, or four weeks between paid performances before a live audience. There are, of course, other ways of defining continuous run, but one should make certain that the agreement is clear as to the continuing right of the producer to produce the play and when those rights cease and terminate.

Right to Assign Option

The producer must have the right to assign the option, since, in all probability, he is going to assign the production rights to a limited liability company, which will be formed to produce the play. The author, on the other hand, has consented to this producer producing the play and will not want him to make a complete assignment to someone else and walk away from the production. The relationship between an author and producer is a very personal relationship, and although in many instances a successful author and the producer are not madly in love, it does make life simpler if they have mutual respect for each other and a working relationship. It is not unusual to provide that the producer may assign the contract to a limited liability company, a partnership, or a corporation in which he or she is one of the principals, but if the producer wishes to make an assignment to an entity in which he or she is not one of the principals, then the author must approve of such assignment.

Arbitration Clause

If there is a dispute with respect to the contract, either party may ask a court of law to resolve the dispute. There is a better way of resolving disputes, however, that I feel is particularly applicable to theatre differences. It may be provided in the agreement that the dispute will be resolved by arbitration. The advantage of arbitration is that (1) the parties can select an arbitrator who is knowledgeable in theatre; and (2) most often a quicker decision may be reached. It is usual to provide that the arbitration will be in accordance with the rules and regulations of the American Arbitration Association.

Agreements of this kind will sometimes provide that disputes may be settled by a party specifically designated by the parties to the agreement. For example, if there is a dispute of an artistic nature, the author and producer may agree that the director will cast the deciding vote. It there is a business dispute, the parties may agree that the dispute will be settled by either the attorney for the production or the general manager.

Script Changes

Almost always the option agreement will provide that there will be no script changes without the approval of the author. Although rarely granted, it is usual to ask the author not to unreasonably withhold such approval. It is most usual to give the author sole and complete control of the script even to the extent that he or she may be unreasonable.

Legal Clauses

There are a few boilerplate legal clauses usually added to the end of an option to produce a play. It may be provided that the agreement will be interpreted under the laws of the state of New York (or any other state where the agreement is being drafted), that this agreement is the entire agreement between the parties and anything previously said or written is invalid, that the parties are not to be considered joint venturers or partners, and such similar provisions.

CHAPTER 3

Movie Deals

Investors Expect to Share in Sale of Movie Rights

MOTION PICTURE RIGHTS deserve special attention. As was pointed out, usually the investors in a show share in the proceeds from the sale of subsidiary rights if the play runs for a certain length of time. One of the most lucrative possible sources of income for a production, its investors, and its adaptors is a share in the sale of the motion picture rights. A distinction must be made between (1) the rights to deal with the motion picture rights in the play, and (2) the rights to base the play in whole or in part on the movie.

If a play is adapted from a work that has already been made into a movie, then the movie rights have already been disposed of and, unless the rights have reverted to the owner of the basic work (which is not likely in most instances), some kind of deal ought to be made with the company owning the movie rights.

Film Company May Also Own Basic Rights in Work

A play and a movie may be based on the same basic work (a novel, a record, etc.). A producer or adaptor may want to base a play on a movie (which, in this instance, would make the movie the basic work). The movie may have been an original, or it may have been based on another basic work that the motion picture company acquired all rights to, including the dramatic rights. In either event, appropriate arrangements should be made. The only difference in these two instances is that if the play is to be based on a movie, then the motion picture company will expect a larger payment. The reason for this is that in addition to permitting the adaptor to deal with the play to make a Movie Sale based on the play, they are also granting the rights to adapt the play based on the movie. If the movie is the basic work, the motion picture company is in a much stronger bargaining position than if it only owned the film rights and the film was based on another work. Why would anyone want the rights to base a movie on a play based on a movie? The answer is simple. The play, although based on the movie, might become a totally different property. If the play is a success, there is surely a market—especially if the play is a musical adaptation of a dramatic work.

One should always be prepared to bargain for the motion picture rights, so that if the play is a success it may then be made into another movie.

Dramatic Rights

If the motion Picture company owns the dramatic rights, that part of the negotiations is the same as negotiating with anyone else for the dramatic rights in a basic work, discussed in detail in Chapter 1, although the price may tend to be steeper.

Film Rights—Option of First Refusal

For the most part, in addition to the compensation for the dramatic rights, one may expect that the company owning the film rights will want an option of first refusal to make a movie based on the play for one-third less than any other bona fide offer. There may also be a fixed amount of $250,000, more or less, set forth in the agreement to purchase the movie rights in the play. In addition, a percentage of the net profits and of the gross box office receipts is negotiable.

Share of Sale to Other Film Company

In addition, if the motion picture company chooses not to make the film based on the play, that is based on the original film, and the rights are sold to someone else, the company will expect one-third of the proceeds of the film sale.

Film Company May Want Cast Album and Publishing Rights

An owner of the motion picture rights may try to get the rights to publish the music and to make the original cast album if the play is a musical. Many of the major film studios have associated companies that do publishing and recording. It is not advisable for a producer or an adaptor to permit them to have these rights unless it is unavoidable. The producer may have to rely on an investment from a record or publishing company in exchange for the rights to make the original cast album, and if these rights have been tied up and are not available, the producer may lose this investment source. It is better to give the motion picture owners an option of first refusal on these rights, so that at the very least they will have to match any other bona fide offers.

Sometimes the motion picture owner will agree to cease distribution of the original movie, and sometimes not. In most instances, they will cooperate in every way, including making copies of the print available for viewing; for if a deal has been made, at this point, they will in fact have a vested interest in the outcome of the play.

The negotiations would be similar whether the play will be a musical or a drama, except with a drama there would be no discussion of music publishing. A dramatic cast album is a possibility, but very unlikely, so that it is less a subject of sharp bargaining. The dollar amounts and percentages might vary, but not substantially. More important, bear in mind that most adaptations are for musicals rather than for dramas.

CHAPTER 4

First-Class Productions

What Does a First-Class Production Mean?

IT'S ALL PRETTY MUCH OF A MESS. It's all so very confusing. Something that was difficult to define in the first place is now in the process of meaning something else. Although there was never a succinct clearly defined definition of the term, those of us in the business knew what it meant, sort of knew, and now with it changing no one knows for sure what it means. I'm talking about a "First-Class Performance" or a "First-Class Production" and you will notice that's a capital "F" with a capital "C" and a capital "P," not to be confused with a first-class performance or first-class production with all lower case letters.

Everyone in the business thinks that their production is "first-class," that it is something very special, something great. But for many years those of us in the business who considered ourselves knowledgeable knew that a "First-Class Production" meant a production with a First-Class Cast, a First-Class Director in a First-Class Theatre. We all knew that a First-Class Cast meant a professional cast, which meant with Actors' Equity actors. We all knew that a First-Class Director meant a professional director, which meant a member of the Society of Stage Directors and Choreographers ("SSD&C"). We all knew that a First-Class Theatre meant Broadway theatres and a bunch of other classy theatres in certain specific cities scattered throughout the United States. We knew the names of some of them and if we weren't sure whether or not the theatre in question was "First-Class" we would call the League of American Theatres and Producers (back then it was the "League of New York Theatres and Producers") or better yet, we would check with Equity and if the Equity contract for that theatre was the Production Contract for a First-Class house, then it was a First-Class Theatre.

So for years we muddled through with this information. We knew the successful big Broadway plays would do a sit-down production (which means it was a run-of-the-play) in First-Class Theatres and the tours of these smash hits also went into the First-Class houses. We also knew that the "Bus and Truck Productions," that is the one or two night stands did not end up in the First-Class houses, but theatres that were other than First-Class. Now they may have been first-class (lower case "f" and "c"), but they weren't First-Class (capital "F" and "C").

And then something happened that messed this all up and as confusing as it was before, now we are really confused and are just not sure what a First-Class Theatre is in other cities outside of New York City. What happened was that a Broadway production company decided to take a big Broadway musical on tour, but not with the original cast and not with Equity actors. Non-Equity tours had toured in the past, and there were many non-Equity productions in theatres throughout the United States. But this time they managed to take this non-Equity cast production into what we all knew were the First-Class Theatres where, up to that time, only a First-Class Cast (Equity) could go with its First-Class Director (the member of the SSD&C).

Suffice it to say that this was a serious threat to the Actors' Equity Association because it had always been anticipated that Equity performers would be performing in the theatres we had always known to be First-Class Theatres. Recent negotiations between the League of American Theatres and Producers and Actors Equity have resolved the question, at least for the time being, with some compromises and concessions acceptable to both sides.

Background

During the 1920s, a Dramatists Guild, Inc. ("Guild") contract was introduced that served as the legal basis for almost all the author-producer First-Class stage productions in this country, including Broadway productions. That practice continued up until the early 1980s. "First-Class Performance" and "First-Class Production" are interchangeable terms that have a specific meaning, albeit sometimes not easy to determine what is and what isn't First-Class. The Dramatists Guild Inc., Approved Production Contract (APC), later discussed, defines a First-Class Performance as a live stage production of a play on the speaking stage, within the territory, under a producer's own management, in a regular evening bill in a First-Class Theatre in a first-class manner, with a first-class cast and a first-class director. What is really meant is the Broadway theatres and the other large theatres in large cities that use a certain Actors' Equity contract for the cast. The use of "first-class" so many times to define First-Class performances lends to the ambiguity.

Starting in the 1980s, the Guild had a difficult time insisting on the use of its author-producer contract because of the continuing question of whether playwrights, as independent contractors, were in violation of the Sherman Antitrust Act by virtue of their joining together in the Guild.

The contract referred to as the Dramatists Guild, Inc., Minimum Basic Production Contract (MBPC) was used (1) to option original plays, and (2) to engage adaptors (bookwriter, composer, and lyricist) when a producer had acquired rights to do an adaptation of a basic work. For many years, there was a Guild agreement form that producers were required to sign, which contained the same contract provisions the producers also entered into with individual authors after 1961.

When the League of New York Theaters and Producers (the "League"), now the League of American Theaters and Producers, negotiated and signed an MBPC contract, it bound all members of the League to use that contract. After the Guild's troubles with the Sherman Antitrust Act, the League no longer signed the MBPC contract binding all its members. Despite this, individual producers usually signed the contract, not because they were bound to do so by the contract between the League and the Guild, but rather because of the bargaining power of the individual Guild members.

Periodically, the League negotiated changes in the contract with the Guild, even though its members had no League imposed obligation to use the Guild contract. However, the contract was almost always used, because Guild members who were in demand had enough bargaining power to (1) insist on its use and (2) to force less powerful members to comply.

The contract basically benefited playwrights, who received pittances as option payments but would get paid during the run of the play by a percentage of the gross weekly box office receipts. Under the contract, the straight-play minimum was 10 percent of the gross weekly box office receipts, and the musical minimum was 6 percent. A straight play breaking even at $200,000 each week, would, if it grossed $200,000 one week, pay the playwright $20,000 that week. Investors would get nothing. Investors only shared in the net profits after all expenses were paid. They would then recoup their investment. With the heavy royalty payments, it was difficult to get to the point where there were net profits to pay to investors.

During the 1970s and 1980s, investors in theatre began examining the wisdom of investing in plays where the playwright could make money while the play itself was just breaking even, and *before* the investors saw a return on their investment.

The Royalty Pool Formulas

The new approach began with the musical and spread quickly. The changes were known as "royalty pool formulas" and represented an attempt to use the initial weekly profits from a play in part to pay back investors.

The royalty pool formula substituted for gross weekly box office royalties (the author's, the director's, the choreographer's, the designer's, and the producer's fee), a pool consisting of part of the weekly net profits. It used part of the weekly net profits to pay back the investors. The formulas varied; for example, in one formula, the size of the royalty pool from which royalty payments were paid was increased after 100 percent recoupment, and again after 150 percent recoupment.

After the royalty pool formulas were embraced, the Guild was forced to give investors a break or find itself losing member support. (The League had commenced a lawsuit charging the Guild with violations of the Sherman Antitrust Act, and the Guild had counterclaimed with claims of violations of the same act by the League.)

The "Grind" Formula and the New Guild Contract

A new Guild contract was being negotiated in earnest in 1984, with the goal of announcing the new contract effective as of January 1985. However, an unforeseen event occurred. A producer not happy with the Guild recommendations was producing a musical play called *Grind*. He put together a formula that differed from what the Guild and the League had agreed upon. When four of the most important creative people in the business signed the *"Grind"* formula, the Guild, which had not been consulted, suspended the four members.

The Guild contract was not ready by January 1, 1985. In fact, it was not until March 1, 1985, that the contract was ready for acceptance, and even then, no copies were available for examination. Late in March 1985, the League was sponsoring seminars on the new contract, which had been labeled the Approved Production Contract (APC). Still, no copies of the contract were ready for distribution. There was a pervading question as to how viable the new APC would actually be, and the doubt lingered that it would be as universally used as the MBPC was.

The APC finally arrived in May 1985. The new contract still left much to be desired. For example, the first six pages of the APC for plays — not for musical plays — contains thirty-three cross-references. And the cross-references run into further cross-references: for instance, Section 2.04 refers to Section 9.01, which then refers to Section 11.01; Section 5.08 refers to Article XX, which refers to Section 7.01, Section 1.02(c) (which refers to Section 2.05), and Section 8.01 (a) and (b). Section 4.02 refers to Article V, which refers to Article XX and Section 9.02. Many sections have cross-references within each section.

It now seems that the dominant position the Guild once had with Broadway productions no longer exists, as some important Guild members have realized that the other formulas are as good or better than the APC and have been willing to make exceptions to the Guild contract limitations. However, even if variations of the APC are not used, when the APC is used, it represents a great improvement over the MBPC and has improved relations with investors. Regardless of how much the APC is used, it made a contribution by serving to settle the antitrust lawsuit between the Guild and the League. The net effect has been an erosion of the strict control that the Guild had been able to impose on First-Class Production contract terms in the past.

The 1985 "Approved Production" contracts are reproduced in their entirety in appendices D and E of this book. The previously used contract, the MBPC, contained the minimum terms acceptable to the Guild, except that the Guild would consent to certain changes when requested by the producer's attorney or representative.

Both sides acknowledge the APC to be a contract setting forth fixed terms — that is, terms that are minimum and maximum. The review of the contracts by the Guild and the League is intended to foster this concept and to permit any changes consistent with the existing APC terms. The thought is that additions to the contract should either clarify unclear terms or add any terms inadvertently omitted.

Since the APC came into effect, there have been a surprising number of clauses proposed to be included in Article XXII, "Additional Production Terms," intended to clarify or add to the contract without changing the nature of it as both a minimum and maximum contract. It didn't work out exactly as a minimum/maximum, as the Guild has gone along with some changes negotiated by agents that benefit a Guild member to which the producer wanting that particular Guild member on the show has had to accede. In all fairness, it should be stated that the Guild, when pressed, has also had to accede to some changes that benefit the producer, especially in the area of changes in the royalty pool formula.

Each individual contract is countersigned by the Dramatists Guild if it approves of the terms. The Guild will not acknowledge that a concession in one agreement binds them on other agreements; however, it is pretty difficult to argue that an item once accepted for one producer is not acceptable for another producer.

Clauses dealing with "publishing rights," the "original-cast recording," "warranties and representations," "the amount of the per-diem," "billing credits," and the like are some of the items that have received special treatment.

Commentary on the Dramatists Guild, Inc., Approved Production Contract for Plays

Initial Grant of Rights

Article I is similar to that of the previous contract in dealing with the granting of rights to produce the play and the services the author will furnish. As with the former agreement, what is most important about this article is that it gives the producer an "option": There is not a contractual obligation to produce the play.

Option Periods and Payments

The option periods as set forth in Article II are essentially the same as in the minimum Basic Production Contract; however, option payments are larger. Section 2.04 is a new provision in that it extends the option during the presentation of a tryout, as a second-class performance or as a developmental production of the play. The extension is for the number of days on which the play was presented plus an additional sixty days, up to a maximum of eight weeks. The acknowledgment of the Guild that it is sometimes in the author's interest to make concessions so that the play may have the advantage of a production to develop the play, without unreasonable expense, is a step in the right direction. This kind of concession is an awakening to the reality that the producer and the author have some common interests, and that their relationship, even on a monetary issue, ought not always be adversarial. Both the author and the producer have to fashion an agreement that will attract investor capital, or neither of them will have a play to produce.

Advance Payments

Deductions from Advance and Royalty Payments

Article III introduces a new concept, the "advance payment," as something separate from the payment for the options. Up until the use of the Approved Production Contract, the author was paid an option "fee" that was usually a nonreturnable advance against the royalties, although on rare occasions part of the advance was considered a fee and not an advance against the royalties.

Under the APC, as set forth in Article VI, option payments for the first and second options are fees, not advances against royalty earnings or against the advance payment. However, the payment for the third option period, if any, is to be deducted from the amount of the advance payment. The advance payments provided for in Article III are payments against the royalties; that is, the amount of such advance payment reduces the first royalties earned by that amount.

The amount of the advance payment is related to the amount of the capitalization of the play and is fixed at 3 percent of the capitalization, less 3 percent of that sum. The maximum advance is fixed at $35,000.

For example, if a play is capitalized for $600,000, the advance would be 3 percent of $600,000, or $18,000, less 3 percent of $18,000, or $540.00, which would result in an advance in the amount of $17,460.

Royalties

Article IV sets forth the amount of the royalties, but states that some of the royalties are subject to the adjustments set forth in Article V. Section 4.01 defines the different kinds of performances, such as "out-of-town" performances and "preview" performances. The significant contribution is in the definition and determination of the royalties for a "fixed-fee" performance.

Prior to the APC, the fixed-fee performances were dealt with in what was known as "Paragraph Tenth" of the MBPC, which was not part of the printed form and was the subject of negotiation for each contract.

With the APC, a fixed fee is paid to a producer when he sells the entire production for presentation by a local promoter, or local sponsor, who pays a flat fee for the entire show, which amount includes payment for the production rights. Since the payment received by the producer is not measured directly by box office receipts, there must be some other measure of the payment to the author for the production rights. Section 4.02 (d) fixes the amount of these payments.

The fixed-fee payments for a First-Class Performance are different than for other than a First-Class Performance. This is a somewhat complicated way to fix the fees payable to the author; but at least this is an attempt, and it will avoid the necessity of negotiating this item each time a contract is made.

Royalty Adjustments

Article V is the Guild's answer to the recognized need for a royalty pool formula. It is an attempt to give the investors an opportunity to recoup their investment during a period when the author accepts a reduced royalty. The author's royalty increases after recoupment.

The adjustment for out-of-town, preview, and regular performances (with the exception of the first three consecutive seven-day periods following the official press opening of the play in New York City) is covered by Section 5.05. It provides that prior to recoupment of production costs the author will be paid a royalty of $1,000 per week, plus 25 percent of the weekly profits, but in no event more than 5 percent of the gross weekly box office receipts during weeks that the gross weekly box office receipts are not over 110 percent of the "weekly breakeven" as defined in Article V. The royalty provided is $1,000 for each of the first three consecutive periods following the official opening.

After recoupment of the production costs, the same kind of formula is used, but the 25 percent of weekly profits is increased to 35 percent during weeks that the gross weekly box office receipts are not over 120 percent of the weekly breakeven; instead of 110 percent. If the director of the play receives, during any week, an amount less than is provided for in the director's agreement, then the author's 35 percent of the weekly profits will be reduced on a pro rata basis, but in no event less than 25 percent. Although it is not clear, it is presumed that the reference to "pro rata basis" means that the author's share will be reduced in the same proportion that the director's share is reduced.

The adjustment for touring performances of the play covered by Section 5.06 is identical with the provisions on adjustments for regular performances (Section 5.05) discussed above.

A new addition is the provision that the royalty is fixed at a flat $1,000 per performance week during any losing week of regular or touring performances. There is also a new provision in Section 5.09 that makes an adjustment that reduces the royalties payable for four weeks around the Christmas season. These are important provisions, because the play needs all the help that it can get during losing weeks, and traditionally plays suffer economically during the Christmas season. Unlike some businesses, theatre is a particularly seasonal business, and a play can experience several losing weeks or months, but if it can weather each storm, it may go on to run for a very long time.

General Payment Provisions

The general payment provisions of Article VII are similar to the provisions in the previous contract and merely designate to whom to make the checks and to whom to send them. That an adaptor of a foreign-language play must receive at least one-third of the compensation payable to the author is not new to this contract.

General Production Provisions

Most of the provisions in Article VIII are similar to provisions that were contained in the printed part of the old MBPC, or were added in Paragraph Tenth, which was the paragraph typed in with terms and conditions that were applicable to that particular play. The cast, director, and designers must be mutually agreeable to the producer and the author, and the straight play contract inadvertently includes "conductor, choreographer and/or dance director" when these would seem to be appropriate only in the contract for a musical play.

The significant part of this article appears in Section 8.01, paragraphs (b) and (c), where it is provided that no one may change a word of the author's script without his or her approval; and, if there are any approved changes, they belong to the author no matter who contributed them. Although the producer may complain to the Guild that the author is arbitrary in not doing rewrites of the play, and the Guild may urge the author to do so, neither the Guild, nor anyone else, can force the author to make any changes unless he or she wishes.

The amount of the per diem paid to the author when he or she is away from home has always been typed in as part of the old Paragraph Tenth. Now this agreement attempts to make a provision that need not be negotiated, but does not really accomplish the purpose and it must now be set forth in Article XXII, which is the equivalent of Paragraph Tenth If this provision is not added to Article XXII, the reference to "reasonable hotel and travel accommodations" of a class "equal to the greater of the class charged to the Company by Producer or Director" may be a source of disagreement and contention that interferes with the hoped-for smooth progress of the play. Ascertaining the "class" of the producer's accommodations is not always easy, since the producer is in charge of paying for them.

Section 8.06, concerning the author not using the designs without the consent of the owners of the designs, is a provision that the United Scenic Artists has insisted upon and that always appeared in Paragraph Tenth of the MBPC. This provision no doubt resulted from authors engaging licensing agents to license the stock and amateur rights and the licensing agents then wanting to designate the stage setup and the costume designs. A designer's work could then be copied in hundreds of theatres around the country and the designer would have no right to the income from such use. This section was intended to prohibit this practice.

"Billing credit," always a strongly negotiated item, is dealt with in Section 8.10, in an attempt to fix some parameters. One should have no trouble with the language as it is stated. An author usually expects that his or her name will be at least 50 percent of the size of the title, so that the 40-percent provision would, of course, be acceptable to the producers. The significant provision is contained in Section 8.10(b) concerning the size of the author's billing credit, if the title of the play appears more than once in any one advertisement. This would seem to permit the producer to use a billing box, which has the title in much smaller type, and all credits are based on the size of the type in the billing box. Since it is provided that Section 8.10 may be modified or supplemented by a provision in Article XXII, one should make sure that this provision applies to posters, billboards, and the like; that is, the reference to "Advertisement" must include such uses or it must be made clear that in addition to an advertisement, such other usage is permissible.

Use of part of the play for radio and television advertising is not a new idea. The amount of an excerpt from a play that may be used has variously been fixed at five minutes or ten minutes, so seven minutes seems a suitable compromise. There is every reason to believe that an author, if approached later, would welcome changing this to provide for a longer time, if the producer was willing to spend the money to arrange it or to have arranged for the kind of program that gives such advertising free as part of its programming.

It's nice for the original producer of the play to get credit as such in later productions and in other media, since billing credits are a very important part of the business and add to one's credibility in the business. Bear in mind that the author need only "use all best efforts" to make this happen, and it is not a contractual obligation that it occur.

House seats are still dealt with individually and are treated in the typewritten Article XXII. House seats, of course, are seats that must be purchased by the recipient. The requirements of section 8.14 were the result of the "ice scandal" investigation which exposed the unlawful sale of tickets at exorbitant prices by some of the box office personnel. This provision is intended to prevent a house-seat holder from trading in tickets for a profit.

Article IX, titled "Additional Production Terms" is an attempt to clarify what up to now has been dealt with in a haphazard manner. In the previous contract, the MBPC was an option for a first-class production. Although there was sometimes a question as to just exactly what was meant by a First-Class Production; nevertheless, the contract gave only First-Class rights.

Most knowledgeable attorneys in the field would provide for second-class tours, in Paragraph Tenth of the MBPC, but there was not usually a provision was not usually a provision that the contract covered all second-class productions. Off-Broadway also was not a part of the contract.

It worked the other way around. The Off-Broadway contract, if properly prepared, provided that the producer could contract for a First-Class Production in one of three ways. He could: (1) enter into an Off-Broadway contract containing an option to enter into a First-Class contract, with a reference to the terms of such First-Class contract; (2) enter into an Off-Broadway contract, with the MBPC annexed, to be signed and become effective when the optionee gives notice and makes the payments required; (3) sign both an Off-Broadway contract and an MBPC at the same time if the producer, at that time, believes that the play could be done in either arena, but is not certain which way to go either for artistic reasons or because he or she is not sure of being able to raise the larger amount of money required for the First-Class Production.

The new APC gives the producer the option to produce a second-class production, as well as a First-Class Production. A second-class production is defined as one that is other than First-Class, stock, amateur, and ancillary performances or Off-Broadway performances. It also sets forth the royalty terms for such a production.

Furthermore, if the producer's rights have "vested" (see below), the APC gives the producer the right to produce the play Off-Broadway, in the British Isles, Australia, and New Zealand.

Definition of "Vested"

In Section 11.02, the APC contains a definition of a concept that was employed throughout the MBPC. The term *vested* means that the producer's production has run a certain period of time so that from then on the producer acquires certain potentially valuable rights.

As in the previous contract, if the play runs the length of one of several specified times, then the producer becomes entitled to certain benefits, namely: (1) the rights to produce the play in "Additional Territories" as they are defined in the "Agreement"; (2) the right to reopen the play; (3) the right to participate in subsidiary rights income and to be consulted on the disposition of such rights; (4) the right to create, manufacture, and sell commercial use products, and at a later date to share in the income from such uses; (5) a preferential bargaining position with respect to the motion picture rights.

There are several alternative ways for becoming vested. The British Isles, Australia, and New Zealand are treated separately.

Participation in Subsidiary Rights

As in the previous contract the producer may acquire a participation in the subsidiary rights income of the author. The producer will assign this potential income to the producing company that will produce the play. As was stated, the play must first run long enough to "vest." Fortunately, what is a "subsidiary right" is defined.

Unlike the previous contract, which had but one plan set forth, the producer under the APC may elect one of four alternative plans for sharing the subsidiary rights income (in the musical APC, there are only three alternatives). If the producer does not elect one of the plans within the time set forth in Section 11.03 (c), then the author may elect one. If neither makes the choice within the time set forth, then Alternative III becomes applicable (see Appendix D). It is, of course, impossible to know which of the four alternatives will be most advantageous to either party without knowing about the specific play. Obviously, some plays will do better as amateur performances, and others will do better in stock. Each play must be judged on its own particular kind of appeal, and a determination made of what is the best market for that particular play. Some plays will be difficult to present as stock or amateur productions.

As before, the producer shares in the author's income, no matter when received, so long as the contract for subsidiary rights income is entered into within the specified period of time after the last performance of the play, pursuant to the Approved Production Contract.

The attempt to deal with "Revival Performances" is very helpful. Up until now, there has been some confusion concerning what rights the producer would have in the proceeds from a revival. It is also useful that the Approved Production Contract has finally tried to define the various kinds of productions, such as First-Class, second-class, stock, amateur, developmental, out of town, and ancillary.

Commercial-Use Products

Unlike the previous contract, which simply gave a producer participating in subsidiary rights income a share of the income from commercial uses, the APC actually grants the producer the rights to exploit the commercial uses. After the producer's right to do so expires, the author controls these rights. When the producer has the rights, he or she shares with the author, and when the author controls these rights, he or she shares with the producer on any contract entered into before the expiration of forty years after the last performance of the play, wherever the producer has vested (British Isles, Australia, New Zealand, U.S.). In each instance, the percentage sharing is the same.

The author will get: (1) 10 percent of the gross retail sales (after the deduction of taxes) for sales in theatres in which the producer presents the play; (2) 50 percent of producer's net receipts from sales (as this term is defined in the APC) for sales in other locations.

The producer will get: (1) 10 percent of the gross retail sales (after the deduction of taxes) for sales in theatres in which the author's play is presented; (2) 50 percent of producer's net receipts from sales (as this term is defined in the APC) for sales in other locations.

It has always been important to a producer of a First-Class stage production that he not be faced with competition from other stage productions and from other media. Section 11.07 attempts to more clearly define the limits of other uses of the play and expands the concept to include productions in other media.

Article XIII is a carryover from the previous contract as is Exhibit B, the "Instructions to the Negotiator." The purpose of this article and Exhibit B is to give some advantage to a film company that may finance the First-Class Production, but at the same time to make sure that there is no double-dealing.

An author bent on taking advantage of the producer could make a separate film deal in which he or she sells the film rights for something less than they are worth in exchange for the author's granting the motion picture company the rights to another play (in which he or she does not have to share the proceeds with a producer) for something more than the author would otherwise receive.

There is also the constant threat that a film producer will acquire the film rights from the author at a reduced figure, in exchange for the promise that his or her play will be produced. Bear in mind that the APC, like the MBPC, is an option and not a contractual obligation to produce the play. In fact, there are an astonishing number of plays optioned that never get produced. So the promise of a production is an attractive lure to convince the author to sell the film rights for something less than they would otherwise be worth.

For these reasons, the APC provides for a film negotiator who is designated by the Guild and whose job it is to prevent such abuses and to make certain that any sale is on fair and reasonable terms for all parties.

Another important difference in the contracts is that the APC addresses audiovisual productions (Article XIII) rather than just motion picture rights.

Since the MBPC was first established, there has been technological development necessitating some of the changes provided in the APC. Television was invented, and then came audiocassettes and videocassettes, but if the producer's attorney was not knowledgeable in this area, he missed them. The new contract fills this gap.

The new provision that a producer of a revival, under certain circumstances, will share in the author's proceeds from a film sale is contained in Section 13.05. The new provision clarifies the terms if the revival is a First-Class Production and also now refers to a second-class revival. The author having given a 40 percent share of the proceeds from the motion-picture-rights to the original producer, would not feel good about giving a similar percentage to the producer from the motion-picture-rights income of the author. Without some interest in subsidiary-rights income for the financers of the revival, the financing would be very difficult; not impossible, but difficult.

Unfortunately, although Section 13.05 deals with this problem, it does not consider the sharing if the revival is Off Broadway or in a middle theatre. See discussion in Chapter 2 about a solution under such circumstances.

The APC provision for a theatrical conciliation council, provided for in Article XV, is something new. The council is to be composed of five author members and five producer members. The purpose of the council is to consider questions and problems that may arise from time to time during the term of the contract. If there is not a majority vote on any issue, the council selects one disinterested third party to resolve the dispute. If a majority cannot agree on the impartial party, the matter may be submitted to arbitration.

What is most interesting is the reference in Section 15.01 to those specific sections that, in addition to the other contract sections, would be subject to consideration of the council. The specific sections singled out for mention are those covering (1) fixed-fee performance payments; (2) review of weekly breakeven and recoupment calculation; (3) author's billing; and (4) producer's lease, or license, of rights to produce the play in Australia or New Zealand.

Although the Guild still wants to certify the contract, there is, in addition to the certification procedure outlined, some very encouraging language as to the prospects of changing the contract terms under the proper circumstances.

It is a good thing that the Guild acknowledges that the terms of the APC are not etched in stone. They will consider reasonable modifications if necessary to counterbalance or neutralize special circumstances because of the nature of the play or its contemplated production, which circumstances could be expected to affect materially the producer's ability to (a) finance the play, or (b) return to investors their capital contributions within a period then prevailing for other productions of similar size and type, or (c) obtain all the benefits to be accorded to the producer as contemplated by the APC. This is progress, the acknowledgment that the investors are an important part of the producing entity and that adjustments must be made to accommodate them.

There is also a method set forth in Section 16.05 for submission of the contract to a joint review board. If either the producer or the author do not agree with suggested revisions of the contract it may be submitted to the board, which consists of one author member and one producer member selected from the Theatrical Conciliation Council.

Probably the most important thing that emerged from the negotiations for the APC is the awareness of the economic facts of 1985 theatre life, which resulted in an attitude on the part of the Guild that did not prevail during the time that the MBPC was being used. Although the MBPC provided for a General Advisory Committee to establish principles concerning the contract, it did little or nothing to improve the contract.

What happened, in fact, was that an attorney for a producer would negotiate with the author's representative until an agreement was reached. Then the producer's attorney would submit the signed contract to the Guild for its countersignature. If the Guild didn't like certain terms that were negotiated, they would instruct the attorney to have them removed from the contract. The attorney could argue with the Guild, but if they stood firm, and if their member author stood firm, the producer had no choice but to accept their edict or abandon the thought of producing that particular play.

With this background, it is no wonder that the theatrical business people welcome the concept of a theatre conciliation council and joint review board, but most of all the acceptance of the fact that the contract ought to be changed under certain circumstances at certain times. It is probable that the Guild had little choice but to accept this intrusion on its formerly held powers, the result of a combination of circumstances, such as the need to have a realistic royalty arrangement to attract investors, plus the awareness that some Guild members were quietly defying the Guild and making separate arrangements to get their plays produced. Sometimes such separate arrangements were made instead of using the MBPC, but most often an MBPC was entered into and then the representatives of the parties made some side letter agreements that the Guild never saw and never knew about. Some Guild members are today doing the same thing under some circumstances and defying the Guild admonition to not work on a First-Class Production without a Guild-certified APC.

The arbitration provisions are still part of the contract as set forth in Article XX, with some minor modifications.

Article XXI contains some miscellaneous provisions, two of which deserve careful reading and awareness of their existence. Section 21.02 settles part of the hassle as to who is responsible for the payments to a not-for-profit theatre that presented the play prior to the producer's production.

It is most usual for such a not-for-profit organization to finance, in whole or in part, a workshop or showcase production, and in exchange, therefore, to receive some part of the gross receipts, and sometimes some part of the net profits of a future commercial production (see discussion in Chapter 2).

The not-for-profit organizations' pitch for a share of the net profits relates to their desire to have some part of the subsidiary rights income. It will be interesting to see whether this provision fixes the amount that is paid to such organizations as 1 1/2 percent of the gross and 5 percent of the subsidiary rights income.

The provision for the gross payments is in a usual amount. The 5 percent of the subsidiary rights income would seem to be a reasonable substitute for the 5 percent of the net profits that was usually asked for and often agreed to.

Commentary on the Dramatists Guild, Inc., Approved Production Contract for Musical Plays

---

Many of the differences between the APC for plays and the APC for musical plays (Appendix E) involve different numbers, both percentages and dollar amounts; adjustment because there may be three parties involved—the bookwriter, the composer and the lyricist (although they may be only one or two persons); and the necessity of dealing with music and lyrics, publishing, and recordings.

In addition, there are a few conceptual differences that are based on the fact that a musical production will be presented in a theatre having a much larger potential box office gross than the gross for a straight play.

In Article I, Section 1.06 sets forth a well-accepted basic principle, namely that the music and lyrics for a musical play belong to the composer and lyricist and they must be the copyright owners. (On some rare occasions a producer will try to encroach on these rights, but when this happens, it is most often a misunderstanding of the role of the producer, sometimes an honest mistake.)

Music publishing rights, small performing rights, and recording rights belong to the composer and lyricist.

In general, the main difference between the musical contract and the play contract is that the musical contract provides for larger advances and for smaller percentage royalty payments. That the percentages are smaller does not mean that the amounts paid are smaller. The following differences should be noted:

1. In Article II, the first-option period payment provided in the musical contract is $18,000 for twelve months and in the play contract is $5,000 for the first six months.

The second-option period in the musical contract is $9,000 for a second consecutive twelve-month period and in the play contract is for $2,500 for the second consecutive six-month period.

The third-option period in the musical contract is $900 per month for a maximum of twelve consecutive months ($10,800) and in the play contract is $5,500 for up to twelve months, payable $2,500 for the first six months of such period and $500 per month thereafter

2. A completed play is defined in Article II, Section 2.03, as at least 110 single-spaced pages; in the musical contract as a book of at least eighty single spaced pages and a score of music and lyrics for at least twelve songs.

3. The additional advance payments based on additional contributions to the capitalization are 3 percent in the play contract and 2 percent in the musical contract, as provided in Article III, Section 3.01, of the musical contract.

4. The maximum advance is $35,000 in the play contract and $60,000 in the musical contract, as provided in Section 3.02.

5. The out-of-town royalty and preview-performance royalty is a straight percentage in the play contract and is a fixed-fee-and-percentage arrangement in the musical contract. The regular-performance royalty is 5 percent until recoupment and 10 percent thereafter in the play contract and 4.5 percent until recoupment and 6 percent thereafter in the musical contract.

6. The fixed-fee performance royalty is 10 percent in the play contract and 6 percent in the musical contract as provided in Article IV, Section 4.02(d), of the musical contract.

7. The limitation on the producer's cash office in the play contract is $500 per week and in the musical contract is $1,500 per week, as provided in Section 4.04 (b) of the musical contract.

8. In computing the weekly breakeven amount, the author's royalties are considered to be $1,000 in the play contract, regardless of the amount actually paid, and are considered to be $3,000 in the musical contract, regardless of

the amount actually paid, as provided in Section 5.01 of the musical contract. The weekly cash-office charge for this purpose is not to exceed $500 in the play contract and $1,500 in the musical contract. The producer's royalty for this purpose is limited to $250 in the play contract and $1,500 in the musical contract.

9. The adjustments for regular performances post-recoupment in Section 5.06 (b) of the musical contract are applicable during weeks that the gross weekly box office receipts for any performance week do not exceed 115 percent of breakeven and is 120 percent in the straight-play contract. The limit on author's fixed-and-percentage royalty for this purpose is 10 percent in the play contract and 6 percent in the musical contract.

10. The adjustments for touring performances, pre-recoupment, as stated in Section 5.07 (a) of the musical contract is for a fixed royalty of $3,000 as opposed to $1,000 in the play contract. In no event can the author's fixed-and-percentage royalty exceed 4.5 percent of the gross weekly box office receipts for each week in the musical contract and 5 percent in the play contract.

The post-recoupment adjustment for any performance week of touring performances refers to a maximum of 115 percent of weekly breakeven in the musical contract and 110 percent of weekly breakeven in the play contract. The fixed royalty is $3,000 in the musical contract and $1,000 in the play contract. In the musical contract, the author's fixed-and-percentage royalty won't exceed 6 percent of the gross weekly box office receipts and in the play contract won't exceed 10 percent.

11. During losing weeks, the author's royalty, as provided in Section 5.08 of the musical contract, is limited to $3,000 per performance week and is limited to $1,000 per performance week in the play contract.

12. The Christmas-period adjustment provided in Section 5.10 of the musical contract provides for an advance to the author of $3,000 per performance week, and this amount in the play contract is $1,000.

13. Section 5.13 of the musical contract provides for a proportionate adjustment in the producer's royalty. For the purpose of calculating recoupment and weekly breakeven, the producer's royalty is computed as therein set forth but not less than $1,500. In the play contract, it is not less than $250.

14. Section 6.02 deals with deductions from royalties, and limits the amount of the deductions to $3,000 per performance week in the musical contract and $ 1,000 per performance week in the play contract.

Section 4.02 (d), (iv) of the musical contract does not appear in the play contract. It provides that, if the producer cannot in good faith arrange for fixed-fee performance payments because the total royalty payments exceed 15 percent of the sums to the producer, the author defers part of the royalty payment so that the author receives the same proportionate share of 15 percent of the sum payable to the producer that he would receive from the total royalty, if paid. The balance over the 15 percent is deferred and payable from other designated receipts.

The musical contract, in Section 5.04, defines "Potential and Actual Gross Ticket Sales," and these definitions do not appear in the Approved Production Contract for Plays. The reason for the definition is that Section 5.06 of the Musical Contract provides for an adjustment in the royalty for regular performances in New York City pre-recoupment, if, in the first 21 performance weeks after the official opening, actual ticket sales in 17 of 21 of such weeks are equal to at least 87 percent of potential gross ticket sales. There is also an adjustment if, thereafter, for any three consecutive performance weeks, actual gross ticket sales fall below 87 percent of potential gross ticket sales. This is labeled the "87% Formula."

The previous Dramatists Guild Minimum Basic Production Contract in the printed form made no provision for royalty adjustments. Producers' attorneys would put in provisions for reductions during losing weeks, if everyone earning a royalty took a similar reduction. The Guild took the position that when you need help with a royalty reduction you should come to them and ask for such help. In fact, reductions were then agreed to by the author and producer during the early weeks of many shows without the approval of the Guild, in fact without the Guild even having knowledge of the waiver of royalties by the author in many cases.

The play contract provides that option payments for all but the third-option period are deducted from the advance payments made to the author. In Section 6.01 of the musical contract, it is provided that the option payments for all but the first-option period are deducted from the advance payment. Why there is this difference is not known, except that it is assumed that this is one of the compromises that resulted from the negotiations between the Guild and the League.

Whereas the play contract provides that the adaptor will receive at least one-third of the compensation otherwise payable to the author, the musical contract, in Section 7.05, makes no such provision, and provides that, unless the adaptor is the English-language "bookwriter," he will not be considered an author or receive any part of the author's royalty.

Since the "author" of a musical (consisting of a book, music, and lyrics) is usually more than one person, and the author of a play is usually one person,

Section 8.03 in each contract has similar but different provisions. There is also a provision in the musical contract that, after three weeks from the first presentation in New York City, if approval for changes or replacements of the author who is bookwriter, composer, and/or lyricist is requested and there is no response within seventy-two hours, the right to vote of such person failing to respond is forfeited. Why this same provision does not appear in the play contract is not known.

Sections 8.17 through 8.21 are not found in the play contract because they deal with items only important to a musical. Music publishing rights, musical scores, the cast album, and music and lyrics deleted from the musical are not proper subjects for a play contract. It should be noted, however, that, although cast albums of plays that do not have music are no longer popular, thirty years ago play albums of straight plays were a very marketable item.

What is significant about sections 8.17, 8.18, and 8.19 of the Approved Production Contract for Musical Plays are the references to what is provided in Article XXII. Article XXII is the provision that is not a part of the printed contract, but is added by the parties after negotiations. Although Sections 8.17 through 8.19 deal with these items, there is still a great deal of leeway as to what will be negotiated and what will end up in Article XXII. The APC was intended to be a minimum-and-maximum contract and not subject to change for the benefit of either party. However, as pointed out, it didn't exactly work out that way. Changes have been made and these sections invite just such negotiation and change.

Traditionally, the producer shares 40 percent of the original cast album and the author 60 percent. The producer's share does not come from the musical running any given length of time, but rather from the producer furnishing the cast for the album. What has never been clearly defined is who has the rights to make the deal for the cast album. There have been various proposals in the past. Sometimes the author had the sole right, sometimes the producer had the sole right, and sometimes both parties would jointly share this right. In each case, of course, the outcome depended on the bargaining power of the respective parties.

What comes as a significant change is the agreement in Section 8.18 that the parties may agree in Article XXII on the terms for disposition of "various music publishing rights in the music and lyrics of the Play." The composer and lyricist have always held these rights in music publishing to be sacrosanct and not subject to encroachment by the producer. Through the years, some producers have tried to encroach on these rights. There is an acknowledgment in this section that, if the producer has the bargaining power, he may end up with some say so and perhaps even some monetary interest in the music publishing rights. This is the acknowledgment of a changed attitude. Whether any producers do in fact end up with any publishing income, or say so with respect to music publishing, remains to be seen.

The sharing of subsidiary rights income is different in each contract. The play contract gives the producer four alternatives and the musical contract gives the producer three alternatives. The percentages are different and the time for sharing is different. It is difficult to speculate which alternative is preferable from the producer's point of view. One can only assume that each play has its own future in different forms, and one must try to evaluate, or guess, where each particular play may be most successful.

The subsidiary rights provision (Article XI) in both contracts is a new concept. Previously, if the producer shared in subsidiary rights income, it was to the extent of 40 percent for the first ten years from the signing of the contract granting such rights, 35 percent for the following two years, 30 percent for the next two years, 25 percent for the next two years, 20 percent for the next two years, and nothing after the eighteenth year.

Since producers are not bound to use the contract, it is no longer widely used as the MBPC was. With respect to its future use, much will depend upon the authors themselves, as to whether they have the bargaining power to insist upon its use and whether they will feel inclined to do so.

Royalty Pool Formulas

The royalty pool formula agreed to for the production of one Broadway musical made an important contribution to the business of financing Broadway plays, particularly musicals. To understand the formula and its ramifications, one ought to have some knowledge of the various elements that go into making up a formula. They are:

1. the amount of any advance against the "contingent compensation," which is determined by all the variables that are set forth in the formula and is usually payable from some percentage of the weekly operating profits or of the net profits of the producing company. The advance may be fixed at the time of the negotiations as noted below in (a), (b), and (c), or may be computed as set forth in (d).

The advance may be:

(a) in a fixed amount, usually a dollar amount such as $250 for each 1 percent of the regular royalty to which the party is contractually entitled (for an Off-Broadway production), or $800 for each 1 percent (for a Broadway production), or some other amount;

(b) computed as some stated percentage of the total capitaliza-tion of the play or of the potential gross weekly box office receipts;

(c) any arbitrary amount arrived at by negotiation between the parties;

(d) computed based on the gross weekly box office receipts, such as an amount equal to half of the regular royalty for such weekly receipts

2. the amount of any fee payable to any of the parties that does not constitute an advance against the contingent compensation;

3. the designation of the parties who will share in the royalty pool formula in some proportion, almost always in the same proportion that they would share in gross weekly box office receipts, sometimes referred to as the pro rata share;

4. any parties, such as the star and the "theatre" (theatre-building owner), who may share in the pool, but in some different way than the other participants, usually in a preferred position. (The theatre arrangement will often provide for the theatre to receive an amount to cover its expenses plus a percentage of the gross weekly box office receipts);

5. the parties, if any, who will not share in the pool, but receive fixed compensation;

6. any provision for minimum weekly guarantees, which may or may not be advances against the contingent compensation;

7. a provision to pay the royalty pool participants pro rata from some percentage of the weekly operating profits (for example, they may be paid a maximum amount equal to half their royalty from 30 percent of such profits until 125 percent of recoupment);

8. an arrangement for increasing the royalty after recoupment of the production costs or some multiple of recoupment, such as 125 percent of recoupment, 150 or 200 percent. For example, the royalty pool participants may be paid a pro rata share from 35 percent of the weekly operating profits until 200 percent of recoupment and a pro rata share from 40 percent of such

profits thereafter; provision may be made for different payments to be made at different multiples of recoupment;

9. any arrangement for payment of deferred royalties, which must also make provision for how the deferrals will be recovered. If a deferral is provided for, there is usually a provision that after recoupment of the total production costs, or 125 percent or 150 percent of recoupment, the deferral will be recovered pro rata by the pool participants from a percentage of some profits—perhaps 25 percent of the weekly operating profits.

10. it is also possible to provide a maximum weekly payment to any royalty pool participants;

11. the royalty pool formula provisions may be fixed, or the producer may have the option during the first few weeks after the New York opening to pay the regular royalties or to invoke the formula; and

12. the formula may be based on the "weekly" operating profits (which term is, of course, defined, as are all the terms necessary to use the formula) or may be based on some other accounting period, such as an average of four consecutive weeks (the reasoning behind a four-week period is that a show may do great business for one week and then have three disastrous weeks, or vice versa. This is an attempt to balance the sharing of the loss or gain by an averaging process).

The different formulas sometimes use different terms to mean the same thing. These terms should be defined in the Limited Partnership Agreement. For example, the "total production costs", "100 percent of the production costs," "production expenses," "100 percent of the production expenses," "total production budget," and "100 percent of the total production budget" are intended to convey the same meaning.

In almost every instance, any of the above terms is followed by language to the effect that the amount is "exclusive of any bonds, deposits and other recoverables." In fact, if this statement is not included, one can be certain that the parties did not know what they were doing, or knew that what they were doing was a mistake. This is understandable when one realizes that the formula concept, and other previous attempts to make investing in theatre more attractive, was created to give the investors back their money before the production costs were increased. At the point that the investors can recoup their total investment is a good time to begin increasing royalties and other percentage payments. Even though the investors may not actually receive their investment back at that time, when this amount is attained by the producing company, they could be paid back in full. The bonds and other recoverables are assets of the producing company and profits are not necessary to cover such amounts in order to make the investors whole.

It is obvious from the above facts that royalty pool formulas may be as various as one's imagination. When structuring the formulas, the ultimate success of the formula will be in whether investors will be satisfied with it enough to part with their money.

CHAPTER 5

The Producing Company

Limited Liability Company, Partnership, Corporation

Why a Limited Liability Company

Tax Benefits and Freedom from Personal Liability for Investors and Producers

A LIMITED LIABILITY COMPANY OR A LIMITED PARTNERSHIP should be used as the producing entity for most theatrical productions. For about seventy years, limited partnerships were used as the producing entity rather than a corporation, a joint venture, or a general partnership. Although there were various complicated schemes for using corporations to accomplish certain specific purposes, by and large the tax advantages of a partnership— namely that the profits are only taxed once, and in the event of losses, they would flow through and be deductible by the partners, subject to the passive-activity-loss rules of the Tax Reform Act were and still are advantages that most investors looked for, expected, and sometimes even insisted upon.

With a corporation, the profits are first taxed as income to the corporation and then, when paid out to the investors as dividends, are again taxed to the investors. Moreover, any losses will not pass through a corporation to the shareholder, other than with a sub-chapter S corporation. Thus the loss would belong to the corporate entity and could not be used until the corporation had income to set off against the loss. A sub-chapter S corporation allows for the pass through of income and losses to shareholders (subject to the passive-activity-loss rules) the same as a partnership. There are reasons why a sub-chapter S corpora-tion is not used for a theatrical production.

It is also possible to arrange for the investors to make loans to a corporation in which the producer is the sole stockholder. Up until 1942, when the Internal Revenue Code was changed, this was a common procedure. This was abandoned for the reason that a non-business bad debt, unless by a corporation regularly engaged in the lending business, is considered a capital loss rather than an ordinary loss.

Limited Liability and The Limited Liability Company Law

A general partnership is seldom used as the producing entity, because it does not give the investors the protection of limited liability, which is the essential feature of a limited partnership. A limited partner's liability is limited to the amount of his or her investment, although the general partner of a limited partnership is personally liable for the obligations of the limited partnership.

A "joint venture" is a fancy name for a kind of general partnership. The investors under such circumstances would be considered general partners with all of the liability of a general partner. There have been some producing companies (one rather well known) that have used joint venture agreements where the investors were led to believe that they enjoyed limited liability. Although he may not have to expend his own funds above the original investment, a joint venturer does not, as a matter of fact, enjoy limited liability and is exposed to the same liability as any other general partner in a general partnership.

The Limited Liability Company Act became effective in 1995 in the state of New York at a time that forty-eight states had such an act. The act provided for the creation of a limited liability company (an "LLC") that would have the tax advantages of a partnership and the freedom from liability for the principals of the company. This meant that the producer as well as the investor could enjoy freedom from personal liability.

Before the Limited Liability Act was passed in an attempt to have the benefit of freedom from personal liability for the producer and the benefits of being taxed as a partnership, some attorneys advised that clients to form a corporation which corporation would become the general partner of the limited partnership. There were risks involved that the partnership might be deemed to be a corporation for tax purposes by the Internal Revenue Service, if the corporation was a shell without substantial assets, but many producers upon advice of counsel assumed this risk.

When the limited liability law was passed, there was no longer the need to run the risk of a corporate general partner since the limited liability company offered a risk free way of combining freedom from personal liability with the tax benefits of a partnership. In spite of this, some attorneys working in theatre refused to learn and use the benefits of the limited liability act, continuing to rely on the limited partnership, probably because it had been done that way for about seventy years and some attorneys are reluctant to accept anything new and different, no matter what the benefits.

Effective January 1, 1997, the Regulations of the Internal Revenue Service made it easy for the producers by giving the producer the option for the producing entity to be taxed as a partnership or as a corporation, whether the producing entity was a limited partnership or a limited liability company.

The test was previously used by the Internal Revenue Service to classify an entity as a corporation for tax purposes was based on four corporate characteristics which distinguish a corporation from other entities: (1) continuity of life, (2) centralization of management, (3) free transferability of interests, and (4) limited liability. Since January 1, 1997, the four characteristics test is no longer used.

Being taxed as a partnership or corporation, whether a limited partnership or a limited liability company, is now the option of the producer.

Limited Liability Company Operating Agreement

There is no standard theatrical limited liability operating agreement. There was a very old and dated limited partnership agreement printed form that some attorneys used and adapted for each particular show. Through the years many changes and additions were made in the form by attorneys working in the business, each having his own particular adaptations. Many of the terms of the limited partnership agreement were incorporated into the limited liability company operating agreement which I prepared. The basic business terms are the same, whether a partnership or a limited liability company, but there are many differences in the agreements.

The following discussion refers specifically to the Limited Liability Company Operating Agreement. However, these same terms, for the most part, would be included in a Limited Partnership Agreement between the General Partners (the "Producers") and the Limited Partners (the "Investors"). The reference to the Managing Member in the Limited Liability Company Operating Agreement is a reference to the Producer, and the reference to the Investor Members is a reference to the Investors.

Basic Provisions

There are certain basics that most limited liability company operating agreements, if properly prepared, will have in common. It is usually these few important elements that the producer knows and discusses with the investor. Many investors who have invested in theatre before are aware of these basic provisions. For example, almost all theatrical limited liability company operating agreements provide that the first net receipts of the company are used to repay the investors their original investment, and after the investors have recouped their investment, all net profits are shared equally with the producer. The producer receives 50 percent and the investors share the other 50 percent in proportion to the amount of their respective investments.

Most limited liability company operating agreements provide that the investors will share in all of the profits of the producing company, including profits from subsidiaries. There are, however, instances where the producer will share only the box office receipts with the investors, just as there are rare instances where the producer will give the investors 60 percent of the profits, rather than 50 percent.

The limited liability company operating agreement is the agreement between the producer, the managing member, and those persons who will sign the agreement as investor members. The agreement is usually signed by the investor at the time the investment in the production is made. After all of the investor members have invested and the production is completely financed, the attorney for the production will prepare a conformed copy of the agreement (a conformed copy is a duplicate of the original with the signatures of each partner indicated) and will forward a copy to each of the investors.

Usual Provisions

The discussion under "Definitions" will cover most of the terms, items, and provisions found in most limited liability company operating agreements. One should bear in mind that each general partner of a "limited partnership" assumes all of the obligations and liabilities of the producing company. The managing members of a "limited liability company" do not have this concern because none of them will assume any personal liability for the obligations to the creditors. The assets of the producing company is what is available to pay debts.

The limited liability company name must contain either the words "Limited Liability Company" or "LLC" or "L.L.C."

If additional funds are needed after the investor members' money is used up, it must come from the managing member. The managing member has the right to make all of the decisions for the company, and is — and should be — responsible as decision maker. The Limited Liability Company Operating Agreement will state that it is being made between the producer and those persons who sign the agreement as "investor members." It will set forth the main address of the company, as well as the name and address of the attorney for the company.

After a show opens, even if it is making money, the production company should not disperse all of the profits to the members, because of the nature of the theatre business. It is not unusual to have a period of very successful business followed by several weeks of more of difficult times. If all of the profits have been paid to the members, then there would be nothing in the company to get over the rough times. Accordingly, most agreements provide that a "sinking fund" (that is, a cash reserve) may be established and retained by the company. The amount of the sinking fund is defined in the agreement and will usually be between $30,000 and $75,000 for an Off-Broadway play and between $150,000 and $350,000 for a Broadway play, the amount depending upon the play's total weekly expenses.

The amount of money the producer intends to raise for the production is known as the "estimated production requirements," or the "total capitalization." It is the amount of cash that, together with any bonds or guarantees furnished, totals the specific dollar amount the producer will attempt to raise. It may be possible for the production to commence with something less than the estimated production requirements, since it might be possible to produce the show for a smaller amount. However, under all circumstances the agreement should state the minimum specific dollar amount that must be raised for a production before the investors' money can be used. Investors want to know that when an investment is made, it will be used only if enough money is raised to produce the show.

The estimated total capitalization required for a dramatic play Off-Broadway will range between $100,000 and $350,000 and for a musical between $400,000 and $1,000,000. The requirements for a Broadway dramatic play will be between $1,000,000 and $2,500,000 and for a musical between $5,000,000 and $9,000,000.

Term of Company

The agreement will usually provide that the company will commence on the day when the articles of organization of the limited liability company is filed in the office of the secretary of state of New York and will terminate upon a specified date, or the death, insanity, or retirement of any individual managing member. The agreement usually provides that the managing member will file such articles. At the present time, it is necessary to publish the articles, or a digest thereof, in two newspapers in the county in which the principal office is located, once a week for six consecutive weeks. An exception to the publishing has been made in the case of a theatrical limited partnership, which need not publish if it is in the business of producing a stage play before a live audience.

Since a theatrical limited liability company should be given the same consideration as a theatrical limited partnership, I have been in communication with the secretary of state of New York to support legislation giving the limited liability company the same exemption from publishing. It is possible that by the time this book is published, the same exception will apply to a limited liability company.

The company may also be terminated when all rights of the company in the play have terminated. Upon termination, the managing member must immediately liquidate the affairs of the company.

The managing member agrees to assign to the company all of the rights held or acquired by him or her in the play. The managing member is generally reimbursed for all legitimate expenditures made prior to the formation of the LLC. The managing member may be reimbursed for the full cost of the option agreement, attorneys' fees, accountants' fees, script duplication costs, and similar expenses. The agreement must state an exact dollar amount that the managing member has expended to date, and should state that he is to be reimbursed for those properly budgeted expenditures he may reasonably make or incur in the future.

Use of Funds Invested

In the agreement, each investor member agrees to contribute to the capital of the company a specific amount, which is set forth in the agreement, which money may be used by the company for the payment of all expenses in connection with the production. An investor may invest by furnishing a bond to Actors' Equity Association, or one of the other unions, or by furnishing the theatre guarantee. The agreement provides that such an investment is the same as a cash investment by the investor member. If the play closes before the investor members' contributions have been repaid to them in full, and before the company has paid any of the obligations covered by the bond deposit, then each investor member who furnished a bond must pay the company the full principal amount that was originally pledged as a guarantee, less any amounts that they already have been called upon to pay.

There is an advantage to furnishing a bond or guarantee, since an association will accept an investment in a savings bank if it is given together with an assignment to the association to be held as security. Under such circumstances a party putting up bond money does not lose the bank interest, whereas all other investors in the producing company would receive no interest on their investment. This provision of the agreement is not intended to substantially discriminate in favor of such bond-furnishing investors, but it does. In the event that the play closes and the other investor members have lost part or all of their investment, a proportionate share will be taken from the bond-furnishing investor members to the extent that it is not used to cover the item for which the bond was posted.

In addition there is also a provision in most agreements that the first net profits received shall be paid to the association or theatre holding the bond for the purpose of releasing the bond. An investor posting a bond would have this additional distinct advantage over the other investors in that his or her funds are returned first. It is most usual for the contract provision to provide that such an arrangement may not reduce the percentage of net profits payable to the investor members. This means that in addition to the amount of the net profits purchased by the bond money, the managing member may have to compensate those persons who furnish bonds by giving them a share of producer's profits. If a producer is having difficulty raising the last money needed for the show, and is very close to being financed, he or she may under such circumstances make such an arrangement for the furnishing of the bond. Most managing members do not want to prefer one investor member over another, but if it means getting the last $50,000 or $200,000 necessary for the production to go on, and it might not otherwise go on, then the managing member might be more inclined to make such an arrangement.

Use of Funds — Smaller Capitalization Finally

The managing member agrees not to use the funds received from the investor members until a specified amount of money, the total capitalization, has been raised. The amount sufficient to produce the show, as noted, is known as the "estimated production requirements," and there may be a maximum and a minimum set forth. The producer may try to raise $400,000, which is set forth as the "maximum estimated production requirements," but may be able to produce the play for $300,000, with a somewhat smaller reserve or by reducing the advertising budget. The amount of $300,000 is considered the "minimum estimated production requirements." The company operating agreement will provide that the company may use the invested funds when between $300,000 and $400,000 has been raised and that under no circumstances may an investment of investor member be used without prior written approval from such investor member, until at least $300,000 has been raised. If the amount necessary to produce the play is not raised within the period of the option to produce the play, the managing member agrees to return to the respective investor members all of the funds collected.

The Arts and Cultural Affairs Law of the state of New York, with the rules and regulations promulgated thereunder by the attorney general of the state of New York, will not permit the difference between the "minimum" and the "maximum" amount raised for a play to be in excess of 25 percent of the amount of the maximum to be raised.

If the play is finally capitalized for less than the maximum estimated production requirements, then instead of returning money to the investors, each investor member will end up with a larger percentage of the show for his investment. For example, if an investor member invests $8,000 for a 1 percent interest in the profits of a $400,000 show, and if the producer later decides to capitalize the show for $300,000, then the $8,000 investment would purchase 1.33 percent of the net profits of the production, and the investor would receive this share. An investor is investing a fixed dollar amount and may get more than 1 percent for the $8,000 investment in such a case, but the investor may not get less than 1 percent for such an amount.

Overcall

The limited liability company operating agreement may provide that each investor member must, upon demand of the managing member, make an additional contribution of 10 percent, 15 percent, or 20 percent of his or her original contribution. This is called an overcall. An overcall provision in the agreement is not recommended. If there are a large number of investors, it can be difficult to collect the overcall from all of them. If one or more refuses to honor the overcall, what is the managing member's obligation? The agreement may provide that the managing member may collect the amount not paid by an investor member from the other investor members, which is sure to make the managing member very unpopular with those having to pay. Or the agreement may provide that the managing member is responsible for any delinquent payments, which is also not a preferred position for the managing member. The managing member can sue for the overcall not paid, but this is both expensive and inconvenient.

Books of Account

The managing member agrees to keep or cause to be kept full and faithful books of account in which all the company transactions will be fully and accurately entered. The books of account as well as the box office statements received from the theatre (or theatres) are available for inspection and examination of the investor members or their representatives. The managing member further agrees to deliver to the investor members a complete statement of production expenses not later than sixty days after the official opening of the play, a monthly unaudited statement of operations, and such other financial statements as may be required by the New York Arts and Cultural Affairs Law and Regulations. The investor members are furnished with all information necessary to prepare their federal and state income tax returns.

Managing Member's Services

The managing member agrees to render the services customarily and usually rendered by theatrical producers and to devote as much time as necessary to the production. It is understood that the producer may engage in other businesses, including other theatrical productions.

The agreement will state that the managing member has complete control of production of the play and the exploitation of all rights in the play. The investor members have no rights to make decisions concerning the business.

Managing Member's Fee and Cash Office Charge

For his services, the producer is paid a producer's fee, which is usually in an amount between 1 and 2 1/2 percent of the gross weekly box office receipts. The producer will also reimburse himself for office facilities furnished to the production; this includes office space, secretarial services, telephone service, stationery, and the like. The amount that the producer takes as reimbursement is known as the "cash office charge" and is usually an amount between $400 and $750 each week for an Off-Broadway show and between $1,000 and $3,000 each week for a Broadway show. The cash office charge does not cover long-distance telephone calls, and if there are unusual expenses that would cause the producer's cost to exceed the amount set forth as the cash office charge, the producer would be entitled to reimbursement for these additional charges.

With the advent of the royalty pool formula, if the author and the other royalty participants agree to be paid as part of a formula, it is usual for the producer's fee to be included as 2, 2 1/2, or 3 points in the pool.

The producer will generally receive the cash office charge and the producer's fee beginning two or three weeks prior to the first rehearsal and continuing through the week after the close of the play. Of course, if the producer's fee is based upon a percentage of gross box office receipts, or is part of the royalty pool, there would be no producer's fee paid until there are box office receipts.

In the event that there is more than one company, the fee and cash office charge is also payable for each additional company for the period two or three weeks prior to the first rehearsal of such additional company and continuing until one week after its close.

Additional Investor Members

The agreement will provide that additional persons may become investor members either before or after the aggregate limited contributions have been obtained. If the managing member needs money above the original amount of the total capitalization, he or she may take on additional investor members, but they cannot reduce the respective shares of the original investor members, so the managing member must pay such additional investor members from the managing member's share of the net profits, just as the managing member would pay for a bond deal from his or her share of the profits.

Advances and Loans

The agreement will usually provide that the managing member has the right to make or receive loans to the company, and these loans will share a certain advantage. If all of the production money has been expended and additional funds are needed to get the show on or to keep the show running, then the managing member may make a loan to the producing company or obtain a loan from someone else, which may be repaid in full prior to the return of any of the contributions of the investor members. It is most usual, however, for the agreement to provide that the company may not incur any expenses in connection with any such loan or advance, and that the percentage of the net profits payable to the investor members must not be affected by such an arrangement.

Additional Services by Producer

The agreement should contain a provision that if the producer finds it necessary to perform any services that would otherwise be performed by a third person, then he may, if he so desires, receive reasonable compensation in the amount that the third person would have received for such services. It may happen, for instance, that the producer has to fill in and direct the show, or act as stage manager, or serve in some other vitally important capacity, and unless this provision appears in the agreement, he could not be paid for such services no matter how well performed and no matter how important to the company.

Share of Profits

As was previously stated, it is most usual for the investor members to share the profits equally with the producer after they have recouped their total investment. The agreement usually states this in the following way: Each investor member will receive that proportion of 50 percent of the net profits that his or her contribution bears to the aggregate limited contributions, excluding, however, from such investor members all persons who may be entitled to compensation as investor members only from the share of the managing member in such net profits and excluding from such aggregate limited contributions the contributions as investor members so made by such persons. Simply stated, this means that an investor member shares the 50 percent of the net profits with the other investor members pro rata in accordance with the size of the investment of each investor member. The excluded investor members for their excluded contributions, as we have stated, would receive compensation from whatever part of the managing member's profits the managing member has agreed to pay them.

In lieu of returning any part of the capital contribution of an investor member to cover the contingency previously referred to — in the event that the play is finally capitalized for less than the maximum estimated production requirements — the percentage of the net profits of each investor is accordingly increased so that each will receive that proportion of 50 percent of the net profits that the contribution made by the investor members bears to the reduced aggregate limited contributions, excluding the same investor members (and their contributions) who are compensated from the producer's share of the profits. This means simply that if the capitalization of the show is less than anticipated, then the investor members' specific dollar amount will purchase a larger percentage than originally anticipated. Each investor member still shares part of the 50 percent of the net profits, and his or her share is pro rata in accordance with the size of the investment; however, if the total budget decreases, this same dollar amount invested is then a proportionately larger percentage of the smaller, reduced capitalization.

Investor Members' Limited Liability

The agreement specifically states that investor members will not be personally liable for any debts, obligations, or losses of the company except from the capital contributed by them. In fact, the managing members, the producers, have the same freedom from personal liability.

Payments in Cash

Unless agreed to, the investor members have no right to demand and receive property other than cash in return for their contributions.

Return of Contributions

Contributions of the investor members are returned to them after the opening of the play and when the company has accumulated a cash reserve in the amount of the sinking fund (plus a reasonable amount for initial expenses in the event that the original company is sent on tour, and plus an amount for any additional company or companies that the producer wishes to organize to present the play), and after the payment of all expenses and provision for contingent expenses. If an investor, instead of investing cash, has given an obligation to Actors' Equity Association or to a similar organization, then in lieu of paying that particular investor's share to him, the company will set aside the amount of each distribution until there is a sum sufficient to release the bond to the investor member, and will then substitute the amount for the investor member's obligation and release the bond security to such investor member.

Distribution of Profits

The agreement will provide that after the investor members' contributions have been returned to them, after accumulating the cash reserve, the amount of the sinking fund plus any reasonable amount for additional companies (if the agreement gives the producer the right to retain profits for the purpose of funding additional companies), and after payment of all expenses and provision for contingent expenses, the net profits are to be paid monthly to the investor members and managing members in accordance with their respective interest in the profits. The monthly financial report prepared by the accountants for the company is used to determine whether or not any contributions are to be repaid or net profits distributed.

Distribution Upon Closing

Upon the closing of all companies and abandonment of further intention of producing the play, the assets of the company are liquidated as promptly as possible. The cash proceeds are used first for the payment of all debts, taxes, and obligations, for the creation of reserves for all contingent obligations, and then for the repayment of the capital contributed by the investor members if they have not been repaid. The balance is then divided among the limited and managing members in the proportion that they share in the net profits.

The agreement will provide that all physical assets of a salable nature belonging to the company must be sold at public or private sale, but that no assets other than the physical assets have to be sold. An investor member and/ or managing member may purchase the physical assets at such a sale.

After the completion of the run of all companies under the management of the company, the managing member has the right to sell or otherwise dispose of the production rights and the company's interest in the subsidiary rights other than the motion picture rights. The limited and/or managing members may be the purchasers at any such sale provided that the amount paid by them as purchasers is a fair and reasonable price. The agreement will sometimes provide that if there is a dispute as to the fairness and reasonableness of the offer, the president of the League of American Theatre and Producers will make the determination.

Return of Contributions or Profits to the Company

Most limited liability company operating agreements provide that if any contribution or distribution of profits is returned to the members and funds are thereafter needed by the company, the managing member may demand the return of any part of the profits or contribution distributed. The managing member and investor members must first repay any profits received by them, and if such profits are insufficient, then the investor members must return their capital contributions. The return to the company of profits and contributions by each partner is in proportion to the respective amounts received as profits by the parties.

Abandonment

The company agreement will provide that the managing member has the right, whenever he deems it necessary, to abandon the production at any time prior to its opening for any reason. In such an event, the production will liquidate all of its funds or accounts and the gross receipts will be distributed in the same manner that they would be distributed if there were no abandonment of the production. This provision is an essential part of any agreement, because although the producer agrees to produce the show and fully intends to do so, show business, like no other business, has unpredictable possibilities that could preclude proceeding with a production.

If the managing member, after the first public performance of the play, determines that continuation of the run is not in the best interests of the company and should be abandoned, he or she has the right to make arrangements with any person to continue the run of the play on such terms that he or she feels are in the best interests of the company.

Substitute Investor Member

An investor member may assign his or her interest in the company to someone else who would be then known as an assignee provided that the assignment maybe made only once and only with the producer's approval.

Additional Company to Produce Here or in Great Britain

The company agreement may provide that the managing member may organize an additional company or companies to present the play in the United States, Canada, or Great Britain (if the rights to produce the play in Great Britain accrue to the Company). Under such circumstances the net profits are not distributed until there is further accumulated in the bank account in addition to the reserve (sinking fund) provided for, a sum that, in the opinion of the managing member, will be sufficient to pay the production expenses of each such additional company. In the event that there is more than one company being presented at the same time, the reserve (sinking fund) provided for shall be maintained for each separate company before the repayment of contributions or distribution of net profits.

Managing Member's Involvement in Other Company

It is not unusual for the agreement to also provide that the company may enter into an agreement concerning the disposition of the British production and subsidiary rights of the play with any company, corporation, or other firm in which the managing member may be in any way interested, provided that such agreement must be on fair and reasonable terms.

There is also likely to be a provision that the managing member may be associated with any person, firm, or corporation which produces or company-produces a second company of the play and may receive compensation for doing so, without any obligation to account to the original producing company or to the members of the original company, provided that the original company receives from any such person, firm, or corporation the customary fees and royalties payable to it as the producer of the original company.

The managing member may have the right in the contract to make arrangements to license the road rights to any other party or parties the managing member may designate, provided that the company receives reasonable royalties, or other reasonable compensation, and the company assumes no obligation in connection with any loss or expenses of the company to which the license is granted. The managing members are not disqualified from participating in the company to which the rights are licensed by investing their funds, or otherwise, as a separate enterprise. A managing member may render services to the entity licensing the rights in connection with the exploitation of such rights.

Managing Member's Acquisition of Rights After Termination of Company

If, after the termination of the original producing company, the managing member purchases the production rights of the play for the United States or Canada, either with or without the physical production of the play, and with or without the company's interest in the proceeds of the subsidiary rights of the play, then the amount which the managing member pays for such rights must be the fair and reasonable market value, or an amount equal to the best offer obtainable, whichever is the higher price.

Motion Pictures

It is not unusual for the agreement to contain a provision to the effect that the parties acknowledge that one or more of the investor members may be a motion picture company, or a person nominated or otherwise controlled by a motion picture company, and that such company may acquire the motion picture rights in the play. In such event the company must be free to deal with the motion picture company without liability on the part of the motion picture company to account to the company or to the managing member or investor members for any profits it may derive from, or in connection with, the rights which it acquires.

Execution of Agreement

There are certain provisions in the agreement that are designed to simplify the execution of the agreement and the filing of the necessary documents. For example, there is a provision that the agreement may be executed in counterparts, all of which taken together will be deemed to be one original. This avoids the necessity of all members actually signing the same copy of the document. Each of the members agrees that the original of the agreement (or set of original counterparts) may be held at the office of the company; that Articles of Organization for the company be filed in the office of the secretary of state of New York and a duplicate original (or set of duplicate original counterparts) may be held at the office of the attorney for the company; and that each investor member will receive a conformed copy of the limited liability company operating agreement. In addition, the investor members give any one of the managing members a power of attorney in his place to make, execute, sign, acknowledge, and file: (1) the Articles of Organization for the limited liability company and to include in the articles all information required by the laws of the state, (2) such amended articles as may be required, and (3) all papers which may be required to effectuate the dissolution of the company after its termination.

Arbitration

The limited liability company operating agreement will almost always contain an arbitration clause which provides, in effect, that if there is a dispute in connection with the making or validity of the agreement, or its interpretation, or any breach of the agreement, then such dispute is determined and settled by arbitration in New York City (if that is the location of the parties, or at least the party with the most bargaining power) pursuant to the rules of the American Arbitration Association. Any award rendered by the Arbitration Association is final and conclusive upon the parties and a judgment may be entered in the highest court of the forum, state or federal, having jurisdiction. Such a provision cannot, however, affect the rights of the investor members under the federal securities laws (later discussed), which govern the offering of a security (a limited liability company interest is considered a security) to the public for sale.

Articles of Organization

The Articles of Organization, previously referred to is the document that is filed in the office of the secretary of state of New York in Albany and the filing fee is $200 to organize the company. The contents of this document, or a digest thereof, must be published once a week for six consecutive weeks in the county in which the company is doing business. The fee for filing the Articles of Organization is $200.

The county clerk in the county where the business is located will designate the newspapers for publication and if it is in the county of New York, one of the papers will be the *New York Law Journal*. The costs of publication in the two papers will be approximately $1,500.

The Articles of Organization contains the following information: (1) the name of the company; (2) the county in which the office is located in the state of New York; (3) the date of dissolution of the company; (4) a designation of the secretary of state of New York as agent of the limited liability company upon whom process against it may be served and the post office address to which the secretary of state will mail a copy of any process against the limited liability company served upon the secretary of state; (5) the name and address of a registered agent of the company, if any; (6) whether the limited liability company is to be managed by one or more members or a class of members; (7) if any specified members are to be liable for any specified dates, obligation or liabilities of the limited liability company; (8) any other provisions not inconsistent with law that the members wish to include for regulation of the affairs of the company, including but not limited to, (a) the business purposes for which the company is formed, or (b) whether there are limitations on the authority of any members.

Contents of Certificate of Limited Partnership in New York State

If the producer and his attorney decide to use a Limited Partnership as the producing entity instead of a Limited Liability Company, then, instead of filing the Articles of Organization with the Secretary of State, a Certificate of Limited Partnership will be filed. The Certificate will contain the following information: (1) the name of the partnership; (2) the nature of the business of the partnership, which is usually stated to be: to act as theatrical producer and to turn to account all rights held in the play; (3) the principal place of business; (4) the date that the partnership commences business and the date of termination; (5) the time when the contribution of each limited partner is returned to him or her; (6) the name and place of residence of each member, general and limited partners being respectively designated, the amount of cash and a description of and the agreed value of any other property contributed by each limited partner, and the percentage of individual profits to be received by each limited partner; (7) additional contributions, if any, agreed to be made by each limited partner and the times at which, or events on the happening of which, they will be made; (8) if a limited partner may substitute an assignee as contributor in his or her place, then this must be set forth together with the terms and conditions of the substitution; (9) the right, if given, of partners to admit additional limited partners; (10) the right, if given, of one or more of the limited partners to priority over other limited partners as to return of contributions or as to income and the nature of such priority; (11) the right, if given, of the remaining general partner or partners to continue the business on the death, retirement, or insanity of a partner; (12) the right, if given, of a limited partner to demand and receive property other than cash in return for his contribution.

CHAPTER 6

Co-producers and Associate Producers

EITHER BEFORE OR AFTER the option is acquired, the producer may decide to produce the play together with a co-producer. Producing a show is a large venture, and it may be advisable to have assistance in the raising of the money, in handling the business details, and in the many areas of decision.

What a producer gives the co-producer and what the producer receives in exchange depends upon the relative bargaining power of the parties.

Co-Producer As Managing Member of a Limited Liability Company

Bear in mind that a co-producer will ultimately also be one of the managing members of the limited liability company. As a managing member he or she may bind the company. Unlike a producer who is the general partner of a limited partnership, the producer who is a managing member of a limited liability company does not have any personal liability. Since the tax benefits of a limited liability company are the same as a limited partnership, and the producer has no personal liability, this is reason enough to use the limited liability company instead of a limited partnership as the producing company.

The co-producers should organize the limited liability company as soon as possible to assure that they have no personal liability. They should also enter into an agreement setting forth the duties and obligations of the producers, which is known as a co-production agreement.

Co-production Agreement

Basic Terms

The co-production agreement will state that the co-producers own a property they wish to produce; that they are going to endeavor to raise the money for the production; and that when the money is raised, they will be the managing members of a limited liability company that will produce the play. This agreement will set forth the basic terms that will be incorporated into the limited liability company operating agreement. There will also be set forth the amount of the budget, the method of sharing profits and losses by each of the members, whether the managing members' profits are related to the amount of money that each raises, how the producer's fees are to be shared, how the cash office charge is shared, and so forth.

The co-producers may agree that they will share equally in the profits of the company irrespective of which managing member is responsible for the raising of most of the money for the show. On the other hand, sometimes co-producers wish to relate the share of the profits more directly to the amount of money that each one raises. If one is going to relate the sharing of the profits to the amount of money that each co-producer raises, one ought also to relate the other important contributions to the production to the sharing of the profits. For example, the managing member who discovered the property could claim a larger percentage of the profits for this contribution, the party influencing the star could claim something extra for that, and so on. The next logical step is an attempt to balance all of the items that each of the co-producers contributes, and to relate the share of the profits to the relative importance of each contribution. Very often when co-producers sit down and try to balance the contribution that each one makes to a production, they discover that the importance of each contribution is difficult to measure. As a result, they end up sharing equally in the profits and losses, with all parties agreeing to contribute their best efforts to the production in all ways.

Who Makes Decisions

The Co-Production Agreement will also set forth how decisions are to be made and what happens if there is a deadlock. It is very important that there be some quick resolution in the event that there is a disagreement. In the case of an artistic decision, two co-producers may provide that, in the event of a dispute between them, the director will make the final determination. They may also provide that in the event of a business dispute, the question will be settled by the attorney, the accountant, or anyone else whose business judgment both producers would respect. Other possibilities exist for settling such disputes and are as various as one's imagination.

Who Signs Checks and Agreements — Billing Credits — Arbitration

The agreement should also set forth who may sign checks and who may sign other obligations of the co-production. The ever-prevailing question of billing credits must be dealt with in this agreement — that is, whose name comes first. It is usual to provide that wherever the name of one co-producer appears, the name of all co-producers will appear in type of the same size, prominence, and boldness. Billing credits are usually in alphabetical order in the absence of other more pressing considerations. An arbitration clause may be included, which, as we know, means that in the event of a dispute, rather than going to court, an impartial person would make the determination.

Personnel Agreed Upon

The Co-production Agreement should also set forth the personnel the producers have agreed upon who will be employed by the show, namely the attorney, the accountant, the general manager, and any other personnel agreed upon at this stage. The terms of the Co-Production Agreement will continue during the run of the play and so long as there are any rights in the play owned by the production company.

Associate Producers — Money

An associate producer may be part of a production, which almost always means that the associate makes a contribution of money. Producers rarely have any say-so in the business, although a smart producer will always consult with the associate, even if he ignores the associate's advice or suggestions.

The associate, in addition to getting billing credit, will generally get a percentage of the producer's profits. It is not unusual to give the associate 1 percent of the producer's share of the company profits for each 4 percent (it could be for each 3% or 5%) of the producing company invested by a party that the associate producer brings to the producer.

Front Money

Amount Needed, and Uses

It may be necessary or advisable for a producer to take a co-producer or an associate producer to assist with the raising of the "front money" (see "Front Money Arrangements" below). Usually one may expect to need between $15,000 and $50,000 in front money for an off-Broadway play, and between $50,000 and $200,000 for a Broadway play, the amount depending upon whether the play is a straight play or a musical, and other factors. Front money is used for the production prior to the receipt of the total capitalization and release of the investors' funds. It is generally used to acquire the property, to engage an attorney and general manager, to print scripts, and to do the other usual pre-production work. The attorney general of the state of New York has issued rules, pursuant to the Arts and Cultural Affairs Law, which specifically set forth what front money may be used for.

Producer Reimbursed for Front Money Not Used to Raise Money

Front money expended is reimbursed to the producer after the play is financed to the extent that the front money was used for properly budgeted items and was not used to raise money. One may not reimburse oneself for money spent to raise money. Thus, the cost of auditions and the like must be borne solely by the producer and may not be recouped as a pre-production expense. If a front money investor, other than the producer, consents to the producer reimbursing himself or herself from the front money invested, the producer may do so; but again, only for properly budgeted items, not for raising money for the production.

Agreement Should Set Forth Facts

Sometimes a co-producer will contribute all of the front money if the other producer furnishes the property, that is the play. The facts should be set forth in the Co-Production Agreement as to which producer is responsible for the front money, and what the party receives for it. Since a front money investor, who is not a producer, will usually get one for one, that is 1 percent of the net profits of the producing company payable from the producer's share of the profits, for each 1 percent that the front money investor invests in the company, this may be used as a starting point in the negotiations between co-producers, one of whom is furnishing the front money.

Front Money Arrangements

The term front money as used herein shall mean funds which may be used only for the following preproduction expenses of the proposed production: fees; advances; deposits or bonds made for the purpose of purchasing options on a book, play or other underlying materials; engaging creative personnel; securing a theatre; retaining legal, accounting, and other professional advisers; preparing offering documents; the costs of a workshop to be presented by the issuer or other purposes reasonably related to the production for which the front money was raised.

One should be cautious about the meaning of "or other purposes reasonably related to the production for which the front money was raised." This would probably include the costs of reproducing scripts, but ought not be extended to include the buying of dinner and drinks at Sardi's — or trips to the West Coast to consult with the author or director. An arrangement for front money must not be confused with the assignment of profits in exchange for raising capital for the production. Front money is risk capital and, as stated, can be used prior to the capitalization of the show. If the show is not produced, then the front money investor loses the money spent by the producer. As set forth above, the person furnishing the front money will usually get one for one, that is 1 percent of the net profits of the producing company payable from the producer's share of the profits, for each 1 percent that the front money investor invests in the company.

One must be extremely careful whenever one is dealing with a percentage of the producer's profits. Usually the producer gets 50 percent of the net profits of the producing company. After giving away shares, he may end up with considerably less. What is important is the understanding that 1 percent of the net profits of the producing company payable from the producer's share of the profits is not the same thing as 1 percent of the producer's share of the net profits. It's the difference between 1 percent of 100 percent of the producing company net profits and 1 percent of the producer's 50 percent of such net profits.

A front money investor might also be given associate producer billing in addition to the percentage interest. Of course, if the front money is left in the production after the budget is raised—that is, if the amount of the budget is reduced by the amount of the front money and that front money was used for properly budgeted items and not used to raise money, the front money investor will receive a share for the amount of the front money from the limited liability company's profits, as well as what he or she receives from the managing member's share. If front money investors want their money returned to them at the time the show is fully financed, then they are left only with their share of the producer's profits, since they leave none of their money in as an investment as an investor member.

CHAPTER 7

Raising Money—Necessary Filings—The Securities and Exchange Commission and Attorney General

The Securities and Exchange Commission and Attorney General for a Production in New York State

IF FUNDS WILL BE RAISED from the public outside of the state of New York, the production must file certain documents with the Securities and Exchange Commission and with the attorney general of the State of New York before any fund-raising occurs. If funds are to be raised solely in the state of New York, then filing with the SEC is unnecessary, but one must still file with the attorney general.

If a producer is making an offering under the federal securities laws in interstate commerce, to satisfy the federal securities laws, he or she may have several options.

The penalties for noncompliance with the Securities Act are severe: in addition to possible criminal penalties, for example, a producer may be held responsible for the total budget if there is noncompliance. This means that he may raise money, open the show, close the show, lose the entire investment for the investors, and then have to reimburse the investors for the total budget. For this reason, if there is any doubt as to whether a filing should be made, it is wise to resolve the decision in favor of filing.

The SEC is careful to point out that they do not actually approve of the facts as submitted to them. What the SEC does is accept or reject a filing. If it is not accepted, appropriate changes must be made in the documents submitted so that the documents will be accepted. They must accept the documents before an offering may be made to the public. However, the SEC makes the fine distinction that acceptance of a filing does not constitute "approval" of the filing.

A person should bear in mind that no sales material of any kind may be given to a prospective investor unless it is filed and accepted by the SEC. Each prospective investor must be given an offering circular or a "prospectus," as it is sometimes called.

Background

The Securities Act of 1933 regulates the offer and sale of securities and interstate commerce. If the offering is not in interstate commerce the federal securities laws do not apply or if what is offered is not a security, the federal securities laws do not apply. Limited liability company and limited partnerships interests constitute "securities" and are thus subject to the Securities Act.

The Securities Act specifically exempts private offerings, but what constitutes a private offering is not always easy to determine. While the Securities Act specifically exempts private offerings of securities from registration, and what constitutes a private offering is not easy to determine, public offerings of securities must be registered with the Securities and Exchange Commission (SEC). The extreme illustrations of what constitutes a "Public Offering" or "Private Offering" are easy to understand, but the wide range of factual situations not at either extreme, sometimes make if very difficult to determine whether the offering is public or private. If one makes an offering to his brother-in-law whom he has known for twenty-five years, and whom he knows to be a sophisticated investor who is financially secure and could easily stand the loss of investment, there is no doubt that this would constitute a private offering.

The difficult area is in the middle. When one makes the offering to friends of a friend of one's brother-in-law, and vaguely knows about their finances, it becomes less like a private offering, and more like a public offering. There is not a quick and easy way to get an advisory opinion from the SEC on this question.

If there is any doubt, it is always safer to treat an offering as a public offering and to do whatever is necessary to satisfy all the applicable securities laws. The penalties for violating the securities laws can be severe, and one ought not assume the risk if there is any question.

What is "in interstate commerce" is easier to determine. If the General Partner is making the offering in more than one state, the offering has been made in interstate commerce. If the play is being produced in one state and money is being raised in another, an interstate offering is involved. If the offerer uses the U.S. mail to make the offering of limited partnership interests, it is engaged in interstate commerce.

In the 1940s and 50s, it was most usual for a producer to raise money from several sources for various reasons, but unless it was a few close friends of the producer, it was necessary for the attorney for the producer to prepare documents in a way that satisfied the securities laws. It meant complying with the New York State Arts and Cultural Affairs Law if the offering was being made to residents of New York or if the play was being produced in or presented in New York, which included most of the plays being presented. In addition, it was necessary to satisfy the Securities and Exchange Commission requirements if the offering was in interstate commerce as well as the Blue Sky laws of any other states in which the offering was being made.

At that time, one either used an option for an offering totally in the state of New York or one also filed with the SEC. If one filed with the SEC, the filing was either an exemption pursuant to Regulation A, or if the amount of the offering exceeded the maximum permissible under Regulation A, the only viable alternative was a full SI filing. Neither of these options was desirable. A Regulation A filing required the response and acceptance of both the Office of the Attorney General of the State of New York and the SEC. One of the problems was that the Regulation A offering was for a limited amount, finally increased to five million dollars, but this was not enough to cover a budget for a Broadway musical in most instances. What was even more disturbing was that if one wished to proceed with a Regulation A filing, the offering documents would be submitted to both the Attorney General of the State of New York and the SEC, and in some instances these two offices were making conflicting demands. In some cases, to satisfy the SEC, it would be necessary to make changes in the documents that conflicted with the instructions of the Office of the Attorney General. But this was what was necessary to comply with the securities laws. Failure to comply meant the imposition of penalties that were not pleasant.

To add to the confusion, the response time of the SEC to an SEC filing in those days was anywhere between one month to six months. The SEC told you what should be changed with the documents that were filed and you went about convincing them they were wrong or you made the changes. The SEC would then examine the changes, and if they were not happy with what you did, you would make more changes and wait for another response so that you could make even more changes if necessary.

Meanwhile, the Office of the Attorney General was going through the same procedure of examining the documents and requesting changes, then examining the changes in the documentation and requiring further changes.

If all of this sounds difficult, this was nothing compared to the chore of a full filing, that is, an SI filing, which was necessary to make a public offering which exceeded the Regulation A maximum dollar amount. The full filing required documentation that was difficult to prepare, and with any luck, the SEC would respond to the documents in less than six months.

The worst part of this all is the fact that the Securities and Exchange Act was originally passed to protect orphans and widows from investing in nonexistent oil wells and manufacturing plants. The documentation required, especially for an S1 filing, had nothing to do with an offering for the production of a play. But when an attorney was presented with a form that had to be completed for a government agency, the attorney did the best he or she could to try and fill in the form, even if the answers were not pertinent to what was intended by the question on the form or if the questions made little sense.

Lawyers struggled with the securities requirements because it was necessary to comply to avoid the client getting into trouble. Some state securities commissions have never seen a "Theatrical Offering," and some will not permit one under any circumstances. These are the states that permit their securities commission to make a determination whether the investment is a good or safe investment for the citizens of their state.

The Attorney General of the State of New York has promulgated specific rules and regulations applicable to theatrical investments. The Arts and Cultural Affairs Law covers offerings for theatrical stage productions and is specifically limited to such offerings. Offerings for a film venture or television production are not covered by The Arts and Cultural Affairs Law, but must comply with the state securities (Blue Sky) laws of the state applicable to other than theatrical offerings.

On October 11, 1996, President Clinton signed into law the National Securities Market Improvements Act of 1996, which he stated to be "the most significant overhaul of the Securities Regulatory structure in decades." The most important change is a provision which preempts state authority over securities offerings under certain circumstances. Under amended Section 18 of the 1933 Act, it was provided that no state may prohibit an offer or sale in the state, oppose additional disclosure requirements, impose "merit" standards, require the registration or qualification of a security or transaction, or prohibit or limit the use of offering documents prepared by or on behalf of an issuer in connection with an offering if the security offered is a "covered" security.

A "covered" security, amongst other things, is defined as a security offered or sold to a "qualified purchaser" as defined by the Commission. It is presumed that the Commission will define such purchasers in a manner similar to that of an "accredited investor" in Rule 501 under the 1933 Act. An accredited investor is defined in Rule 501 of the Rules and Regulations under the Securities Act of 1933 as, amongst other things, any natural person whose individual net worth or joint net worth with that person's spouse, at the time of his purchase, exceeds $1,000,000, or any natural person who had an individual income in excess of $200,000 in each of the two most recent years or joint income with that person's spouse in excess of $300,000 in each of those years and has a reasonable expectation of reaching the same income level in the current year. The Act did not preempt the states from enforcing the fraud provisions of any state law in connection with any securities transactions.

It should be born in mind that if an offering is made solely within the state of New York, the Arts and Cultural Affairs Laws and the Rules and Regulations promulgate thereunder would be applicable. This means that an offering may be made within the state with waivers or under the proper circumstances using just the investment agreement as the offering document. The states may continue to impose filing requirements for documents filed with the Commission and have certain annual and periodic reports. The states may also require filing of consents to service of process and may impose filings fees in the amount provided by state law on the day before the Act became effective.

With respect to theatrical offerings subject to the law of the state of New York, the amendment affects only offerings made pursuant to Rule 506 of Regulation D under the Federal Securities Act of 1933. If the offering is pursuant to Rule 506, in order to comply with the New York law, Form 99 must be filed together with a copy of the Offering Document prepared in accordance with Rule 506.

It is appropriate to proceed under Rule 506 of Regulation D, except in the following circumstances: if the offering is in the state of New York and is not for more than $500,000, and the offerer wants to proceed using only the Investment Agreement as the offering document, avoiding the preparation and use of an Offering Circular; or if: (1) the offering is going to be sold to more than thirty-five non-accredited investors, which cannot be done under Rule 506; (2) the offering is a public offering solely in New York State or in more than one state, since Regulation D and Rule 506 are only for private offerings; (3) the offering is made solely in the state of New York and is made with waivers of filing with the Attorney General.

One might assume wrongly that since the NSMIA preempted state authority over certain filings that none of the rules and regulations of the states would be applicable to an offering. For example, the New York State Rules and Regulations limit the number of persons to not more than four to whom an offering may be made for front money. A person making an offering pursuant to Regulation D, Rule 506 would be mistaken to assume that this limitation does not apply. Front money is raised before the filing for the Regulation D offering is made so that one cannot claim that the State of New York lacks jurisdiction. The rule would apply until the Regulation D offering is filed. It would make sense to assume that the jurisdiction of the State of New York or any other state is not preempted until the Regulation D, Rule 506 filing is complete and it is, in fact, an offering pursuant to this Regulation. This reasoning should apply to any other limitations that would not apply after the filing, but are limitations that are applicable prior to the filing with the SEC.

Neither the SEC nor the Attorney General suggests any changes that should be made in the offering documents as either would do if the offering were not pursuant to Regulation D, Rule 506. The onus is on the attorney, as it always has been, to prepare the offering documents so that they comply with what the SEC and the Attorney General would want if, in fact, they were reviewing the documentation and demanding certain changes. Other states have other requirements. Sometimes a fee is required and sometimes the offering documents may have an endorsement with a specific requirement of the state, such as a limitation on transferability of the interest in the production company.

At this time, as was stated, almost all security offerings of an interest in a theatrical producing company are offerings of an interest in a limited liability company, which are made pursuant Regulation D of the Federal Securities Exchange Act under Rule 506. Unless one is making an offering only in the State of New York or unless the offering must be a public offering or sold to more than thirty-six non-accredited investors, the only reasonable way to proceed with the offering is in accordance with Rule 506.

How to Make an Offering Today

Before one can raise money, that is, make an offering to potential investors to invest in a play, it is necessary to satisfy the applicable securities laws. Counting federal law, the law of the District of Columbia and the fifty states, there are fifty-two different laws with which to be concerned. There is the Uniform Securities Act, but there is little uniformity in the various states' laws, even those that have adopted the Uniform Securities Act, although some do have specific features in common.

Since almost all offerings of securities to finance the production of stage plays are now made in one way, it seems appropriate to put in perspective all of the information about securities filings. It is likely that someone at some time will want to utilize the information contained in one or another of the various ways set forth to prepare an offering of an interest in a production company. Stated simply, it is a fact that almost all offerings now being prepared are for a limited liability company as the producing entity that is making the offering pursuant to Rule 506 of Regulation D.

If the producer is not extremely happy with the limitations of Rule 506, when faced with the problems of the other alternatives, in almost all cases the producer will make the compromise and go with a Rule 506 offering, even if it means the limitations of a private offering and the limitation on the number of non-accredited investors. The alternatives are just too complicated, too time consuming, to expensive and not feasible, unless the offering is limited solely to the state of New York.

One preparing documentation for an offering of interests in a company producing stage plays, which offering will be subject to both federal and state jurisdiction, should do the following:

1. Prepare and file with the secretary of state, the Articles of Organization for a limited liability company. See FORM.

2. Prepare a co-production agreement if there is more than one producer. See FORM 122-1.

3. Prepare an Operating Agreement. See FORM.

4. Prepare a Private Placement Memorandum. See FORM.

5. Prepare a Form D, Notice of Sale of Securities pursuant to Regulation D. See FORM.

6. Prepare a New York State Form 99. See FORM.

7. Prepare a letter to the Securities and Exchange Commission sending five copies of the Form D, with copies of the Operating Agreement, the Private Placement Memorandum and Form 99.

8. Prepare a letter to the Attorney General of the State of New York sending copies of Form 99 and the Private Placement Memorandum. The Operating Agreement is not required, but there is nothing wrong with also including it with the documents forwarded to the Attorney General.

9. Check the Blue Sky Laws of every State in which funds will be offered and make sure there is compliance with the laws of each State.

10. Make certain that the letters to the SEC and the other securities office request acknowledgment of receipt and always include a Self Addressed Stamped Envelope so that there is evidence of filing.

If the offering is to be made to residents of other states, one must examine the requirements for an exemption in each of those states.

Rule D

A "Rule D" offering is a private offering. Rule D, like all of the other provisions of the federal securities laws, requires that the offerer comply with the state laws in each state in which the offering is being made.

Although the transactions under Rule D are exempted from the registration requirements of Section 5 of the Securities Act of 1933, such transactions are not exempt from the antifraud, civil liability, or other provisions of the federal securities laws.

- Rule 504 of Rule D, applies to offerings not exceeding $500,000, within the 12 months before the start of and during the offering of the securities,

- Rule 505 applies to offerings not exceeding $5,000,000, during such period, and

- Rule 506 applies to offerings exceeding $5,000,000, during such period.

Blue Sky Laws

Before the NSMIA was enacted, satisfying several of the state securities laws could be a minor catastrophe, especially if it meant doing the substantial amount of work that could be required for a small Off-Broadway show with a limited budget. If the producer of the play can work within the limitations of a Regulation D, Rule 506 Offering, the satisfaction of the securities laws in many states can be greatly eased. The NSMIA, in preempting state authority over certain securities offerings, prompted many states to promulgate rules that are similar to one another in many respects. Some states even have a provision that makes satisfying the law "self-executing," which means that, under certain circumstances, one does not even have to file anything. Of course, the fraud provisions of the states must be strictly complied with.

One provision that many states have adopted is particularly useful: it is not necessary to file anything until a sale is made and then the filing must be within fifteen days of the sale in the state. An example of a self-executing state is Virginia. If there are no more than thirty-five investors, not just in Virginia, but anywhere, the offering is self-executing. If there are more than thirty-five investors anywhere one may file a Notification under Regulation D and pay the fee of $250. The state of Pennsylvania is a self-executing state if the offering is made to just two accredited investors. This is labeled an "isolated transaction." Again, if the offering does not qualify as self-executing, Regulation D may be used.

Examples of states that require a filing within fifteen days of the first sale in that state are New Jersey, Connecticut, and Pennsylvania, but there are many others. This is a distinct advantage since the offerer can go into the state and try to make a sale, and if unsuccessful, nothing need be done. If a sale is made in a state, it is then worth the trouble to file whatever is required, which is usually something not too complicated. It is important to examine the law of each state at the time of the offering because these laws change. The number of investors that may qualify for a self-executing offering can change from thirty-five to twenty-five and the filing fee of $250 can become $350. Also, it must be remembered that a Regulation D offering is a private, not a public, offering and some states require an affirmation that there will be no public solicitation and that the purchase is for an investment. Other states require a statement that the offerer received no compensation for the sale. Still others require an additional document to be filed (the filing fees varying in all of the states).

The Attorney General

If the money for the production is going to be raised only in the state of New York, an SEC filing may be avoided. In all cases, however, there must be a filing with the office of the attorney general.

New York, like all of the other states in the union, has what are known as "blue sky laws" (security laws designed to protect investors). In addition to the New York law, there are the New York State theatre financing regulations that govern a theatrical financing. It may be necessary to file in other states in which money will be raised. The production attorney will make this decision as to where filings are necessary.

If a filing has been made with the SEC, the filing with the attorney general is greatly simplified, since the attorney general will accept the offering circular filed with the SEC with one or two minor additions that will have been included at the time the SEC filing was made.

Offering Solely within New York State

If one is making an offering solely within the state pursuant to the Arts and Cultural Affairs Law, the offerer may have several options, depending on certain factors. They are:

- A private offering in which the offerees waive the filing of offering documents (offering with waivers).

- An offering made with an investment agreement only, not requiring the use of an Offering Circular, sometimes referred to as a Prospectus.

- A public offering requiring the filing and use of an Offering Circular.

A discussion of each of the three follows. Bear in mind that, which of the three is used will depend upon the facts of each offering, such as whether the play may be financed by a private offering without the necessity of a public offering, the amount of the offering, and the limitations of time in commencing the offering.

[1]—Offering with Waivers

If the offering is being made to thirty-five persons or fewer, the offerer may have each of the investors sign a waiver of filing with the Attorney General and avoid the filing of Offering Documents acceptable to the Attorney General. The waiver provision was ostensibly provided to accommodate a producer who wanted to make the offering to a very few close friends, whom it is assumed would have all of the facts necessary to satisfy the requirements of a "full and fair" disclosure without the necessity of an offering circular or private placement memorandum.

Since an investment agreement is required, it would be useful to incorporate some information into this document to accomplish a disclosure of facts thought to be material. It makes sense that if the operating agreement is the only document used whether by reason of the fact that the offering is for $500,000 or less, or by reason of the fact that it is done by waivers, the information that may be included should be the same.

It should be noted that the offering may only be made to thirty-five persons or fewer, and does not mean that the offering may be made to more than thirty-five persons so long as there are thirty-five investors or fewer. There is a distinction between the number to whom an offering may be made (offerees) and the number to whom the sale is actually made (purchasers). The New York law focuses upon the number of offerees not the number of purchasers.

The provision for a waiver of filing is in the nature of a private offering and it is for this reason that the offering may be made to only thirty-five persons or less.

[2]—Offering Using Only an Investment Agreement

If the offering is for $500,000 or less, including the right to an involuntary overcall, the offerer may use an investment agreement as the only offering document and would not use an offering circular. The Attorney General's intention providing for this regulatory exemption is to decrease the costs of a filing with the Attorney General for these small offerings. It would be contrary to this cost-saving purpose if all the information which would otherwise be required in the offering circular, prospectus or private placement memorandum were simply included in a bulked-up investment agreement, thus creating the same number of pages which would have been in two documents. Nevertheless, one may now include language in the investment agreement that will constitute a full and fair disclosure of the risks involved, without having to put this material in an offering circular or prospectus.

[3] — Public Offering with Offering Circular

An offering circular prepared for an offering in the State of New York is similar to the offering circular used for a Regulation A filing with the SEC. For this reason, if the budget for the play is for $5,000,000 or less and if a Regulation D, Rule 506 offering cannot be made, it is suggested that a Regulation A filing be made so that one would be able to take advantage of an investor in another state.

The National Securities Market Improvement Act of 1966 (NSMIA) has made the filing of a Regulation A filing in the State of New York using a state supervised offering document impractical, providing the offering may be made within the limitations of a Regulation D, Rule 506 offering.

Six Items Required in Every Investment Agreement

The law provides that all investment agreements must contain the following items (which also includes filings with the Securities and Exchange Commission that are accepted as filed by the Department of Law):

(1) A statement that all monies raised from this offering and sale of syndication interests shall be held in a special bank account in trust until actually employed for pre-production or production purposes of this particular theatrical production company or until returned to the investor or investors.

(2) A statement that financial statements will be furnished to all investors and the Department of Law pursuant to the provisions of Article 23 and the regulations issued by the Attorney General thereunder.

(3) If the offering is for one or more specified productions, a representation that the issuer or other offerer has acquired the right to develop, produce or invest in the theatrical production or productions which are the subject of the offering, the date or dates on which such right or rights were acquired and the expiration date of such right or rights. If the offering is for or includes one or more non-specified theatrical productions, a representation that the issuer or other offerer will acquire the rights to the first production to be presented, or the right to invest in a production, or will enter an agreement to develop a production before expending any of the proceeds of the offering, provided, however, that the proceeds of the offering may be used for the limited purpose of acquiring such production rights, costs reasonably related to such acquisition, and organizational and offering expenses.

(4) A statement, where permitted by this Part, that where authorized by investors, contributions may be used for pre-production or production purposes prior to the completion of the offering. If the issuer or other offerer intends to use the interest earned in investors' contributions, when permitted to do so by the individual investors, this option must be fully explained. State whether and under what circumstances the issuer or other offerer agrees to refund such contributions and any interest earned thereon. No authorization for such use shall be effective unless and until the signature of the investor has been obtained on a separate signature page in the investment agreement. Investors shall not, however, be required to authorize use of their contributions or any interest earned thereon prior to the completion of the offering as a condition of their investment. Such authorization shall be set forth in capital letters in boldface roman type or if typed, in capital letters with underlining, as follows:

INVESTOR MEMBERS AUTHORIZING IMMEDIATE
USE OF FUNDS NOT WAIVING REFUND

THE FOLLOWING SIGN THE FOREGOING AGREEMENT AS INVESTOR MEMBERS AND AGREE THAT THEIR CONTRIBUTIONS MAY BE USED FORTHWITH BY THE MANAGING MEMBERS FOR PRODUCTION OR PRE-PRODUCTION PURPOSES. THE UNDERSIGNED DO NOT WAIVE THEIR RIGHT OF REFUND OF ANY PORTION OF SUCH CONTRIBUTION EXPENDED FOR SUCH PURPOSES AND RELY ON THE MANAGING MEMBERS TO REFUND THEIR CONTRIBUTION IN THE EVENT THE OFFERING IS ABANDONED PRIOR TO FULL

CAPITALIZATION OF THE COMPANY. SUCH REFUND IS THEREFORE CONTINGENT UPON THE MANAGING MEMBERS' FINANCIAL ABILITY TO MEET THIS OBLIGATION. THE UNDERSIGNED OBTAIN NO ADVANTAGE BY ENTERING INTO THIS ARRANGEMENT UNLESS SUCH ADVANTAGE HAS BEEN NEGOTIATED WITH THE MANAGING MEMBER OR MEMBERS.

INVESTOR MEMBERS AUTHORIZING IMMEDIATE
USE OF FUNDS AND WAIVING RIGHT OF REFUND

THE FOLLOWING SIGN THE FOREGOING AGREEMENT AS INVESTOR MEMBERS AND AGREE THAT THEIR CONTRIBU-TIONS MAY BE USED FORTHWITH BY THE MANAGING MEMBERS FOR PRODUCTION OR PRE-PRODUCTION PURPOSES. THE UNDERSIGNED WAIVE THEIR RIGHT OF REFUND OR ANY PORTION OF SUCH CONTRIBUTION EXPENDED FOR SUCH PURPOSES IN THE EVENT THE OFFERING IS ABANDONED PRIOR TO FULL CAPITALIZATION OF THE COMPANY. THE UNDERSIGNED OBTAIN NO AD-VANTAGE BY ENTERING INTO THIS ARRANGEMENT UNLESS SUCH ADVANTAGE HAS BEEN NEGOTIATED WITH THE MANAGING MEMBER OR MEMBERS.

INVESTOR MEMBERS AUTHORIZING IMMEDIATE
USE OF INTEREST EARNED ON THEIR CONTRIBUTION
AND WAIVING THEIR RIGHTS TO A REFUND THERETO

THE FOLLOWING SIGN THE FOREGOING AGREEMENT AS INVESTOR MEMBERS AND AGREE, ONLY, THAT THE INTEREST EARNED ON THEIR CONTRIBUTIONS MAY BE USED FORTHWITH BY THE MANAGING MEMBERS FOR PRODUC-TION OR PRE-PRODUCTION PURPOSES. THE UNDERSIGNED WAIVE THEIR RIGHT OF REFUND TO ANY PORTION OF THE INTEREST EARNED ON THEIR CONTRIBUTIONS WHICH HAS BEEN EXPENDED FOR SUCH PURPOSES IN THE EVENT THE OFFERING IS ABANDONED PRIOR TO FULL CAPITALIZATION OF THE COMPANY. THE UNDERSIGNED

OBTAIN NO ADVANTAGE BY ENTERING INTO THIS ARRANGEMENT UNLESS SUCH ADVANTAGE HAS BEEN NEGOTIATED WITH THE MANAGING MEMBER OR MEMBERS.

If the theatrical production company will use the proceeds for more than one production or for one or more nonspecified production and offering literature is filed pursuant to the Regulations, the authorization of investors to use their contributions for the limited purpose of acquiring production rights, costs reasonably related to such acquisition, and organizational and offering expenses may be set forth by amending the first sentence in the above legends to read as follows:

THE FOLLOWING SIGN THE FOREGOING AGREEMENT AS INVESTOR MEMBERS AND AGREE THAT THEIR CONTRIBU-TIONS MAY BE USED FORTHWITH FOR THE LIMITED PURPOSE OF ACQUIRING PRODUCTION RIGHTS, COSTS REASONABLY RELATED TO SUCH ACQUISITION, AND ORGANIZATIONAL AND OFFERING EXPENSES.

If the form of the theatrical production company is other than a Limited Liability Company, the above stated legend language shall be appropriately altered.

(5) There must also be disclosed the total amount of expenses that have been advanced at the date of filing the agreement with the Department of Law, which are to be reimbursed out of the capitalization, with an itemized breakdown and the conditions of repayment of such advances.

(6) The producer's residence must be set forth, but it is not necessary to disclose information concerning previous theatrical experience.

Additional Items Required If Offer Is by Waiver

If the filing is by waivers, two additional items are required as follows:

(1) Information including the name and residence of the producers and where the producer is a corporation owned or controlled by another corporation, information as to the name and address of the other corporation, and who

will control the management and affairs of the theatrical production company. If there is an executive producer or person with a similar title, he must be identified and his functions stated.

(2) A statement on the front cover page in capital letters printed in 10-point modern type and at least two points leaded (or if typed, with underlining):

PURSUANT TO THEIR WRITTEN WAIVER, SUBSCRIBERS TO THIS AGREEMENT ARE NOT RECEIVING A PROSPECTUS OR OFFERING CIRCULAR FILED WITH THE ATTORNEY GENERAL WHICH WOULD OTHERWISE BE REQUIRED UNDER NEW YORK LAW. THE INFORMATION IN THIS DOCUMENT OR ANY OTHER DOCUMENT SUBMITTED TO INVESTORS IN CONNEC-TION WITH THIS OFFER HAS NOT BEEN REVIEWED BY THE ATTORNEY GENERAL FOR THE ADEQUACY OF DISCLOSURE AND THE ATTORNEY GENERAL DOES NOT PASS ON THE MERITS OF THIS OFFERING.

Front Money for Developmental Production

A producer may, without filing with the attorney general, make an offering to fewer than five persons for the sole purpose of raising "front money." Front money may only be used for the specific purposes hereinafter set forth. This provision is very specific in that the offering may only be made to four persons or fewer.

A front money investor will usually get 1 percent of the net profits of the producing company from the Producer's (Managing Member's) share of the profits for each 1 percent invested as front money. For an example, if an Off-Broadway show is capitalized for $500,000, $10,000 will purchase one percent of the net profits of the Limited Liability Company that will be formed to produce the play. If a front money investor invests $10,000, then in addition to the 1 percent of the net profits that he would purchase as an investor member in the limited liability company, he would get an additional 1 percent of the company from the producer's (managing member's) share of such profits.

The important contribution of the amendment to the regulations effective January 1 1985, is the inclusion of "the costs of a workshop" as a proper use of front money. "Front money" is now defined in the regulations as ". . . funds which may be used only for the following pre-production expenses of the proposed production: fees; advances; deposits or bonds made for the purpose of purchasing options on a book, play or other underlying materials; engaging creative personnel; securing a theatre; retaining legal, accounting and other professional advisors; preparing offering documents; the costs of a workshop to be presented by the issuer or other purposes reasonably related to the production for which the front money was raised."

The importance of this new definition stems from the fact that, on occasion, a producer may want to have a workshop or other developmental production of a play, which under the Actors' Equity Workshop Code can be produced for about one-eighth of what an Off-Broadway production would cost, and for about one-twentieth of what a Broadway production would cost. By first doing such a production, the producer gets an opportunity to see the play, and to develop it less expensively, and at the same time gets the opportunity to expose potential investors to the play on the stage. The arguments against doing such a production first is that it is a rather expensive "backer's audition," and second, if the producer merely did a reading in someone's home, or in a hotel room, it would serve the same purpose of exposing the investors to the property.

What is significant is that, if a producer now wants to do a workshop or other developmental production, since he or she can properly use the front money for this purpose, the front money investor can end up with a percentage interest in the play as finally capitalized for the Broadway or Off-Broadway production.

Under these circumstances, it is usual for the producer to have completed the necessary securities filings when the workshop or other developmental production is presented, so that he can pass out the offering literature to prospective investors at the showcase production and actually take their investment at that time, rather than having to wait until some later date to receive the investments.

Public Offerings for a Theatrical Production Company

A new contribution added to the regulations in 1988 and preserved in the regulations as adopted on June 28, 1989 was a provision that permits an offering for the purpose of investing in one or more specified productions or, in the alternative, making an offer for investment in a production company which will be developing and producing an unspecified play or plays.

This addition to the regulations may seem important, however, making a successful offering for the purpose of investing in more than one play or in a company that will develop and produce an unspecified play or plays is not a very likely prospect. When you take into consideration the great difficulty involved in convincing enough investors to invest in a known designated play, to convince investors to invest in a play or plays that are not even yet determined is not just difficult, but close to impossible.

The only way this might conceivably work is if the producer owns the rights to one or more plays of a very very successful playwright and the producer plans on the producing company producing these plays in succession. But even this is difficult since there are so few playwrights who enjoy the reputation of having written plays that cannot fail to garner great reviews and make money for the producing company and investors.

The only other way this could be helpful is if an already hugely successful producer wants to set up a producing company and finance it for plays for which he will later obtain rights to produce. But even this is difficult as no matter how famous a producer may be, it is a very difficult chore for a production company to have continuing successes. It is understandable then why most investors would want to know the play in which they are investing rather than just knowing who will be making the decision for them as to what their money will be used to produce.

Exemption from the Accounting Requirements

It should be noted that all issuers of theatrical syndications in New York, no matter what method of filing they used or whether such filing is exempted by NSMIA from review by the Attorney General, are subject to the financial reporting requirements set for in the Arts and Cultural Affairs Law and its Regulations, which provide in detail the requirements of Accounting for plays, including the necessity of furnishing a "certified statement." A certified statement can be very costly, and there is a provision for exemption from the accounting requirements concerning certified statements if the production is capitalized for $250,000 or less or if the offering is made to fewer than thirty-six persons. The producer must still comply with all the other requirements of maintaining extensive books and records.

Part 50 as amended provides for investment in a producing company, not just in a single production. The accounting regulations (Part 51), under the

Arts and Cultural Affairs law, have been appropriately amended to reflect this change.

Essentially, the amended regulations apply the rules governing a production to a theatrical production company.

The amended regulations contain a provision granting production companies the same exemption opportunity. Rule 51.6 provides:

In those cases where all of the proceeds of the production company are used to invest in specified or non-specified productions, such theatrical production company shall be exempted from filing certified statements provided that it forwards to its investors all the financial reports of the theatrical productions in which it has invested which are required by this Part.

CHAPTER 8

The League of American Theatres and Producers, Inc.

THE BROADWAY PRODUCER must deal with a number of different craft unions and associations. On January 30, 1930, the producers and theatre owners founded their own association, which is now known as the League of American Theatres and Producers. The League has offices at 226 West 47th Street in New York City. The League's 400 member constituency consists of theatre owners and operators, producers, presenters, and general managers of Broadway and touring legitimate theatrical productions in New York and over ninety major cities across the United States and Canada.

Purpose of the League

The League's overall goals are to oversee and promote the common interest of its members; to increase awareness of, and interest in, Broadway theatre across North America; and to provide a full range of support for more profitable theatrical productions.

One of the principle and ongoing responsibilities of the League is to act as bargaining representative for theatre owners and producers with the various craft unions and associations. Each contract is negotiated and entered into for a specific limited period, often three years. Negotiations in the past decade seem to have been extremely protracted and unions will often be working under an "old" contract for sometimes a year or more before the new agreement is signed and put in place. In recent years, it has not only been the issue of salaries but providing for new technologies and negotiating more efficient work rules that has made the labor relations responsibilities of the League increasingly complex and demanding.

Collective Bargaining Agreements

Although virtually all the contracts include language which contracts between the League and the applicable union or guild, certain employees are considered in practice employees of the theatre and others are employees of the producer. The collective bargaining agreements the League has negotiated can be divided into three categories:

- Agreements between the unions and the theatre owners or lessees

- Agreements between the unions and the producers

- Agreements between the unions and the League on behalf of the theatre owners and producers

Agreements for Theatre Owners or Lessees

The contracts of unions with the theatre owners or lessees negotiated by the League include the following:

- Theatrical Protective Union, Local No. 1, IATSE represents the basic house crew of a theatre covering the carpentry, electrical, property, and other related work including "taking in" and "taking out," handling, assembling, and dismantling all equipment used in the show. This covers the curtain men, sound men, fly men, carpenters, electricians, property men, and the like.

- Treasurers and Ticket Sellers Union, Local No. 751, as its name implies, represents treasurers, assistant treasurers, and other box office personnel involved in ticket selling, and telephone operators. Local No. B-741 is aligned with the Treasurers and Ticket Sellers.

- Legitimate Theatre Employees Union, Local No. B-183, represents the ushers, directresses, chief ushers, front doormen, ticket takers, and backstage doormen.

- Theatre, Amusement, and Cultural Building Service Employees, Local No. 54, represents building service employees such as porters, elevator operators, cleaners, and matrons.

- International Union of Operating Engineers, Local No. 30, affiliated with the AFL-CIO, represents employees engaged in the operation and maintenance of heating boilers, heating systems, mechanical refrigerating systems, air circulation (which is part of the mechanical refrigerating system), standpipes, and fire pumps.

Agreements for Producers

The contracts of unions with the producers negotiated by the League include the following:

- Actors' Equity Association, covering actors and stage managers.

- Theatrical Wardrobe Attendants Union, Local No. 764, covering the wardrobe crew of wardrobe supervisors and dressers.

- The Society of Stage Directors and Choreographers, covering directors and choreographers.

- The United Scenic Artists, Local 829, covering set designers, lighting designers, costume designers, and assistant designers.

- Make-up Artists and Hair Stylist Union, Local 798, IATSE, AFL-CIO, which covers make-up artists and hair and wig stylists employed in the production of legitimate shows.

- The Dramatists Guild, Inc., Approved Production Contract, previously discussed in detail, is also negotiated by the League for the producers, but a contract is not signed by the League and the Guild.

- Theatrical Sound Designers, Local 922, IATSE, AFL-CIO.

Agreements for Both Theatre Owners and Producers

The contracts of unions with the theatre owners or lessees and producers negotiated by the League include the following:

- Association of Theatrical Press Agents and Managers, Union No. 18032, AFL-CIO, which as the name states, covers press agents (often hired by the producer or theatre owner, but most usually the producer alone), company managers (hired by the producer), and house managers (hired by the theatre).

- Associated Musicians of Greater New York, Local No. 802, American Federation of Musicians, which covers the musicians, arrangers, copyists, and librarians.

Employer and Employee Also Sign Agreement—Term of Employment

The League has entered into a bargaining agreement with all the above-listed associations and unions. Those with a bargaining agreement still have separate agreements that must be entered into by the employee and the employer. The theatre owners generally hire their employees under a one-year contract during each season, usually the period Labor Day to Labor Day. A producer enters into an agreement with an employee for a particular production.

Members of the League are continually informed and updated on labor activities and, through the League's labor department, have access to copies of all relevant contracts and documentation. The League is a repository for labor information and keeps members advised on past practice, consulting with producers and general managers regarding issues pertinent to day-to-day operations. In addition, League members serve as trustees on the pension and welfare funds of all theatrical unions, overseeing the interests of the industry and the community.

Government Relations

The League's department of government relations helps to develop and maintain relationships with elected officials at the city, state, and federal level and keeps abreast of all regulations and legislation of potential importance to the commercial theatre. Current and recent issues of interest include legislation to restrict ticket-scalping activity, sales tax abatement for scenery constructed in New York; federal, state, and local support of nonprofit theatres; laws to restrict illegal street peddling in the Broadway district; and the forestallment of an admissions tax.

Research Services

The League's Research department generates and maintains extensive records and databases pertaining to the business of Broadway and touring theatrical productions, including comprehensive archives of legitimate-theatre reviews dating back four decades. The League also works with outside market research companies to broaden industry knowledge of audience demographics and habits.

Public Relations

The League has an in-house public relations department whose goal is to promote Broadway across the country. Specific objectives include maximizing coverage of Broadway in the national press and in broadcast media, reaching out to tourists traveling to New York City, informing and educating audiences about Broadway theatre across the county and promoting Broadway both as a business and as a form of mainstream entertainment.

http://www.broadway.org

The League has made the leap into the computer age with its own web site on the World Wide Web members can gain exclusive access to a variety of League resources, including databases, committee actions, and upcoming events.

The Tony Awards

The Antoinette Perry (Tony) Awards is perhaps the most visible endeavor of the League. Since 1967 the League has co-presented the Tony Awards with the American Theatre Wing. The League plays an integral role in the governance, production, and presentation of the awards and related events.

CHAPTER 9

Contracts with the Theatre

IN HIRING THE CREW, a producer ought to try to find a group that is compatible socially as well as on a working basis. There are persons in the business who usually work together. A certain electrician may work with a particular carpenter most of the time as a team, so a producer would hire both. This is desirable since it is to the advantage of a production to have persons on the show who know the working habits of their fellow workers. Liking the people one works with is also most helpful especially in theatre when often the work is under extreme pressure and in close quarters.

As was pointed out in the Preface to this book, publishing the terms of the Union contracts is an exercise in futility since they are constantly changing. It makes more sense to list the address and telephone number of each so that a person interested in a contract can obtain it by communicating with the Union directly. It should be noted that most of the Unions also have a website which in many instances will make the contracts available for downloading.

Theatrical Protective Union, Local #1, IATSE

Jurisdiction

This union has jurisdiction over carpenters, electricians, and property men, and includes "taking in" and "taking out," handling, assembling, and dismantling of any and all equipment, property, chairs, seats, furniture hardware, all electrical fixtures and appliances, staging, scenery, masking, unloading, loading of vehicles, and the like. The minimum basic house crew for each theatre consists of a head carpenter, head electrician, head property man, and curtain man, and in the Minskoff, the Gershwin, and the Winter Garden the basic crew in addition includes an assistant electrician.

Theatrical State Employees
Local #1, IATSE
320 West 46th Street, 3rd Floor
New York, NY 10036
212-333-2500 (Phone)
212-586-2437 (Fax)

Treasurers and Ticket Sellers Union, Local # 751

Jurisdiction

As the name implies, this union governs the hiring of treasurers and ticket sellers within the five boroughs of the city of New York. The League members must negotiate special terms, wages, and hours for theatres outside this area.

Treasurers and Ticket Sellers Union
Local #751, IATSE
1430 Broadway
New York, NY 10018
212-302-7300 (Phone)
212-944-8687 (Fax)

Legitimate Theatre Employees Union Local # 306

Jurisdiction

This union agreement controls the hiring of ushers, ticket takers, directors, head ushers, and doormen. The union shop provision is to the effect that the union will supply the employer with applicants in the operation of "legitimate" theatres and vaudeville or motion picture theatres or theatres having a "reserved seat" policy, as distinguished from a "grind" policy in the city of greater New York. If the union cannot supply help, then the employer may engage help in the open market.

Moving Pictures, Projection Operators, Radio Technicians, Theatrical Employees, and Allied Crafts
Local #306
545 West 45th Street, 2nd Floor
New York, NY 10036
212-956-1306 (Phone)
212-956-9306 (Fax)

Theatre, Amusement, and Cultural Building Service Employees, Local # 54

Jurisdiction

This agreement covers custodians, roundsmen/porters, elevator operators, twenty-six-hour custodians, and matrons. In 1986, Local 54 had about 400 members working in Broadway theatres.

Theatre, Amusement and Cultural Development Division Service Employees Division of Local #32 BJ, Local #54, S.E.I.U.
1650 Broadway, Room 510
New York, NY 10019
212-265-6556 (Phone)
212-314-5161 (Fax)

Mail and Telephone Order Clerks Union, Local B-751

Jurisdiction

This agreement covers all mail clerks, telephone operators and head mail clerks, and head telephone operators employed in any and all theatres.

Mail and Telephone Order Clerks Union
Local B-751
P.O. Box 492
Times Square Station
New York, NY 10108-2103
917-804-8957 (Phone and Fax)

Local Union #30 of the International Union of Operating Engineers

Jurisdiction

Local #30 is the collective bargaining agent for employees engaged in the operation and maintenance of the heating and air-conditioning systems in the theatres.

International Union of Operation Engineers
Local Union #30
115-06 Myrtle Avenue
Richmond Hill, NY 11418
718-847-8484 (Phone)
718-805-2172 (Fax)

CHAPTER 10

Contracts with the Producers

Actors' Equity Association

Casting

USUALLY THE STAGE MANAGER, the casting director, and the choreographer (if one is hired) take charge of the casting, so that the director, author, and producer are insulated from seeing persons totally impossible for the parts. The good possibilities are brought back for the director, author, and the producer to see, and a decision is then made. The decision, as it should be, is largely the director's, but the entire cast must be approved by the author (and composer and lyricist if it is a musical) and the producer, who does the hiring (see Article VIII of the Approved Production Contract for Plays, Appendix D).

In most instances, the negotiations for the cast are carried on by the general manager for the production. Equity requires that there be an open call at which any Equity member so desiring may audition for any part.

Contracts Include Agreement with League and Equity Rules

The Actors' Equity contracts are very simple one-page documents. The standard minimum contracts and the run-of-the-play contracts are 8 1/2-by-11-inch paper. The type is small but easily readable. However, each of these agreements states on it that all the provisions contained in the basic agreement entered into between Equity and the League, and the Equity rules governing employment, is part of the agreement as if it were set forth at length. The Equity rules governing employment are set forth in a small pamphlet of 130 pages. The rules are very detailed and set forth most of the provisions governing the employment of an actor.

Actors' Equity Association
1560 Broadway @ 46th Street
New York, NY 10036
212-869-8530 (Phone)
212-719-9815 (Fax)

Theatrical Wardrobe Attendants Union, Local # 764

Jurisdiction

This agreement is applicable to every New York production, and every production originating in New York, and governs the employment of wardrobe supervisors, assistants, and dressers. Each show must have a minimum wardrobe crew of one wardrobe supervisor, except on: (1) "one-man shows" and (2) on special shows where no wardrobe other than the performers' street clothes are worn and no wardrobe changes requiring the assistance of any other person are to be made.

Wardrobe supervisors and assistants may not perform dressers' duties, and dressers engaged in a production may not perform the duties of supervisors or assistants except in places of extreme emergencies, limited to one performance.

A performer may not assist another performer in dressing nor may the stage manager or his or her assistants perform the duties of a dresser.

Wardrobe, Stars, Duties Defined

Wardrobe is considered to be all clothing, hats, shoes, and the like, worn in the production, whether personally owned by the performers or purchased or rented. The term "stars" is defined to mean performers whose names appear above the title of the show or carry the label "starring" or "also starring" before their names. The duties of employees covered by the contract include maintaining, cleaning, dying, pressing, sorting, handling, distributing, hanging, packing, repacking, repairing, altering, transporting, and the general supervision of all items, costumes, wardrobes, and costume-wardrobe accessories, as well as the dressing of, and making changes for, all performers. The duties also include making, executing, fitting, and remodeling of such items, as well as the control, disposition, and organization of costumes and wardrobe for their efficient and artistic utilization.

Theatrical Wardrobe Union
Local #764, IATSE
545 West 45th Street, 2nd Floor
New York, NY 10036
212-957-3500 (Phone)
212-957-3232 (Fax)

Society of Stage Directors and Choreographers

Directors—Extra Payment for Rewriting

Nowadays directors pick up extra money by participating in the writing of the show. Although a director may not get program writing credit, he or she may get as much as 1 1/2 or 2 percent of the gross receipts for the writing, in addition to the directing fee. In addition, the director who helps with the writing would share in the writer's receipts from the movie sale as well as from the sale of the other subsidiaries. This could mean big money.

Jurisdiction

The collective bargaining agreement of the Society of Stage Directors and Choreographers governs, as the name implies, employment of directors and choreographers in first-class productions in the United States. First-class productions do not include vaudeville-type shows, concert-type shows, readings, nightclub acts, theatre restaurants (Las Vegas shows, however, are considered first-class where so classified by Actors' Equity as part of a road tour), ballets, symphonic and musical importations, and any production not under the jurisdiction of Actors' Equity. In exchange for recognition of the Society for first-class productions, the Society has agreed that it will not attempt to seek recognition to bargain with the producers for other than the first-class presentations just noted. A theatrical production, to be covered by this agreement, must also be presented on the speaking stage in a first-class theatre.

Society of Stage Directors and Choreographers (SSDC)
1501 Broadway, 17th Floor
New York, NY 10036
212-391-1070 (Phone)
212-302-6195 (Fax)

United Scenic Artists, Local # 829

Jurisdiction

The United Scenic Artists, Local #829, Agreement applies and is limited in its application to scenic designers, costume designers and lighting designers, and assistant designers employed by or engaged in a theatrical production produced for Broadway. If an individual designs the scenery and/or the lighting and/or the costumes, he or she must have a separate contract for each.

Definition of Services

Scenic Designer

The scenic designer designs the production and completes either a working model of the settings to scale or completes color sketches or color-sketch models of the settings and necessary working drawings for the constructing carpenter. The designer also supplies the contracting painter with color schemes and designs, and selects or approves properties required for the production, including draperies and furniture, and designs and supervises special scenic effects for the production, including projections. The designer will also supply specifications for the constructing carpenter, supervise the building and painting of sets and the making of properties, and, at the request of the producer, discuss estimates for the set construction with the bidding contractors. In addition, the designer will be present at pre-Broadway and Broadway set-ups, technical and dress rehearsals, the first public performances and openings out-of-town, the first public performance and opening in New York, and will conduct scenic rehearsals for these as may be required.

Costume Designer

The costume designer designs the costumes and will submit a costume plot listing costume changes by scene for each character in the cast; provide color sketches of all costumes; and supply the contracting costume shop complete color sketches of all costumes or outline sketches with color samples attached. The designer will participate in not more than three estimating sessions with costume shops of the producer's choice. If the designer is required to obtain more than three estimates for the same costumes, extra compensation, agreed upon by the designer and producer and subject to the union's approval, will be paid. The designer selects and coordinates all contemporary costumes, including selections from performers' personal wardrobes when the situation arises. The supervision of all necessary fittings and alterations, the selection and approval of an costume accessories (such as headgear, gloves, footwear, hose, purses, jewelry, umbrellas, canes, fans, bouquets, etc.), and the supervision and approval of hair styling and selection of wigs, hairpieces, mustaches, and beards are responsibilities of the costume designer. The designer should be present at pre-Broadway and Broadway technical and dress rehearsals, the first public performances and openings out-of-town, the first public performance and opening in New York, and will conduct costume rehearsals when required.

Lighting Designer

The lighting designer designs the lights, provides a full equipment list and lighting plot drawn to scale, showing type and position of all instruments, and provides a color plot and all necessary information required by the contracting electrician. A control plot showing allocation of instruments for lighting control must be provided by the designer. The lighting designer will supervise and plot special effects and supervise hanging and focusing of the lighting equipment and the setting up of all lighting cues. Up to three estimates may be obtained by the designer for the producer. If the producer requires the designer to obtain more than three estimates, extra compensation will be paid as agreed upon between designer and producer subject to the union's approval. The designer will be present at pre-Broadway and Broadway set-ups, technical and dress rehearsals, the first public performances and openings out-of-town, the first public performance and opening in New York, and will conduct lighting rehearsals as may be necessary.

United Scenic Artists
Local #829
29 West 38th Street, 15th Floor
New York, NY 10018
212-581-0300 (Phone)
212-977-2011 (Fax)

CHAPTER 11

Contracts with the Producers and Theatres

Association of Theatrical Press Agents and Managers, Union # 18032

Jurisdiction

THE ASSOCIATION IS COMMONLY KNOWN AS ATPAM and covers the employment of press agents and managers. Managers include house managers employed by the theatre and company managers who are employed by the production.

In fact, the agreement specifically provides that a contract of employment must be entered into with each employee and that a press agent, a house manager, and a company manager must be employed at all times that a production is playing within the union's jurisdiction.

The agreement states that the jurisdiction of the union is intended to include not only stage productions, but variety and vaudeville attractions, summer theatre, burlesque, road show picture presentations, theatrical entertainment, opera, musical presentations, concerts, ballets, carnivals, circuses, sport expositions, and similar exhibitions and events. The jurisdiction is not confined to the New York metropolitan area.

Association of Theatrical Press Agents and Managers Union
Local 18032, IATSE, AFL-CIO, CLC
1560 Broadway, Suite 700
New York, NY 10036
212-719-3666 (Phone)
212-302-1585 (Fax)

Associated Musicians of Greater New York, Local # 802 American Federation of Musicians

Hiring of Musicians

All musicians are hired by the theatre, that is, they are signed by the theatre even though the payment of the musicians may be shared by the theatre and producer as discussed in the chapter on the theatre license agreement. A contractor selects and hires the musicians and signs the contract with the theatre. Very often the composer or conductor has someone that he would like in the orchestra, so this will influence the actual selection.

Jurisdiction

The League of American Theatres and Producers has entered into a collective bargaining agreement with the musicians union that sets forth the minimum rates of pay as well as other provisions of employment.

Associated Musicians of Greater New York
American Federation of Musicians
Local #802
322 West 48th Street

New York, NY 10036
212-245-4802 (Phone)
212-489-6030 (Fax)

Music Preparation

Extensive terms, conditions, and payment schedules governing the arranging, orchestration, copying, transposing, and proofreading of music are attached to the AEM collective bargaining agreement.

Makeup Artists and Hair Stylists Union, Local 798, IATSE, AFL-CIO

Jurisdiction

The contract recognizes Local 798 as the sole and exclusive bargaining agent for makeup artists and hair stylists employed in the presentation of legitimate shows in the Broadway area. Membership in Local 798 is not a condition of hiring an individual; however, once employed by the production, the individual must join the union.

Makeup Artists and Hair Stylists Union
Local 798, IATSE, AFL-CIO
152 West 24th Street, 2nd Floor
New York, NY 10011
212-627-0660 (Phone)
212-627-0664 (Fax)

CHAPTER 12

Out-of-Town Pre-Broadway

Purpose—Audience Response

U P UNTIL THE EARLY 1960s, almost every Broadway show would go out-of-town for a pre-Broadway run prior to the Broadway opening. The purpose of an out-of-town tryout was to get audience response so that the show could be fixed before it was subjected to the grueling attention of the Broadway critics. Since taking a show out of town is an expensive operation, someone eventually came up with the idea that it wasn't really necessary.

It Depends on the Play

In fact, there are some plays that definitely should be tried out of town, and others where it would make little difference. If a play does not have a pre-Broadway tryout, it will probably preview on Broadway for a longer period of time so that the Broadway preview audience response may be utilized to fix anything that needs fixing, to the extent that it can be fixed, in the available time.

Dramatic Show Differs from Musical

A dramatic show probably should not go out-of-town unless there is a star in the show, a star with out-of-town drawing power. The dramatic show without a star on a pre-Broadway tour is likely to have difficulty finding that audience from which a response is to be measured.

A musical, without a star, likewise should not go out of town on a pre-Broadway tour unless there is a subscription audience waiting to see the show when it arrives. If the theatre wants the show, then the theatre will make arrangements for you to take advantage of the subscription patrons that some theatres have, which can mean guaranteed box office receipts. The Fisher Theatre in Detroit, the Mechanic in Baltimore, the O'Keefe in Toronto are theatres, for example, that have subscription patrons.

A show — dramatic or musical — with a star, or a musical with a subscription ticket sale, may give consideration to a pre-Broadway tour.

How Long on the Road — And Previews

Most usually a straight dramatic show will stay on the road for from four to six weeks before coming to Broadway, and a musical will generally stay out for between six and ten weeks. After the show comes in to New York, it may preview for a few days or a week, or, if it is in trouble and needs a lot of fixing, for several weeks if the money holds out. The very least is a run-through, the dress rehearsal, prior to the official opening.

If the show does not go out-of-town, it may preview in New York for between one and three weeks. In most instances, it will be difficult to preview the show for more than a week or two, as this costs money. Do not count on making money during the previews. It can happen, but only if you have that big-box-office-drawing star, or if the play is written by a currently "hot" or famous author, or some other such unusual situation.

There have been instances recently where big musicals with superstars have gone on the road for extended tours of a year or more, and they have done big business. The object in such instances is to have such a successful run on the road that by the time the show comes to Broadway it has recouped the entire investment in the production. Sometimes this works. Sometimes it doesn't and the show has flopped on Broadway.

Sets and Props Moved by Truck or Train

Although the cast and crew may be flown between stops, the sets and props are almost always moved overland. If it is a big hop, it is possible that the sets and props will also be flown, but this is not usual on most moves. It is not usual to risk the chance of bad weather in transporting the sets, or a certain amount of time is required to set up after arrival. Overland means that a certain number of hours will be required from the time the play is out of the theatre; most likely the last truck will leave at about 8:00 a.m. following the last evening performance. There is no assurance if the sets are flown that they will arrive in time to be installed and ready to go for the next scheduled performance.

Desirable Musical Houses

The most desirable musical houses are the very large houses. Weekly operating expenses for a musical are so great that unless the show is in a large theatre, there is little chance of making money. The O'Keefe Theatre in Toronto and the Fisher in Detroit are ideal, since they are immense and can easily gross over $500,000 a week if you come in with a hot property.

Moving a Show — Deck Complicates Move

Moving a show is an expensive, complicated procedure. The main complication arises from the fact that the last thing out of one theatre has to be the first thing into the next theatre. The last truck to arrive with the floor (or deck, as it is called) must be the first to go into the new house. What sometimes happens is that some of the other parts of the set can be unloaded and flown while the deck is being put down.

A deck is a platform (usually eight-inches deep) that contains all of the turntables and winches. Although some shows do not require a deck, almost all musicals — and many dramatic shows — need one.

Some Shows Own Two Decks

Sometimes a successful road company will own two decks, so that one can be disassembled while, at the next stop, the other is being installed.

Out-of-Town — Union Requirements

The union requirements are different in each out-of-town theatre. One pays more for the cast, and there is a per diem expense payment that must be made to the cast and crew.

Out-of-Town Advertising

While it is out-of-town, a show advertises in all of the major dailies, as the cost is relatively small. All of the out-of-town advertising for a large musical during a three-week stay in a city, for instance, might amount to a total of $150,000.

New York Advertising

In New York City, at the present time, the only really important newspaper for theatre advertising is the New York Times. Some small amount is sometimes spent on the New York Post because it is an afternoon paper, and because it has an audience that, in some instances, responds to a particular kind of show.

Out-of-Town — When to Fold

A show will never close out of town unless the producer runs out of money and has to close, or unless, in that most rare instance, a producer with loads of money decides that the show is so bad that it hasn't a chance and, for his reputation's sake, he must deliver the *coup de grâce*. There are countless show-biz tales of out-of-town flops going on to become theatre history greats, so producers generally keep their shows alive and bring them in to New York for the opening night reviews if at all possible.

Musicians — On the Road

Usually a musical will carry five or six musicians and pick up enough others on the road to make twenty-five or twenty-six in all. The union does not really care whether the production carries the musicians with them or hires them on the road; however, since some of the out-of-town houses have contracts with the local musicians' union to hire a certain number of musicians, it is wise to leave room for the hiring of that number to fulfill the requirements. Then, too, it is more costly to carry the musicians with the production, and usually unnecessary, especially when very competent musicians may be employed in all of the towns booked into. There are usually between twenty-five to thirty musicians on most musicals.

Out-of-Town Advance Man

The advance man on a show that goes out of town is the press agent. If the show is on a road tour, the advance man never sees the company, since he is always a week or two ahead of them. His job is to make sure that as many people as possible learn of the show's coming. To accomplish this, he sets up press interviews for the stars and does whatever else he can to obtain publicity.

On a pre-Broadway tour, the advance man will go out of town two or three weeks ahead of time, but will usually only stay for a day or two in each town. He may come back for any important interviews and will come back for opening night. In his absence, the press agent will ask the company manager to act as the clearing house for the local newspaper and radio people. This may be difficult in some instances, for it is not always easy for the company manager to go to a star, who may at the time feel harassed and overworked, and ask him or her to get up an hour early for an interview with a newspaper reporter the star has never heard of and that one cannot know the possible results of.

Out-of-Town License Agreement

The out-of-town license agreement is discussed in detail after the discussion of the Broadway license agreement, in Chapter 13. If one has an understanding of the Broadway license agreement, it is easier to understand the out-of-town license agreement.

First-Class Productions

It's all so very confusing. Something that was difficult to define in the first place is now in the process of meaning something else. Although there was never a succinct, clearly defined definition of the term, persons working in the business knew what it meant, and now with it changing no one knows for sure what it means. A "First-Class Performance" or a "First-Class Production" that's a capital "F" with a capital "C" and a capital "P," not to be confused with a first-class performance or first-class production with all lower case letters, is a term that's meaning has always been elusive and is now even more so.

Everyone in the business thinks that their production is "first-class," that is something very special, something great. But for many years people in the business knew that a "First-Class Production" meant a production with a First-Class Cast, a First-Class Director in a First-Class Theatre. A First-Class Cast meant a professional cast, which meant with Actors' Equity actors. A First-Class Director meant a professional director, which meant a member of the Society of Stage Directors and Choreographers ("SSD&C"). A First-Class Theatre meant Broadway theatres and many other class theatres in certain specific cities scattered throughout the United States. The names of some of them were known and if it was not a certainty whether or not the theatre in question was "First-Class," the League of American Theatres and Producers (back then it was the "League of New York Theatres and Producers") or Actors' Equity would have the answer. If the Equity contract for that theatre was the Production Contract for a First-Class house, then it was a First-Class Theatre.

For years this information sufficed. The successful big Broadway plays would do a sit-down production (which means it was a run-of-the-play) in First-Class Theatres and the tours of these smash hits with Equity actors also went into the First-Class houses. The "Bus and Truck Productions," that is the one or two night stands did not end up in the First-Class houses, but theatres that were other than First-Class. They many have been first-class (lower case "f" and "c"), but they weren't First-Class (capital "F" and "C").

And then something happened that made it next to impossible to know what a First-Class Theatre is in other cities outside of New York City. What happened was that a Broadway production company decided to take a big Broadway musical on tour, but not with the original cast and not with Equity actors. Non-Equity tours had toured in the past, and there were many non-Equity productions in the other than First-Class Theatres throughout the United States. But this time they managed to take this non-Equity cast production into what was known as a First-Class Theatre where, up to that time, only a First-Class Cast (Equity) could go with its First-Class Director (member of the SSD&C).

This was a serious threat to the Actors' Equity Association because it had always been anticipated that Equity performers would be performing in the theatres always known to be First-Class Theatres. Recent negotiations between the League of American Theatres and Producers and Actors' Equity have resolved the question, at least for the time being, with some compromises and concessions acceptable to both sides. The contract settled on is known as the Experimental Touring Program, which means they are going to give it a chance to see how it works for both sides.

Experimental Touring Program

The Experimental Touring Program ("ETP") is designed to allow lower budget musicals that qualify under stringent criteria to tour under the Equity/League Production Contract. The ETP offers Producers six tiers of salary rates. Criteria used to determine if a production qualifies include, but are not limited to, itinerary, number of traveling company, and average weekly guarantees. Equity has the right to unilaterally revoke this Experimental Touring Program in June of 2007, and the program expires in June of 2008.

CHAPTER 13

Broadway and Out-of-Town Theatre Licenses

Theatre Arrangement

THE THEATRE should be arranged for as soon as possible after one is certain that the production will proceed. If there is a booking jam-up, it is possible for a show to wait around for one or two months for a theatre to open up. This could be expensive.

Broadway Theatre License Agreement

License Agreement—Not a Lease

The agreement to use a Broadway theatre is not a lease as one would expect, but rather a license agreement. Theatre owners, not wanting to have the occupancy of their property burdened with the large number of "landlord and tenant" laws that are tenant-oriented, have opted for a license agreement to avoid this.

The Theatre License Agreement for many years traditionally provided a modest weekly guarantee plus a payment to the theatre of 25 to 30 percent of the gross weekly box office receipts, or some combina-tion of amounts in this neighborhood. There were also elaborate arrangements for sharing certain of the expenses of the theatre, usually at the same percentage rate as the sharing of receipts. The sharing was for different periods of time for different items. These included a sharing of the take-in and take-out, advertising of various kinds, the musicians, ticket sales — that is, extra personnel needed in the event of a smash — and such items. At that time, the theatre owner and the producer were more partnered than they are now.

The theatre owners in the late Seventies decided that if they wanted to invest in the production they would do so by giving the producer cash or the equivalent thereof, but that they did not want to be, in a sense, a co-producer of every play that came into their theatre. Hence, the theatre owners increased the amount of the weekly guarantee to cover all of their weekly expenses of running the theatre and decreased the amount of the weekly gross that was shared. The concept of sharing expenses also mostly disappeared.

The Broadway theatres are owned by three entities, the Shubert Organization, Inc., Nederlander Associates, Inc., and Jujamcyn Theaters Corporation.

The license agreement of each entity is different in some respects, but each has many similar provisions. Some of the terms are negotiable, and the producer's lot is dependent upon the attractiveness of his play compared to the desirability of other plays that are angling to get into the theatre at that particular time.

A license agreement for a Broadway theatre is set forth in the Appendix of this book. There is also a form for a somewhat unique situation. Sometimes a smaller theatre will be licensed on an arrangement that if less than 500 seats are used the license fees will be something less than otherwise. This arrangement usually provides that the producer may at a later date utilize more than 499 seats, and at that time the license fees will change. This would permit the producer to produce the play for a smaller amount and to operate at a smaller weekly operating cost. If the play turns out to be successful and 499 seats are not enough, the producer can then increase the number of seats that are available.

As noted above, some of the items are negotiable. The following are those clauses that need clarification or are the subject of negotiation:

- The amount of the up-front guaranteed payment that must be made to obtain the license, which is usually equal to twice the weekly guarantee of rental. It is usual that the weekly guarantee to the theatre will cover all of the costs of operating the theatre. However, sometimes the producer can convince the theatre owner to delay the giving of a guarantee up front.

- The amount of the weekly rental, or fixed fee. Whether the payment is labeled a fee or rental is unimportant. The thing to bear in mind is that the rental and fee and all other payments for expenses of the theatre will be in an amount that is sufficient to cover all of the operating and running expenses of the theatre, as can be seen in the provisions in the forms.

- The percentage of the box office receipts that the theatre will claim. The percentage of the gross box office receipts is the theatre's profits and will usually be 5 percent, or something between 5 and 10 percent.

- The length of time that the producer has to remove his or her belongings at the termination of the agreement. The producer usually has forty-eight hours to vacate the premises at the termination of the license, but this can be as little as six hours or as much as seventy-two hours. The time will depend upon whether or not the theatre has a backup production waiting to occupy the theatre.

- The amount that triggers the "stop clause." The stop clause can be triggered by varying amounts. This amount depends entirely on the bargaining power of the parties (see the forms for examples of this amount). Although the stop clause may be invoked by either party, it is mostly for the protection of the theatre, since the producer has other ways of terminating the agreement. The paragraph refers to the dollar amount falling below a certain specified amount for any week. This can be negotiated to two weeks, and maybe even for two consecutive weeks, depending upon the producer's bargaining power.

- The number of house seats that the theatre will get (see the forms in the Appendix for numbers that are typical).

- The theatre owner must employ the box office personnel as the theatre license issued by the state of New York requires this. The legislature of the state felt it would be wiser to have the theatre caring for the money received for tickets, rather than the producer, many of whom are believed to be more transient than the theatre owners with their existing real estate.

- What the producer will furnish. There is sometimes a provision that could be very important to the theatre owner, the identity of the "star." Theatre owners make money when the theatre is occupied for a long period of time. Thus the hit shows mean more money, and the theatres strive to bring in hits. Although a star cannot alone make a hit, under certain circumstances the presence of a particular star may make the difference between a hit and a flop. For this reason, the theatre owner wants to know who the star will be and that the star represented to be part of the production will in fact be part of the production.

- The amount of security deposit with the theatre. This is usually a figure not too far from the weekly guarantee multiplied by two. Sometimes the agreement permits the producer to substitute securities satisfactory to the theatre in lieu of cash as the security deposit. This is very important, because the usual theatrical Limited Partnership Agreement makes provision for special treatment to one furnishing a bond or security deposits (see reference to bond or security contained in the discussion of the Limited Partnership Agreement).

- Provision for an additional payment for the air conditioning ($200 per performance is not unusual).

- The time for presentation of the play, which is a negotiable item and may be extended to a period more than two weeks after the preview date.

A producer should try to get reciprocal provisions in the agreement with respect to (1) violations—if caused by the theatre they should promptly remove them; and (2) indemnification to the producer for the theatre's noncompliance with violations.

The provision appearing in one of the forms that the theatre in its sole discretion may determine whether the producer has sufficient funds and, if not, may terminate the license, is harsh and ought to be modified.

It is important to the producer that the theatre be responsible for complying with all governmental rules and regulations for the theatre, namely that there is a valid Certificate of Occupancy for the purpose it is being licensed and that the theatre will continue to keep the premises in condition so that there will be no violations.

The result of the negotiations will be dependent upon the availability, or scarcity, of theatre space at the time that the negotiations take place.

Simply stated, the present arrangement provides that the theatre owner will recoup all of the expenses required to maintain the theatre and will receive a share of the gross box office receipts in addition, which will be the theatre owner's profit. Thus the theatre has no risk, except that the theatre will be unoccupied.

Out-of-Town License Agreement

Sharing of Gross Receipts

The Out-of-town First-Class Theatre License Agreement is very similar to the Broadway License Agreement. It is most usual that the producer pays $25,000 guaranteed (to cover the theatre expenses) plus 10 percent of the gross weekly box office receipts.

Guarantee and Deposit

The amount of the weekly guarantee and the amount of the security deposit vary with the size of the house, whether it is a musical or a nonmusical coming into the theatre, and other factors. The weekly guarantee will vary between $15,000 and $35,000, and the security deposit is usually the amount of the one-week guarantee.

Stop Clause Not Usual

There is no reason to have a stop clause, since in most instances the play tries out of town only for a very limited engagement.

Equipment Must Comply with Laws

The electrical equipment brought into the theatre by the producer must comply with all local statutes and laws.

P. A. System Furnished but Not Operator

The producer may use the public address system in the theatre at no additional charge; however, it is most usual for the producer to pay for the operator who operates the P.A. system.

Souvenir Book Sales

The license agreement sets forth the maximum that may be charged for souvenir books, and also provides that the theatre must be given either a 10 or 20 percent commission, which is paid to the house concessionaire. All other concessions are reserved for the theatre.

Penalty to Producer If Star Out

In the out-of-town license agreement, there is also a penalty provision in the event that the star or featured player leaves the show or cannot perform.

Theater Furnishes Treasurer and Assistant

The theatre will furnish a treasurer and assistant treasurer, but if it is necessary to engage a second assistant treasurer in the box office, the salary of the second assistant is shared by the parties in the same percentage that they share the receipts. Any additional box office help required is paid for solely by the producer.

Theatre Use Before Opening

Some out-of-town license agreements will provide that for a stated period prior to opening a fixed licensing fee is paid. This may be between $3,000 and $6,000 per week. When a fixed sum is paid for the theatre prior to opening, the producer must usually also pay the cost of electricity during that period. Bear in mind that the theatre must (or ought to at any rate) be used for rehearsals for a few days prior to the opening.

Theatre Designates Newspaper for Advertising— Insurance—Fireproofing Sets—and Miscellaneous

It is not unusual to provide that the theatre may designate the newspapers in which the advertising appears. The theatre maintains jurisdiction of the sale of the tickets at all times. The producer agrees that he will carry liability and compensation insurance during the time that the play is at the theatre. Scenery and paraphernalia must be fireproofed. An out-of-town lease also contains certain limitations on the appearance of the company in clubs, restaurants, or other places patronized by the public. If the show closes for further rehearsals, or due to the sickness or inability of the principal performer to perform, there is a provision that the producer must pay a fixed amount each week that it is closed.

CHAPTER 14

Pre-opening—
During Run—After Opening

Star and Director—Raising Money

WITH BUT ONE OR TWO EXCEPTIONS, having a particular star or director helps very little in raising money for a production. The one or two exceptions are those very rare persons whose names have become household words and who cannot possibly do anything that does not make money, even if the production is somewhat less than good.

Record Company Financing

Record companies have in the past invested large sums of money in musicals in exchange for the right to do the original cast album. Original cast albums are no longer in vogue, and investments by record companies are almost nonexistent.

Film Company Investing

Some film companies do make investments in and do actually produce plays. Such a company expects a preferred bargaining position on the film rights (usually an option of first negotiation and an option of first refusal). Sometimes a film company will make an outrageous offer for the film rights of a play in exchange for the investment, and sometimes they don't get it.

Insurance

Most Broadway producers will find it advisable to have the following insurance coverage:

- Workmen's compensation (this coverage is mandatory).

- Disability insurance (mandatory in New York).

- A theatrical floater policy. This is an all-risk policy (with some minor exceptions) covering costumes, electrical equipment, sets, and basically all the other personal property of the show except buildings and improvements.

- Business interruption coverage. This is coverage for an indirect profit loss caused by loss of the theatre, loss of sets, or some other similar happening.

- Personal effects insurance (required by Actors' Equity Association). This is an Inland Marine Form Policy, which covers actors and stagehands, jewelry, clothing, furs, and personal property.

- Liability insurance covering injuries to the public and the cast and crew. The coverage includes bodily injury and property damage.

- Nonappearance coverage for a star. If the star does not appear for one reason or another, the producer may suffer a large loss. This insurance coverage may range between $200,000 and $500,000.

Of course, there are many other kinds of insurance to cover special things and special events.

The theatres will, in most instances, have the following insurance coverage:

- Workmen's compensation for all theatre personnel.

- Fire and allied-peril coverage on the building.

- Fire and allied-peril coverage on the contents of the building.

- Boiler and machinery insurance covering the heating and air-conditioning equipment.

- Business interruption (rental insurance) to compensate for the theatre being dark because of fire or other peril.

- Broad form money and securities coverage inside and outside, which would cover box office hold-up and payroll hold-up.

- Fidelity bond.

There is a large variety of miscellaneous insurance policies that a theatre owner might carry to cover glass, signs, marquees, and numerous other parts of the theatre. In most cases, however, there is a very small market for this kind of insurance, and, in some instances, it is not easy to place it.

Bonds Required

Before the show goes into production, the producer will be required to furnish certain bonds and guarantees that have been previously discussed. The following will be required:

- Actors' Equity Association—two weeks' salary.

- ATPAM— two weeks' salary.

- Stagehands, payable to IATSE for Local No. I—one week's salary.

- American Federation of Musicians—one week's salary.

- American Federation of Musicians—Arrangers, and Copyists— bond varies in amount, usually between $2,500 and $5,000.

- Wardrobe Attendants, Local 764 — one week's salary.

- United Scenic Artists — payment for the entire set, costume, and lighting design must be made in advance to the union.

- The theatre — a deposit usually in the amount of one or two weeks of the guaranteed rental.

Independent Booking Office, Out-of-Town Booking

Up until March of 1985, the Independent Booking Office, a not-for-profit corporation, arranged for the booking of tours, took care of the contracts and the other details of a pre- or post-Broadway tour. The office charged a regular weekly fee payable by both the theatre and the producer, but it wasn't enough. The fees were too low for too long, and it was inevitable that insolvency would force them to go out of business. The void that was created was filled by the League of American Theatres and Producers.

The Independent Booking Office had certain information that had been accumulated through the years, and this formed the basis of the Theatre Specifications File in the League's computer. The League did not take over the function of booking tours, but the information in the computer was the information needed by producers to book tours. With the help of the information in the computer, the tours are booked through the producer's office by a staff member or the company manager, or by one of three booking agents who charge a fee based on the weekly receipts. The booking agents are Columbia Artist Theatricals Corporation, National Artist Management Company, and Road Works Productions.

The Theatre Specifications File contains the following useful information for the major theatres and art centers throughout the country that present Broadway tours and tryouts:

- seating capacity

- stage dimensions

- electrical configurations

- stage and pit dimensions

- information on in-house laundry facilities to comply with union requirements

- location of sound booth

- location of dressing rooms

- showers

- information on star dressing rooms

- taxi companies available

- in-house doctors

The League's providing this information serves a useful purpose for producers wanting to take their shows on tour or outside of New York for tryouts.

Play Doctor—Payment

Rarely does a production call someone in to rewrite a show, as most doctoring comes from directors or persons acting as directors. Generally, what is needed is a point of view about the script, and this comes from the director, not from rewriting. If a top director is called in to doctor a show, it can cost as much as $3,000 per day for his services. Expensive, yes, but if it means saving the show, it is money well spent. Usually, the doctor-director will be paid $25,000 or $30,000 as a fee plus 2 percent of the gross receipts. Directors have also done doctoring for different considerations. On one occasion, the "doctor" was given a well-known European sports car for the job. (It happens to have been a used car at that.) Other gifts are sometimes settled on.

Billing

The billing credits are often a hassle when there is a director replacement. Often the new director does not want his name on the billing, and often the original director agrees with him. If the new director wants billing and the original director will not permit the removal of his name, the producer has just one more problem to deal with and to settle. But then this is a producer's role.

Advertising

Most usually the first big ad for a show is run during the second or third week of rehearsal; however, if the show has a big star, the first big ad might be as early as four or five months before the scheduled opening.

Advance Sale

The treasurer handles the money and is personally responsible if there is a shortage or if the show closes, and there are insufficient funds to make refunds for the advance sale. Although tickets are printed as far in advance as needed, on a dramatic show it is unlikely that they would be printed further in advance than ten weeks (sometimes six weeks, or something between six and ten) unless the show has a lot of theatre parties signed. A musical show would most likely start with tickets for twelve weeks in advance, unless there is indication of a huge advance sale and a long run.

A large advance sale by itself is not enough to provide a producer with a great feeling of security. What is important is how far the advance sale is spread out. Even a three million dollar advance on a big musical might not by itself spell success. In a theatre grossing $800,000, that would mean that the equivalent of less than four weeks' tickets are sold in advance. If the equivalent of four weeks' tickets is spread over thirty weeks or more, and there is little sale at the window, the show would be in big trouble—three million dollar advance sale notwithstanding.

Ticket-Sale Deductions

There are no amusement or other taxes on the sale of theater tickets. The only deduction is 5 percent, which once was a New York City amusement tax. It is now used for the union pension-and-welfare plans and is shared by the unions in accordance with an arbitration award made on April 23, 1963.

Ticket Brokers

The box office personnel deal with the ticket brokers. By and large, ticket brokers can do very little to make or break a show, since they more or less cater to the demand for tickets rather than being a very moving force in creating the demand.

Theatre Parties

In a Shubert house, the theatre takes care of the theatre party arrangements. In other houses, the general manager or the producer arranges an audition for the theatre party agents. It is then necessary to find out what dates each may want and shuffle things around so that everyone is happy.

A theatre-party contract will specify the name of the star, and if that star does not appear in the show, the party may be canceled and the money must be refunded.

During Run

Range of Production Costs

The range of costs of a dramatic show is between $1,000,000 and $2,000,000, and a musical between $7,000,000 and $12,000,000.

Potential Weekly Gross and Weekly Net

One can plan on a dramatic show grossing between $300,000 and $600,000 at capacity, depending upon the size of the theatre, and a musical at capacity grossing between $600,000 and $1,000,000. A dramatic production will likely break even when it grosses between $150,000 and $200,000, and a musical between $350,000 and $500,000.

After Opening

Reviews—What to Do

The morning after the opening, there is customarily a meeting in the office of the advertising agency to plan the expenditure of money for advertising. The producer, the press agent, the general, or company, manager, and sometimes the attorney are present. If the show gets raves, the job is an easy one. If the show gets unanimous pans, although painful, the job is once again an easy one. The difficult area is when a play gets mixed reviews and there is a chance that it could make it, but it's hard to tell how good that chance is and therefore difficult to know how much money to spend to try to keep the show alive.

When to Close

It is not an easy decision to close a show if there is the possibility of business developing at a later date. One has to weigh the amount of the advance sales and the number and size of the theatre parties against the current box office sales and try to come up with some kind of divination of what the future holds. It isn't always easy. Usually when a show starts downhill, there is very little chance that it will make it, and often ego, or what have you, motivates keeping it open.

National Company

If a show is a big hit in New York, then there is no problem at all with a national company, since the show will probably get guarantees of a certain amount everywhere it goes.

Generally, the production must be simplified technically—that is, the scenery and props—so that it may be moved in and out of towns with some degree of speed. The staging is most generally a duplication of the Broadway production. Usually, the stage manager puts the show together, and then the original director comes in for the last week of rehearsals and takes it out of town through the opening night.

Most often the show will have a dress rehearsal with the Broadway set before it leaves New York, with an invited audience, for the first performance out of town is generally with a paid audience.

Producer

A producer ought to do what the name implies, "produce." Strangely enough, show biz happens to appeal to a wide assortment of people. Sometimes people go into the business for the wrong reasons. Playboys should restrict their activities to other than theatre.

Sharpies who want to "cash in quick" should stick to the racetrack. One ought not practice being a dilettante while producing. Producing means making a lot of difficult decisions and carrying them out. Painful as it may be, it sometimes means firing your favorite star, or even your favorite person—if he or she happens to be the director and is not right for the show.

A producer has to be able to select wisely, raise money, hire, fire, influence people, convince people that they should or should not do something, mediate disputes, encourage and assist people to work together and to get along together, buy wisely, sell sharply, hold hands and soothe heads, comfort the sick, assist the needy, and to be all things to all people. In a word, to "produce."

APPENDIX A

Front Money Agreement

(Name and address of organizer)

(Date)

Dear (name of front money investor):

1. We plan to organize a limited liability company (the "Company") under the laws of the state of New York to present and produce, on Broadway in New York City and elsewhere, a musical stage play, currently entitled "Happy Days," based on the novel of the same name. We are writing the book, music and lyrics and are the anticipated managing members of the Company, although others may be admitted as such. The investor members of the Company will share pro rata in fifty percent (50%) of the net profits of the Company, and the managing members will receive fifty percent (50%) of such net profits, all to be defined in the limited liability company operating agreement. The amount of capital to be raised by and for the Company is yet undetermined, but will not exceed $9 million.

2. You have agreed to advance to us the sum of $140,000, which shall constitute front money. We shall have the right to use these funds immediately, but only in connection with the Play, for the following preproduction expenses

of the proposed production: fees; advances; deposits, or bonds made for the purpose of purchasing options on a book, play, or other underlying materials; engaging creative personnel; securing a theatre; retaining legal, accounting, and other professional advisers; preparing offering documents; the costs of a workshop to be presented by the issuer or other purposes reasonably related to the production for which the front money was raised.

3. (a) In consideration of the foregoing, if and when the Company is formed, and the offering of Company interests is allowed to commence, you may be designated as an investor member thereof, at your option, to the extent of the amount of front money so advanced by you, and you shall be entitled to such portion of the investor members' share of the net profits of the Company as your investment bears to the total capital raised for the production of the Play. For example, you will receive one percent (1%) of the net profits of the Company, if any, if an offering of $7,000,000 of Company interests were to be made.

(b) In addition, you shall be entitled to an interest in the Company's net profits equal to your portion of the investor members' share of the net profits of the Company, but payable only from the managing members' share of such net profits as, when and if received by the managing members (and subject to all rights of refund, rebate and return as are applicable to the managing members' share under the operating agreement).

(c) If you elect not to be designated as an investor member of the Company, prior to exercising your option to be so designated, you will (a) receive a full refund of your front money contribution, without interest, in the event and at such time as the Company is fully capitalized; and (b) in lieu of the consideration referred to in subclauses "a" and "b" of this Clause "3," you will be entitled to receive such portion of fifty percent (50%) of the net profits of the Company as your front money contribution bears to the total capital raised for the production of the Play, but payable only from the managing members' share of such net profits as, when, and if received by the managing members (and subject to all rights of refund, rebate and return as are applicable to the managing members' share under the operating agreement).

4. You understand that the front money advanced hereunder is high-risk capital and that if the Play is abandoned, at any stage, for any reason whatsoever, our only obligation will be to account to you for the funds spent, and to return to you, and the other parties advancing money, any unused balance of such funds on deposit, pro rata and pari-passu. We agree to furnish you with an accounting for all front money advanced to us hereunder, but not more than once every six months and then only until such money has been fully expended, or the Play abandoned, and the provisions of this Clause "4" fully satisfied.

5. At such time, if any, as the Company is to be formed and you elect to be designated as an investor member thereof, you hereby irrevocably authorize, nominate, and appoint each of us as your attorney-in-fact to execute the operating agreement on your behalf, to the extent of the amount of front money advanced by you under Clause "2," above, and to take any and all further steps which we may deem necessary or appropriate to effectuate your investment in the Company in accordance with the foregoing provisions. You will be furnished with a copy of the definitive offering documents, if required by law, the operating agreement and any other offering material at that time.

6. You are aware that while offering literature may be filed with the Securities and Exchange Commission and the Department of Law of the State of New York, the Company's offering has not yet been declared effective or allowed to commence by these securities agencies.

7. Your liability in respect to the Play shall be limited to the amount of front money advanced by you under paragraph "2" hereof. We agree to indemnify you against any and all claims, liabilities or expenses, including reasonable attorneys' fees, arising out of any claim by third parties asserting that you are liable for any sum beyond such amount.

8. Except as herein specifically set forth, you shall not have any rights by reason of your making this advance of front money.

9. This letter, when countersigned by you, shall constitute a binding agreement between us which shall be construed in accordance with the laws of the state of New York. Our agreement hereunder may not be modified orally.

If this letter correctly sets forth your understanding, please sign and return a copy of same.

Very truly yours,

AGREED TO AND ACCEPTED:

Social Security or
Federal I.D. Number

APPENDIX B

Literary Purchase Agreement[1]

AGREEMENT made as of this   day of   19 , between
            , residing at

                                    , (hereinafter
sometimes referred to as the "Purchaser") and
                        , residing at

                            ,
            (hereinafter sometimes referred to as the "Owner"),
with respect to the original literary work entitled

              .

In consideration of the covenants and conditions herein contained and other good and valuable consideration, it is agreed:

<u>FIRST</u>: The Owner does hereby warrant and represent that:

---

[1] The agreement is for a literary property in which the television and motion pictures rights have already been sold. The purchaser, in such a case, must find the owner of and negotiate the option and rights to purchase the motion picture and television rights in the newly created musical stage play. Without such rights, it is not likely that a top bookwriter, composer, and lyricist would want to work on the play. Very often the literary property agreement is for all rights, including the stage, film, and TV rights. If such is the case, the use of the film and TV rights is conditioned upon the play running a certain period of time, usually the time needed to "Vest" as provided in the Dramatists Guild, Inc. Approved Production Contract. Of course, the owner's royalty will be less than if the film and TV rights were also included.

(a)   is the sole author of an original literary (type of work)
          entitled

          (hereinafter sometimes referred to as the "Work"); that the Work was
          registered for copyright in the Copyright Office on the   day of
                          under Entry No.   , in the name of   .

(b) The aforesaid copyright was renewed in the Copyright Office
    in the name of   on the day of   19   , under Entry
    No.   .

(c) Motion picture and television rights in the Work have been conveyed
    to   .

                          .

(d) The Owner has full right and authority and is free to enter into this
    Agreement and to grant, upon the terms and conditions hereof, the
    rights herein granted and no right, title, and interest now valid or
    outstanding for or to the Work or the rights herein granted by which
    such rights or the full enjoyment and exercise thereof might be
    encumbered or impaired heretofore has been conveyed or granted to
    any other person, firm, or corporation by the Owner or his predecessor
    in interest.

(e) No adverse claim has been made on him with respect to the rights
    herein granted in the Work, and he knows of no claim that has been
    made that the Work infringes upon the copyright in any other work or
    violates any other rights of any person, firm, or corporation, and the
    Work was not copied in whole or in part from any other work.

(f) The Owner has the sole unencumbered, unrestricted, and lawful right
    to enter into this Agreement and to make the grant hereinafter provided
    for and has the full right, power, and authority to make, enter into and
    to fully perform this Agreement in each and every respect; no consent
    or permission of any authors' society, performing rights society, firm,
    or corporation whatsoever is required in connection with the grant in
    this Agreement made, or in connection with any of the subject matter
    of this Agreement.

(g) At the present time there are no outstanding rights to present a stage adaptation or radio production and the only rights (other than the publishing rights) that are still in effect are the motion picture and television production rights heretofore referred to.

(h) There is no claim or litigation concerning or purporting to affect the Owner's right or title in or to the Work as herein presented or conveyed.

SECOND: The owner does hereby convey, grant and assign to the Purchaser the sole and exclusive rights to use, adapt, translate, subtract from, add to, and change the Work and the title thereof in the production of a legitimate musical stage presentation, and to use the Work or any part or parts thereof and the title and any similar title and any or all of the characters and characterizations of the Work in connection with such legitimate musical stage presentation (hereinafter sometimes referred to as the "Play") based upon the Work; together with the further sole and exclusive rights, by mechanical or electrical means, to record, reproduce, and transmit sound, including the spoken words, dialogue, music, and songs, whether extracted from the Work or otherwise, and to change such spoken words, dialogue, music, and songs in or in connection with or as part of the production, performance, and presentation of such Play; the sole and exclusive right to make, use, license, and vend any and all records required and desired for such purpose; to produce or cause the musical Play to be produced upon the regular speaking stage throughout the world, and to use, sell, lease, or otherwise dispose of the musical Play and all rights of every kind and nature therein now or hereafter ascertained and to authorize others so to do for any and all purposes and by any and all means throughout the world, subject further, however, to the rights in the Work previously granted as hereinabove set forth; and, subject to the reservations of rights or reverter to the Owner hereunder, the exclusive right to copyright the Play in the name of the Purchaser or his nominee, and to obtain extensions and renewals of such copyright. The right to use the title is granted exclusively only for and in connection with the Play, based in whole or in part upon the Work, and the owner makes no warranty with respect to the rights of the Purchaser so to use such title, except insofar as same is affected by owner's acts or omissions.

THIRD: The Purchaser will cause a completed musical play to be written and composed, and upon completion of the Play, any and all rights therein, whether presently known or hereafter ascertained, of any kind, nature, and description, including but not limited to, television, radio, motion picture, foreign, commercial, second-class touring, stock, amateur, tabloid, sequel, remake, shall become the sole and exclusive property of the Purchaser.

FOURTH: The Purchaser has paid to the Owner, upon the execution hereof, the sum of five thousand dollars ($5,000) as a nonreturnable advance payment on account of the following royalties, also to be paid to the Owner:

(a) One and one-half percent (1.5%) of the gross box office receipts from all first-class stage presentations of the musical in the United States of America, the Dominion of Canada, and Great Britain, authorized or licensed hereunder as provided in the Dramatists Guild, Inc., Approved Production Contract for a musical,

(b) That proportion of the Authors' ("Author" and "Authors" as used in this agreement refers to the bookwriter, composer, and lyricist collectively) share of all proceeds, emoluments, and other things of value received from the sale, lease, and disposition of any and all other rights in the musical, including, but not limited to, motion picture publication of libretto, radio, television, stock, amateur, foreign, commercial, operetta, grand opera, second-class touring, "remake," "sequel," and condensed tabloid versions and all other rights now known or hereinafter to be known in the proportion that 1.5 percent shall bear to the total percentage of gross box office receipts payable as royalties to the Bookwriter, Composer, Lyricist, and Owner.

(c) Anything to the contrary herein notwithstanding if the Authors and all other royalty participants, including the Purchasers with respect to the Producer's fee, agree to a Royalty Pool Formula, then Owners agree that they will accept the same proportion in the pool in accordance with the terms of the formula. If there is a dispute as to what constitutes the "same proportion," the decision of the Accountant for the Production Company shall be binding upon the parties.

FIFTH: The rights herein granted shall cease and terminate and shall automatically revert to the Owner without any obligation of any kind to the Purchaser:

(a) Unless the Purchaser shall have written or cause to have written a completed play based on the Work.

(b) Unless the Play is presented on the stage, before a paying audience, on or before the   day of   19 .

Nothing herein contained shall be deemed to obligate the Purchaser to produce the Play. The time period herein provided may be extended as hereinafter provided for in Paragraph "SIXTH" of this Agreement.

SIXTH: The Purchaser shall have the option of extending the time within which to cause the completed Play to be produced, as hereinabove provided, for an additional year, that is, until, upon serving written notice upon the Owner of the exercise of such option on or before, and by paying to the Owner the additional sum of $5,000 as a further nonreturnable advance against royalties.

SEVENTH: It is mutually agreed that:

(a) The Author shall be deemed to be the sole Author of the musical for all purposes hereof and shall have full and exclusive rights and privileges as Author with respect to all matters relating to the production of the musical (such as, but not limited to, choice of cast, director, and sale of motion picture [if not in conflict with any existing contracts concerning the motion picture rights] and other subsidiary rights, etc.). No signatures of the Owner shall be necessary in connection with any of the foregoing, provided, however, that the Author will furnish to the Owner fully conformed copies of each Agreement made regarding any sale or other disposition upon the execution of any such Agreement.

(b) Commencing with the date hereof and continuing until the termination of all the Purchaser's rights hereunder, the Owner will not grant the right to adapt or redramatize the Work or any part thereof in any form and will not sell, lease, license, assign, or otherwise dispose of any performing rights in or to said story.

(c) Upon the presentation of the musical for the number of performances that would cause the rights to vest in the producer, in accordance with the terms of the Dramatists Guild, Inc., Approved Production Contract (the "APC"), the musical and the Work shall be deemed merged forever and in perpetuity in the sense that the Owner shall not convey or dispose of any rights in or to the Work, including the copyrights therein and thereto, without the prior written consent of the Author. Under no circumstances shall the sale of the Work be limited anywhere. Notwithstanding any such merger, however, the Owner and their assignees and licensees may continue exclusively to exercise their respective rights of publishing and selling copies of the Work (as distinguished from the musical) in any and all territories of the world and to derive and retain for their account all royalties and proceeds therefrom, and, in this connection, the Owner's rights in the copyrights of the Work or any part thereof shall continue to be vested in the owner, subject, however, in all respects, to the terms and conditions of this Agreement. If the Work shall merge in the Play as herein provided, then the Author shall have the sole right to sell, lease, license, or otherwise dispose of the motion picture and subsidiary rights therein (subject to any previous grant by the Owner). In extension and not in limitation of the foregoing, it is specifically understood and agreed that the Author's rights in motion picture, subsidiary rights, British Isle production rights and other related rights shall be effective upon a merger of the Work and Play as herein provided. If the original run of the musical shall terminate prior to the aforementioned minimum period, the owner shall thenceforth be completely free to exploit any and all of his respective rights in such story for the sole and exclusive benefit of himself, his successors, licensees, and assigns.

(d) All leases, licenses, or other dispositions of any right or interest in or in connection with the musical and/or the subsidiary and/or the motion picture rights thereof shall be in writing and made in good faith on the basis of the best efforts and interests of all concerned.

(e) All contracts executed by the Purchaser and Author of the musical in connection with any of the rights in the musical or pertaining thereto, which are the subject of this Agreement, or the rights of the owner therein or herein, shall acknowledge the interest of the Owner pursuant to the terms of this Agreement. In instances where the Owner is entitled to any of the proceeds, Purchaser will exercise his best efforts to provide in any contract that express provision shall be made for payments directly to the Owner through his agent as hereinafter provided and copies of all such contracts relating to the rights herein, confirming, affecting, or relating to any of the Owner's rights hereunder shall be furnished to the Owner through his agent, as hereinafter provided, promptly upon the execution thereof.

(f) The Owner shall not be entitled to receive any share from, nor to receive any accounting for, any and all royalties and other compensation from publication of the original lyrics and music in and of the musical, mechanical reproductions, and original cast album and other recordings including statutory and copyright royalties, and so-called small rights arising out of the music publication and recording contracts by the Purchaser or anyone else for his original music and lyrics, and all royalties and dividends, etc., that may be derived by the Purchaser or anyone else, as lyricist(s) and composer(s), from such organizations as the American Society of Composers, Authors, and Publishers; Broadcast Music, Incorporated; and other similar organizations. It is understood, however, that any sale or disposition of synchronization rights for use in connection with the making of a motion picture and/or of a television program shall be deemed a disposition of motion picture and/or television rights, as the case may be, and the Owner shall share in the proceeds therefrom in accordance with his rights to share in the disposition of motion picture and television rights as herein provided for.

EIGHTH: If the musical shall not be produced on the legitimate speaking stage, pursuant to the terms hereof, on or before the date herein provided for, as the same may be extended pursuant hereto, or if the rights do not merge as herein provided, then:

(a) All rights in the Work granted to or acquired by the Purchaser hereunder shall forthwith revert to the Owner with the same force and effect as if this Agreement had never been entered into.

(b) All rights in such portion of the musical as shall not be contained in or taken from or incidental to the Work shall forthwith revert to the Purchaser.

(c) The Purchaser shall be free to make such use and disposition of his original music and lyrics of the musical as he sees fit, but it is expressly understood and agreed that the Purchaser or his assignee shall not have any right to retain or use the name of the Play (or any title of which such name or title is part) as the title of any works or rights which may revert to them hereunder, or in any way have the right to capitalize on the fact that such right and/or music and/or lyrics were once a part of the musical and/or associated with any version of such play.

NINTH: The Purchaser agrees that the name of Owner shall appear in all advertising and publicity issued by or with the consent or under the control of the Purchaser wherever the Author's name shall appear, with the same size and prominence as Author's name. If the title is not used as the title of the Play, then that title will appear in the credits as the story on which the Play is based.

TENTH: The Purchaser agrees to hold in the name of the Owner two (2) pairs of house seats for each performance of the Play in New York City (except theatre parties and benefit performances), which seats shall be held until noon of the day preceding the performance with respect to a matinee performance and until seventy-two (72) hours preceding the performances, which seats shall be paid for at the regularly established box office prices therefor. The Owner shall also have the right to purchase ten (10) pairs of house seats for the New York opening. Author acknowledges and agrees that the theatre tickets made available hereunder cannot, except in accordance with the regulations promulgated by the office of the Attorney General of the State of New York, be resold at a premium or otherwise, and that complete and accurate records will be maintained by them, which may be inspected at reasonable times by a duly designated representative of Producer and/or the Attorney General of the State of New York, with respect to the disposition of all tickets made available hereunder.

ELEVENTH: Subject to the terms and conditions hereof, the terms of this Agreement shall be for the period of the copyright of the musical.

TWELFTH: Purchaser will advise or cause the Owner to be advised in writing, in full and complete detail, of all offers for the purchase of the motion picture and/or television rights to the musical as soon as possible after the receipt of such offers but not later than forty-eight (48) hours prior to the acceptance of any such offer.

THIRTEENTH: Purchaser will keep and maintain, or by contract cause to be kept and maintained, full and correct books and records relating to the presentation of the musical hereunder and all transactions in which the Owner may have an interest hereunder and the proceeds derived therefrom. Such books and records will be kept in New York, New York. The Owner and/or his agent and/or representatives shall have access to such books and records during all regular business hours and may take or cause to be taken excerpts and/or extracts therefrom. Payments herein required to be made to the Owner shall be made at the same time and in the same manner as payment to Author and pursuant to the terms and conditions of the Option Agreement. Payments to the Owner shall be accompanied by copies of all such statements as are required to be furnished to Authors by the Dramatists Guild, Inc., Approved Production Contract and such rules and regulations.

FOURTEENTH: The addresses of the parties herein shall be for all purposes as follows: Copies of all notices shall be mailed to Donald C. Farber, Esq., Farber & Rich LLP, 1370 Avenue of the Americas, New York, New York 10019. All notices required to be given hereunder shall be in writing and sent by certified mail addressed as above provided, except as may, from time to time, be otherwise directed in writing by the respective parties.

FIFTEENTH: Any claim, dispute, misunderstanding, or controversy or charge of unfair dealing arising under, or in connection with, or out of this Agreement, or the breach thereof, shall be submitted to arbitration before one arbitrator to be held under the rules and regulations of the American Arbitration Association. Failure by the Producer to pay any amount claimed to be due by the Owner is evidence of a dispute entitling the claimant to an arbitration. Judgment upon the award rendered may be entered in the highest court of the forum, State or Federal, having jurisdiction. The arbitrator is empowered to award damages against any party to the controversy in such sums as they shall deem fair and reasonable under the circumstances. The arbitrator is also empowered to require specific performance of a contract, or in the alternative money damages, and have power to grant any other remedy or relief, injunctive or otherwise, which they deem just and equitable.

The arbitrator is also empowered to render a partial award before making a final award and grant such relief, injunctive or otherwise, in such partial award as they deem just and equitable. The arbitrator may determine and indicate in his written award by whom and in what proportion the cost of arbitration shall be borne.

SIXTEENTH: The Owner hereby acknowledges that (*name of agent or attorney*) (hereinafter referred to as "the Agent" or "the Attorney") has acted for the Owner in the negotiation and consummation of this Agreement, and the Owner therefore agrees that so long as the Owner or their assignees shall have any rights under this Agreement or any extensions of renewals hereof or under any agreements amendatory hereof or in substitution hereof or under any first-class dramatic production agreement which may proceed from this Agreement, shall be the sole exclusive and irrevocable agent of the Owner with respect to the Owner's interest in this Agreement and in the rights and privileges granted herein, with the sole and exclusive right and power to deal therewith for the Owner and, further, that as such agent, shall be entitled to receive any and all monies due the Owner pursuant hereof and to deduct and retain for itself ten percent (10%) thereof, except where such monies are applicable to an exercise of the amateur rights of the musical, in which case it may deduct and retain for itself twenty percent (20%) of such monies. This designation as sole and exclusive agent for the Owner shall be irrevocable and Purchaser hereby is directed by the Owner to make payment of any and all sums payable to the Owner hereunder. The Owner acknowledges that all such payments by the Purchaser to when made, shall be deemed to be payments by the Purchaser to the Owner hereunder.

SEVENTEENTH: This Agreement, irrespective of its place of execution, shall be construed and interpreted in accordance with the laws of the State of New York as though, and with the same effect, as if it had been actually executed and delivered within such State.

EIGHTEENTH: This Agreement shall be binding upon and shall inure to the benefit of the parties hereto and their respective heirs, executors, administrators, personal representatives, successors, and assigns.

NINETEENTH: Purchaser shall have the right to assign this Agreement, provided, however, that the assignee shall in all respects be subject to, and assume in writing directly to the Owner, each and every term, provision, condition, and obligation herein contained.

TWENTIETH: This Agreement constitutes the entire understanding between the parties hereto and no warranty, representation, inducement, or agreement not contained herein shall be binding on the parties. This Agreement can be modified only by a written instrument duly authorized by the parties hereto or the authorized representatives of each of the parties.

    IN WITNESS WHEREOF, the parties hereto have executed this Agreement as of the day and year first above written.

Owner

Purchaser

Co-production Agreement

AGREEMENT made as of this   day of   1996, between John Jones (hereinafter sometimes referred to as "Jones") and Henry Smith (hereinafter sometimes referred to as "Smith").

FIRST: The parties will co-produce Off-Braodway in New York City the play "Happy Happy" written by John Jones (hereinafter sometimes referred to as the "Play").

SECOND: The parties have formed the "Happy Happy LLC" Limited Liability Company under the laws of the State of New York (hereinafter sometimes referred to as the "Company") to produce the said Play.

(a) The parties hereto will be the Managing Members of the Company, and the parties contributing to the capital thereof will be the Investor Members of the Company.

(b) The capital of the Company will be in an amount not more than one million dollars ($1,000,000) and not less than eight hundred thousand dollars ($800,000), or such other amount as may mutually be agreed upon between the parties to this Agreement. The parties contemplate producing the Play in an off-Broadway or middle theatre.

(c) The Limited Liability Company Operating Agreement shall be based on a theatrical Limited Liability Company Operating Agreement as prepared by Donald C. Farber, Esq., of counsel to Jacob, Medinger & Finnegan LLP.

(d) Each party agrees to use his best efforts to raise as much of the capital of the Company as possible. In the event that the parties hereto cannot raise the complete capital necessary for the Company and it is necessary to pay someone any money or share of the Managing Members' profits, for the raising of any part of said capital, if the parties hereto are in agreement with respect to such an arrangement, then the amount so paid to said party(s) shall be contributed equally by the parties hereto.

(e) The Investor Members shall receive fifty percent (50%) of the net profits of the company, and the Managing Members shall receive the remaining fifty percent (50%) of the net profits. The net profits shall first be used to repay the Investor Members to the extent of their investment in the Company before the profits are shared with the Managing Members.

If any star(s) or other person(s) are entitled to receive any part of the gross receipts or net profits, the same shall be deemed to be an expense and deducted before computing the net profits to be divided between the Managing and Investor Members.

(f) Regardless of the amount of capital raised or contributed by each party to this Agreement, the producers' share of any net profits shall be divided equally between them, that is fifty percent (50%) to Jones and fifty percent (50%) to Smith.

(g) The parties agree to assign to the Company, at their original cost, all rights in and to the option to produce the play which they have heretofore acquired and any other agreement entered into for the purpose of producing the Play.

(h) The producers' fee payable by the Company shall be in the amount of two percent (2%) of the gross weekly box office receipts until the production budget is recouped and will, thereafter, be in the amount of three percent (3%) of the gross weekly box office receipts. The cash office charge shall be seven hundred fifty dollars ($750.00) each week for each company and shall commence three weeks prior to rehearsals and shall terminate one week after the close of each production. Both the producers' fee and the cash office charge will be shared by the parties equally.

THIRD: Any and all obligations of any kind or nature for the Joint Venture and for the Company shall be incurred only upon the consent of both parties to this Agreement.

FOURTH: All contracts and all checks on behalf of the Joint Venture and on behalf of the Company may be signed by either party to this Agreement, or someone delegated to so sign by both parties to this Agreement.

FIFTH: Wherever producers' credits are given, the credits shall be as mutually agreed to by the parties to this Agreement.

SIXTH: Each party shall devote as much time as is reasonably necessary for the production and presentation of the Play, it being recognized and agreed that each party may be engaged in other activities, whether or not of a competing nature, so long as he devotes sufficient time to the Joint Venture and to the Company, and to the proper running of the business of producing and presenting the Play.

SEVENTH: The Joint Venture shall terminate upon the happening of the first of the following:

(a) The formation of the LLC;

(b) Such date as the parties hereto may mutually agree upon;

(c) The withdrawal of any of the parties hereto.

EIGHTH: It is agreed that the pre-production money, that is the front money, shall be furnished equally by the parties to this Agreement, and in the event that it is necessary to assign any share of the producers' profits to someone else in exchange for front money, then the assignment shall be made equally by the parties to this Agreement.

All front monies so advanced, by the parties to this Agreement, as well as other budgeted expenditures on behalf of the Joint Venture, by either party, approved by the other party, shall be repaid to the party expending such sum immediately upon full capitalization of the Company.

NINTH: It is agreed that the following parties will be engaged by the Joint Venture and the Company in the following capacities:

(a) Donald C. Farber, Esq., 1270 Avenue of the Americas, 31st Floor, New York, New York 10020.

TENTH: It is agreed that all decisions, artistic and business, will be made by the parties jointly. In the event that there is a dispute of an artistic nature which cannot be resolved, then the final decision will be made by the director, and his decision shall be final and binding. In the event of a dispute of a business nature which cannot be resolved, the decision of Donald C. Farber shall be final.

ELEVENTH: Other than those decisions specifically covered in this Paragraph TENTH of this Agreement, any and all disputes or differences in connection with this Agreement, or the breach or alleged breach thereof, shall be submitted to arbitration to be held in New York City, by one arbitrator, under the rules and regulations of the American Arbitration Association then obtaining, and each of the parties hereto agrees to be bound by the determination of the arbitrator. Judgment on the award rendered may be entered in the highest court of the forum having jurisdiction.

TWELFTH: If any party(s) wish to terminate the run of the Play and the other party(s) wish to continue it, the party(s) wishing to continue (the "continuing party(s)") shall assume complete control of the production and presentation of the Play commencing immediately upon giving written notice to such effect after the party(s) seeking to terminate the run (the "retiring party(s)") shall have given notice thereof, and the continuing party(s) shall thereafter bear all the expenses and liabilities of the production of the Play and be entitled to receive all of the net profits in connection therewith as well as the management fee and office charge. The continuing party(s) shall indemnify the retiring party(s) from any liability incurred after the takeover and shall evidence such indemnity by appropriate instruments. The retiring party(s) shall forfeit all rights, title and interest in and to the production of the Play and the proceeds therefrom commencing with such takeover, but this shall not affect proceeds accrued prior thereto but not received, including proceeds from subsidiary rights in the Play.

THIRTEENTH: The provisions of this Agreement shall survive the termination of the Joint Venture and shall continue to bind the parties hereto. This Agreement shall be binding and shall inure to the benefit of the parties, their respective successors and assigns. This Agreement sets forth the entire Agreement of the parties and may not be changed except by an instrument in writing signed by each of the parties. The validity, construction, interpretation and effect of this Agreement shall be determined by and in accordance with the laws of the State of New York.

IN WITNESS WHEREOF, the parties hereto have set their hands and seals to this Agreement as of the day and year first above written.

_____

John Jones

_____

Henry Smith

APPENDIX D

Approved Production
Contract for Plays[1]

APPROVED PRODUCTION CONTRACT FOR PLAYS

THIS CONTRACT, made and entered into as of the day of
, 19 ("*Effective Date*") by and between

whose address is

hereinafter referred to jointly and severally as "*Producer*," and

whose address is

hereafter referred to as "*Author*."

W I T N E S S E T H:

Whereas, The Dramatists Guild, Inc. has promulgated this form of
agreement known as the Approved Production Contract ("*APC*") which it has
recommended to its members as being fair and reasonable to both authors and
producers; and

---

[1] ©1985 The Dramatists Guild, Inc.

Whereas, Author, a member of The Dramatists Guild, Inc. ("***Guild***") has been or will be writing a certain play or other dramatic property, now entitled hereinafter referred to as the "***Play***"; and

Whereas, Producer is or will be in the business of producing plays and desires to acquire the sole and exclusive rights to produce the Play in the United States, its territories and possessions, including Puerto Rico, and Canada (the "***Territory***") and to acquire Author's services in connection therewith;

Now, therefore, in consideration of the mutual covenants herein contained and other good and valuable consideration, the parties hereto agree as follows:

ARTICLE I
Initial Grant of Rights

SECTION 1.01 **Initial Grant of Rights to Produce Play**. Author hereby grants to Producer the sole and exclusive rights, subject to the terms of this Contract, to present the Play for one or more First-Class Performances. For the purposes of this Contract, the term "***First-Class Performances***" shall mean live stage productions of the Play on the speaking stage, within the Territory, under Producer's own management, in a regular evening bill in a first-class theatre in a first-class manner, with a first-class cast and a first-class director. The terms "***produce***" and "***present***" (and their derivatives) shall be used interchangeably.

SECTION 1.02 **Grant of Author's Services**. Author hereto agrees to:

(a) perform such services as may be reasonably necessary in making revisions in the Play;

(b) assist in the selection of the cast and consult with, assist and advise the Producer, director, scenic, lighting and costume designers and the choreographer and/or dance director, conductor and sound designer, if any, regarding any problem arising out of the production of the Play;

(c) attend rehearsals of the Play as well as out-of-town performances prior to the Official Press Opening (as defined in SECTION 2.05 herein) of the Play in New York City, provided, however, that Author may be excused from such attendance on showing reasonable cause.

SECTION 1.03 **Termination of Rights if No Production**. Although nothing herein shall be deemed to obligate Producer to produce the Play, nevertheless, unless Producer presents the first paid public First-Class Performance of the Play within the applicable Option Period described in Article II herein for which the prescribed payment has been made, Producer's rights to produce the play and to the services of Author shall then automatically and without notice terminate.

SECTION 1.04 **Continuous Production Rights.** If the first paid public First-Class Performance of the Play hereunder is presented within one of the Option Periods (including the extensions, if any, set forth in SECTIONS 2.03 and 2.04 herein), the rights granted to present the Play shall continue subject to the reopening provisions of ARTICLE X herein.

SECTION 1.05 **Definition of Author**. For the purposes of this Contract, the term "*Author*" shall mean each dramatist, collaborator, adaptor, bookwriter, composer, lyricist, novelist and owner of underlying rights whose literary or musical material is used in the Play. The term "Author" shall include any person who is involved in the initial stages of a collaborative process and who is deserving of billing credit as an Author and whose literary or musical contribution will be an integral part of the Play as presented in subsequent productions by other producers. It shall not include a person whose services are only those of a literal translator.

SECTION 1.06 **Reservation of Rights**. Author shall retain sole and complete title, both legal and equitable, in and to the Play and all rights and uses of every kind except as otherwise specifically herein provided. Author reserves all rights and uses now in existence or which may hereafter come into existence, except as specifically herein provided. Any rights reserved shall not be deemed competitive with any of Producer's rights and may be exercised by Author at any time except as otherwise specifically provided herein.

ARTICLE II
Option Periods and Payments

SECTION 2.01 **Option Periods/Option Payments**. In considera-tion of the foregoing grant of rights and of Author's services in writing the Play and Author's agreement to perform services in connection with the production of the Play as hereinabove provided, Producer agrees to pay Author the following sums ("*Option Payments*") in order to maintain Producer's rights to present the Play, provided that the first paid public First-Class Performance of the Play occurs prior to the expiration of the applicable "*Option Period*" described below;

(a) "*First Option Period*"—$5,000 for the period of 6 months following the Effective Date of this Contract, payable upon the execution of this Contract by Author and Producer.

(b) "*Second Option Period*"—$2,500 for a second consecutive 6-month period, payable on or before the last day of the First Option Period.

(c) "*Third Option Period*"—$5,000 for an additional period of up to 12 consecutive months, payable in the following manner: $2,500 for the first 6 months of such period, payable on or before the last day of the Second Option Period and $500 per month thereafter, for up to 6 months, payable on or before the last day of the preceding month. In order to exercise this right to extend for a Third Option Period, Producer must give Author written notice, on or before the last day of the Second Option Period, of the intended date of the first paid public First-Class Performance together with copies of commitments representing actual or proposed contributions of Equity Capital (as defined in SECTION 3.03(b) (i) herein) which, in the aggregate, equal at least 50% of Production Costs (as defined in SECTION 3.03 herein); plus copies of documents representing one of the following:

(i) a commitment for the licensing of a first-class theatre, with occupancy to occur before the end of the Third Option Period; or

(ii) a contract for the engagement of a star, featured actor or director pursuant to which such person agrees to tender services before the end of the Third Option Period; or

(iii) if Producer and Author mutually agree in *ARTICLE XXII* herein that Producer shall have the rights, in the Territory, to present Developmental Productions (as defined in *SECTION 4.01(f)* herein), then a contract with a theatre or organization for the presentation of a Developmental Production of the Play, the first performance of which is to be presented before the end of the Third Option Period.

The extension of Producer's rights and option for the Third Option Period shall not be prevented or affected by the fact that any of these commitments or contracts may be made subject to conditions, including, but not limited to, the availability of a person or theatre, the attainment of full capitalization of the production, further negotiations regarding material terms, or the execution of a formal agreement or the fact that any of these commitments or contracts may later be breached or held to be unenforceable.

SECTION 2.02 **Option Payments Non-Returnable**. Each of the foregoing Option Payments made by Producer shall be non-returnable (except to the extent described in ARTICLE XVI herein) but shall be deductible, to the extent permitted by the terms of ARTICLE VI herein, from the Advance Payments and Royalties (as defined respectively in SECTIONS 3.01 and 4.02 herein) otherwise payable to Author.

SECTION 2.03 **Extension of Option Until Delivery of Completed Play**. If this Contract provides in ARTICLE XXII that the Play has not been completed at the Effective Date of this Contract, the payment for the First Option Period shall be made at the time and in the manner set forth in ARTICLE XXII herein , but the expiration of the Option Periods and the due dates for the subsequent Option Payments otherwise specified in this ARTICLE shall be extended and measured from the date on which the Completed Play is delivered to Producer. Producer shall maintain the sole and exclusive rights and option to present the Play while Producer awaits delivery of the Completed Play. Unless otherwise defined in ARTICLE XXII herein, a "*Completed Play*" shall mean the Play consisting of a script of at least 110 single spaced pages. If the Completed Play is not delivered within 6 months after the Effective Date of this Contract, Producer may, at any time thereafter, terminate this Contract upon written notice to Author. Author agrees that time is of the essence with respect to such delivery date.

SECTION 2.04 **Extension of Option for Try-Out Performances**. If, during one of the Option Periods, Producer presents Second-Class Performances (as defined in SECTION 9.01 herein) or Developmental Productions of the Play, the expiration of the Option Periods and due dates for subsequent Option Payments shall be extended for a period equal to the number of days on which performances of the Play were so presented (up to a maximum of 8 weeks) plus an additional 60 days.

SECTION 2.05 **Definition of "Official Press Opening"**. For the purposes of this Contract, the term "*Official Press Opening*" shall mean the performance of the Play which Producer has publicly announced as the opening and to which the press is invited.

ARTICLE III
Advance Payments

SECTION 3.01 **Calculation and Due Dates of Advance Payments**.

(a) Producer shall pay Author the following "*Advance Payments*," at the stated times, subject to the provisions of *SECTIONS 3.04* and *6.01* herein:

  (i) On the first day of rehearsal at which Producer requires the attendance of all cast members of the Principal Company (as defined in SECTION 3.01(b) herein), but in no event later than 5 business days before the initial First-Class Performance of the Play, Producer shall pay Author a sum equal to 3% of the amounts constituting Capitalization (as defined in SECTION 3.03 herein) at such date.

  (ii) Thereafter, at such times as additional amounts are contributed towards Capitalization, Producer shall pay Author, within 10 business days after Producer's receipt thereof, a sum equal to 3% of such additional contributions.

  (iii) The sums otherwise payable by Producer pursuant to the foregoing calculation in this SECTION shall be reduced by an amount equal to 3% of such sums. The net amounts paid to Author shall constitute the Advance Payments.

(b) For the purposes of this Contract, a "*Company*" shall mean each unit of actors assembled to present the Play hereunder. "*Principal Company*" shall mean the first Company funded in an amount sufficient to present First-Class Performances of the Play.

SECTION 3.02 **Maximum Advance**. The aggregate amount of Advance Payments payable by Producer pursuant to SECTION 3.01 herein shall not exceed $35,000, regardless of the amount of Capitalization.

SECTION 3.03 **Definition of "Production Costs," "Capitalization" and "Equity Capital"**.

(a) For the purposes of this Contract, "***Production Costs***" shall mean the estimated costs of producing the Principal Company (including any contingency reserves) as described in the documents used in connection with the financing of such Company, including costs that may be paid, if permitted by the terms of such documents, by an overcall demand on investors, but not including any weekly operating expenses.

(b) For the purposes of this Contract, "***Capitalization***" shall mean:

(i) the aggregate of the following sums actually received by Producer (after all necessary bank clearances) for the purpose of paying Production Costs:

(A) all amounts contributed as Equity Capital. For the purposes of this Contract, "***Equity Capital***" shall mean the amounts contributed by investors in order to pay Production Costs and obtain an ownership interest in the venture producing the Principal Company, including all amounts received by Producer pursuant to an overcall demand made on the investors who previously contributed Equity Capital to such venture, but only to the extent such sums exceed 10% of the total Equity Capital contributions received by Producer from all investors immediately prior to the date on which the demand for such overcall is issued and only to the extent such sums are used by Producer to pay Production Costs; and

(b) should Producer find it necessary to obtain loans to pay Production Costs, then the amount of such loan proceeds shall also be included to the extent such proceeds are in excess of 20% of the estimated Production Costs (or if the documents used in connection with the financing of the Principal Company set forth an amount representing minimum estimated Production Costs, then such amount); however, if

Producer receives no Equity Capital pursuant to an overcall (whether or not an overcall demand is made), then the amount of such loan proceeds shall be included to the extent such proceeds are in excess of 30% of such estimated Production Costs;

(ii) but not including the foregoing sums to the extent allocated to pay the following items of Production Costs:

(A) all security bonds, deposits and other guarantees to be provided to any union or other collective bargaining organization, theatre or other entity;

(b) all Option Payments to Author;

(C) advertising, promotional and press related costs in excess of 10% of the minimum estimated Production Costs; and

(D) all sums described in SECTION 6.01(b) herein which are included as Production Costs and paid to a third party who presented the Play in the Territory as a Developmental Production or as other non-First-Class Performances.

(c) All sums received by Producer to pay the operating costs of paid public Performances of the Play (rather than Production Costs) shall be excluded in determining the amount of Capitalization, regardless of the source of any such sums or the manner in which such sums may be contributed.

SECTION 3.04 **Advance Payments Non-Returnable**. All Advance Payments made by Producer shall be nonreturnable but shall be deductible, to the extent permitted by the terms of ARTICLE VI herein, from Royalties otherwise payable to Author.

ARTICLE IV
Royalties

SECTION 4.01 Definitions. For the purposes of this Contract, the following terms shall have the indicated meanings:

(a) *"Out-of-Town Performances"* — First-Class Performances of the Play outside of New York City prior to presentation of Preview or Regular performances.

(b) *"Preview Performances"* — First-Class Performances of the Play in New York City prior to the Official Press Opening in New York City. For the purposes of calculating Royalties under this Contract, the Official Press Opening in New York City shall be deemed a Preview Performance.

(c) *"Regular Performances"* — First-Class Performances of the Play in New York City commencing with the first performance of the play following the Official Press Opening of the Play in New York City.

(d) *"Touring Performances"* — First-Class Performances of the Play hereunder outside of New York City, presented by a Company simultaneously with or subsequent to Out-of-Town, Preview or Regular Performances.

(e) *"Fixed-Fee Performances"* — All performances of the Play hereunder (other than Preview and Regular Performances) produced by or pursuant to a grant of rights from Producer, in return for which Producer receives compensation based in whole or in part on a fixed (i.e., guaranteed) fee.

(f) *"Developmental Productions"* — Productions of the Play presented pursuant to Actors' Equity Workshop Agreements.

(g) *"Backers' Auditions"* — Performances of the Play presented pursuant to the Actors' Equity Association Backers' Audition Code, or, if the performances are outside the United States then pursuant to any other similar code, contract or agreement in effect in such location.

(h) *"Performance Week"* — The 6- or 7-day period, beginning on either Monday or, if there is no scheduled performance on Monday, then on Tuesday and continuing through Sunday, during which one or more performances of the Play are presented hereunder.

(i) *"Full Performance Week"* — Any Performance Week during which no fewer than 8 performances of the Play are presented.

(j) *"New York City"* — The theatrical district of the Borough of Manhattan of the City of New York unless the parties modify the definition, in Article XXII herein, to include any other location in the Borough of Manhattan.

SECTION 4.02 **Description of Royalties**. Author shall earn the following aggregate *"Royalties"* for each week of performances, described below, during which the Play is presented hereunder:

(a) *Out-of-Town Performances and Previous Performances* — 5% of the Gross Weekly Box Office Receipts (as defined in SECTION 4.03 herein) from Out-of-Town and Preview Performances up to and including the Performance Week in which the costs of presenting such Company have been Recouped (as defined in SECTION 4.04 herein) and 10% thereafter. This Royalty is not subject to the Royalty Adjustment provisions of ARTICLE V herein until and unless such Company has attained Recoupment.

(b) *Regular Performances* — 5% of the Gross Weekly Box Office Receipts from Regular Performances up to and including the Performance Week in which the costs of presenting such Company have been Recouped and 10% thereafter. This Royalty is subject to the Royalty Adjustment provisions of ARTICLE V herein.

(c) *Touring Performances* — 5% of the Gross Weekly Box Office Receipts earned from Touring Performances up to and including the Performance Week in which the costs of presenting such Company have been Recouped and 10% thereafter. This Royalty is subject to the Royalty Adjustment provisions of ARTICLE V herein.

(d) *Fixed-Fee Performances* — For the purposes of this SECTION 4.02(d), the term "Producer" shall mean Producer's grantee in those cases where Fixed-Fee Performances are produced by such grantee.

   (i) Except s provided in SECTION 4.02(d)(ii) herein, Author's Royalty for Fixed-Fee Performances of the Play shall be calculated in the following manner:

      (A) 10% of any fixed fee paid to Producer by such local promoter or sponsor for such Performances; plus

(b) 10% of Producer's share of box office receipts and any profits for such Performances (including box office receipts and profits paid as a salary, fee, royalty or other type of compensation for Producer's services) paid to Producer by such local promoter or sponsor.

    (ii) With respect to first-class theatres which have, after January 1, 1977, presented First-Class Performances of plays pursuant to which the authors of such plays have customarily received royalties for such performances based on a percentage of gross weekly box office receipts (rather than on fixed fees), Author's Royalty for Fixed-Fee Performances of the Play presented in such theatres shall be calculated in the following manner:

        (A) 10% of any fixed fee paid to Producer by the so-called "local promoter" or "local sponsor" for such Performance; plus

(b) if the local promoter or sponsor pays Producer a percentage of box office receipts and any profits for such Performances (including box office receipts and profits paid as a salary, fee, royalty or other type of compensation for Producer's services), then Author shall be paid, from up to 50% of Producer's share of such box office receipts and profits, a sum equal to 25% of the amounts paid to Author in (A); plus

        (C) 10% of the balance of Producer's share of box office receipts and any profits set forth in (b) above (after deduction of the sum paid to Author in (b) above);

    (iii) The calculations set forth above may be made on a weekly basis or on a theatre-by-theatre basis at Producer's option.

    (iv) If there is any dispute between Author and Producer as to whether a particular theatre should be classified under SECTION 4.02(d)(i) or (ii), the parties shall submit the matter for resolution to the Theatrical Conciliation Council. The decision of the Council shall be final and binding on the parties.

    (v) If Producer licenses the Play to an entity in which Producer has any financial or other interest, or if the Play is presented in a theatre in which Producer has a similar interest, the arrangements made between Producer and such entity or theatre shall not be materially different from the arrangements made in the industry between unrelated parties under similar circumstances. Furthermore, irrespective of whether there is any financial or other interest between Producer and such entity or theatre, the weekly operating expenses of such Fixed-Fee Performances which are customarily paid by the producer (e.g. compensation to actors), rather than by the local promoter or sponsor, shall be reflected in the amount of the fixed fee for the purpose of computing and paying Author's Royalties under this SECTION 4.02(d). If Author or the Guild believes that any such arrangements made by Producer are materially different, or that the fixed fee does not reflect the weekly operating expenses customarily paid by the producer rather than the local promoter or sponsor then, in either case, Author, or the Guild, on behalf of Author, shall submit such matter to the Theatrical Conciliation Council which shall determine whether the arrangements are appropriate under the circumstances or whether the fixed fee reflects the weekly operating expenses customarily paid by producers, as the case may be. The decision of the Council shall be final and binding on the parties.

(e) ***Developmental Productions*** — If the rights to present Developmental Productions of the Play are granted in ARTICLE XXII herein, Author shall earn a Royalty equal to the minimum compensation paid to an actor for such Developmental Production, excluding any per diem, travel and other allowances, if any, paid to the actor. Author and Producer shall not modify any provision of this Contract as a condition to the granting of rights to present Developmental Productions.

(f) ***Backers' Auditions*** — No Royalties to Author.

SECTION 4.03 **Definition of "Gross Weekly Box Office Receipts"**. (a) Where Author's Royalties, as provided herein, are based upon "Gross Weekly Box Office Receipts", the Royalties for such Performance Week shall be computed upon all sums received by Producer from all ticket sales to the Play, allocable to performances given in such week, less the following deductions:

(i) federal or other admission taxes;

(ii) customary commissions and fees, as may be prevailing from time to time, paid to or retained by third parties in connection with theatre parties, benefits, American Express or other similar credit card plans, telephone sales, automated ticket distribution or remote box offices, e.g., Ticketron and Ticket World (but not ticket brokers), and commissions or fees for group sales;

(iii) commissions and fees paid to or retained by credit card companies for sales of tickets;

(iv) those sums equivalent to the former 5% New York City Amusement Tax, the proceeds of which are now paid to the pension and/or welfare funds of various theatrical unions;

(v) subscription fees;

(vi) receipts from Actors' Fund Benefit performances provided the customary payments are made by the Actors' Fund to The Dramatists Guild Fund, Inc.;

(vii) receipts from two performances of the Play in each calendar year to the extent such receipts are contributed for theatre-related eleemosynary purposes; and

(viii) if applicable, library discounts, value added taxes and entertainment taxes, if any.

(b) Producer may also deduct from Gross Weekly Box Office Receipts allocable to any Performance Week any sums included as Gross Weekly Box Office Receipts in a prior Performance Week and which were included in Author's Royalty calculation but which sums subsequently are refunded or uncollectible due to dishonored checks, invalidated credit card receipts or for any other reason.

(c) If the Play is presented simultaneously by more than one Company, Gross Weekly Box Office Receipts received by each such Company shall be computed and paid separately.

SECTION 4.04 **Definition of "Recouped" and "Recoupment".** (a) For the purposes of this Contract, the terms *"Recouped"* or *"Recoupment"* shall mean, with respect to each Company presenting the Play, the recovery of all costs incurred in presenting such Company after payment or accrual (but not prepayment) of all operating expenses for such Company.

   (b) For the purposes of determining Recoupment, the costs incurred in presenting a Company shall include the following *"Production Expenses"*: fees of designers, directors, general and company managers; cost of sets, curtains, drapes and costumes; cost or payments on account of properties, furnishings, lighting and electrical equipment; premiums for bonds and insurance; unrecouped option and advance payments to persons other than Author; rehearsal charges, transportation charges, reasonable legal and accounting expenses, advance advertising, publicity and press expenses and other expenses and losses actually incurred in connection with the production and presentation of the Play up to and including the Official Press Opening of such Company and all sums described in SECTION 6.01(b) herein to be paid, as Production Costs, to a third party who presented the Play in the Territory as a Developmental Production or as other non-First-Class Performances; but there shall not be included any compensation paid to Producer or to any person rendering the services of a producer other than a cash office charge not to exceed $500 per week (regardless of the amount actually paid) commencing 4 weeks before the opening of rehearsals and continuing until the Official Press Opening of the Company and other than Producer's Royalty (as defined in SECTION 5.12 herein). No amounts charged as Production Expenses shall be charged again as operating expenses, or vice versa.

   (c) Recoupment shall be calculated separately for each Company presenting the Play so that the profits or losses attributable to one Company shall not affect the calculation of Recoupment for any other Company. Recoupment shall be determined by the accountant engaged by Producer and, subject to SECTION 5.08 herein, the determination made by such accountant shall be final and binding as among the parties hereto. Promptly upon the making of such determination by the accountant, Producer shall send Author written notice that Recoupment has occurred.

(d) In calculating Recoupment for the purposes of this Contract, the amounts of bonds, deposits or other items which, by their terms, are returnable to the Company shall not be included as costs to be recovered. Recoupment of the amounts incurred in presenting any Company shall be deemed final so that, once Recoupment has been attained, subsequent expenses that may be incurred by such Company will not alter the fact that such Company has Recouped within the meaning of this Contract.

(e) All expenses incurred by any Company to finance Touring or Off-Broadway Performances by that same Company must be Recouped before Author shall be entitled to post-Recoupment Royalties with respect to such Touring or Off-Broadway Performances. It is understood that the incurring of such expenses shall not affect or otherwise alter the payment of post-Recoupment Royalties, if any, by such Company for performances which precede such Touring or Off-Broadway Performances.

ARTICLE V
Royalty Adjustments

SECTION 5.01 **Definition of "Weekly Breakeven"**. (a) For the purposes of this Contract, the term *"Weekly Breakeven"* shall mean, for each Company presenting the Play hereunder, the operating expenses of such Company for each Performance Week as set forth in the accounting reports as customarily prepared by the accountant engaged by Producer. For the purpose of determining Weekly Breakeven, operating expenses shall consist of the following: $1,000 of Author's Royalty (regardless of the total Royalty actually paid to Author), compensation paid to the cast, director, stage manager, general and company managers, press agents, orchestra, and miscellaneous stage personnel, transportation charges, weekly cash office charge not to exceed $500 (regardless of the total cash office charge actually paid to Producer), advertising, press and publicity costs, legal and accounting expenses, the costs of exhibiting television commercials, theatre guaranty and expenses, rentals, miscellaneous supplies and all other reasonable expenses of whatever kind actually incurred in connection with the weekly operation of the Play, as distinguished from Production Expenses, but not including any compensation to Producer or a person rendering services of a producer, other than $250 of Producer's Royalty, or any money paid to Producer by way of a percentage of the Gross Weekly Box Office Receipts or otherwise for the making of any loan or the posting of any bond, or any cost incurred in producing the first television commercial (or any other type of audio-visual promotion), or any sum paid by Producer to any trade association of producers and/or theatre owners.

(b) Notwithstanding the foregoing, the costs incurred in producing any subsequent television commercials or any other type of audio-visual promotions shall be included in determining Weekly Breakeven, but shall be amortized over a period of no fewer than 13 weeks

SECTION 5.02 **Definition of "Weekly Profits"**. For the purposes of this Contract, the term "*Weekly Profits*" shall mean the amount by which Gross Weekly Box Office Receipts for a particular Performance Week exceed the Weekly Breakeven for such week.

SECTION 5.03 **Definition of "Losing Week" and "Weekly Losses"**. For the purposes of this Contract, the term "*Losing Week*" shall mean any Performance Week for which the Gross Weekly Box Office Receipts do not exceed the Weekly Breakeven for such week, and the term "*Weekly Losses*" shall mean the amount by which Weekly Breakeven for a particular Performance Week exceeds the Gross Weekly Box Office Receipts for such week.

SECTION 5.04 **Adjustments for Out-of-Town and Preview Performances**. With respect to each Performance Week of Out-of-Town and Preview Performances, commencing with the week after the costs of presenting such Company have been Recouped, the Royalties payable to Author for such Out-of-Town and Preview Performances shall be subject to adjustment in the same manner as is applicable to Regular Performances as described in SECTION 5.05(b) herein.

SECTION 5.05 **Adjustments for Regular Performances**. With respect to each Company presenting Regular Performances, the Royalties payable to Author for such Regular Performances shall be subject to adjustment in the following manner:

(a) **Pre-Recoupment**—(i) If the Gross Weekly Box Office Receipts for any Performance Week of Regular Performances (except for the first

3 consecutive 7-day periods following the Official Press Opening of the Play in New York City and the Split Week, if any, as defined in SECTION 5.05(a)(ii) herein), up to and including the Performance Week in which the costs of presenting such Company have been Recouped, do not exceed 110% of Weekly Breakeven, Author's Royalty for such week, in lieu of the Royalties otherwise payable, shall be comprised of a fixed Royalty of $1,000 per Full Performance Week, plus a percentage Royalty equal to 25% of the Weekly Profits, if any, for such week; provided, however, in no event shall Author's fixed and percentage Royalty exceed a sum equal to 5% of the Gross Weekly Box Office Receipts for such week.

(ii) The Royalties payable to Author for each consecutive 7-day period of performances, commencing with the day following the Official Press Opening in New York City, shall be (in lieu of the Royalties otherwise payable) $1,000 for each such 7-day period, pro-rated based on the number of performances, fewer than 8, presented in any such period. This Royalty shall apply for no more than 3 consecutive 7-day periods unless the day following the third such period (i.e., the 22nd day following the Official Press Opening in New York City) is not the first day of a Performance Week, in which case the Royalty for the number of performances of the Play presented for the partial week as measured from such 22nd day up to the beginning of the next Performance Week ("Split Week") shall continue to be at the rate of $1,000 per 7-day period, pro-rated as described in the preceding sentence; however, if the Gross Weekly Box Office Receipts for the Performance Week in which the Split Week occurs exceed 110% of Weekly Breakeven for such week, Author's Royalty for such Split Week shall be 5% of the Gross Weekly Box Office Receipts for the performances presented in such Split Week. The Royalty adjustment described in this SECTION 5.05(a)(ii) shall be applicable only to the extent that the three 7-day periods and Split Week, if any, occur prior to or during the Performance Week in which the costs of presenting such Company have been Recouped.

(b) **Post-Recoupment**—If the Gross Weekly Box Office Receipts for any Performance Week of Regular Performances, occurring after the Performance Week in which the costs of presenting such Company have been Recouped, do not exceed 120% of Weekly Breakeven, Author's Royalty for such week, in lieu of Royalties otherwise payable, shall be comprised of a fixed Royalty of $1,000 per Full Performance Week, plus a percentage Royalty equal to 35% of Weekly Profits, if any, for such week; provided, however, in no event shall Author's fixed and percentage Royalty exceed a sum equal to 10% of the Gross Weekly Box Office Receipts for such week. Notwithstanding the foregoing sentence, if the Director of the Play receives for any such week a royalty which is less than the full royalties payable pursuant to the Director's agreement with Producer, then Author's percentage Royalty described in the preceding calculation shall, for such week, be reduced, on a pro-rata basis, from 35% of such Weekly Profits (but in no event to less than 25% of Weekly Profits), with the other provisions of such calculation remaining unchanged.

SECTION 5.06 **Adjustments for Touring Performances**. With respect to each Company presenting Touring Performances of the Play, the Royalties payable to Author for such Touring Performances shall be subject to adjustment in the following manner:

(a) *Pre-Recoupment*—If the Gross Weekly Box Office Receipts for any Performance Week of Touring Performances, up to and including the Performance Week in which the costs of presenting the Touring Company have been Recouped, do not exceed 110% of Weekly Breakeven for such Touring Company, Author's Royalty for such week, in lieu of the Royalties otherwise payable, shall be comprised of a fixed Royalty of $1,000 per Full Performance Week, plus a percentage Royalty equal to 25% of the Weekly Profits, if any, for such week; provided, however, in no event shall Author's fixed and percentage Royalty exceed a sum equal to 5% of the Gross Weekly Box Office Receipts for such week.

(b) *Post-Recoupment*—If the Gross Weekly Box Office Receipts for any Performance Week of Touring Performances, occurring after the Performance Week in which the costs of presenting the Touring Company have been Recouped, do not exceed 120% of Weekly Breakeven for such Touring Company, Author's Royalty for such week, in lieu of Royalties otherwise payable, shall be comprised of a fixed Royalty of $1,000 per Full Performance Week, plus a percentage Royalty equal to 35% of the Weekly Profits, if any, for such week;

provided, however, in no event shall Author's fixed and percentage Royalty exceed a sum equal to 10% of the Gross Weekly Box Office Receipts for such week. Notwithstanding the foregoing sentence, if the Director of the Play receives for any such week a royalty which is less than the full royalties payable pursuant to the Director's agreement with Producer, then Author's percentage Royalty described in the preceding calculation shall, for such week, be reduced, on a pro-rata basis, from 35% of such Weekly Profits (but in no event to less than 25% of Weekly Profits), with the other provisions of such calculation remaining unchanged.

SECTION 5.07 **Adjustments for Losing Weeks**. If any Company has Weekly Losses in any week of Regular or Touring Performances, Author's Royalty for performances by such Company for such Losing Week shall, in lieu of Royalties otherwise payable, be $1,000 per Full Performance Week.

SECTION 5.08 **Review of Weekly Breakeven and Recoupment Calculation**. Should either Author or Producer wish to challenge the accountant's determination of Weekly Breakeven or Recoupment, the challenging party, upon notice to the other party, shall, in lieu of commencing in arbitration proceeding, present the matter, in writing, for resolution to the Theatrical Conciliation Council, whose decision shall he advisory in nature. After receiving such decision, either party may bring the matter to arbitration as provided in ARTICLE XX herein.

SECTION 5.09 **Yearly Royalty Adjustment**. For a period of 4 consecutive Performance Weeks occurring during the months of December and/or January wherein one such Performance Week is the week in which Christmas occurs ("*Christmas Period*"), Producer may, provided he gives written notice to Author on or before December 1 of each such year, specifying which 4 consecutive Performance Weeks will constitute the Christmas Period for that year, adjust Author's Royalties otherwise payable in the following manner:

(a) *Pre-Recoupment*—The aggregate Weekly Losses incurred in up to 3 Losing Weeks, if any, occurring during such Christmas Period may be deducted from the Gross Weekly Box Office Receipts earned during any one Performance Week during such Christmas Period.

(b) *Post-Recoupment*—Author's Royalty for all 4 Performance Weeks during such Christmas Period may be calculated by separately aggregating the Gross Weekly Box Office Receipts for such weeks and the Weekly Breakeven for such weeks and then dividing each of those two sums by 4. The resulting amounts shall be treated as if they were the Gross Weekly Box Office Receipts and Weekly Breakeven for a single week. The Author's applicable post-Recoupment Royalty (which would otherwise be payable, without reference to this SECTION, after taking into account any other appropriate Royalty Adjustments set forth in this ARTICLE) shall be calculated based on such amounts and then multiplied by 4 to determine the Author's Royalty for the entire Christmas Period.

(c) The foregoing calculations shall be made and adjusted Royalties for such Christmas Period shall be paid within 7 days following the end of the last Performance Week during the Christmas Period. During the Christmas Period, Producer shall pay Author $1,000 for each Full Performance Week as an advance against the adjusted Royalties payable for such Christmas Period.

(d) The provisions of this SECTION may be applied by Producer in one or more years and to any or all (or none) of the Companies presenting the Play and Producer may choose a different Christmas Period for each Company; provided, however, that if Producer chooses to apply this Royalty Adjustment provision to a Company presenting Touring Performances, all performances by such Company during the applicable Christmas Period must be presented in one theatre.

(e) If any Company attains Recoupment during a Christmas Period, then Producer must, with respect to such Company, calculate Author's Royalties for the entire Period either on the basis of SECTION 5.09(b) or without reference to this SECTION, as Producer, in his sole discretion, may decide.

(f) The provisions of this SECTION shall not apply to Fixed-Fee Performances.

SECTION 5.10 **Pro-rata Adjustment for Fixed Royalties.** In any instance in which this Contract provides that Royalties payable to Author for a given Full Performance Week of a Company are to be, in whole or in part, a fixed-dollar amount, and if fewer than 8 performances of the Play are presented by such Company during such week, then the fixed dollar Royalties otherwise payable to Author hereunder shall be reduced by an amount equal to one-eighth of such fixed-dollar dollar Royalties for each performance of the Play, fewer than 8, given in any such Performance Week.

SECTION 5.11 **Pro-rata Adjustment for Repertoire Perfor-mances**. If the Play is to be presented in repertoire with one or more other plays, Author and Producer shall agree on the method in which Author's Royalties shall be prorated and such method shall be set in ARTICLE XXII herein.

SECTION 5.12 **Proportionate Adjustment in Producer's Royalty**. (a) Regardless of the amount of royalties received by Producer for any week of performances, for the purposes of calculating Recoupment and Weekly Breakeven, "*Producer's Royalty*" shall be deemed to be limited to the following amounts but may not be deemed to be less than $250:

Producer's Royalty shall be calculated in the following manner:

   (i)   divide the amount of Royalties earned by Author for such week by an amount equal to 10% of the Gross Weekly Box Office Receipts for such week, then

  (ii)   multiply that number by an amount equal to the lesser of,.

     (A) 2.5% of the Gross Weekly Box Office Receipts for such week or

(a) the amount of royalties (but not the cash office charge) payable to Producer for such week as set forth in the documents used in connection with the financing of the Play.

(b) For the purposes of the calculation described in SECTION 5.12(a) herein, the amount of Royalties earned by Author shall be the full amount of Royalties otherwise payable to Author prior to the deduction of any Advance or Option Payments as permitted by this Contract.

(c) If Producer presents Off-Broadway Performances of the Play pursuant to the terms of SECTION 9.02 herein, then in making this adjustment for such performances, Author's 10% Royalty referred to in SECTION 5.12(a)(i) shall be Author's post-Recoupment Off-Broadway Royalty set forth in ARTICLE XXII herein.

SECTION 5.13 **Pro-rata Adjustment of Weekly Breakeven**. If more than one Royalty calculation is applicable for performances presented in any Performance Week and one such calculation is to be made based on Weekly Profits or Weekly Losses (for example, it there are both Touring Performances and Fixed-Fee Performances presented in one Performance Week), the determination of the amount of such profits or losses to be allocated to such performances shall be made in the following manner: the amount of Weekly Breakeven applicable to such calculation shall be the actual Weekly Breakeven for the entire Performance Week, prorated, based on the ratio that the number of performances to which the Weekly Profits or Losses calculation is to be applied bears to the total number of performances presented during such Performance Week; and the amount of Gross Weekly Box Office Receipts used in calculating the profits or losses shall be only those receipts earned for the performances as to which the Weekly Profits or Losses calculation applies.

ARTICLE VI
Deductions from Advance and Royalty Payments

SECTION 6.01 **Deductions from Advances**. (a) Option Payments made for the Third Option Period, if any, shall be deducted from the Advance Payments otherwise payable to Author. Option Payments for the First and Second Option Periods shall not be deducted from Advance Payments.

(b) If a third party has previously produced the Play in the Territory as a Developmental Production or as other non-First-Class Performances and if Producer is required to make any payment to such third party in order to acquire all of the rights in the Play contemplated by this APC then, to the extent that such sums are included as Production Costs, Producer shall deduct from the Advance Payments otherwise payable to Author so much of such sums as equal the aggregate of all monies directly or indirectly paid to Author for such prior production (less customary per-diem and transportation expenses), but in no event more than the sums paid by Producer to such third party. Author and such third party shall give Producer a complete and accurate statement, signed by both Author and such third party, setting forth all monies paid to Author in connection with such prior production. The total sums payable by Producer to such third party and deductible from Author's Advance Payments shall be set forth in ARTICLE XXII herein.

SECTION 6.02 **Deductions from Royalties**. (a) All Option and Advance Payments received by Author may be deducted from Royalties earned by Author from any or all Companies presenting the Play, at the rate of up to 50% of such Royalties per Performance Week, commencing for the Performance Week in which such Company has reached Recoupment.

(b) The foregoing deductions shall be permitted only in such amounts as will not cause Author to earn, for any week in which such deductions are made, Royalties of less than $1,000 per Full Performance Week.

ARTICLE VII
General Payment Provisions

SECTION 7.01 **Royalty Due Dates/Box Office Statements**. (a) The portion of any Gross Weekly Box Office Receipts or Weekly Profits due to Author shall belong to Author and shall be held in trust by Producer as Author's property until payment. The trust nature of such funds shall not be questioned, whether the monies are physically segregated or not. In the event of breach of treat hereunder, Author may, at his option, pursue his remedies at law or in equity in lieu of the arbitration procedure established by this Contract.

(b) Within 7 days after the end of each Performance Week, Producer shall send to the Guild for Author's account, the amount due as Author's Royalties for such week, together with the daily box-office statements (for each person comprising Author) of each performance of the Play during such week, signed by the treasurer or treasurers of the theatre in which the performances are given and signed by Producer or Producer's duly authorized representative.

(c) Box-office statements and payments due for performances, in the United States, presented more than 500 miles from New York City shall be sent within 14 days after the end of each Performance Week, and for performances presented in Canada or in any location outside the Territory, within 21 days after the end of each such week, unless such payments are delayed or blocked due to the action or inaction of government authorities, in which case the payments shall be made as soon thereafter as possible.

(d) In cases where Author's compensation depends on the calculation of Weekly Breakeven of Weekly Profits, weekly operating statements shall be sent to the Guild (for each person comprising Author), at the same time Author's check is due.

(e) Producer shall also send to the Guild the actual production expense statements provided to investors as well as the periodic accounting reports as prepared by the accountant for the production.

(f) All reports and statements sent to the Guild pursuant to this ARTICLE shall be held confidential by Author, the Guild, and any Author's representative.

(g) Notwithstanding the provisions of SECTION 7.01(c) herein, Royalties for performances of the Play given in repertoire with one or more other plays shall be sent no later than 4 days after the end of every 4 Performance Weeks during which the Play is so performed, regardless of the number of performances presented.

SECTION 7.02 **Method of Payment**. All checks shall be sent to the Guild. Checks for payments due under ARTICLES II and IX herein shall be drawn to the order of the Guild. All other checks shall be drawn to the order of Author or, where Author indicates in writing to Producer and the Guild that Author is represented by an agent who is a member in good standing of the Society of Author's Representatives, Inc., then to the agent.

SECTION 7.03 **Separate Calculations**. If the Play is presented simultaneously by more than one Company, Royalties accruing from each Company shall be computed and paid separately.

SECTION 7.04 **Author's Division of Payments**. If Author is comprised of more than one person, all sums set forth herein as being payable to Author represent the aggregate of all amounts payable to all persons comprising Author. Such aggregate sums shall be divided equally unless otherwise provided in ARTICLE XXII herein.

SECTION 7.05 **Adapter's Compensation**. If the Play is an English language adaptation made from a foreign language play or from other literary property, the adaptor shall receive at least one-third of the compensation otherwise payable to Author pursuant to the terms of the APC with the amounts to be paid to be set forth in ARTICLE XXII herein.

SECTION 7.06 **Deductions**. No deductions shall be made from compensation due by Producer to Author on account of a debt due by Author to Producer unless an agreement in writing providing therefor shall have been made between Author and Producer and filed with the Guild; except, however, that such deduction may be made if it is less than $200 and a memorandum, signed or initialed by Author acknowledging his indebtedness, and receipted by Producer or his representative, accompanies the statement for the week in which the deduction is made.

ARTICLE VIII
General Production Provisions

SECTION 8.01 **Producer's Undertaking**. Producer, recognizing that the Play is the artistic creation of Author and that as such Author is entitled to protect the type and nature of the production of Author's creation, hereby agrees:

(a) Under his own management to rehearse, present and continue to present the Play, with a cast, director, scenic, lighting, costume and, where appropriate, sound designer, conductor, choreographer and/or dance director mutually agreeable to Producer and to Author, and to announce the name of Author as sole Author of the Play upon all programs and in all advertising matter in accordance with the terms of SECTION 8.10 herein. Any change in the cast or any replacement of a director, conductor, choreographer and/or dance director shall likewise be subject to the mutual consent of the parties. Author may designate another person to act on his behalf with respect to such approvals and appointments. If Author is not available for consultation in the United States (or wherever else the Play is being produced), the provisions of this SECTION shall not apply unless Author shall have designated another person to act on his behalf who is available for consultation where the Play is being produced.

(b) To rehearse, produce, present and continue to present the Play, including Touring Performances thereof, with neither Author nor Producer making or causing to be made any addition, omission or alteration in the manuscript or title of the Play as contracted for production without the consent of the other. Producer warrants that any change of any kind whatsoever in the manuscript, title, stage business or performance of the Play made by Producer or any third party and which is acceptable to Author shall be the property of Author. Producer shall cause to be prepared, executed and delivered to Author, not later than the Official Press Opening in New York City, such documents as may be necessary to transfer to Author all rights in any such changes in the manuscript or title of the Play; however, Producer shall not be responsible to deliver documents to Author for any materials or changes solicited by Author from any third party. Author shall not be obligated to make payment to any person suggesting or making any such changes unless Author has entered into a bona fide written agreement to do so; similarly, Producer shall not be required to make payment to any person solicited by Author to suggest or make changes unless Producer has entered into a bona fide written agreement to do so. Subject to SECTION 8.16 herein, Author shall, without any obligation to Producer, be entitled to use any pans of the Play omitted.

(c) Producer may complain to the Guild that Author is unreasonable in refusing to make changes or additions. In such event the Guild shall appoint a representative or representatives and, if they so advise, shall lend its best efforts to prevail upon Author to make the suggested changes, it being understood, however, that the Guild shall have no power to compel Author to agree to such changes.

SECTION 8.02 **Author's Right to Attend Rehearsals/Author's Availability**. (a) Author shall have the right to attend all rehearsals and performances of the Play prior to the Official Press Opening in New York City.

(b) Author shall use all best efforts to be available one month ahead of scheduled rehearsal dates to perform the services required pursuant to the terms of this Contract.

SECTION 8.03 **Author's Exercise of Approval Rights**. If more than one person constitutes Author, then, where the approval or consent of Author is required anywhere in this Contract, and such persons cannot agree, the President of the Guild shall, upon the request of Producer or any person comprising Author, appoint a single arbitrator to pass on such unresolved disagreements.

SECTION 8.04 **Expenses**. (a) Producer shall reimburse Author for such hotel and travel expenses as Author may incur in making trips to attend rehearsals and up to 12 weeks of Out-of-Town Performances and the Official Press Opening in New York City, and at any other time when the presence of Author is required by Producer.

(b) In addition to the expenses to be reimbursed pursuant to SECTION 8.04(a) herein, if Author is a resident of the City of New York, Producer shall reimburse Author for such local travel expenses as Author may incur during the time when the Play is in rehearsal in New York City or being presented for Preview Performances, and shall also reimburse hotel expenses for an Author who resides in the City of New York but outside of the Borough of Manhattan, if such expenses are reasonably necessary due to Producer's rehearsal or production schedule.

(c) Unless specific dollar amounts are provided in ARTICLE XXII herein, the amounts reimburse able by Producer under this SECTION shall be the cost of reasonable hotel and travel accommodations. In any event, Author's hotel and travel accommodations shall be of a class equal to the greater of the class charged to the Company by Producer or Director.

(d) If Author is unavailable and designates another person to act on his behalf in connection with the consultations set forth in SECTION 8.01(a) herein, Author and Producer may agree in ARTICLE XXII to specify the extent to which such designee's expenses may be reimbursed, if at all.

SECTION 8.05 **Copying Expenses**. Producer shall pay all costs incurred in making copies of the Play and any revisions thereof prior to the Official

Press Opening in New York City and shall use best efforts to provide facilities, in or near any theatre in which the Play is presented, for the purpose of copying Author's revisions of the Play.

SECTION 8.06 **Designs**. Pursuant to the rules and regulations of the United Scenic Artists Local 829, Author undertakes and agrees that Author will not sell, lease, license or authorize the use of any of the original designs of scenery, lighting or costumes created by the designers, without the written consent of the owner of such designs.

SECTION 8.07 **Artwork**. If Producer owns the artwork and/or logo for the production of the Play, Producer grants to Author the right to use such artwork and logo in connection with Author's exploitation of the Play (but not for the purpose of creating Commercial Use Products as defined in SECTION 11.01 herein), subject to all restrictions which may exist in connection with such uses and subject to all payments which must be made to any third party, which payments shall not be the responsibility of Producer. Author shall not use or grant to others the right to use such artwork and logo without first giving Producer 60 days prior written notice. Author shall indemnify Producer for any liability which may arise in connection with any such use.

SECTION 8.08 **Production Script**. Prior to the last performance of the Play under this Contract or prior to one month after the Official Press Opening in New York City, whichever is earlier, Producer shall deliver to Author or Author's representative, as Author's property, a neat and legible script of the Play, as currently presented.

SECTION 8.09 **Rights to Promote**. Author hereby grants to Pro-ducer and Producer's licensees and permitted assigns, the right to use Author's name, biography, photographs, likeness or recorded voice (referred to in this SECTION as "materials"), and the title of and excerpts from the Play for advertising, press and promotional purposes by any means or medium. Producer shall submit to Author, for approval, all materials which Producer intends to use. If Author does not advise Producer, within 72 hours of receipt of the materials, of desired changes therein, the material shall be deemed approved as submitted by Producer. Producer shall include Author's biography in all programs used by Producer in which any other biography appears.

SECTION 8.10 **Author's Billing**. (a) Author shall receive billing credit whenever Producer or Director is accorded billing credit; provided, however, with respect to ABC listings and "teaser" advertisements, radio and television advertisements and marquees, billing credit may be accorded to any one or more of Producer, Author or Director without according billing credit to the others), if such person(s) has achieved a level of prominence greater than those not receiving billing credit and such that the use of the name(s) of the person(s) excluded would not enhance the commercial value of the Play. If Producer and Author are unable to agree, then, upon the written request of Producer, the determination of whether such level of prominence has been achieved shall be made by a theatrical press agent designated by the Theatrical Conciliation Council. Such determination must be made prior to the publication of such credits. The designation of the press agent and such agent's determination shall be final and binding on the parties hereto.

(b) Author's billing shall be on a separate line beneath the title of the Play. It shall be in a type size no less than 40% of the type size used for the title of the Play (other than logo titles); provided, however, if the title of the Play appears more than once in any one advertisement, the placement and size of Author's billing shall be in relation to the title where used in closest proximity to the billing accorded to others involved in the Play. In no event shall Author's billing be smaller than the type size used for the billing accorded to Director and/or Producer (except where Producer's name appears as part of the name of the theatre).

(c) Author and Producer may supplement the provisions of SECTION 8.10(b) in ARTICLE XXII herein but shall not modify or supplement in any way the provisions of SECTION 8.10(a) herein.

SECTION 8.11 **Radio and Television Publicizing**. Producer shall have the right to authorize one or more radio and/or television excerpts of the Play, not exceeding 7 minutes each, for the purpose of exploiting and publicizing the theatre industry, performances of the Play, any person performing in the Play and for use on awards programs, without any additional approval by or payment to Author, provided Producer receives no compensation therefrom other than reimbursement of out-of-pocket expenses; however, Author shall have approval of any change in the script made in an excerpt produced under the control of Producer.

SECTION 8.12 **Producer's Credit**. (a) If Producer has presented the Play for its Official Press Opening, Author shall use all best efforts to require that Producer receive conspicuously placed billing credit in the following circumstances:

(i) if all or any portion of the Play is published, the credit shall appear on a page preceding the first page of the text of the Play;

(ii) if a motion picture or television production is produced based on the Play, the credit shall appear on the screen separately with no other credit; and

(iii) in the case of any Revival, Stock, Amateur or Ancillary Performances, as those terms are defined in SECTION 11.01 herein, the credit shall appear on the first page of credits in all programs used therefor.

(b) The credit referred to above shall contain the name(s) of Producer and co-producers, if any, and shall state that the Play was originally produced by them. The order, title and relative size and spacing of the names of Producer (and co-producers, if any) shall be identical to the billing contained in the program for the Play at the time of the Official Press Opening.

(c) No casual or inadvertent failure to comply with the provisions of this SECTION shall be deemed a breach of this Contract unless such failure can, but shall not, be rectified as soon as practicable.

SECTION 8.13 **Approval of Use of Producers' Names**. Producer shall not use the name of any other person, firm or corporation as a producer of the Play unless Author has consented in writing.

SECTION 8.14 **House Seat Records**. If Author receives an allocation of house seats pursuant to ARTICLE XXII herein, Author agrees to maintain a true, complete and accurate record, in accordance with the requirements of the Arts and Cultural Affairs Law of the State of New York and the regulation promulgated thereunder, of Author's disposi-tion of such house seats. Author agrees not to dispose of such house seats at a price above the regular box office prices for such tickets.

SECTION 8.15 **Debt by Author**. If Author is indebted to the Guild or to Producer, the Guild may file with the Negotiator (as described in ARTICLE XII herein) a memorandum to that effect, and the Negotiator shall thereupon withhold from Author's share of income held by the Negotiator, the amount of such indebtedness and shall pay the same over to the Guild and/or Producer as their interests may appear. The foregoing shall not limit Producer's rights to pursue other remedies in connection with the collection of any indebtedness.

SECTION 8.16 **Revue Sketches**. (a) Any sketch or number of a revue and any song or musical number in the Play which shall not have been used on the Official Press Opening in New York or within 3 weeks thereafter, or having been so used shall be omitted from the Play for 3 successive consecutive Performance Weeks, may be withdrawn by Author and used by him for any purpose, free of any claim by Producer, subject only to such financial interest in additional uses as Producer may theretofore have acquired.

(b) If a sketch, song or other contribution of one or more persons constituting Author is omitted from a condensed or tabloid version of the Play, then such person whose work is so omitted shall nevertheless share in the proceeds from such version, provided his contribution shall have been included in at least one-half of the then prior performances of the Play. In such case, each such person shall share in the proceeds of the condensed or tabloid version in the same proportion that his original compensation hereunder bears to the total compensation due hereunder to all persons constituting Author.

ARTICLE IX
Additional Production Rights

SECTION 9.01 **Grant of Second-Class Performance Rights**. (a) Author hereby grants Producer the sole and exclusive rights to produce one or more Second-Class Performances of the Play on the speaking stage in the Territory during the time that Producer continues to have rights to present the Play hereunder. For the purposes of this Contract, the term "Second-Class Performance" shall mean all performances of the Play other than Stock, Amateur and Ancillary Performances (as those terms are defined in SECTION

11.01 herein), Off-Broadway Performances (as defined in SECTION 9.02 herein), and First-Class Performances and Developmental (i.e., "workshop") Productions.

(b) Author's Royalties for Second-Class Performances shall be calculated and paid in the manner set forth in SECTION 4.02(d) herein with respect to Touring Performances, unless Author's Royalty is calculated in whole or in part on the basis of a fixed fee payable to Producer, in which case the Royalty shall be calculated and paid in the manner set forth for Fixed-Fee Performances.

SECTION 9.02 **Grant of Off-Broadway Performance Rights**. (a) Author hereby grants Producer the sole and exclusive rights to produce one or more Off-Broadway Performances of the Play during the time that Producer continues to have rights to present the Play hereunder. The foregoing grant is subject to the conditions precedent that Producer has Vested (as defined in SECTION 11.02 herein) in the Territory and that Producer is not simultaneously presenting any other performances of the Play in New York City. For the purposes of this Contract, the term "Off-Broadway Performances" shall mean performances of the Play in theatres which are classified as Off-Broadway pursuant to the Actors' Equity Association Agreement Governing Employment Off-Broadway, as that agreement may be amended from time to time.

(b) Author's Royalties for Off-Broadway Performances shall be calculated and paid in the manner set forth in ARTICLES IV and V herein with respect to Touring Performances except that Author's post-Recoupment Royalties shall be such amount as may be agreed upon by Author and Producer and set forth in ARTICLE XXII herein, but in no event more than 10% of the Gross Weekly Box Office Receipts.

SECTION 9.03 **Grant of Rights in the British Isles, Australia and New Zealand**. (a) Author hereby grants to Producer the sole and exclusive rights to produce one or more productions of the Play for a consecutive run, as theatrically understood, in a regular evening bill, in a first-class manner, in a first-class theatre, on the speaking stage in one or more of the following "*Additional Territories*":

(i) The United Kingdom of Great Britain (i.e., England, Northern Ireland, Scotland and Wales) and in Ireland (collectively the "*British Isles*")

(ii) Australia

(iii) New Zealand

(b) The foregoing grant is subject to the conditions precedent that Producer has Vested in the Territory and is not in breach of any provision of this Contract.

(c) Producer's rights to present the Play in the Additional Territories shall include the right to present "tryout" performances prior to the presentation of the Play in the Additional Territory equivalent of first-class theatres.

(d) The terms of this Contract applicable to First-Class Perfor-mances in the Territory shall apply to performances of the Play in the British Isles except as may be provided to the contrary herein.

(e) If Producer chooses to produce the Play pursuant to a lease or license to a third party in Australia or New Zealand, Producer's rights shall be subject to the following procedure: Producer shall give Author written notice of the terms of any third party offer for the production of the Play in such Additional Territory. Producer may accept the offer unless Author shall, within 5 business days after receipt of Producer's notice, give Producer written notice, delivered either in person or by wire communication, that the offer is unacceptable, stating Author's reasons therefor, together with a definite offer from a third party, on terms at least as favorable to Producer as those contained in the offer which Producer is willing to accept. If within the prescribed period of time Author submits such an offer, Author may accept such offer. If within the prescribed period of time Author fails to submit such an offer, then Producer may accept the original offer. If the offer presented by Author is from a producer or other entity or person in which Author has any financial or other interest, or if a dispute arises as to whether such offer is at least as favorable to Producer as the offer which Producer obtained, or if any other dispute arises under this SECTION 9.03(e), the parties shall submit the matter to the Theatrical Conciliation Council for the purposes of (i) determining whether of not such offer is the result of good-faith arm's length negotiations, or (ii) determining whether the offer presented by Author is at least as favorable to Producer, or (iii) resolving any other dispute, as the case may be. If the Council determines that the offer is the result of good-faith arm's length negotiations or is at least as favorable to Producer, as the case may be, then Author may accept such offer; however, if the Council determines that such offer is not the result of such negotiations, or is not at least as favorable to Producer, as the case may be, the offer presented by Producer shall be accepted. The decision of the Council in connection with any matter presented under this SECTION 9.03(e) shall be final and binding on the parties hereto.

SECTION 9.04 **Payments Required to Extend Rights in the Additional Territories**. The following provisions of this SECTION shall apply separately to each Additional Territory;

(a) Unless Producer presents the first paid public performance of the Play in an Additional Territory within 6 months after the date on which Producer has Vested in the Territory, Producer's rights to present the Play in such Additional Territory shall automatically terminate unless such rights are extended as provided in this SECTION.

(b) Producer shall be entitled to three consecutive 6-month exten-sions of such rights upon payment of $1,000 for the first extension, $1,500 for the second extension and $2,000 for the third extension, which payment must be made prior to the expiration of the rights period then in effect, provided, however, that for the third extension, Producer must give Author, simultaneously with the payment of $2,000, written notice of the intended date of the first paid public performance together with copies of documents representing one of the following:

(i) a commitment for the licensing of the Additional Territory equivalent of a first-class theatre, with occupancy to occur before the end of the third extension period or

(ii) contracts for the engagement of the principal members of the cast or the director, pursuant to which such person(s) agrees to render services before the end of the third extension period.

The last paragraph of SECTION 2.01(c) shall also apply to the extension of Producer's rights under this SECTION.

SECTION 9.05 **Royalty Payments in the Additional Territories**. (a) Author's Royalties for performances of the Play in the British Isles shall be calculated and paid in accordance with the provision of ARTICLES IV and V applicable to Touring and Fixed-Fee Performances, except that all references to fixed dollar amounts in' such ARTICLES shall be reduced to one-third of the stated amounts. Author's Royalties for performances in Australia and New Zealand shall be 10% of the Gross Weekly Box Office Receipts.

(b) The payments made pursuant to SECTION 9.04 herein for an Additional Territory may be deducted from the Royalties earned by Author from any Company presenting the Play in such Additional Territory at the rate of up to 50% of such Royalties per Performance Week commencing for the Performance Week in which such Company has reached Recoupment. Such deductions shall be permitted only in such amounts as will not cause Author to earn, for any week in which such deductions are made, Royalties of less than the foreign currency equivalent (at the time of payment) of $300 per Full Performance Week.

(c) Sums payable to Author in connection with Performances of the Play in any Additional Territory shall be paid after deduction of all withholding and other taxes due thereon pursuant to the laws of the applicable Additional Territory, all conversion and remittance costs applicable to such payments and all payments required to be made to any author's society or similar organizations. Producer shall not be liable for losses incurred due to fluctuations in the exchange rate.

(d) In addition to the Royalties payable pursuant to this SECTION, if Author earns in any Performance Week Royalties equal to less than 10% of the Gross Weekly Box Office Receipts for such week from productions in Australia or New Zealand, Producer shall, simultaneously with the payment of Author's Royalties for such week, pay to the Guild, on Author's behalf (for the benefit of Author's representatives), a sum equal to 10% of the difference between the amount of Author's Royalties and a sum equal to 10% of the Gross Weekly Box Office Receipts.

SECTION 9.06 **Transfer of Rights to an Additional Territory Producer**. Provided Producer has complied with the provisions of SECTION 9.03(b) herein, Producer may produce the Play alone or in association with or under lease or license to an Additional Territory producer or manager, subject to Author's written consent. In such case, Producer's obligations to make the payments herein provided shall remain unimpaired. The contract between Producer and the Additional Territory producer or manager shall require the Play to be produced in the manner and on the terms provided herein with respect to productions in the Additional Territory.

SECTION 9.07 **Advances for Performances in the Additional Territories**. If the Play is produced in any Additional Territory in association with or under lease or license to an Additional Territory producer or manager pursuant to the provisions of this ARTICLE, and if, in connection therewith, Producer receives an advance payment applicable against royalties payable to Producer, or a lump sum in lieu of a portion of such royalties, Author shall receive 50% of such advance or lump sum as an advance against Royalties payable for such production. Author's share of the advance or lump sum received by Producer with respect to an Additional Territory may be deducted from the payments due pursuant to SECTION 9.05 herein with respect to such Additional Territory.

SECTION 9.08 **Author's Presence in the Additional Territories**. If the Play is presented in any Additional Territory by or under grant of rights from Producer, Author shall have the right to be present for up to 3 weeks in order to attend rehearsals, tryouts and the opening of the first production of the Play in such Additional Territory. Producer shall reimburse Author for hotel and travel expenses during such period and at any other time when the presence of Author is required by Producer. Unless specific dollar amounts are provided in ARTICLE XXII herein, the amounts reimbursable by Producer under this SECTION shall be the cost of reasonable hotel and travel accommodations. In any event, Author's hotel and travel accommodations shall be of a class equal to the greater of the class charged to the Company by Producer or Director.

SECTION 9.09 **Producer's Financial Participation in Additional Territory Uses**. (a) If the Play is not presented in any Additional Territory by or under grant of rights from Producer within the period set forth in SECTION 9.04 herein, then Author shall thereafter have the sole right to produce or authorize the production of the Play in any such Additional Territory in which Producer's rights have lapsed and, provided that Producer has Vested in the Territory and is not in breach of any provision of this Contract, Author shall pay Producer the following amounts:

(i) with respect to the British Isles, 25% of the compensation earned by Author (after deduction of agents' commissions, if any) regardless of when paid, in connection with each contract for the production of the Play (including any contracts for British Isles Subsidiary Rights, other than Media Productions in which Producer will have previously acquired a worldwide interest) entered into on or after the Effective Date of this Contract but prior to the expiration of 7 years from the date on which Producer has Vested in the Territory; provided, however, that with respect to each contract for the presentation of the British Isles equivalents of First or Second-Class Performances, Author shall pay Producer 10% of the compensation earned by Author (after deduction of agents' commissions, if any) regardless of when paid, in connection with each such contract entered into after said 7-year period or after the close of the first First-Class Performance in the British Isles, whichever first occurs, but before the expiration of 40 years from the date on which Producer Vested in the Territory; and

(ii) with respect to Australia and New Zealand, 35% of the compensation earned by Author (after deduction of agents' commissions, if any) regardless of when paid, in connection with each contract for the production of the Play (including any contracts for Australian or New Zealand Subsidiary Rights, other than Media Productions in which Producer will have previously acquired a worldwide interest) entered into on or after the Effective Date of this Contract but prior to the expiration of 6 years from the date on which Producer has Vested in the Territory;

(b) If the Play has been presented in any Additional Territory by or under a grant of rights from Producer in accordance with the provisions of this ARTICLE and Producer has Vested in such Additional Territory and is not in breach of any provision of this Contract, Producer's financial interest in Author's compensation derived from the disposition of Subsidiary Rights (as defined in SECTION 11.01 herein) in such Additional Territory (other than Media Productions in which Producer will have previously acquired a worldwide interest), will be as follows:

(i) with respect to the British Isles, Producer will have the same financial interest in British Isles Subsidiary Rights as Producer has with respect to such Subsidiary Rights in the Territory, and the time periods described in the applicable Producer's Alternative (as defined in SECTION 11.03(c) herein) shall be measured from the last performance of the Play in the British Isles; and

(ii) with respect to Australia and New Zealand, Producer's financial interest in Australian and New Zealand Subsidiary Rights shall be equal to 40% of the compensation earned by Author (after deduction of agents' commissions, if any) regardless of when paid, in connection with each contract for the disposition of such Subsidiary Rights entered into on or after the Effective Date of this Contract but prior to the expiration of 7 years from the date on which Producer Vested in such Additional Territory or 4 years from the last performance of the Play in the Additional Territory, whichever is later.

SECTION 9.10 **Additional Rights to Present Backers' Auditions**. While Producer has the rights to present the Play hereunder, Producer shall also have the rights to present Backers' Auditions of the Play.

ARTICLE X
Reopening Rights

SECTION 10.01 **Reopenings in the Territory**. (a) Provided Producer has Vested in the Territory, Producer may, within 4 months after the last performance of the Play in the Territory, notify Author in writing of Producer's intention to reopen the Play in the Territory. In such case Producer may so reopen the Play within 12 months following such last performance; provided, however, that if the Play is not reopened within 4 months from such last performance, Producer must, in order to retain his rights to reopen the Play, pay Author the following sums (as non-returnable advances against the Royalties payable): $500 per month for up to 4 months, commencing with the fourth month following the last performance, and $1,000 per month for up to an additional 4 months.

(b) If Producer presents the Play in the Territory but closes the Play prior to having Vested, Producer may reopen the Play provided he gives the Author written notice, within 30 days after such closing, of Producer's intention to reopen the Play, pays Author $500 per month (as non-returnable advances against the Royalties payable), commencing one month following the closing until the Play has reopened, and commences rehearsals for such production no later than 3 months after the closing.

(c) All the provisions of this SECTION shall apply to each reopening in the Territory. Such reopenings may be First-Class, Second-Class or Off-Broadway Performances.

SECTION 10.02 **Reopenings in the Additional Territories.** (a) Provided Producer has Vested in the British Isles, Producer may, within 4 months after the close of the last performance in the British Isles, notify Author in writing of Producer's intention to reopen the Play in the British Isles. In such case Producer may reopen the Play in the British Isles, within 12 months following such list performance, in accordance with the provisions of SECTION 10.01(a) herein.

(b) If Producer presents the Play in the British Isles but closes the Play prior to having Vested in the British Isles, Producer may reopen the Play in the British Isles in accordance with the provisions of SECTION 10.01(b) herein.

(c) Provided Producer has Vested in Australia or New Zealand, Producer may retain the rights to reopen the Play in such Additional Territory upon paying Author (as non-returnable advances against the Royalties payable) $500 per month, for up to 6 months, commencing one month following the last performance in such Additional Territory. In no event may Producer reopen the Play after 7 years from the date on which Producer Vested in such Additional Territory.

(d) If Producer presents the Play in Australia or New Zealand but closes the Play prior to having Vested in such Additional Territory, Producer may reopen the Play in such Additional Territory in accordance with the provisions of SECTION 10.01(h) herein.

(e) All the provisions of this SECTION shall apply to each reopening of the Play in the applicable Additional Territory. Such reopenings must be the Additional Territory equivalent of First-Class Performances.

SECTION 10.03 **Closing.** Producer shall in each instance, immed-iately upon determining to close a ran of the Play, give written notice thereof to Author.

ARTICLE XI
Subsidiary Rights

SECTION 11.01 **Definitions Relating to Subsidiary Rights**. For the purposes of this Contract, the term *"Subsidiary Rights"* shall mean those rights in the Play relating to the following methods of exploitation:

(a) *"Media Productions"*—shall mean Audio-Visual Productions (as defined below), audio-only recordings and radio uses.

(b) *"Audio-Visual Productions"*—shall mean motion picture, television, video cassette, video disc and all other kinds of visual and audio-visual productions in connection with the Play, whether now existing or developed in the future. All of the foregoing shall be considered Audio-Visual Productions, regardless of the method or mode of reproduction, projection, transmission, exhibition or delivery used. However, Audio-Visual Productions shall not include Foreign Local Television Productions. For the purpose of this Contract, the term *"Foreign Local Television Productions"* shall mean all television productions of the Play in a foreign language produced and distributed exclusively for television exhibition outside the Territory and the Additional Territories.

(c) *"Commercial Use Products"*—shall mean wearing apparel; toys; games; figures; dolls; novelties; books; souvenir programs; and any other physical property representing a character in the Play or using the name, character or the title of the Play or otherwise connected with the Play or its title.

(d) *"Stock Performances"*—shall mean all performances of the Play presented in the English language pursuant to one of the Actors' Equity Association agreements governing employment of actors in productions classified, pursuant to the terms of such agreements, as "stock," "resident theatre," "university resident theatre," "dinner theatre," or "guest artist contract" productions (and the equivalents of such performances outside the United States).

(e) *"Amateur Performances"*—shall mean all performances of the Play presented in the English language and using only non-professional actors (i.e., an actor who is not a member of a performing arts union or guild in the Territory or outside the Territory, as the case may be).

(f) **"*Ancillary Performances*"**—shall mean all performances of the Play presented in the English language as condensed and tabloid versions, so-called concert tour versions and musical comedy, operetta and grand opera versions based on the Play as well as foreign language performances of all kinds in the Territory or each Additional Territory, as the case may be, and performances of the Play pursuant to one of the Actors' Equity Association agreements governing employment of actors in productions classified pursuant to the terms of such agreements as: "theatre for young audiences", "small professional theatre", and "non-profit theatre code" productions (and their equivalents outside the United States).

(g) **"*Revival Performances*"**—

   (i) In the City of New York—all First-Class, Second-Class and Off-Broadway Performances of the Play in the City of New York and all performances at Lincoln Center (regardless of how classified), presented after the expiration of Producer's rights to present the Play in the Territory; and

   (ii) Outside the City of New York—all First and Second-Class Performances of the Play in the Territory, presented after the expiration of Producer's rights to present the Play in the Territory and presented outside the City of New York, provided that, with respect to each contract entered into for such production, the Play is presented in at least 3 cities throughout the Territory. Notwithstanding the foregoing, if any of such cities is the City of New York, the 3-city minimum shall automatically be waived. Until the Play is presented in the third city or in the City of New York, whichever first occurs, Author shall pay all sums due to Producer from such Revival Performances to the Guild, which shall hold such sums until the first presentation of the Play in the third city or the City of New York, whichever first occurs, and then pay such sums to Producer. No interest shall accrue to Producer's benefit on such sums held by the Guild.

   (iii) In the Additional Territories—all performances of the Play in any of the Additional Territories (which are the Additional Territory equivalents of First or Second-Class Performances in the Territory), presented after the expiration of Producer's rights to present the Play in such Additional Territory.

SECTION 11.02 **Definition of Vested**. For the purposes of this Contract, the term "*Vested*" shall mean that Producer has presented the Play in one of the manners described below:

(a) With respect to the Territory, for the following number of consecutive (as customarily defined in the theatre industry) paid public First-Class Performances:

  (i) 10 Preview Performances plus the Official Press Opening of the Play in New York City, or

  (ii) 5 Preview Performances plus the Official Press Opening in New York City plus 5 Regular Performances, or

  (iii) 5 Out-of-Town and 5 Preview Performances plus the Official Press Opening in New York City, provided there are no more than 28 days between the last Out-of-Town Performance and the first Preview Performance, or

  (iv) 5 Preview Performances plus the Official Press Opening in New York City if the Play has been presented previously by someone other than Producer and is presented by Producer hereunder with substantially the same cast and scenic designs as existed in the prior presentation.

Each Preview Performance given in New York City within 10 days of the Official Press Opening in New York City (even though not consecutive) shall be considered a "consecutive" performance for the purpose of this paragraph, provided that the scale of box office prices of each such Preview Performance is at least 65% of the scale of box-office prices announced for the Regular Performances and that each such Preview Performance is publicized in advance in the paid "ABC" listings of The New York Times and a similar listing in any other newspaper, magazine or other periodical of general circulation in the City of New York. Any Preview Performance given more than 10 days before the Official Press Opening shall not be considered a "consecutive" performance for the purpose of this paragraph.

(b) With respect to the Territory, for 64 consecutive paid public Out-of-Town Performances, whether or not the Play has its Official Press

Opening in New York City, provided that breaks may be made in performances outside of New York City because of the necessities of travel so long as the 64 performances shall have been given within 80 days of the first performance.

(c) With respect to the Territory, for 64 consecutive Out-of-Town Performances in arenas or auditoriums if, because of the nature of the Play or the size or complexity of its contemplated production, the performance of the Play in a traditional first-class theatre would not be feasible or desirable. The same provisions of SECTION 11.02(b) shall apply in connection with breaks for travel.

(d) With respect to the British Isles, for the following number of first-class performances:

   (i) if the Play is first produced in London, then for 21 consecu-tive performances in London, or

   (ii) if the Play is first produced outside of London, for 64 per-formances within 80 days after the first performance, presented either outside of London, or partly in London and party outside of London.

(e) With respect to Australia, for 21 consecutive performances, including an Official Press Opening, provided such performances are the Australian equivalent of First-Class Performances in the Territory.

(f) With respect to New Zealand, for 21 consecutive performances, including an Official Press Opening, provided such performances are the New Zealand equivalent of First-Class Performances in the Territory.

SECTION 11.03 **Participation in Subsidiary Rights**. Although Producer is acquiring rights in the Play and Author's services solely in connection with the production of the Play, Author recognizes that by a successful production Producer makes a contribution to the value of other rights in the Play. Therefore, although the relationship between the parties is limited to play production as herein provided, and Author alone owns and controls the Play with respect to all other uses, nevertheless, if Producer has Vested in the Territory and Producer is not in breach of any provision of this Contract, Author hereby agrees that:

(a) *No Outright Sale*—Author will not authorize or permit any outright sale of the right to use said Play for any of the Subsidiary Rights purposes during the period therein specified without Producer's prior consent. In no event shall there be any outright sale of any such rights prior to the first paid public First-Class Performance of the Play, except that an outright sale of rights for Audio-Visual Productions may be permitted if made subject to the provisions of Section 13.07 herein.

(b) *Best Efforts*—Author will use best efforts to exploit the Play for Subsidiary Rights purposes.

(c) *Producer's Alternatives*—

(i) Producer shall have the right to choose one of the 4 Producer's Alternatives set forth in this SECTION and shall give Author and the Guild written notice of such choice on or before 12 o'clock midnight on the first day of rehearsal at which Producer requires all cast members of the Principal Company. If Producer fails to give such notice in a timely manner, Author may choose which Producer's Alternative will apply upon giving Producer and the Guild written notice of such choice on or before 12 o'clock midnight on the next business day following said rehearsal date. If both Producer and Author fail to choose a Producer's Alternative in a timely manner, Producer's Alternative III will apply.

(ii) Participation in Territory—With respect to the exploitation of Subsidiary Rights in the Territory, Author shall promptly pay to Producer, based on the applicable Producer's Alternative, the designated percentage of Author's compensation directly or indirectly earned (after deduction of agents' commissions, if any), from the disposition of the specified Subsidiary Rights anywhere in the Territory, pursuant to each contract entered into on or after the Effective Date of this Contract but prior to the expiration of the periods described in the applicable Producer's Alternative (regardless of when such compensation is paid); provided, however, that with respect to Media Productions, Producer's participation shall be in Author's compensation earned from exploitations anywhere in the world:

Under Producer's Alternative #	If any of the following Subsidiary Rights are disposed of	Author will promptly pay Producer, based on the following percentages of Author's Compensation directly or indirectly earned (after deduction of agent's commissions, if any from such dispositions pursuant to each contract entered into on or after the Effective Date of this Contract but prior to the expiration of the specified periods of time after the last performance of the Play hereunder (regardless of when such compensation is paid):
I	Media Productions	50% in perpetuity
	Stock Performances	50% for the first 5 years then 25% for the next 3 years
	Amateur and Ancillary Performances	0%
	Revival Performances	20% for 40 years
	Commercial Use Products	See *SECTION 11.05*
II	Media Productions	50% in perpetuity
	Stock and Ancillary Performances	0%
	Amateur Performances	50% for the first 5 years then 25% for the next 3 years
	Revival Performances	20% for 40 years
	Commercial Use Produces	See *SECTION 11.05*
III	Media Productions	50% in perpetuity
	Stock, Amateur and Ancillary Performances	10% for the first 5 years then 25% for the next 5 years
	Revival Performances	20% for 40 years
	Commercial Use Products	*See SECTION 11.05*
IV	Media Productions	30% in perpetuity
	Stock, Amateur and Ancillary Performances	30% for the first 20 years then 25% for the next 10 years and 20% for the next 10 years (total of 40 years)
	Revival Performances	20% for 40 years
	Commercial Use Products	See *SECTION 11.05*

provided, however, that if this Alternative IV is chosen, Producer hereby assigns to Author the first $100,000 otherwise payable to Producer pursuant to this Alternative.

(d) ***Revival Participation***—In paying Producer's financial participa-tion in Revival Performances, Author shall secure the payment of one-half of such sum (i.e., 10%) from the producer of the Revival Perfor-mances.

(e) ***Foreign Participation***—Author shall have the exclusive right to negotiate and contract for all performances of the Play and for other Subsidiary Rights purposes described in this ARTICLE outside the Territory and outside the Additional Territories, and Author shall promptly pay Producer 25% of the compensation earned by Author (after deduction of agents' commissions, if any), regardless of when paid, in connection with each such contract (other than contracts for Media Productions in which Producer will have previously acquired a worldwide interest) entered into on or after the Effective Date of this Contract but prior to 7 years from the date on which Producer Vested in the Territory. With respect to contracts for Foreign Local Television Productions, Author shall pay Producer 50% of such compensation earned by Author (after deduction of agents' commissions, if any) for such contracts entered into on or after the Effective Date of this Contract but prior to 15 years from the date on which Producer Vested in the Territory.

(f) ***Participation in Audio-Visual Sequels***—If the producer of the Audio-Visual Production, in the original contract for Audio-Visual Production rights, is granted the right to make one or more Audio-Visual Production remakes, prequels, sequels or spin-offs upon the payment of additional compensation, then, if and when such additional compensation is paid, Producer's share of such compensation shall be one-half of the Media Productions percentage set forth in the applicable Producer's Alternative.

SECTION 11.04 **Author's Share of Subsidiary Rights**. No person who is not an Author (as specifically defined in SECTION 1.05 herein) may participate in Author's share of any Subsidiary Rights proceeds.

SECTION 11.05 **Producer's Rights Regarding Commercial Use Products**. (a) Anything to the contrary herein notwithstanding, Author hereby grants to Producer the sole and exclusive rights to create, manufacture and sell (or have created, manufactured and sold) Commercial Use Products, during the time that Producer retains any rights to present the Play hereunder, except that if on the last day of such period a contract exists with a third party for the creation, manufacture or sale of Commercial Use Products, then such contract will continue in full force and effect until the expiration of its term, but in no event for more than 5 years from the date of such contract (or the last extension thereto. This grant of rights shall be for the Territory and for each Additional Territory in which Producer presents or licenses the rights to present the Play. Producer shall pay Author the following amounts, regardless of when paid, in connection with each contract entered into for the exploitation of Commercial Use Products:

  (i) with respect to sales of such products on the premises of theatres in which Producer presents the Play, a sum equal to 10% of the gross retail sales (after deduction of taxes);

  (ii) with respect to sales of such products in other locations, a sum equal to 50% of Producer's net receipts from such sales (i.e.,, the gross amounts paid to Producer less all customary third party costs actually incurred in the creation, manufacture and sale of such Commercial Use Products).

(b) After the expiration of Producer's rights to exploit Commercial Use Products in the Territory or any Additional Territory, Author may exploit or enter into contracts for the exploitation of Commercial Use Products in such locations in which Producer's rights have expired, subject to any contracts which may continue in effect as described in SECTION 11.05(a) herein. Author will pay Producer the following amounts (after deduction of agents' commissions, if any) regardless of when paid, in connection with each such contract entered into before the expiration of 40 years after the last performance of the Play in the Territory or such Additional Territory, as the case may be, provided Producer has Vested in such location:

  (i) with respect to sales of such products on the premises of theatres in which Author's Play is presented, a sum equal to 10% of the gross retail sales (after deduction of taxes);

  (ii) with respect to sales of such products in other locations, a sum equal to 50% of Author's net receipts from such sales (i.e., the gross amounts paid to Author less all customary third party costs actually incurred in the creation, manufacture and sale of such Commercial Use Products).

(c) In addition to Producer's rights and financial interest described in SECTIONS 11.05(a) and (b) herein, provided Producer has Vested in the Territory, Producer shall also have such rights and financial interest on a worldwide basis in those cases where the rights to exploit Commercial Use Products are disposed of together with Author's dispositions of rights to exploit any or all Media Productions.

(d) If there are Revival Performances in the Territory or any Addi-tional Territory, Producer's right to share in Commercial Use Products income, from contracts entered into simultaneously with or subsequent to those Performances in such location (other than contracts which are related to the disposition of rights to Media Productions), shall revert to Author; provided, however, that Producer shall have the right to make arrangements with the producers of Revival Performances with respect to the exploitation of Commercial Use Products created or manufactured by Producer, and to retain all sums derived therefrom.

(e) None of the sums described in this SECTION, paid to or retained by Producer in connection with the exploitation of Commercial Use Products, shall be included in the calculation of Recoupment hereunder.

SECTION 11.06 **Producer's Rights to Consult in Dispositions of Subsidiary Rights**. If Producer shall be entitled to share in Author's Subsidiary Rights income with respect to the Territory, or with respect to any of the Additional Territories, Author will not undertake to grant any Subsidiary Rights in the Territory and the applicable Additional Territories, during the periods in which Producer is entitled to share in such income, without giving Producer the reasonable opportunity to consult fully with Author in connection with the exploitation of all such rights.

SECTION 11.07 **Restrictions on Dispositions by Author**. (a) In addition to Producer's rights as set forth in SECTION 11.06 herein, Author represents that, except to the extent set forth in ARTICLE XXII herein, Author has not authorized or permitted, and covenants that Author shall not authorize or permit, unless Producer first consents in writing, the exploitation (or publicity regarding future exploitations) of any of the rights hereinbelow described, prior to the dates specified below:

Rights	**Specified Date**
(i) Worldwide Media Productions (other than radio) and Foreign Local Television Productions:	the Effective Date of this Contract, subject to the provisions of ARTICLE XIII herein.
(ii) Separately with respect to the Territory and each Additional Territory: First and Second-Class, Stock, Amateur and Ancillary Performances, Off-Broadway and Revival Performances (and their equivalents outside the Territory); and radio;	the date on which all of Producer's rights to produce the play have expired in the Territory or such Additional Territory, as the case may be, or the date on which Producer has in writing declared that he will not reopen the Play.
(iii) Separately with respect to the Territory and each Additional Territory: Commercial Use Products:	the date on which all of Producer's rights to produce the play have expired in the Territory or such Additional Territory, as the case may be, subject to any contracts which may continue in effect as described in SECTION 11.05 herein.

(b) If Author has disposed of any rights in the Play outside the Territory prior to the Effective Date of this Contract then, provided Producer Vests in the Territory, Producer will receive a sum equal to one-half the amount Producer would have been entitled to receive hereunder had Producer Vested in the Territory prior to the disposition of such rights. Except to the extent that such sums have been previously paid by Author, such sums shall be paid to Producer from Author's share of the first monies, if any, received by Author on or after the Effective Date of this Contract from all Subsidiary Rights exploitations.

SECTION 11.08 **Reservation of Audio-Visual Production Rights Outside the Territory**. If Author disposes of any rights outside the Territory, other than Audio-Visual Production rights, Author shall reserve in Author's contract therefor, and for Author's own use, all Audio-Visual Production rights in such foreign area (including the Additional Territories) and such contract shall provide that the exercise of such reserved rights in such foreign area, by Author or any person authorized by Author, shall not be deemed restricted in any way by the terms of such contract or competitive with any rights so disposed of.

ARTICLE XII
The Negotiator

SECTION 12.01 **Choice of Negotiator**. Edward E. Colton is appointed as Negotiator.

SECTION 12.02 **Alternate Negotiator**. Franklin R. Weissberg is appointed as Alternate Negotiator. The Alternate Negotiator shall have all the rights and duties of the Negotiator and shall have the power to act in the Negotiator's absence.

SECTION 12.03 **Disqualification of Negotiator**. If it appears that the Negotiator and/or the Alternate Negotiator by reason of his relations with any Producer who has received motion picture financing, directly or indirectly, or his representation of any Author or Producer of the Play or for any other reason whatsoever, might, in the disposition of the Audio-Visual Production rights in the Play, act in a dual capacity or copy a position possibly conflicting with complete representation of Author, the Dramatists Guild Council may, upon the request of Author or Producer involved, replace the Negotiator and/or the Alternate Negotiator with a Temporary Negotiator, for the purposes of disposing of the Audio-Visual Production rights in connection with the Play.

SECTION 12.04 **Selection of New Negotiator**. The Negotiator and Alternate Negotiator shall each serve until he resigns, is removed by action of the Theatrical Conciliation Council or otherwise becomes unable to perform his services. Any new Negotiator and any new Alternate Negotiator (other thin a Temporary Negotiator) shall be appointed by action of the Theatrical Conciliation Council.

SECTION 12.05 **Duties of Negotiator**. (a) The Negotiator shall act as the representative of the Author in connection with the disposition of Audio-Visual

Production rights in the Play, and shall have the right generally to conduct negotiations therefor subject to such written instructions as may be issued to him by the Theatrical Conciliation Council. Whenever Author and Producer are represented by an agent in connection with the disposition of such rights, the Negotiator shall cooperate with and work in conjunction with said agent. The Negotiator shall have the right to consummate such sale or lease after consultation with Producer and subject to the approval of Author and after according Producer all the rights to which Producer is entitled pursuant to the terms of this Contract. The Negotiator shall also receive and distribute the monies resulting therefrom as provided herein. All contracts shall be signed by the Negotiator or, in his absence, the Alternate Negotiator and countersigned by a person designated by the Guild. In order to aid Author and Producer in obtaining the best possible terms, the Negotiator shall keep Producer apprised of current practices in the sale of Audio-Visual Production rights.

(b) If such rights are disposed of prior to the production of the Play, the Audio-Visual Production rights contract must be signed before the beginning of rehearsals. In such a case the contract shall be on the basis of a minimum guaranteed payment or an advance, plus or on account of percentage payments based on the receipts of the Audio-Visual Production or the box-office receipts of the Play, or both, and shall be subject to the approval of the Guild and Producer.

SECTION 12.06 **Disposition of Proceeds**. All monies received from the disposition of Audio-Visual Production rights in the Play shall be forthwith deposited by the Negotiator in a special account entitled "The Dramatists Guild Negotiator's Account" in a bank located in New York City as may be designated from time to time by the Guild. All withdrawals therefrom shall be made by check signed by the Negotiator or, in his absence, the Alternate Negotiator or, if appointed, the Temporary Negotiator, and countersigned by a person designated by the Guild.

SECTION 12.07 **Compensation of Negotiator**. Prior to making any withdrawals from the proceeds deposited in the Dramatists Guild Negotiator Account in connection with the Play, there shall first be deducted 1¼% of such sums so deposited. Said 1¼% shall be deducted from the amounts payable to the agents in respect of the agents' commission or, if there are no agents, then from the total sums on deposit prior to making any payments to Author or Producer. Said 1¼% shall be divided 85% to the Negotiator and 15% to the

Guild as full and complete compensation for their services in connection with the disposition of the Audio-Visual Production rights in the Play.

SECTION 12.08 **Instructions to Negotiator**. The Negotiator shall, in connection with the disposition of Audio-Visual Production rights in the Play, follow the procedures set forth in EXHIBIT B attached hereto and made a part of this Contract.

ARTICLE XIII
**General Provisions Regarding
Audio-Visual Productions**

SECTION 13.01 **Cooperation by Author**. Author agrees to co-operate and shall cause his agent to cooperate with the Negotiator and shall promptly transmit to the Negotiator all offers for Audio-Visual Production rights received directly by or on behalf of Author and shall disclose to the Negotiator any arrangements, actual or contemplated, between Author and any third party with whom negotiations may be pending for the disposal of the Audio-Visual Production rights. Moreover, Author agrees that unless Producer shall consent thereto, Author will not insist on any commitment or agreement with any such third party for Author's personal services as author, actor, director, or in any other capacity, as a condition of disposition of the Audio-Visual Production rights to such third party.

SECTION 13.02 **Conflicts**. The release date of the Audio-Visual Production rights production shall not interfere with either the Regular or Touring Performances of the Play. Such release date shall be fixed by Author, and Producer shall be given written notice thereof. If Producer files no objection with the Negotiator within 3 business days after such notice is sent, the release date will be deemed to be satisfactory to Producer. If within such 3-day period, Producer states in writing his reasons for objecting, the Negotiator shall give due consideration to Producer's objections and shall then fix a release date which shall be binding and conclusive on the parties.

SECTION 13.03 **Rights of Producer**. If Producer deems himself aggrieved by any disposition of Audio-Visual Production rights, his sole recourse shall be against Author and then only for fraud or willful misconduct; Author's refusal to grant the right to make a motion picture or other Audio-Visual Production remake, prequel, sequel or spin-off or the Play or of the picture or other Audio-Visual Production made therefrom shall not be a basis for Producer deeming himself aggrieved; and in no event shall Producer have any recourse, in law or in equity, against any purchaser or lessee of such rights, or against anyone claiming thereunder, or against the Negotiator, the Guild, or others who voted for the Selection of the Negotiator.

SECTION 13.04 **Revues**. A separate song or sketch from a revue may be disposed of for Audio-Visual Production rights purposes only at the expiration of 18 months after the end of Producer's rights to present the Play hereunder. Author shall give Producer notice of such proposed disposition. If Producer, within 5 days after notice to him thereof, objects thereto, then the approval of the Theatrical Conciliation Council hereof shall first be obtained before such disposition can be made. Unless otherwise agreed among those constituting Author, Author's share of the proceeds (after deduction of Producer's share, if any is owing) shall be participated in only by the authors of the song or sketch so disposed of.

SECTION 13.05 **Rights in Case of New Producer**. (a) If the Audio-Visual Production rights have not been disposed of within 5 years after the date on which Producer has Vested in the Territory, and if a third party presents Revival Performances commencing after said 5-year period, then the compensation which Producer shall be entitled to receive from Author's disposition of rights in Audio-Visual Productions as provided in SECTION 11.03(c) herein shall be reduced in the following manner provided that Author pays the amount of such reduction to the producer of the Revival Performances: if the producer of such Revival Performances presents at least the same number of First-Class Performances and at least the same number of Second-Class Performances (counted separately) as Producer, Producer's share of Audio-Visual Production rights proceeds earned after the date on which such performances are equaled shall be reduced by 25%; if the number of First-Class and the number of Second-Class Performances (counted separately) presented by the producer of the Revival Performances exceeds by more than 15% the number of each such class of Performances presented by Producer, Producer's share of Audio-Visual Production rights proceeds earned after the date on which the number of

Producer's Performances (of both classes) are so exceeded, shall be reduced by 50%; if neither of the foregoing occurs, then Producer's share of such proceeds shall remain unchanged.

(b) The foregoing reduction in Producer's share of Audio-Visual Production rights proceeds may occur only once, regardless of the number of producers presenting Revival Performances.

SECTION 13.06 **Defaults by Producer**. (a) If Producer is in default to a member of the Guild in the payment of compensation or other monies accruing from the production of the Play, the Guild may file with Producer and the Negotiator a memorandum to that effect, and the Negotiator shall thereupon withhold from Producer's share of Audio-Visual Production rights proceeds the amount stated in such memorandum and shall forthwith notify Producer in writing thereof. Unless Producer demands arbitration thereon within 10 days from Producer's receipt of such notice, the Negotiator shall make payment to Author of the amount shown to be due in such memorandum.

(b) If Producer shall have furnished a bond, and the Guild shall have drawn on such bond because of Producer's defaulted obligations on the Play, and Producer shall have failed to replenish the bond after notice and demand according to its terms, the Guild may file with Producer and the Negotiator a memorandum to that effect, stating the amount so to be replenished, and the Negotiator shall thereupon withhold from Producer's share the amount stated in such memorandum, and shall forthwith notify Producer in writing thereof. Unless Producer demands arbitration thereon within 10 days after Producer's receipt of such notice, the Negotiator shall make payment to Author of the amount shown to be due in such memorandum.

(c) In either case, if arbitration is demanded, the Negotiator will hold the amount in question until the arbitration award is rendered and final and shall then pay such amount in accordance with the film award.

SECTION 13.07 **Prior Disposition of Audio-Visual Production Rights**. If Author shall have sold any of the Audio-Visual Production rights in the Play to Producer prior to entering into this Contract, then Author and Producer may not enter into this Contract until one year following the date of the agreement for the disposition of such Audio-Visual Production rights.

ARTICLE XIV
Agents

SECTION 14.01 **Employment of Agent/Commissions**. Author may employ an agent for the disposition of rights in the Play, The commission of such agent shall not exceed 10% of the amounts received from such dispositions except for Amateur Performances, for which the commission shall not exceed 20%. The commissions paid to such agents may be deducted from the proceeds of any disposition in which Producer shares before payment is made to Producer (except for cast album proceeds payable hereunder to Producer from which no commission shall be deducted and except in relation to motion picture uses from which the commissions may be deducted only if Producer has consented to the agent's representation of Producer as provided in SECTION 14.02 herein).

SECTION 14.02 **Producer's Consent to Agent for Sale of Motion Picture Rights**. If Producer has not consented to the agent's also representing Producer with respect to motion picture uses, the agent's commission with respect thereto shall not exceed 10% of the proceeds of such disposition to which Author is entitled after payment of Producer's share, and shall be deducted only from Author's share of such proceeds. If Producer shall consent to the agent's also representing him, then the agent's commission shall not exceed 10% of the proceeds of such disposition and shall be deducted from all such proceeds before payment is made to Producer. In either case, the agent's commission for motion picture uses shall be reduced in accordance with the provisions of SECTION 12.07 herein.

SECTION 14.03 **Restrictions in Appointments**. In no event shall Author appoint Producer, or any corporation in which Producer has an interest, or any employee of Producer, or the attorney for Producer, or a member of a firm of attorneys representing Producer, as Author's agent or representative. No Author's agent or officer, directing head or employee of an agent shall, with respect to the Play, act in the dual capacity of agent and producer (the word "producer" as used in this SECTION shall include any person having executive direction or any stock interest in Producer, if a corporation, or who is one of the general partners of any partnership, general or limited) in connection with this Contract; and if he does so act, his agency shall be abandoned insofar as the Play is concerned, and he shall not be entitled to collect or receive any monies or commissions in connection with this Contract.

SECTION 14.04 **Payments**. All monies derived from the disposal of rights in the Play shall be paid to Author's agent, but only if the agent is the Dramatists Play Service, Inc., or is a member in good standing of the Society of Author's Representatives, Inc. Otherwise such monies shall be paid to the Guild which shall pay such monies directly to Author, agent and Producer as their respective interests shall appear.

SECTION 14.05 **No Deductions Other Than Agent's Commissions**. Neither Author nor Producer shall make any claim for commissions in connection with any disposition of the Play for any purpose; nor shall Producer be reimbursed by Author for any expenses or disbursements claimed by Producer unless Author, prior to the expenditure thereof, shall have agreed upon the repayment of such disbursements in writing and such agreement has completed the Certification Procedure described in ARTICLE XVI herein.

ARTICLE XV
Theatrical Conciliation Council

SECTION 15.01 **Theatrical Conciliation Council**. The Theatrical Conciliation Council (*"Council"*), an association of professionals in the theatre industry, shall meet for the purposes and at the times set forth in this Contract and at any other time, at the request of Author or Producer, to consider questions and problems that may arise from time to time during the term of this Contract (including, without limitation any issue which may arise under SECTIONS 4.02(d), 5.08, 8.10 and 9.03(e) herein. Each submission to the Council shall be made in a writing describing the matter to be considered with a copy thereof sent to the other party to this Contract.

SECTION 15.02 **Membership of Council**. The Council shall be comprised of two groups of members, i.e., Author Members and Producer Members. Author Members shall consist of playwrights, who have had First-Class Performances of at least one of their plays produced in New York City, and the executive director of the Guild. Producer Members shall consist of theatrical producers and/or theatre owners or operators, who have produced or presented First-Class Performances of at least one play in New York City, or executive directors (or other persons holding similar positions) of theatrical producer/owner-operator organizations.

SECTION 15.03 **Members of Council**. The members of the Council shall be those persons listed in EXHIBIT A attached hereto.

SECTION 15.04 **Replacement of Members**. If a member of either group resigns, is removed in accordance with the by-laws of the Council, or otherwise becomes unable to perform his services, a new member, meeting the qualifications set forth in SECTION 15.02 herein, shall be chosen by a majority of the remaining members of such group.

SECTION 15.05 **Action by Council**. Any decision or other action by the Council, as contemplated by this Contract, shall require a majority vote of all members voting in person at a meeting at which no less than and no more than 5 members of each group are in attendance. If this Contract provides, or if the parties have agreed in writing, that the decision of the Council shall be binding on the parties, then if the 10 members referred to above cannot be assembled within 7 days after the Council has received written notice of the matter to be considered, the matter may be submitted to arbitration by either Author or Producer in accordance with the provisions of ARTICLE XX herein. If the 10 members of the Council are assembled in a timely manner but cannot reach a decision within 7 days after all parties have presented their arguments in support of their positions, then, prior to adjourning the meeting, the Council shall select, by majority vote of those members present, a disinterested third party to resolve the dispute. If a majority of such Council members cannot agree on such third party, then the matter may be submitted to arbitration by either Author or Producer in accordance with the provisions of ARTICLE XX herein.

SECTION 15.06 **Binding Nature of Council Decisions**. If this Contract provides, or if the parties have agreed, in ARTICLE XXII or elsewhere in writing, that the decision or other action of the Council on a particular matter shall be binding on the parties, then once such matter is decided or action taken by the members constituting the Council on the date of such decision or action, neither of the parties hereto may resubmit the same matter to the Council at a later date for any reason including, without limitation, that the membership of the Council has changed.

SECTION 15.07 **Members of Council Held Harmless**. Producer and Author each represents and covenants (a) that neither of them will directly or indirectly undertake or threaten to undertake any claim, action or proceeding of any kind against any Council member in connection with the action or inaction of any such person in his capacity as a member of the Council or the Joint Review Board (as defined in SECTION 16.06 herein), and (b) that Producer and Author will hold each Council member harmless from any liability in connection with such actions or inactions.

ARTICLE XVI
Certification Procedure

SECTION 16.01 **Submission of Contract to the Guild**. For the purposes of this ARTICLE, the term "Contract" shall include this Contract and any written amendment thereto. On the first business day following the full execution of this Contract, Author shall commence the "*Certification Procedure*" described in this ARTICLE by submitting two copies of the Contract to the Guild in order to obtain the Guild's opinion as to whether this Contract, as signed, conforms with or is reasonably equivalent to (as described below) the form of Approved Production Contract.

SECTION 16.02 **Standards for Certification**. If this Contract, as signed, does not modify any of the provisions of the APC, the Guild shall certify that this Contract conforms therewith. If, however, this Contract, as signed, does modify any of the provisions of the APC, the Guild shall certify that this Contract is reasonably equivalent to the APC only if the modifications are reasonably necessary to counterbalance or neutralize special circumstances relating to or arising from the nature of the Play or its contemplated production, which circumstances could reasonably be expected to affect materially Producer's ability to (a) finance the Play, or (b) return to investors their capital contributions within a period then prevailing for other productions of similar size and type, or (c) obtain all the benefits to be accorded to Producer as contemplated by the APC.

SECTION 16.03 **Response from Guild**. Within 10 business days following the full execution of this Contract, the Guild shall notify both Author and Producer of its opinion by sending each of them either:

(a) one copy of this Contract bearing the Guild's signature thereby certifying that, in the opinion of the Guild, this Contract conforms with or is reasonably equivalent to the APC; or

(b) a letter advising that it is the Guild's opinion that this Contract neither conforms with nor is reasonably equivalent to the APC. Such letter must specify the reasons for the Guild's opinion and shall contain suggested revisions, which shall be set forth in detail and which would, in the Guild's opinion, make this Contract reasonably equivalent to the APC. This Contract shall automatically terminate 10 business days following the receipt by Producer of the Guild's letter unless, prior to the expiration of such 10 business-day period, one of the following events occurs:

   (i) Producer sends the Guild a copy of this Contract to which is affixed a copy of the Guild's letter signed by both Author and Producer, thereby indicating their agreement with the suggested revisions, in which case this Contract as so revised shall thereupon be deemed to have been certified by the Guild as being reasonably equivalent to the APC; or

   (ii) Producer submits this Contract and the Guild's letter to the Joint Review Board (as defined in SECTION 16.06 herein) in which case this Contract shall continue in full force and effect, as signed, and the provisions of SECTION 16.05 herein shall be applicable; or

   (iii) Producer sends the Guild a letter signed by both Author and Producer amending this Contract to eliminate the automatic termination provisions contained in this SECTION 16.03(b), in which case this Contract shall continue in full force and effect, as signed, notwithstanding the lack of certification. The signing of such letter by Author will be considered by the Guild as the tendering of Author's resignation from the Guild, which the Guild may accept.

If this Contract shall automatically terminate due to the operation of this SECTION 16.03(b), Author shall immediately return all Option Payments received from Producer, less a sum equal to the pro-rata portion of the Option Payment allocable to that portion of the Option Period measured from the Effective Date of this Contract through the date of termination, which sum may be retained by Author.

SECTION 16.04 **Guild's Failure to Respond**. If the Guild fails to send Author and Producer one of the foregoing responses within the applicable

10-business-day period, the Guild shall be deemed to have certified that this Contract is in conformity with or reasonably equivalent to the APC.

SECTION 16.05 **Submission of Contract to Joint Review Board**. If Producer or Author does not agree either with the Guild's suggested revisions or with the Guild's opinion that this Contract neither conforms with nor is reasonably equivalent to the APC, and if Producer and Author do not send the Guild the letter referred to in SECTION 16.03(b) (iii) herein, then, in order to prevent the termination of this Contract pursuant to the terms of SECTION 16.03(b) herein, Producer shall submit this Contract and the Guild's letter to the Joint Review Board (as described in SECTION 16.06 herein) within the applicable 10-business-day period. The Joint Review Board, in making its determination as to whether this Contract conforms with or is reasonably equivalent to the APC, will apply the Standards for Certification set forth in SECTION 16.02 herein. Within 10 business days after its receipt of such documents, the Joint Review Board will send to Author, Producer and the Guild a written decision either:

(a) that this Contract, as signed, conforms with or is reasonably equivalent to the APC in which case this Contract shall be deemed to have been certified by the Guild; or

(b) that specific revisions, which shall be set forth in detail by the Joint Review Board in its decision, are required to make this Contract reasonably equivalent to the APC. This Contract shall automatically terminate 10 business days following the receipt by Producer of such decision unless, prior to the expiration of such 10-business-day period, one of the following events occurs:

   (i) Producer sends the Guild a copy of this Contract to which is affixed a copy of the decision of the Joint Review Board signed by both Author and Producer, thereby indicating their agreement with the suggested revisions, in which case this Contract as so revised shall thereupon be deemed to have been certified by the Guild as being reasonably equivalent to the APC; or

   (ii) Producer sends the Guild a letter signed by both Author and Producer amending this Contract to eliminate the automatic termination provision of this SECTION 16-05(b), in which case this Contract shall continue in full force and effect as signed, notwithstanding the lack of certification. The signing of such letter by Author will be considered by the Guild as the tendering of Author's resignation from the Guild, which the Guild may accept.

If this Contract shall automatically terminate due to the operation of this SECTION 16.05(b), Author shall immediately return all Option Payments received from Producer, less a sum equal to the pro-rata portion of the Option Payment allocable to that portion of the Option Period measured from the Effective Date of this Contract through the date of termination, which sum may be retained by Author; or

(c) that the Joint Review Board cannot reach agreement in which case Author shall have 5 business days, following receipt of the decision, to send Producer written notice that Author rescinds this Contract. If Author does not send Producer notice of rescission within said 5-business-day period, this Contract shall continue in full force and effect, as signed, notwithstanding the lack of certification.

SECTION 16.06 **Joint Review Board**. (a) The *"Joint Review Board"* shall consist of two persons (and two alternates) chosen from the then current membership of the Theatrical Conciliation Council. Promptly upon the submission of this Contract to the Joint Review Board, the Author Members shall choose one person and one alternate from their group, and the Producer Members will choose one person and one alternate from their group. The alternates may attend meetings of the Joint Review Board, but shall not cast a vote unless the designated member is unavailable to do so. All decisions of the Joint Review Board shall be made by agreement between the Author Member and Producer Member.

(b) The decision of the Board, pursuant to SECTION 16.05 (a), (b) or (e) herein, shall be final and binding on the Author, Producer and the Guild, subject to the right of Author and Producer to amend this Contract to eliminate the termination provision of SECTION 16.05(b).

SECTION 16.07 **Expedited Review Procedure**. If Producer and Author agree that the review of this Contract contemplated by the foregoing provisions must be accelerated, they may jointly petition the Guild and, if necessary, the Joint Review Board, in writing, to tender its opinion as promptly as possible, but in no event later than 5 business days after its receipt of the documents specified above.

SECTION 16.08 **Notices**. All notices and other communications to be given pursuant to the provisions of this ARTICLE XVI shall be in writing, addressed to the party receiving the notice at the address indicated at the beginning of this Contract (or such other address as shall have been designated by written notice), and shall be sent only by (a) personal delivery with receipt acknowledged in writing, or (b) registered or certified mail, return receipt requested. Notices shall be deemed given on the day received (at any time prior to 5 p.m. on such day) at the address specified for the delivery of notices.

ARTICLE XVII
Warranties, Representations and Covenants

SECTION 17.01 **Scope of Warranties, Representations and Covenants**. Author hereby makes the following warranties representations, and covenants with respect to the Play.

(a) Author is the sole and exclusive Author, owner and the copyright proprietor of the Play and of all rights of every kind or nature therein, and Author has the right and authority to enter into this Contract and to grant the rights granted herein.

(b) Author makes such additional warranties, representations, covenants and indemnities, if any, as may be set forth in ARTICLE XXII herein.

ARTICLE XVIII
Claims for Infringement

SECTION 18.01 **Conduct of Defense**. If any infringement or interference with the rights of any third party is claimed because of the production of the Play, then Producer and Author shall jointly conduct the defense of any action arising therefrom unless either of them choose to engage separate counsel. In no event shall Author be responsible for any material in the Play supplied by

Producer. Upon any suit being brought against Author or Producer alone, such person shall promptly inform the other of such fact.

SECTION 18.02 **Expenses of Defense**. If Producer and Author conduct a joint defense of any such third party action, they shall share equally the expenses thereof; however, if Producer or Author engage separate counsel, they shall each bear their own expenses. When Author writes the Play at the request of Producer from material supplied him by Producer and an action is brought on the grounds of plagiarism, then Producer shall defend the action at his own expense and pay all damages that may be incurred as the result of the plagiarism and pay any judgment rendered against Author on account thereof. If the act or omission upon which any claim is based shall be found to have been caused by either Author or Producer alone, then no part of the expenses shall be paid by the party not at fault, who shall be entitled to all legal remedies that may be available against the party at fault.

ARTICLE XIX
Termination

SECTION 19.01 **Failure to Pay Royalties**. If Producer at any time fails to make any Royalty payment when due (time being of the essence of this Contract) Author may, at Author's option, send Producer written notice to correct such failure or breach within 5 business days after the receipt of such notice. Producer shall either correct such breach within said 5 days or, if Producer disagrees with Author's allegations, Producer shall send Author written notice thereof within said 5 days and either party, or the Guild on behalf of Author, shall immediately submit the dispute to arbitration as provided in ARTICLE XX herein. The award of the arbitrator shall require the party losing such dispute to pay the costs of the arbitration plus the prevailing party's reasonable legal fees. If Producer does not, within said 5-day period, correct such breach or send Author the above-mentioned notice, or if Producer does send the notice and the arbitrator determines that all or part of such Royalties should be paid and Producer does not make the payments due as required by the award within 10 business days after Producer's receipt of a copy of such award, then all of Producer's rights granted pursuant to this Contract shall cease, terminate and revert to Author upon the expiration of said 5-day or 10-day period, as the case may be, unless the Guild agrees m writing to extend Producer's time to make such payment. If Producer's office or place of business shall be more than 100 miles from the place from which the notice is sent, then the notices set forth in this SECTION shall be sent by wire communication.

SECTION 19.02 **Failure to Produce Play/Improper Assignment**. All rights granted to Producer under this Contract shall terminate automatically and without notice if Producer: fails to produce the Play within the time and in the manner provided in SECTION 1.03 herein; or fails to Vest prior to the expiration of Producer's production rights hereunder; or fails to make any Option Payment or Advance Payment when it becomes due; or if Producer assigns the rights herein except as permitted in SECTION 21.01.

SECTION 19.03 **Effects of Termination**. If the rights of Producer to present the Play shall cease and terminate in the manner provided in this ARTICLE, Producer shall immediately cease dealing with the Play in any manner and shall forthwith return to Author all literary materials relating to the Play which are in Producer's possession or control, except that Producer may retain one copy of such materials, but not for commercial use or sale. To the extent that termination occurs due to Producer's failure to make any Advance Payments to Author, Author shall return to Producer all Advance Payments theretofore made.

ARTICLE XX
Arbitration

SECTION 20.01 **Obligation to Arbitrate**. (a) Any claim, dispute, or controversy arising between Producer and Author under or in connection with or out of this Contract, or the breach thereof, shall be submitted to arbitration pursuant to the terms of this ARTICLE unless Author selects other remedies as permitted by SECTION 7.01 herein or unless otherwise specifically provided in the APC. The Guild shall receive notice of such arbitration and shall have the right to be party to the same. Failure by Producer to pay any amount claimed to be due by Author or by the Guild is evidence of a dispute entitling the claimant to an arbitration. Judgment upon the award rendered may be entered in the highest Court of the forum, State or Federal, having jurisdiction.

(b) All arbitrations shall be conducted in the City of New York before arbitrators selected from the Theatrical Production Arbitration Board herein created and in accordance with the procedures herein set forth except where Author and Producer agree to hold the arbitration outside New York. In such event, the arbitrators shall be selected from the panel of the American Arbitration Association and the arbitration shall be held in accordance with the rules of said Association.

SECTION 20.02 **Theatrical Production Arbitration Board**. The Theatrical Production Arbitration Board (*"Board"*) shall Consist Of 24 permanent members. Eight shall be chosen by the Guild Council (to be known as the *"Author's Slate"*) and 8 by a majority of the Producer Members of the Theatrical Conciliation Council (to be known as the *"Producer's Slate"*). Within 20 days thereafter, a majority of the 16 persons so chosen shall appoint 8 additional persons as public members (to be known as the *"Public Slate"*), provided such persons have never been a member of the Guild or produced a play or owned or operated a theatre. All such persons shall serve until replacement is required as set forth in SECTION 20.03 herein.

SECTION 20.03 **Replacements**. In the event of the death, resignation, illness, incapacity or unavailability of any member, or if a member of the Public State shall produce or have a play produced or become a theatre owner or operator, such member shall be replaced by a temporary or permanent successor to be appointed in the following manner: by the Council of the Guild, if the vacancy is in the Author's Slate; by the Producer Members of the Theatrical Conciliation Council if it is in the Producer's Slate; by a majority of the members of the Author's and Producer's Slates, jointly, if it is in the Public Slate.

SECTION 20.04 **Rules**. The Board, by a majority vote of all members, shall have full power to establish such rules and procedures as it may deem necessary, not inconsistent herewith. In the absence of such rules, the procedure under this ARTICLE shall be in accordance with the commercial arbitration rules then obtaining of the American Arbitration Association, except as hereinbelow otherwise provided.

SECTION 20.05 **The Complaint**. The party aggrieved, whether Author, Producer or Guild (hereinafter referred to as the *"Complainant"*) shall file with the American Arbitration Association 5 copies of a written complaint setting forth the claim, dispute, difficulty, misunderstanding, charge or controversy to be arbitrated and the relief which the Complainant requests, A copy of the complaint shall be mailed by the American Arbitration Association to the Perry complained against (hereinafter referred to as the "*Respondent*") and another to the Guild, if the Guild is not the Complainant.

SECTION 20.06 **The Answer**. The Respondent shall, within 8 days of the mailing to him of the complaint, file 5 copies of a written answer with the American Arbitration Association, and the American Arbitration Association shall mail one copy to the Complainant and another to the Guild, if the Guild is not the Complainant. Where the copy or the complaint is mailed to a Respondent at an address more than 500 miles from New York, he shall have 3 additional days to file his answer. If no written answer is filed within such period, the Respondent nevertheless will be deemed to have entered a general denial of the allegations of the complaint.

SECTION 20.07 **Participation by the Guild**. The Guild may file a complaint and demand arbitration, with or without Author's consent; and Author, in such event, shall be a party to the arbitration, and shall not discontinue the arbitration without the consent of the Guild.

SECTION 20.08 **Selection of Arbitrators**. (a) Author, or the Guild, if it has initiated the arbitration, shall appoint one arbitrator from the Author's Slate and Producer shall appoint one arbitrator from the Producer's Slate. These two arbitrators shall be appointed within 10 days from the date of the mailing of the complaint to the Respondent.

(b) If either the Author or the Producer fails to appoint an arbitrator within 10 days after the mailing of the complaint as aforesaid, then such appointment shall be made promptly from the Author's State by the Guild and from the Producer's Slate by the American Arbitration Association. If the Guild initiated the arbitration and fails to appoint an arbitrator within said 10-day period, then such appointment shall be made from the Author's State by the American Arbitration Association.

(c) Immediately after the appointment of the aforesaid 2 arbitrators, the third arbitrator shall be appointed within 5 days by the 2 arbitrators to be chosen from among the persons on the Public Slate. The American

Arbitration Association shall appoint from members of its panels any arbitrator or arbitrators required where for any reason appointment has not been made from the Slates herein provided for.

SECTION 20.09 **Power of Arbitrators**. The arbitrators are empowered to award damages against any Perry to the controversy in such sums as they shall deem fair and reasonable under the circumstances to require specific performance of a contract, to grant any other remedy or relief, injunctive or otherwise, which they deem just and equitable. The arbitrators are also empowered to tender a partial award before making a final award and grant such relief, injunctive or otherwise, in such partial award as they deem just and equitable. Subject to the provisions of SECTION 19.01 herein, the arbitrators shall determine and indicate in their written award by whom and in what proportion the cost of arbitration shall be borne.

SECTION 20.10 **Special Arbitration**. If the Author or Producer demands an immediate arbitration upon a complaint by either alleging violation of SECTION 1.02(c) or SECTION 8.01(a) or (b) and 5 copies of the complaint are filed with the Guild at any time after 10 days before the date for which rehearsals have been scheduled, the arbitration procedure outlined in this ARTICLE shall be accelerated as follows:

(a) The arbitration hearing shall be held within 3 days after the filing of the complaint.

(b) The complaint shall be delivered or telegraphed to the Respond-ent by the American Arbitration Association. The Respondent must file 5 copies of his answer with the American Arbitration Association within 24 hours thereafter.

(c) The name of the arbitrator appointed by the Complainant shall be set forth in the complaint and the name   of the arbitrator appointed by the Respondent shall be set forth in the answer. If either person so named shall be unavailable, a substitute shall be forthwith named by Author or Producer, as the case may be. The third arbitrator shall be appointed by the persons so Selected within 24 hours after the receipt of the answer by the American Arbitration Association. The American Arbitration Association shall appoint from members of its panels any arbitrator or arbitrators required where for any reason appointment has not been made from the Slates herein provided for.

ARTICLE XXI
Miscellaneous Provisions

SECTION 21.01 **Assignability of Rights**. Except as provided below, neither this Contract nor the rights granted herein to Producer shall be licensed or assigned by Producer without his first having obtained the consent in writing of the Author. Notwithstanding the foregoing, Producer may, without Author's consent, license or assign this Contract or any of the rights contained herein to a corporation, partnership or member entity of which any person comprising Producer is a controlling party or controlling shareholder or has a controlling interest, provided that any licensee or assignee shall assume all of the obligations of this Contract and that Producer shall remain personally liable for the fulfillment thereof in the same manner as though no such license or assignment had been made. A copy of any such license or assignment shall be filed with the Guild.

SECTION 21.02 **Obligations to Not-for-Profit Theatre Organiza-tions**. Notwithstanding the provisions of SECTION 11.04 herein, with respect to amounts owed to a not-for-profit theatre organization which has presented the Play prior to Producer's production hereunder, where such amounts are measured as a percentage of Subsidiary Rights income or Gross Weekly Box Office Receipts (or both), Producer and Author shall share such payments in the following manner:

> (a) Subsidiary Rights income payments of up to 5% of 100% of such income shall be shared by Producer and Author in the same percentages as they share in such income;

> (b) Gross Weekly Box Office Receipts payments of up to 1 1/2% shall be shared equally by Producer and Author.

SECTION 21.03 **Inspection of Contracts**. Author and Producer shall each have the right to inspect contracts entered into by the other if such contracts would affect the inspecting party's financial interest hereunder.

SECTION 21.04 **Equal Employment Opportunity**. Author and Producer agree, that in connection with the presentation of the Play, they will promote equal employment opportunities in consonance with the artistic integrity of the Play.

SECTION 21.05 **Non-Applicability of APC**. The APC shall not apply to any agreement relating to the purchase of rights in the Play made on the basis such that no part of the consideration is contingent upon the production of the Play upon the speaking stage in the Territory.

SECTION 21.06 **Notices**. All notices given pursuant to this Contract shall be in writing and delivered either in person, by wire communication or by registered or certified mail, return receipt requested, to the party being notified, at the address first above written (or such other address as may be designated by written notice). A copy of each notice shall be sent (at the same time and in the same manner as the original notice is sent) to the Guild and to the persons, if any, specified in ARTICLE XXII herein. Unless specified to the contrary herein, notices shall be deemed given on the day received (at any time prior to 5 p.m. on such day) at the address specified for delivery of such notices.

SECTION 21.07 **Proof of Execution**. In making proof of the execution of this Contract or of any of the terms hereof, for any purpose, the use of a copy of this Contract filed with the Guild shall be sufficient, provided that at any time after 2 years from the Effective Date there may be produced from the files of the Guild, in lieu of the copy of this Contract originally deposited therein, a microfilm of said copy.

SECTION 21.08 **Counting of Business Days**. Whenever this Contract provides for the measurement of time by the passage of *"business days,"* Saturdays, Sundays and legal holidays in the Territory, and if applicable in any Additional Territory, shall not be counted. If such measurement is made in *"days,"* then only such legal holidays shall not be counted.

SECTION 21.09 **Binding Nature of Contract**. This Contract shall be binding upon and inure to the benefit of the respective parties hereto and their respective successors in interest and permitted assigns, but shall be effective only after having completed the Certification Procedure set forth in ARTICLE XVI herein.

SECTION 21.10 **Changes in Writing**. This Contract may not be amended and no amendment will be effective unless and until the amendment is reduced to writing, signed by the panics hereto and has completed the Certification Procedure set forth in ARTICLE XVI herein. This Contract may not be amended orally under any circumstances. Any attempted oral amendment of this Contract shall be null and void and of no legal effect.

SECTION 21.11 **Permissible Variation in Certification Proce-dure**. (a) If the following two conditions exist at the time this Contract is presented to the Guild for Certification, the Guild reserves the right to certify this Contract regardless of the terms contained herein:

   (i)   this Contract is entered into with a producer who has, after the date of the promulgation of the APCs, entered into a contract (or amendment of such a contract) for the presentation in New York City of First-Class Performances of a play written by an author who, at the date of signing such contract (or amendment) was a member of the Guild, and

   (ii) on the date of signing this Contract, such prior contract (or amendment) has not been determined by either the Guild or the Joint Review Board to conform with or to be reasonably equivalent to the APC (other than by reason of the Guild's failure to respond timely, as provided in SECTION 16.04 herein, or the Joint Review Board's inability to reach a decision).

In such case, the Guild's decision to certify under the foregoing circumstances shall be final and unreviewable by the Joint Review Board, and the provisions of *SECTION 16.05* herein shall not apply to that certification.

   (b) The foregoing provisions of this SECTION shall not apply if the prior contract (or amendment) was not in conformity with or reasonably equivalent to the APC due to, in whole or in part, the existence of provisions which were less favorable to the producer than those contained in the APC.

SECTION 21.12 **Severability**. Should any part, term or provision of this Contract be decided by the courts to be in conflict with any law of the state where made of the United States, the validity of the remaining parts, terms or provisions shall not be affected thereby.

SECTION 21.13 **Applicable Law**. Unless the parties specify to the contrary in ARTICLE XXII herein, this Contract shall be governed by and construed in accordance with the substantive laws of the State of New York without reference to rules regarding the conflict of laws.

SECTION 21.14 **Counterparts**. This Contract may be executed in several counterparts and all counterparts so executed by all the parties hereto and affixed to this Contract shall constitute a valid and binding agreement, even though all of the parties have not signed the same counterpart. The Guild's certification of this Contract, pursuant to the Certification Procedure described in ARTICLE XVI herein, shall be affixed to any one of the counterparts signed by Producer,

SECTION 21.15 **Headings and Captions**. The headings and captions of the ARTICLES and SECTIONS of this Contract are inserted for convenience only and shall not be used to define, limit, extend or describe the scope or intent of any provision herein.

SECTION 21.16 **Pronouns**. Whenever the context may require, any pronoun used herein shall include the corresponding masculine, feminine or neuter forms.

ARTICLE XXII
Additional Production Terms

(Producer and Author may add to this Contract certain additional terms provided that such terms do not conflict with or modify any of the provisions of this APC unless such provisions of the APC expressly permit modification in this ARTICLE. Examples of acceptable additional terms are the following: Rights to Present Developmental Productions; Revised Definition of Completed Play; Author's Billing Credits; Author's Travel Expenses; House Seats; Special Arrangements Among Persons Comprising Author; Merger of Rights with Underlying Rights; Royalty Adjustments for Repertoire Performances; Persons to Whom Copies of Notices Should be Sent and Agency Clause. Modifications in the terms of the APC may also be made in order to counterbalance or neutralize special circumstances as described in SECTION 16.02 herein.)

SECTION 22.01

Signature Page For Approved Production Contract for Plays
for the Play Entitled

_____

IN WITNESS WHEREOF, each of the parties has signed this Contract as of the Effective Date of this Contract.

Producer(s)*	Date of Signing	Author(s)	Date of Signing
_____	_____	_____	_____
_____	_____	_____	_____

This Contract is Certified by the Guild in accordance with the provisions of *ARTICLE XVI* herein.

The Dramatists Guild, Inc.

By _____

Date of Signing _____

(If Producer is a corporation, the following must be signed by the person or persons in control thereof, i.e., the person or persons (a) owning or controlling a majority of its stock or a majority of its voting stock; or (b) using their name as part of the corporate title; or (c) rendering services in connection with the Play as Producer; or (d) whose name is included in publicity advertising or programs as Producer or co-Producer of the Play.)

In consideration of the execution of this Contract by Author, the undersigned (if more than one, then the undersigned jointly and severally) hereby agrees to jointly be liable with Producer for the full performance of each and every covenant and provision of this Contract on Producer's part to be Performed, including but not limited to the payment of all monies due Author hereunder.

_____

_____

*Where the Contract is signed by a corporate Producer, the officer signing should state his office and the corporate seal should be affixed. Where the officer signing for the corporation is other than the President, a certified copy of a resolution should be furnished showing the authority of said person so to sign.

Where this Contract is signed by a partnership, all the general partners must sign and the partnership name should also be stated.

EXHIBIT A
MEMBERS OF THE
THEATRICAL CONCILIATION COUNCIL

<u>Author Members</u>   <u>Producer Members</u>

James Goldman   Richard Barr
Garson Kanin   Bernard B. Jacobs
Arthur Kopit   Norman Kean
David E. LeVine   James M. Nederlander
Peter Stone   Robert E. Nederlander
Stephen Sondheim   Harvey Sabinson
Terrence McNally   Gerald Schoenfeld

EXHIBIT B
Instructions to the Negotiator

Procedure to Be Followed in the Sale or Lease of Plays for Audio-Visual Production

It is recognized that with regard to the procedure to be followed in the disposition of motion picture rights to plays, theatrical productions are divided into two groups, those completely or substantially financed by motion picture producers and those not so financed (herein referred to as "financed independently of the motion picture industry"). The distinction takes on significance where the disposition of motion picture rights is concerned. The significance lies in the fact that the producer who has motion picture backing (by reason of financial, employment or other contractual relations) occupies a dual position. He is both buyer and seller. As a result of this dual role, it is impossible for him, however strict and unexceptionable his conduct, to escape criticism. This duality does not exist, however, for the producer whose production is financed independently of the motion picture industry. You should bear this distinction in mind in carrying out your duties. It is suggested that you request every producer to make a voluntary disclosure to you of any relationship that he may have which conflicts with the basic relationship of being jointly interested with Author in the proceeds of motion picture monies.

The same possibility of conflict of interests may exist with respect to the disposition of any other Audio-Visual Production rights the proceeds of which are shared by the producer of the stage production. The principles set forth in this Exhibit shall apply as well, to the extent practicable, to the disposition of such rights and all references contained herein to the term "motion pictures" shall also be deemed to refer to Audio-Visual Productions where the context and industry practices appear to the Negotiator to warrant it.

I.   Plays Produced by Producers Independently of Motion Picture Backing

You will offer Producer full opportunity to satisfy you that he is certain of his own knowledge that neither all nor my substantial part of his financial backing is directly or indirectly derived from any motion picture producer. You will not, in this connection, be required to exact any onerous legal proof of Producer, but will rely on your own best judgment, remembering, however, that the burden of proof is on Producer. In the event of Producer's electing to take advantage of this opportunity and of his satisfying you that no substantial part of the financing of the Play was derived from the motion picture industry, it is recognized that his interest in securing the highest price, or the best conditions of sale, or both, is identical with that of Author and that it is to Author's advantage to have the constant benefit of Producer's advice and experience throughout the negotiations of the motion picture rights to the Play.

In the event of Producer's refusal or failure to satisfy you as above, you will decide all questions of his participation in negotiations according to your own best judgment. As provided in *SECTION 13.03* of the APC, you are not to be in any way liable for the exercise of discretion.

The Producer having Vested in the Territory, you shall, upon request of either Author (or his agent) or Producer, call a conference between Author (or his agent), Producer and yourself to the end of fixing a price at which the Play may be offered for sale for motion picture purposes; and shall thereafter offer the Play for such sale at the price established.

If at any time during the negotiations for the sale or lease of the Play it is, in your opinion or in the opinion of either Author (or his agent) or Producer, advisable either to reduce or to raise the price at which the Play is to be held for sale, you will again call for a conference for the establishment of a new price. At no time shall the holding price of the Play be changed in either direction without affording Author and Producer full opportunity to confer. Any offer received by you must be forthwith communicated to Author, or his agent, and Producer.

It is desirable that the sales price shall be mutually satisfactory to both Author and Producer. In the event Author decides to accept a definite offer which is unsatisfactory to Producer then, except in the event of the contingency provided for in the second succeeding paragraph, the following procedure shall be followed: You shall forthwith advise Producer by telegram of the price, method of payment and release date. This offer may be accepted by you unless Producer shall, within 2 business days after receipt of the notice, advise you by telegram that the offer is rejected, giving his reasons therefor. If Producer rejects the offer he shall have a period not to exceed 5 business days from the date of the notification from Producer above referred to in which to submit to you a definite "better offer" which shall mean an offer (a) from a party of financial standing capable of making the payments set forth in the offer at the respective times therein provided for, (b) for a price in excess of that contained in the offer which Author is willing to accept, and (c) on other terms at least as favorable to Author as those contained in the offer which Author is willing to accept.

If within the prescribed period of time Producer brings in a "better offer," such offer shall be accepted. If, however, the "better offer" is from Producer or an entity in which Producer has any financial or other interest, Producer shall so notify the Author of such offer specifying the price, method of payment and release date. The Author shall then have 10 business days from receipt of Producer's notice to try to obtain a "better offer" by offering the Play in the open market with the Producer's offer as a minimum. If within the prescribed period of time the Author brings in a "better offer", such offer shall be accepted, unless the Producer gives notice within one business day after receipt of Author's notice of an intention to make a higher bid, which shall be made within 2 business days after receipt of Author's notice. This bidding procedure may continue indefinitely until the highest acceptable offer is received. In the event Author and Producer do not agree as to whether or not the offer brought in by Producer is (a) from a party of financial standing capable of making the payments set forth in the offer at the respective times therein provided for, (b) for a price in excess of that contained in the offer which Author is willing to accept, (c) in terms at least as favorable to Author as those contained in the offer which Author is willing to accept, and (d) from an entity in which Producer has no financial or other interest, then it is agreed as follows:

You shall have the right in your sole discretion (i) to determine said issue or (ii) to request the American Arbitration Association to appoint two persons who, together with you will constitute the arbitrators to determine said issue. If you, by reason of your relationship with either Author or Producer or for my other reason whatsoever, occupy a position as a result of which you may not be able inbiasedly to determine said issue then, if requested by either Author or Producer or on your own volition, you shall request the American Arbitration Association to appoint three persons who, without you, will constitute the arbitrators to determine said issue, which determination shall hereafter also be referred to as a determination under (ii) hereof. The determination by you under the contingency provided for in (i) or the determination of the majority of the three persons referred to in (ii) shall be binding and conclusive upon

Author and Producer. In the event alternative (ii) is adopted, the arbitration shall take place on two days' notice, Sundays and holidays excluded, and the cost of said arbitration shall be borne by Author and Producer in equal proportion. Except as hereinbefore provided for, the rules and regulations of the American Arbitration Association shall apply to any determination made under alternative (ii), but any determination made under (i) shall be made by you without any formal hearing. You shall have the right to make the decision under alternative (i) except in such situations where in your uncontrolled determination the question involved is a close one.

The exception referred to in the second preceding paragraph is as follows: In the event Producer is associated with or employed by a motion picture producer or has been financed wholly or in substantial part by a motion picture producer or an officer thereof, then you shall not be obligated to offer Producer any period in which to bring in a definite offer in excess of that acceptable to Author, but except as aforesaid, the provisions of the foregoing paragraph shall apply.

If at my time during the negotiations for the sale or even after the consummation of the sale year or Author find any reasonable grounds for doubting the veracity of Producer's statement of his financial backing, you or Author shall forthwith report said doubts to the Council of the Guild and either Author or the Guild may then demand an arbitration under the terms of *ARTICLE XX* of the APC to establish the fact of misrepresentation, if any.

II. Plays Financed by Motion Picture Producers in Whole or in Part

The phrase *"motion picture backer"* as hereinafter employed is construed as describing any film or television producer, subsidiary or affiliate or officer or employee thereof, contributing, in whole or in part, to the financing of the stage production of the Play. The phrase *"motion picture backed producer"* as hereinafter employed is construed as describing any producer whose production is financed in whole or in substantial part by a motion picture backer or a producer who has had a past or present executive employment relationship of other significant contractual or business relationship with a motion picture backer.

Such productions fall into three classifications, as follows;

(1) That in which Producer has in writing disclosed to Author, upon signing the APC for the Play, the fact that he is, or desires to be, motion picture financed;

(2) That in which Producer does not make such disclosure upon signing the APC, but makes it before the date of the Play's first full cast rehearsal;

(3) That in which Producer has made no such disclosure at any time but is not, at the time of negotiations for the Play's sale to motion pictures, able to satisfy the Negotiator of his complete independence of motion picture financing.

The object of such classification is to protect the interests of all three parties and to avoid the complications which result from motion picture financing of which Author is not aware.

III. Procedure in Case Production Falls Under Above Classification (1)

It is desirable from all points of view that Producer whose production is to be financed by motion picture capital should, prior to the signing of the APC, disclose in writing to Author either the fact of such financing, or his desire or intention to obtain such financing. When such disclosure is made and Author signs the APC, it shall be assumed that Author is satisfied with such financing and you will accord the motion picture backers the protection provided in the following procedure.

The Producer having Vested in the Territory, you shall decide when, in your judgment, acting as Author's representative, a holding price at which the motion picture rights to the Play are to be offered for sale or lease should be fixed and after full consultation with both Producer and Author you will arrange with Author to fix that price.

If the fixing of this price gives you any reason to suspect collusion between the motion picture producer and Author which might operate against the spirit and content of the APC or the interest of Producer, or Author's best financial interest, you will forthwith report your suspicions to the Theatrical Conciliation Council as a violation of the APC.

The price being fixed to your satisfaction, however, you will:

(a) Immediately offer the rights at this price to the motion picture backer, with the stipulation that he shall have 2 days in which to accept or reject the price named.

(b) If at the end of said 2 days the motion picture backer does not accept the Play at the price named, then the Play may be offered in the open market with the rejected price as a minimum, and no further opportunity will be given to, or bids received from the motion picture producer to meet or better any other bids from any other motion picture corporation in excess of the price rejected by him.

(c) If the Play is not sold in the open market at the price named, or better, you and Author may by agreement reduce the holding price one or more times. If you do so, however, the procedure hereinbefore outlined must be repeated.

If at any time following a rejection by the motion picture backer, Author and Negotiator elect to demand of the motion picture backer an offer as evidence of its interest in the property and the motion picture backer does not submit any such offer within one week after receipt of the Negotiator's request to do so, then the Play shall be considered free and clear of any obligation to the motion picture backer which financed it and shall be offered in the open market and no further opportunity will be given to, or bids received from, the motion picture backer to meet or better any other bids from any other motion picture producer in excess of the price rejected by him.

If the motion picture backer does so manifest its interest by making an offer, this offer must be submitted as a fixed sum, or a fixed sum plus a percentage of receipts, together with a summary of the terms of the proposed contract which shall be acceptable to the Negotiator. Author shall, by the terms of such offer, have one week after receipt in which to give notice as to whether Author accepts or rejects it. If Author rejects it, however, he may still use it as a minimum holding price at which to offer the property on the open market, but no bid will be received from the motion picture backer in excess of such holding price. If, however, no offers are received in excess of this holding price, Author may, if he wishes, offer the Play in the open market at a sum at or below the price set by the motion picture backer and rejected by Author. In this instance, however, the motion picture backer will be free to file offers with you in competition with any other motion picture company, and no bid from such backer shall be received in such competition in excess of such minimum holding price. But if Author receives a bid from any other motion picture company at the same price as that offered by the backer, the backer's bid (if kept open) shall receive preference, provided that the other terms of the contract offered by the backer are as favorable as those offered by the other motion picture company.

In all cases of such motion picture financed productions, you will at all times keep Author fully informed of all facts relating to sale or lease, including (but not by way of limitation) offers received, steps in negotiation, execution of the contract and consummation of the sale, but you will not reveal any such facts to anyone other than Author and the Guild; and you will particularly caution Author against disclosing any such information to the motion picture backed producer,

IV. Procedure Under Classification (2)

When Producer has made no written disclosure of motion picture financing upon signing the APC, but has made it between that date and the date of the first rehearsal of the Play, then Author shall have the right to choose between instructing the Negotiator either to follow the above procedure or instructing him to proceed as in the ensuing paragraph.

V. Procedure Under Classification (3)

Where Producer has not at any time in writing disclosed to Author the fact of any motion picture financing, or cannot, at the time of the negotiations for the Play's sale or lease to pictures, satisfy the Negotiator of his independence of motion picture financing, or has received motion picture backing at some time after the date of the first rehearsal and prior to the offering for sale or lease, whether such backing is disclosed or not, then the Negotiator shall use his utmost efforts to secure a competitive open market for the picture rights to the Play without any of the advantages to the motion picture backer as set

APPENDIX E

Approved Production Contract for Musical Plays[1]

APPROVED PRODUCTION CONTRACT FOR MUSICAL PLAYS

THIS CONTRACT, made and entered into as of the   day of   , 19
("*Effective Date*") by and between

whose address is

hereinafter referred to jointly and severally as "*Producer*," and the following
person residing at the indicated addresses:

"*Bookwriter*":

"*Composer*":

"*Lyricist*":

hereinafter referred to jointly as "*Author*".

WITNESSETH:

Whereas, The Dramatists Guild, Inc. has promulgated this form of agreement known as the Approved Production Contract ("*APC*") which it has recommended to its members as being fair and reasonable to both authors and producers; and

Whereas, Author, a member of The Dramatists Guild, Inc. ("*Guild*") has been or will be writing the book, music and lyrics of a certain musical play or other dramatic property, now entitled

hereinafter referred to as the "*Play*"; and

Whereas, Producer is or will be in the business of producing plays and desires to acquire the sole and exclusive rights to produce the Play in the United States, its territories and possessions, including Puerto Rico, and Canada (the "*Territory*") and to acquire Author's services in connection therewith;

Now, therefore, in consideration of the mutual covenants herein contained and other good and valuable consideration, the parties hereto agree as follows:

ARTICLE I
Initial Grant of Rights

SECTION 1.01 **Initial Grant of Rights to Produce Play**. Author hereby grants to Producer the sole and exclusive rights, subject to the terms of this Contract, to present the Play for one or more First-Class Performances. For the purposes of this Contract, the term "*First-Class Performances*" shall mean live stage productions of the Play on the speaking stage, within the Territory, under Producer's own management, in a regular evening bill in a first-class theatre in a first-class manner, with a first-class cast and a first-class director. The terms "*produce*" and "*present*" (and their derivatives) shall be used interchangeably.

SECTION 1.02 **Grant of Author's Services**. Author hereto agrees to:

(a) perform such services as may be reasonably necessary in making revisions in the Play;

(b) assist in the selection of the cast and consult with, assist and advise the Producer, director, scenic, lighting and costume designers and the choreographer and/or dance director, conductor and sound designer, if any, regarding any problem arising out of the production of the Play;

(c) attend rehearsals of the Play as well as out-of-town performances prior to the Official Press Opening (as defined in SECTION 2.05 herein) of the Play in New York City, provided, however, that Author may be excused from such attendance on showing reasonable cause.

SECTION 1.03 **Termination of Rights if No Production**. Although nothing herein shall be deemed to obligate Producer to produce the Play, nevertheless, unless Producer presents the first paid public First-Class Performance of the Play within the applicable Option Period described in Article II herein for which the prescribed payment has been made, Producer's rights to produce the Play and to the services of Author shall then automatically and without notice terminate.

SECTION 1.04 **Continuous Production Rights.** If the first paid public First-Class Performance of the Play hereunder is presented within one of the Option Periods (including the extensions, if any, set forth in SECTIONS 2.03 and 2.04 herein), the rights granted to present the Play shall continue subject to the reopening provisions of ARTICLE X herein.

SECTION 1.05 **Definition of Author**. For the purposes of this Contract, the term "*Author*" shall mean each dramatist, collaborator, adaptor, bookwriter, composer and lyricist whose literary or musical material is used in the Play. The term "Author" shall include any person who is involved in the initial stages of a collaborative process and who is deserving of billing credit as an Author and whose literary or musical contribution will be an integral part of the Play as presented in subsequent productions by other producers. It shall not include a person whose services are only those of a literal translator.

SECTION 1.06 **Reservation of Rights**. Author shall retain sole and complete title, both legal and equitable, in and to the Play and all rights and uses of every kind except as otherwise specifically herein provided. Author reserves all rights and uses now in existence or which may hereafter come into existence, except as specifically herein provided. Any rights reserved shall not be deemed competitive with any of Producer's rights and may be exercised by Author at any time except as otherwise specifically provided herein. All contracts for the publication of the music and lyrics of the Play shall provide that the copyright be in the names of the Composer and Lyricist.

ARTICLE II
Option Periods and Payments

SECTION 2.01 **Option Periods/Option Payments**. In consideration of the foregoing grant of rights and of Author's services in writing the Play and Author's agreement to perform services in connection with the production of the Play as hereinabove provided, Producer agrees to pay Author the following sums ("*Option Payments*") in order to maintain Producer's rights to present the Play, provided that the first paid public First-Class Performance of the Play occurs prior to the expiration of the applicable "*Option Period*" described below:

(a) "*First Option Period*" — $18,000 for the period of 12 months following the Effective Date of this Contract, payable upon the execution of this Contract by Author and Producer.

(b) "*Second Option Period*" — $9,000 for a second consecutive 12-month period, payable on or before the last day of the First Option Period.

(c) "*Third Option Period*" — $900 per month for a maximum of 12 consecutive months. Payment for the first such month shall be made on or before the last day of the Second Option Period; thereafter, payment for each additional month of such extension shall be made on or before the last day prior to the commencement of such month.

SECTION 2.02 **Option Payments Non-Returnable**. Each of the foregoing Option Payments made by Producer shall be non-returnable (except to the extent described in ARTICLE XVI herein) but shall be deductible, to the extent permitted by the terms of ARTICLE VI herein, from the Advance Payments and Royalties (as defined respectively in SECTIONS 3.01 and 4.02 herein) otherwise payable to Author.

SECTION 2.03 **Extension of Option Until Delivery of Completed Play**. If this Contract provides in ARTICLE XXII that the Play has not been completed at the Effective Date of this Contract, the payment for the First Option Period shall be made at the time and in the manner set forth in ARTICLE XXII herein, but the expiration of the Option Periods and the due dates for the subsequent Option Payments otherwise specified in this ARTICLE shall be extended and measured from the date on which the Completed Play is delivered to Producer. Producer shall maintain the sole and exclusive rights and option to present the Play while Producer awaits delivery of the Completed Play. Unless otherwise defined in ARTICLE XXII herein, a "***Completed Play***" shall mean the Play consisting of a book of at least 80 single-spaced pages plus a score consisting of music and lyrics for at least 12 songs.. If the Completed Play is not delivered within 6 months after the Effective Date of this Contract, Producer may, at any time thereafter, terminate this Contract upon written notice to Author. Author agrees that time is of the essence with respect to such delivery date.

SECTION 2.04 **Extension of Option for Try-Out Performances**. If, during one of the Option Periods, Producer presents Second-Class Performances (as defined in SECTION 9.01 herein) or Developmental Productions of the Play, the expiration of the Option Periods and due dates for subsequent Option Payments shall be extended for a period equal to the number of days on which performances of the Play were so presented (up to a maximum of 8 weeks) plus an additional 60 days.

SECTION 2.05 **Definition of "Official Press Opening"**. For the purposes of this Contract, the term "***Official Press Opening***" shall mean the performance of the Play which Producer has publicly announced as the opening and to which the press is invited.

ARTICLE III
Advance Payments

SECTION 3.01 **Calculation and Due Dates of Advance Payments**.

(a) Producer shall pay Author the following "***Advance Payments***," at the stated times, subject to the provisions of SECTIONS 3.04 and 6.01 herein:

    (i) On the first day of rehearsal at which Producer requires the attendance of all cast members of the Principal Company (as defined in SECTION 3.01(b) herein), but in no event later than 5 business days before the initial First-Class Performance of the Play, Producer shall pay Author a sum equal to 2% of the amounts constituting Capitalization (as defined in SECTION 3.03 herein) at such date.

(ii) Thereafter, at such times as additional amounts are contributed towards Capitalization, Producer shall pay Author, within 10 business days after Producer's receipt thereof, a sum equal to 2% of such additional contributions.

(iii) The sums otherwise payable by Producer pursuant to the foregoing calculation in this SECTION shall he reduced by an amount equal to 2% of such sums. The net amounts paid to Author shall constitute the Advance Payments.

(b) For the purposes of this Contract, a *"Company"* shall mean each unit of actors assembled to present the Play hereunder. *"Principal Company"* shall mean the first Company funded in an amount sufficient to present First-Class Performances of the Play.

SECTION 3.02 **Maximum Advance**. The aggregate amount of Advance Payments payable by Producer pursuant to SECTION 3.01 herein shall not exceed $60,000, regardless of the amount of Capitalization.

SECTION 3.03 **Definition of "Production Costs," "Capitalization" and "Equity Capital"**. (a) For the purposes of this Contract, *"Production Costs"* shall mean the estimated costs of producing the Principal Company (including any contingency reserves), as described in the documents used in connection with the financing of such Company, including costs that may be paid, if permitted by the terms of such documents, by an overcall demand on investors, but not including any weekly operating expenses.

(b) For the purposes of this Contract, *"Capitalization"* shall mean:

(i) the aggregate of the following sums actually received by Producer (after all necessary bank clearances) for the purpose of paying Production Costs:

(A) all amounts contributed as Equity Capital. For the purposes of this Contract, *"Equity Capital"* shall mean the amounts contributed by investors in order to pay Production Costs and obtain an ownership interest in the venture producing the Principal Company, including all amounts received by Producer pursuant to an overcall demand made on the investors who previously contributed Equity Capital to such venture, but only to the extent such sums exceed 10% of the total Equity Capital contributions received by Producer from all investors immediately prior to the date on which the demand for such overcall is issued and only to the extent such sums are used by Producer to pay Production Costs; and

(B) Should Producer find it necessary to obtain loans to pay Production Costs, then the amount of such loan proceeds shall also be included to the extent such proceeds are in excess of 20% of the estimated Production Costs (or if the documents used in connection with the financing of the Principal Company set forth an amount representing minimum estimated Production Costs, then such amount); however, if Producer receives no Equity Capital pursuant to an overcall (whether or not an overcall demand is made), then the amount of such loan proceeds shall be included to the extent such proceeds are in excess of 30% of such estimated Production Costs;

(ii) but not including the foregoing sums to the extent allocated to pay the following items of Production Costs:

(A) all security bonds, deposits and other guarantees to be provided to any union or other collective bargaining organization, theatre or other entity;

(B) all Option Payments to Author;

(C) advertising, promotional and press related costs in excess of 10% of the minimum estimated Production Costs; and

(D) all sums described in SECTION 6.01(b) herein which are included as Production Costs and paid to a third party who presented the Play in the Territory as a Developmental Production or as other non-First-Class Performances.

(c) All sums received by Producer to pay the operating costs of paid public Performances of the Play (rather than Production Costs) shall be excluded in determining the amount of Capitalization, regardless of the source of any such sums or the manner in which such sums may be contributed.

SECTION 3.04 **Advance Payments Non-Returnable**. All Advance Payments made by Producer shall be non-returnable but shall be deductible, to the extent permitted by the terms of ARTICLE VI herein, from Royalties otherwise payable to Author.

ARTICLE IV
Royalties

SECTION 4.01 **Definitions**. For the purposes of this Contract, the following terms shall have the indicated meanings:

(a) *"Out-of-Town Performances"* — First-Class Performances of the Play outside of New York City prior to presentation of Preview or Regular Performances.

(b) *"Preview Performances"* — First-Class Performances of the Play in New York City prior to the Official Press Opening in New York City. For purposes of calculating Royalties under this Contract, the Official Press Opening in New York City shall be deemed a Preview Performance.

(c) *"Regular Performances"* — First-Class Performances of the Play in New York City commencing with the first performance of the play following the Official Press Opening of the Play in New York City.

(d) *"Touring Performances"* — First-Class Performances of the Play hereunder outside of New York City, presented by a Company simultaneously with or subsequent to Out-of-Town, Preview or Regular Performances.

(e) *"Fixed-Fee Performances"* — All performances of the Play hereunder (other than Preview and Regular Performances) produced by or pursuant to a grant of rights from Producer, in return for which Producer receives compensation based in whole or in part on a fixed (i.e., guaranteed) fee.

(f) *"Developmental Productions"* — Productions of the Play presented pursuant to Actors' Equity Workshop Agreements.

(g) *"Backers' Auditions"* — Performances of the Play presented pursuant to the Actors' Equity Association Backers' Audition Code or, if the performances are outside the United States, then pursuant to any other similar code, contract or agreement in effect in such location.

(h) *"Performance Week"* — The 6- or 7-day period, beginning on either Monday or, if there is no scheduled performance on Monday, then on Tuesday and continuing through Sunday, during which one or more performances of the Play are presented hereunder.

(i) *"Full Performance Week"* — Any Performance Week during which no fewer than 8 performances of the Play are presented.

(j) *"New York City"* — The theatrical district of the Borough of Manhattan of the City of New York unless the parties modify the definition, in *Article XXII* herein, to include any other location in the Borough of Manhattan.

SECTION 4.02 **Description of Royalties**. Author shall earn the following aggregate *"Royalties"* for each week of performances, described below, during which the Play is presented hereunder:

(a) *Out-of-Town Performances and Preview Performances* —

    (i) *Pre-Recoupment* — (A) $4,500 per Full Performance Week for the first 12 Performance Weeks of Out-of-Town Performances and for each week of Preview Performances. This Royalty is subject to the Royalty Adjustment provisions of ARTICLE V herein.

    (B) 4.5% of the Gross Weekly Box Office Receipts (as defined in SECTION 4.03 herein) for each Performance Week of Out-of-Town Performances commencing for the 13th such week, if any, and for each subsequent Performance Week of Preview Performances continuing until the earlier of the Official Press Opening in New York City or the end of the Performance Week in which the costs of presenting such Company have been Recouped. This Royalty is subject to the Royalty Adjustment provisions of ARTICLE V herein.

(ii) Post-Recoupment — 6% of the Gross Weekly Box Office Receipts from Out-of-Town and Preview Performances commencing for the first Performance Week after the week in which the costs of presenting such Company have been Recouped. This Royalty is subject to the Royalty Adjustment provisions of ARTICLE V herein.

(b) *Regular Performances* — 4.5% of the Gross Weekly Box Office Receipts from Regular Performances up to and including the Performance Week in which the costs of presenting such Company have been Recouped and 6% thereafter. This Royalty is subject to the Royalty Adjustment provisions of *ARTICLE V* herein.

(c) *Touring Performances* — 4.5% of the Gross Weekly Box Office Receipts from Touring Performances up to and including the Performance Week in which the costs of presenting such Company have been Recouped and 6% thereafter. This Royalty is subject to the Royalty Adjustment provisions of *ARTICLE V* herein.

(d) *Fixed-Fee Performances* — For the purposes of this SECTION 4.02(d), the term "Producer" shall mean Producer's grantee in those cases where Fixed-Fee Performances are produced by such grantee.

(i) Except as provided in SECTION 4.02(d)(ii)   herein, Author's Royalty for Fixed-Fee Performances of the Play shall be calculated in the following manner:

(A) 6% of any fixed fee paid to Producer by such local promoter or sponsor for such Performances; plus

(B) 6% of Producer's share of box office receipts and any profits for such Performances (including box office receipts and profits paid as a salary, fee, royalty or other type of compensation for Producer's services), paid to Producer by such local promoter or sponsor.

(ii) With respect to first-class theatres which have, after January 1, 1977, presented First-Class Performances of plays pursuant to which the authors of such plays have customarily received royalties for such performances based on a percentage of gross weekly box office receipts (rather than on fixed fees), Author's Royalty for Fixed-Fee Performances of the Play presented in such theatres shall be calculated in the following manner:

(A) 6% of any fixed fee paid to Producer by the so-called "local promoter" or "local sponsor" for such Performances; plus

(B) if the local promoter or sponsor pays Producer a percentage of box office receipts and any profits for such Performances (including box office receipts and profits paid as a salary, fee, royalty or other type of compensation for Producer's services), then Author shall be paid, from up to 50% of Producer's share of such box office receipts and profits, a sum equal to 25% of the amounts paid to Author in (A); plus

(C) 6% of the balance of Producer's share of box office receipts and profits set forth in (B) above (after deduction of the sum paid to Author in (B) above);

(iii) The calculations set forth above may be made on a weekly basis or on a theatre-by-theatre basis at Producer's option.

(iv) If Producer cannot, in good faith, arrange for the presentation of Fixed-Fee Performances because the royalty participants connected with the Play, including Author and Producer, are entitled to receive, by the terms of their contracts, royalties which, in the aggregate, exceed 15% of the sums payable to Producer by such local promoter or sponsor (without reference to SECTION 4.02(d)(ii) (B) above), Author hereby agrees to accept the following Royalty in lieu of Author's Royalty described above: Author's Royalty for such Fixed-Fee Performances shall be calculated by multiplying 15% by Author's pro-rata share of the total royalties all the royalty participants were otherwise entitled to receive. (For purposes of example only, if all royalty participants were entitled to receive aggregate royalties of 18% of the sums payable to Producer and Author's 6% royalty represents one-third of such amount, then Author will receive a Royalty equal to one-third of 15%, i.e., 5%.) Provided, however, that if Producer elects this Royalty calculation, Author shall accrue the amount of the difference between the amount of Royalties paid pursuant to such calculation and the amount of Royalties which would have been paid for such Performances if such calculation were not used, and Producer shall pay Author the amount of such unpaid Royalties from 50% of the sums, if any, set forth in SECTIONS 4.02(d)(ii)(C) and 4.02(d)(i)(B) above (remaining after payment of Author's Royalty referred to in such SECTIONS), payable pari passu with the other royalty participants similarly sharing in such sums, but only to the extent such sums are earned from the Performances as to which this Royalty calculation is used.

(v) If there is any dispute between Author and Producer as to whether a particular theatre should be classified under **SECTION** 4.02(d)(i) or (ii), the parties shall submit the matter for resolution to the Theatrical Conciliation Council. The decision of the Council shall be final and binding on the parties.

(vi) If Producer licenses the Play to an entity in which Producer has any financial or other interest, or if the Play is presented in a theatre in which Producer has a similar interest, the arrangements made between Producer and such entity or theatre shall not be materially different from the arrangements made in the industry between unrelated parties under similar circumstances. Furthermore, irrespective of whether there is any financial or other interest between Producer and such entity or theatre, the weekly operating expenses of such Fixed-Fee Performances which are customarily paid by the producer (e.g. compensation to actors), rather than by the local promoter or sponsor, shall be reflected in the amount of the fixed fee for the purpose of computing and paying Author's Royalties under this SECTION 4.02(d). If Author or the Guild believes that any such arrangements made by Producer are materially different, or that the fixed fee does not reflect the weekly operating expenses customarily paid by the producer rather than the local promoter or sponsor then, in either case, Author, or the Guild, on behalf of Author, shall submit such matter to the Theatrical Conciliation Council which shall determine whether the arrangements are appropriate under the circumstances or whether the fixed fee reflects the weekly operating expenses customarily paid by producers, as the case may be. The decision of the Council shall be final and binding on the parties.

(e) ***Developmental Productions*** — If the rights to present Developmental Productions of the Play are granted in *ARTICLE XXII* herein, Author shall earn a Royalty equal to the minimum compensation paid to an actor for such Developmental Production, excluding any per diem, travel and other allowances, if any, paid to the actor. Author and Producer shall not modify any provision of this Contract as a condition to the granting of rights to present Developmental Productions.

(f) ***Backers' Auditions*** — No Royalties to Author.

SECTION 4.03 **Definition of "Gross Weekly Box Office Receipts"**. (a) Where Author's Royalties, as provided herein, are based upon "***Gross Weekly Box Office Receipts***", the Royalties for such Performance Week shall be computed upon all sums received by Producer from all ticket sales to the Play, allocable to performances given in such week, less the following deductions:

(i) federal or other admission taxes;

(ii) customary commissions and fees, as may be prevailing from time to time, paid to or retained by third parties in connection with theatre parties, benefits, American Express or other similar credit card plans, telephone sales, automated ticket distribution or remote box offices, e.g., Ticketron and Ticket World (but not ticket brokers), and commissions or fees for group sales;

(iii) commissions and fees paid to or retained by credit card companies for sales of tickets;

(iv) those sums equivalent to the former 5% New York City Amusement Tax, the proceeds of which are now paid to the pension and/or welfare funds of various theatrical unions;

(v) subscription fees;

(vi) receipts from Actors' Fund Benefit performances provided the customary payments are made by the Actors' Fund to The Dramatists Guild Fund, Inc.;

(vii) receipts from two performances of the Play in each calendar year to the extent such receipts are contributed for theatre-related eleemosynary purposes; and

(viii) if applicable, library discounts, value added taxes and entertainment taxes, if any.

(b) Producer may also deduct from Gross Weekly Box Office Receipts allocable to any Performance Week any sums included as Gross Weekly Box Office Receipts in a prior Performance Week and which were included in Author's Royalty calculation but which sums subsequently are refunded or uncollectible due to dishonored checks, invalidated credit card receipts or for any other reason.

(c) If the Play is presented simultaneously by more than one Company, Gross Weekly Box Office Receipts received by each such Company shall be computed and paid separately,

SECTION 4.04 **Definition of "Recouped" and "Recoupment"**. (a) For the purposes of this Contract, the terms "*Recouped*" or "*Recoupment*" shall mean, with respect to each Company presenting the Play, the recovery of all costs incurred in presenting such Company after payment or accrual (but not prepayment) of all operating expenses for such Company.

(b) For the purposes of determining Recoupment, the costs incurred in presenting a Company shall include the following "*Production Expenses*": fees of designers, directors, general and company managers; cost of sets, curtains, drapes and costumes; cost or payments on account of properties, furnishings, lighting and electrical equipment; premiums for bonds and insurance; unrecouped option and advance payments to persons other than Author; rehearsal charges, transportation charges, reasonable legal and accounting expenses, advance advertising, publicity and press expenses and other expenses and losses actually incurred in connection with the production and presentation of the Play up to and including the Official Press Opening of such Company and all sums described in SECTION 6.01(b) herein to be paid, as Production Costs, to a third party who presented the Play in the Territory as a Developmental Production or as other non-First-Class Performances; but there shall not be included any compensation paid to Producer or to any person rendering the services of a producer other than a cash office charge not to exceed $1,500 per week (regardless of the amount actually paid) commencing 4 weeks before the opening of rehearsals and continuing until the Official Press Opening of the Company and other than Producer's Royalty (as defined in SECTION 5.13 herein). No amounts charged as Production Expenses shall be charged again as operating expenses, or vice versa.

(c) Recoupment shall be calculated separately for each Company presenting the Play so that the profits or losses attributable to one Company shall not affect the calculation of Recoupment for any other Company. Recoupment shall be determined by the accountant engaged by Producer and, subject to SECTION 5.09 herein, the determination made by such accountant shall be final and binding as among the parties hereto. Promptly upon the making of such determination by the accountant, Producer shall send Author written notice that Recoupment has occurred.

(d) In calculating Recoupment for the purposes of this Contract, the amounts of bonds, deposits or other items which, by their terms, are returnable to the Company shall not be included as costs to be recovered. Recoupment of the amounts incurred in presenting any Company shall be deemed final so that, once Recoupment has been attained, subsequent expenses that may be incurred by such Company will not alter the fact that such Company has Recouped within the meaning of this Contract.

(e) All expenses incurred by any Company to finance Touring or Off-Broadway Performances by that same Company must be Recouped before Author shall be entitled to post-Recoupment Royalties with respect to such Touring or Off-Broadway Performances. It is understood that the incurring of such expenses shall not affect or otherwise alter the payment of post-Recoupment Royalties, if any, by such Company for performances which precede such Touring or Off-Broadway Performances.

ARTICLE V
Royalty Adjustments

SECTION 5.01 **Definition of "Weekly Breakeven"**. (a) For the purposes of this Contract, the term "*Weekly Breakeven*" shall mean, for each Company presenting the Play hereunder, the operating expenses of such Company for each Performance Week as set forth in the accounting reports as customarily prepared by the accountant engaged by Producer. For the purpose of determining Weekly Breakeven, operating expenses shall consist of the following: $3,000 of Author's Royalty (regardless of the total Royalty actually paid to Author), compensation paid to the cast, director, stage manager, general and company managers, press agents, orchestra, and miscellaneous stage personnel, transportation charges, weekly cash office charge not to exceed $1,500 (regardless of the total cash office charge actually paid to Producer), advertising, press and publicity costs, legal and accounting expenses, the costs of exhibiting television commercials, theatre guaranty and expenses, rentals, miscellaneous supplies and all other reasonable expenses of whatever kind actually incurred in connection with the weekly operation of the Play, as distinguished from Production Expenses, but not including any compensation to Producer or a person rendering services of a producer, other than $1,500 of Producer's Royalty, or any money paid to Producer by way of a percentage of the Gross Weekly Box Office Receipts or otherwise for the making of any loan or the posting of any bond, or any sum paid by Producer to any trade association of producers and/or theatre owners.

(b) The costs incurred in producing television commercials and any other type of audio-visual promotions shall be included in determining Weekly Breakeven, but the costs of each such commercial or Audio-Visual promotion shall be amortized at the rate of $3,000 per Performance Week.

SECTION 5.02 **Definition of "Weekly Profits"**. For the purposes of this Contract, the term "*Weekly Profits*" shall mean the amount by which Gross Weekly Box Office Receipts for a particular Performance Week exceed the Weekly Breakeven for such week.

SECTION 5.03 **Definition of "Losing Week" and "Weekly Losses"**. For the purposes of this Contract, the term "*Losing Week*" shall mean any Performance Week for which the Gross Weekly Box Office Receipts do not exceed the Weekly Breakeven for such week, and the term "*Weekly Losses*" shall mean the amount by which Weekly Breakeven for a particular Performance Week exceeds the Gross Weekly Box Office Receipts for such week.

SECTION 5.04 Definition of **"Potential and Actual Gross Ticket Sales"**. For the purpose of this Contract, the term *"Potential Gross Ticket Sales"* shall mean the dollar amount of total ticket sales that would be earned, without discounts or deductions of any kind, if every seat in the theatre, available for purchase as specified in the applicable ticket manifest, were sold for each performance during a given Full Performance Week. *"Actual Gross Ticket Sales"* shall mean the aggregate amounts received by Producer from total tickets sold in a given Performance Week.

SECTION 5.05 **Adjustments for Out-of-Town and Preview Performances**. (a) Author may earn additional Royalties for the first 12 Performance Weeks of Out-of-Town Performances and any number of Performance Weeks of Preview Performances (other than the performance constituting the Official Press Opening in New York City) under the following circumstances:

> (i) provided Producer has presented Out-of-Town Performances of the Play and, provided further, that after adding the aggregate Weekly Profits, if any, earned for each Performance Week of Out-of-Town Performances (up to the first 12 such weeks) and Preview Performances, and subtracting therefrom the aggregate losses, if any, theretofor incurred for each Losing Week of Out-of-Town Performances (up to the first 12 such weeks) and Preview Performances, there exists a cumulative net operating profit for such Performances, then Author shall earn additional Royalties equal to the amount by which the Royalties which Author would have earned if they were calculated pursuant to SECTION 4.02(c) herein (after taking into account the applicable Royalty Adjustments set forth in this ARTICLE), exceed the amount of Royalties actually earned by Author for such Performances. Such additional Royalties shall be payable only from and shall not exceed 50% of the cumulative net operating profits of such Out-of-Town and Preview Performances. If Producer is required to pay to one or more third parties any portion of such cumulative net operating profits, then the 50% of cumulative net operating profits, otherwise available to pay additional Royalties, shall be reduced by one-half of such third-party payments, with such reduction not

to exceed an amount equal to 5% of 100% of such cumulative net operating profits. In no event shall the total Royalties payable to Author pursuant to this SECTION for such Out-of-Town and Preview Performances exceed 4.5% of the Gross Weekly Box Office Receipts of such Performances.

(ii)   The calculation described in this SECTION shall be made by the accountant engaged by Producer. In making this calculation, such accountant shall not include any income or expense attributable to the performance constituting the Official Press Opening in New York City. The additional Royalties, if any, which may be due shall be paid to Author no later than 60 days following the Official Press Opening of the play in New York City and shall be accompanied by a statement from such accountant describing the calculation of such additional Royalties.

(b)   With respect to each Performance Week of Out-of-Town and Preview Performances commencing with the 13th week of Out-of-Town Performances, if any, the Royalties payable to Author for such Out-of-Town Performances and all subsequent Preview Performances shall be subject to adjustment in the same manner as is applicable to Regular Performances as described in SECTION 5.06(a)(i) and, if the costs of presenting such Company have been Recouped, then as described in SECTION 5.06(b) herein.

SECTION 5.06 **Adjustments for Regular Performances**. With respect to each Company presenting Regular Performances, the Royalties payable to Author for such Regular Performances shall be subject to adjustment in the following manner:

(a)   *Pre-Recoupment* —

(i)   If the Gross Weekly Box Office Receipts for any Performance Week of Regular Performances, up to and including the Performance Week in which the costs of presenting such Company have been Recouped, do not exceed 110% of Weekly Breakeven, Author's Royalty for such week, in lieu of the Royalties otherwise payable, shall be comprised of a fixed Royalty of $3,000 per Full Performance Week, plus a percentage Royalty equal to 25% of the Weekly Profits, if any, for such week; provided, however, in no event shall Author's fixed and percentage Royalty exceed a sum equal to 4.5% of the Gross Weekly Box Office Receipts for such week.

(ii) With respect to Regular Performances in New York City only, if, in the first 21 Performance Weeks of Regular Performances, commencing with the first Performance Week following the Official Press Opening of the Play in New York City, Producer has received Actual Gross Ticket Sales in 17 of 21 such weeks equal to at least 87% of Potential Gross Ticket Sales, then, commencing for the Performance Week following such 17th Performance Week, Author's Royalty shall increase from 4.5% to 6% of the Gross Weekly Box Office Receipts, subject to the adjustments specified in the preceding SECTION 5.06(a)(i). However, if at any time thereafter, Actual Gross Ticket Sales for any 3 consecutive Performance Weeks of Regular Performances fall below 87% of Potential Gross Ticket Sales for each of such weeks, then, commencing for the first Performance Week thereafter, Author's Royalty will revert to 4.5% of the Gross Weekly Box Office Receipts until the Play has subsequently earned Actual Gross Ticket Sales during 17 of any consecutive 21 Performance Weeks of Regular Performances, equal to 87% of Potential Gross Ticket Sales for each of such weeks, at which point, Author's Royalties shall increase again to 6% subject to the same calculation above described (the "**87% Formula**"). The 87% Formula shall continue to apply up to and including the Performance Week in which the costs of presenting the Principal Company have been Recouped, at which point, the 87% Formula shall cease and be of no further force or effect regardless of the number of weeks that may have accrued to the benefit of either producer or Author at such date.

(b) ***Post-Recoupment***—If the Gross Weekly Box Office Receipts for any Performance Week of Regular Performances, occurring after the Performance Week in which the costs of presenting such Company have been Recouped, do not exceed 115% of Weekly Breakeven, Author's Royalty for such week, in lieu of Royalties otherwise payable, shall be comprised of a fixed Royalty of $3,000 per Full Performance Week, plus a percentage Royalty equal to 35% of Weekly Profits, if any, for such week; *provided, however,* in no event shall Author's fixed and percentage Royalty exceed a sum equal to 6% of the Gross Weekly

Box Office Receipts for such week. Notwithstanding the foregoing sentence, if the Director of the Play receives for any such week a royalty which is less than the full royalties payable pursuant to the Director's agreement with Producer, then Author's percentage Royalty described in the preceding calculation shall, for such week, be reduced, on a pro-rata basis, from 35% of such Weekly Profits (but in no event to less than 25% of Weekly Profits), with the other provisions of such calculation remaining unchanged.

SECTION 5.07 **Adjustments for Touring Performances**. With respect to each Company presenting Touring Performances of the Play, the Royalties payable to Author for such Touring Performances shall be subject to adjustment in the following manner:

(a) *Pre-Recoupment*—If the Gross Weekly Box Office Receipts for any Performance Week of Touring Performances, occurring at any time prior to and including the Performance Week in which the costs of presenting the Touring Company have been Recouped, do not exceed 110% of Weekly Breakeven for such Touring Company, Author's Royalty for such week, in lieu of the Royalties otherwise payable, shall be comprised of a fixed Royalty of $3,000 per Full Performance Week, plus a percentage Royalty equal to 25% of the Weekly Profits, if any, for such week; *provided, however,* in no event shall Author's fixed and percentage Royalty exceed a sum equal to 4.5% of the Gross Weekly Box Office Receipts for such week.

(b) *Post-Recoupment*—If the Gross Weekly Box Office Receipts for any Performance Week of Touring Performances, occurring after the Performance Week in which the costs of presenting the Touring Company have been Recouped, do not exceed 115% of Weekly Breakeven for such Touring Company, Author's Royalty for such week, in lieu of Royalties otherwise payable, shall be comprised of a fixed Royalty of $3,000 per Full Performance Week, plus a percentage Royalty equal to 35% of the Weekly Profits, if any, for such week; *provided, however,* in no event shall Author's fixed and percentage Royalty exceed a sum equal to 6% of the Gross Weekly Box Office Receipts for such week. Notwithstanding the foregoing sentence, if the Director of the Play receives for any such week a royalty which is less than the full royalties payable pursuant to the Director's agreement with Producer, then Author's percentage Royalty described in the preceding calculation shall, for such week, be reduced, on a pro-rata basis, from 35% of such Weekly Profits (but in no event to less than 25% of Weekly Profits), with the other provisions of such calculation remaining unchanged.

SECTION 5.08 **Adjustments for Losing Weeks**. If any Company has Weekly Losses in any week of Regular or Touring Performances, Author's Royalty for performances by such Company for such Losing Week shall, in lieu of Royalties otherwise payable, be $3,000 per Full Performance Week.

SECTION 5.09 **Review of Weekly Breakeven and Recoupment Calculation**. Should either Author or Producer wish to challenge the accountant's determination of Weekly Breakeven or Recoupment, the challenging party, upon notice to the other party, shall, in lieu of commencing in arbitration proceeding, present the matter, in writing, for resolution to the Theatrical Conciliation Council, whose decision shall he advisory in nature. After receiving such decision, either party may bring the matter to arbitration as provided in ARTICLE XX herein.

SECTION 5.10 **Yearly Royalty Adjustment**. For a period of 4 consecutive Performance Weeks occurring during the months of December and/or January wherein one such Performance Week is the week in which Christmas occurs (*"Christmas Period"*), Producer may, provided he gives written notice to Author on or before December 1 of each such year, specifying which 4 consecutive Performance Weeks will constitute the Christmas Period for that year, adjust Author's Royalties otherwise payable in the following manner:

(a) *Pre-Recoupment*—The aggregate Weekly Losses incurred in up to 3 Losing Weeks, if any, occurring during such Christmas Period may be deducted from the Gross Weekly Box Office Receipts earned during any one Performance Week during such Christmas Period.

(b) *Post-Recoupment*—Author's Royalty for all 4 Performance Weeks during such Christmas Period may be calculated by separately aggregating the Gross Weekly Box Office Receipts for such weeks and the Weekly Breakeven for such weeks and then dividing each of those two sums by 4. The resulting amounts shall be treated as if they were the Gross Weekly Box Office Receipts and Weekly Breakeven for a single week. The Author's applicable post-Recoupment Royalty (which would otherwise be payable, without reference to this SECTION, after taking into account any other appropriate Royalty Adjustments set forth in this ARTICLE) shall be calculated based on such amounts and then multiplied by 4 to determine the Author's Royalty for the entire Christmas Period.

(c) The foregoing calculations shall be made and adjusted Royalties for such Christmas Period shall be paid within 7 days following the end of the last Performance Week during the Christmas Period. During the Christmas Period, Producer shall pay Author $3,000 for each Full Performance Week as an advance against the adjusted Royalties payable for such Christmas Period.

(d) The provisions of this SECTION may be applied by Producer in one or more years and to any or all (or none) of the Companies presenting the Play and Producer may choose a different Christmas Period for each Company; provided, however, that if Producer chooses to apply this Royalty Adjustment provision to a Company presenting Touring Performances, all performances by such Company during the applicable Christmas Period must be presented in one theatre.

(e) If any Company attains Recoupment during a Christmas Period, then Producer must, with respect to such Company, calculate Author's Royalties for the entire Period either on the basis of SECTION 5.10(b) or without reference to this SECTION, as Producer, in his sole discretion, may decide.

(f) The provisions of this SECTION shall not apply to Fixed-Fee Performances.

SECTION 5.11 **Pro-rata Adjustment for Fixed Royalties.** In any instance in which this Contract provides that Royalties payable to Author for a given Full Performance Week of a Company are to be, in whole or in part, a fixed-dollar amount, and if fewer than 8 performances of the Play are presented by such Company during such week, then the fixed-dollar Royalties otherwise payable to Author hereunder shall be reduced by an amount equal to one-eighth of such fixed-dollar Royalties for each performance of the Play, fewer than 8, given in any such Performance Week.

SECTION 5.12 **Pro-rata Adjustment for Repertoire Performances**. If the Play is to be presented in repertoire with one or more other plays, Author and Producer shall agree on the method in which Author's Royalties shall be prorated and such method shall be set forth in ARTICLE XXII herein.

SECTION 5.13 **Proportionate Adjustment in Producer's Royalty.** (a) Regardless of the amount of royalties received by Producer for any week of performances, for the purposes of calculating Recoupment and Weekly Breakeven, "***Producer's Royalty***" shall be deemed to be limited to the following amounts but may not be deemed to be less than $1,500:

Producer's Royalty shall be calculated in the following manner:

(i) divide the amount of Royalties earned by Author for such week by an amount equal to 6% of the Gross Weekly Box Office Receipts for such week, then

(ii) multiply that amount by an amount equal to the lesser of:

(A) 3% of the Gross Weekly Box Office Receipts for such week or

(B) the amount of royalties (but not the cash office charge) payable to Producer for such week as set forth in the documents used in connection with the financing of the Play.

(b) For the purposes of the calculation described in SECTION 5.13(a) herein, the amount of Royalties earned by Author shall be the full amount of Royalties otherwise payable to Author prior to the deduction of any Advance or Option Payments as permitted by this Contract.

(c) If Producer presents Off-Broadway Performances of the Play pursuant to the terms of SECTION 9.02 herein, then in making this adjustment for such performances, Author's 6% Royalty referred to in SECTION 5.13(a)(i) shall be Author's post-Recoupment Off-Broadway Royalty set forth in ARTICLE XXII herein.

SECTION 5.14 **Pro-rata Adjustment of Weekly Breakeven.** If more than one Royalty calculation is applicable for performances presented in any Performance Week and one such calculation is to be made based on Weekly Profits or Weekly Losses (for example, if there are both Touring Performances and Fixed-Fee Performances presented in one Performance Week), the determination of the amount of such profits or losses to be allocated to such performances shall be made in the following manner: the amount of Weekly Breakeven applicable to such calculation shall be the actual Weekly Breakeven for the entire Performance Week, prorated, based on the ratio that the number of performances to which the Weekly Profits or Losses calculation is to be applied bears to the total number of performances presented during such Performance Week; and the amount of Gross Weekly Box Office Receipts used in calculating the profits or losses shall be only those receipts earned for the performances as to which the Weekly Profits or Losses calculation applies.

ARTICLE VI
Deductions from Advance and Royalty Payments

SECTION 6.01 **Deductions from Advances**. (a) Option Payments made for all but the First Option Period shall be deducted from the Advance Payments otherwise payable to Author.

(b) If a third party has previously produced the Play in the Territory as a Developmental Production or as other non-First-Class Performances and if Producer is required to make any payment to such third party in order to acquire all of the rights in the Play contemplated by this APC then, to the extent that such sums are included as Production Costs, Producer shall deduct from the Advance Payments otherwise payable to Author so much of such sums as equal the aggregate of all monies directly or indirectly paid to Author for such prior production (less customary per-diem and transportation expenses), but in no event more than the sums paid by Producer to such third party. Author and such third party shall give Producer a complete and accurate statement, signed by both Author and such third party, setting forth all monies paid to Author in connection with such prior production. The total sums payable by Producer to such third party and deductible from Author's Advance Payments shall be set forth in *ARTICLE XXII* herein.

SECTION 6.02 **Deductions from Royalties**. (a) All Option and Advance Payments received by Author may be deducted from Royalties earned by Author from any or all Companies presenting the Play, at the rate of up to 50% of such Royalties per Performance Week, commencing for the Performance Week in which such Company has reached Recoupment.

(b) The foregoing deductions shall be permitted only in such amounts as will not cause Author to earn, for any week in which such deductions are made, Royalties of less than $3,000 per Full Performance Week.

ARTICLE VII
General Payment Provisions

SECTION 7.01 **Royalty Due Dates/Box Office Statements**. (a) The portion of any Gross Weekly Box Office Receipts or Weekly Profits due to Author shall belong to Author and shall be held in trust by Producer as Author's property until payment. The trust nature of such funds shall not be questioned, whether the monies are physically segregated or not, In the event of breach of trust hereunder, Author may, at his option, pursue his remedies at law or in equity in lieu of the arbitration procedure established by this Contract.

(b) Within 7 days after the end of each Performance Week, Producer shall send to the Guild for Author's account, the amount due as Author's Royalties for such week, together with the daily box-office statements (for each person comprising Author) of each performance of the Play during such week, signed by the treasurer or treasurers of the theatre in which the performances are given and signed by Producer or Producer's duly authorized representative.

(c) Box-office statements and payments due for performances, in the United States, presented more than 500 miles from New York City shall be sent within 14 days after the end of each Performance Week, and for performances presented in Canada or in any location outside the Territory, within 21 days after the end of each such week, unless such payments are delayed or blocked due to the action or inaction of government authorities, in which case the payments shall be made as soon thereafter as possible.

(d) In cases where Author's compensation depends on the calculation of Weekly Breakeven of Weekly Profits, weekly operating statements shall be sent to the Guild (for each person comprising Author), at the same time Author's check is due.

(e) Producer shall also send to the Guild the actual production expense statements provided to investors as well as the periodic accounting reports as prepared by the accountant for the production.

(f) All reports and statements sent to the Guild pursuant to this ARTICLE shall be held confidential by Author, the Guild, and any Author's representative.

(g) Notwithstanding the provisions of SECTION 7.01(c) herein, Royalties for performances of the Play given in repertoire with one or more other plays shall be sent no later than 4 days after the end of every 4 Performance Weeks during which the Play is so performed, regardless of the number of performances presented.

SECTION 7.02 **Method of Payment**. All checks shall be sent to the Guild. Checks for payments due under ARTICLES II and IX herein shall be drawn to the order of the Guild. All other checks shall be drawn to the order of Author or, where Author indicates in writing to Producer and the Guild that Author is represented by an agent who is a member in good standing of the Society of Author's Representatives, Inc., then to the agent.

SECTION 7.03 **Separate Calculations**. If the Play is presented simultaneously by more than one Company, Royalties accruing from each Company shall be computed and paid separately.

SECTION 7.04 **Author's Division of Payments**. If Author is comprised of more than one person, all sums set forth herein as being payable to Author represent the aggregate of all amounts payable to all persons comprising Author. Subject to the provisions of SECTION 8.20 herein, such aggregate sums shall be divided equally unless otherwise provided in ARTICLE XXII herein.

SECTION 7.05 **Adaptor's Compensation**. If the Play is an English language adaptation made from a foreign language play or from other literary property, and if the adaptor is not the English language Bookwriter, then notwithstanding the provisions of SECTION 1.05 herein, the adaptor shall not be deemed to be one of the persons comprising Author and neither the adaptor nor the author of the foreign language play or other literary property shall receive any portion of Author's Royalty hereunder.

SECTION 7.06 **Deductions**. No deductions shall be made from compensation due by Author to Producer on account of a debt due by Author to Producer unless an agreement in writing providing therefor shall have been made between Author and Producer and filed with the Guild; except, however, that such deduction may be made if it is less than $200 and a memorandum, signed or initialed by Author acknowledging his indebtedness, and receipted by Producer or his representative, accompanies the statement for the week in which the deduction is made.

ARTICLE VIII

General Production Provisions

SECTION 8.01 **Producer's Undertaking**. Producer, recognizing that the Play is the artistic creation of Author and that as such Author is entitled to protect the type and nature of the production of Author's creation, hereby agrees:

(a) Under his own management to rehearse, present and continue to present the Play, with a cast, director, scenic, lighting, costume and, where appropriate, sound designer, conductor, choreographer and/or dance director mutually agreeable to Producer and to Author, and to announce the name of Author as sole Author of the book, music and lyrics of the Play upon all programs and in all advertising matter in accordance with the terms of SECTION 8.10 herein. Any change in the cast or any replacement of a director, conductor, choreographer and/or dance director shall likewise be subject to the mutual consent of the parties. Author may designate another person to act on his behalf with respect to such approvals and appointments. If Author is not available for consultation in the United States (or wherever else the Play is being produced), the provisions of this SECTION shall not apply unless Author shall have designated another person to act on his behalf who is available for consultation where the Play is being produced.

(b) To rehearse, produce, present and continue to present the Play, including Touring Performances thereof, with neither Author nor Producer making or causing to be made any addition, omission or alteration in the book, music, lyrics or title of the Play as contracted for production without the consent of both Producer and only the Author of the affected portion of the Play (i.e., Bookwriter, Composer, or Lyricist), with any change in the title requiring approval of a majority of Bookwriter, Composer and Lyricist. Producer warrants that any change of any kind whatsoever in the manuscript, title, stage business or performance of the Play made by Producer or any third party and which is acceptable to Author shall be the property of the Bookwriter, Composer or Lyricist, as the case may be. Producer shall cause to be prepared, executed and delivered to Author, not later than the Official Press Opening in New York City, such documents as may be necessary to transfer to Author all rights in any such changes in the manuscript or title of the Play; however, Producer shall not be responsible to deliver documents to Author for any materials or changes solicited by Bookwriter, Composer, or Lyricist from any third party. Neither Bookwriter, Composer nor Lyricist shall not be obligated to make payment to any person suggesting or making any such changes unless he has entered into a bona fide written agreement to do so; similarly, Producer shall not be required to make payment to any person solicited by Bookwriter, Composer or Lyricist to suggest or make changes unless Producer has entered into a bona fide written agreement to do so. Subject to SECTION 8.16 herein, Author shall, without any obligation to Producer, be entitled to use any parts of the Play omitted.

(c) Producer may complain to the Guild that Author is unreasonable in refusing to make changes or additions. In such event the Guild shall appoint a representative or representatives and, if they so advise, shall lend its best efforts to prevail upon Author to make the suggested changes, it being understood, however, that the Guild shall have no power to compel Author to agree to such changes.

SECTION 8.02 **Author's Right to Attend Rehearsals/Author's Availability**. (a) Author shall have the right to attend all rehearsals and performances of the Play prior to the Official Press Opening in New York City.

(b) Author shall use all best efforts to be available one month ahead of scheduled rehearsal dates to perform the services required pursuant to the terms of this Contract.

SECTION 8.03 **Author's Exercise of Approval Rights**. (a) Where the approval or consent of Author is required, the Bookwriter, Composer and Lyricist of the Play shall vote as 3 separate units (regardless of the number of persons constituting each such unit), with each unit having one vote and with a majority of such votes controlling, unless otherwise provided in ARTICLE XXII herein. Where the approval or consent of Author is required anywhere in this Contract, and such persons cannot agree, the President of the Guild shall, upon the request of Producer or any person comprising Author, appoint a single arbitrator to pass on such unresolved disagreements.

(b) If, after the Play has been presented for at least 3 weeks in New York City, Producer, because of some emergency, requests the approval of Author to make changes or replacements as provided in SECTION 8.01 herein and Producer is unable to obtain any response from Bookwriter, Composer or Lyricist, within 72 hours after requesting same, then the right to vote of such person failing to timely respond shall be forfeit and the votes of the others shall control.

SECTION 8.04 **Expenses**. (a) Producer shall reimburse Author for such hotel and travel expenses as Author may incur in making trips to attend rehearsals and up to 12 weeks of Out-of-Town Performances and the Official Press Opening in New York City, and at any other time when the presence of Author is required by Producer.

(b) In addition to the expenses to be reimbursed pursuant to SECTION 8.04(a) herein, if Bookwriter, Composer or Lyricist is a resident of the City of New York, Producer shall reimburse such person for such local travel expenses as such person may incur during the time when the Play is in rehearsal in New York City or being presented for Preview Performances, and shall also reimburse hotel expenses for an such persons who reside in the City of New York but outside of the Borough of Manhattan, if such expenses are reasonably necessary due to Producer's rehearsal or production schedule.

(c) Unless specific dollar amounts are provided in ARTICLE XXII herein, the amounts reimbursable by Producer under this SECTION shall be the cost of reasonable hotel and travel accommodations. In any event, Author's hotel and travel accommodations shall be of a class equal to the greater of the class charged to the Company by Producer or Director.

(d) If Author is unavailable and designates another person to act on his behalf in connection with the consultations set forth in SECTION 8.01(a) herein, Author and Producer may agree in ARTICLE XXII to specify the extent to which such designee's expenses may be reimbursed, if at all.

SECTION 8.05 **Copying Expenses**. Producer shall pay all costs incurred in making copies of the Play and any revisions thereof prior to the Official Press Opening in New York City and shall use best efforts to provide facilities, in or near any theatre in which the Play is presented, for the purpose of copying Author's revisions of the Play.

SECTION 8.06 **Designs**. Pursuant to the rules and regulations of the United Scenic Artists Local 829, Author undertakes and agrees that Author will not sell, lease, license or authorize the use of any of the original designs of scenery, lighting or costumes created by the designers, without the written consent of the owner of such designs.

SECTION 8.07 **Artwork**. If Producer owns the artwork and/or logo for the production of the Play, Producer grants to Author the right to use such artwork and logo in connection with Author's exploitation of the Play (but not for the purpose of creating Commercial Use Products as defined in SECTION 11.01 herein), subject to all restrictions which may exist in connection with such uses and subject to all payments which must be made to any third party, which payments shall not be the responsibility of Producer. Author shall not use or grant to others the right to use such artwork and logo without first giving Producer 60 days' prior written notice. Author shall indemnify Producer for any liability which may arise in connection with any such use.

SECTION 8.08 **Production Script**. Prior to the last performance of the Play under this Contract or prior to one month after the Official Press Opening in New York City, whichever is earlier, Producer shall deliver to Author or Author's representative, as Author's property, a neat and legible script of the Play, as currently presented.

SECTION 8.09 **Rights to Promote**. Author hereby grants to Pro-ducer and Producer's licensees and permitted assigns, the right to use the names of

Bookwriter, Composer and Lyricist, and each of their biographies, photographs, likeness or recorded voice (referred to in this SECTION as "materials"), and the title of and excerpts from the Play for advertising, press and promotional purposes by any means or medium. Producer shall submit to Bookwriter, Composer and Lyricist, for approval, all materials which Producer intends to use. If Bookwriter, Composer and Lyricist does not advise Producer, within 72 hours of receipt of the materials, of desired changes therein, the material shall be deemed approved as submitted by Producer. Producer shall include Author's biography in all programs used by Producer in which any other biography appears.

SECTION 8.10 **Author's Billing**. (a) Author shall receive billing credit whenever Producer or Director is accorded billing credit; provided, however, with respect to ABC listings and "teaser" advertisements, radio and television advertisements and marquees, billing credit may be accorded to any one or more of Producer, Author or Director without according billing credit to the other(s), if such person(s) has achieved a level of prominence greater than those not receiving billing credit and such that the use of the name(s) of the person(s) excluded would not enhance the commercial value of the Play. If Producer and Author are unable to agree, then, upon the written request of Producer, the determination of whether such level of prominence has been achieved shall be made by a theatrical press agent designated by the Theatrical Conciliation Council. Such determination must be made prior to the publication of such credits. The designation of the press agent and such agent's determination shall be final and binding on the parties hereto.

(b) Author's billing shall be on one or more separate lines beneath the title of the Play. It shall be in a type size no less than 40% of the type size used for the title of the Play (other than logo titles); *provided, however*, if the title of the Play appears more than once in any one advertisement, the placement and size of Author's billing shall be in relation to the title where used in closest proximity to the billing accorded to others involved in the Play. In no event shall Author's billing be smaller than the type size used for the billing accorded to Director and/or Producer (except where Producer's name appears as part of the name of the theatre).

(c) Author and Producer may supplement the provisions of SECTION 8.10(b) in ARTICLE XXII herein but shall not modify or supplement in any way the provisions of SECTION 8.10(a) herein.

SECTION 8.11 **Radio and Television Publicizing**. Producer shall have the right to authorize one or more radio and/or television excerpts of or based on the Play, not exceeding 12 minutes each, for the purpose of exploiting and publicizing the theatre industry, performances of the Play, any person performing in the Play and for use on awards programs, without any additional approval by or payment to Author, provided Producer receives no compensation therefrom other than reimbursement of out-of-pocket expenses; however, Author shall have approval of any change in the book, music or lyrics made in an excerpt produced under the control of Producer.

SECTION 8.12 **Producer's Credit**. (a) If Producer has presented the Play for its Official Press Opening, Author shall use all best efforts to require that Producer receive conspicuously placed billing credit in the following circumstances:

>   (i)   if all or any portion of the Play is published, the credit shall appear on a page preceding the first page of the text of the Play;

>   (ii) if a motion picture or television production is produced based on the Play, the credit shall appear on the screen separately with no other credit; and

>   (iii) in the case of any Revival, Stock, Amateur or Ancillary Performances, as those terms are defined in SECTION 11.01 herein, the credit shall appear on the first page of credits in all programs used therefor.

>   (b)   The credit referred to above shall contain the name(s) of Producer and co-producers, if any, and shall state that the Play was originally produced by them. The order, title and relative size and spacing of the names of Producer (and co-producers, if any) shall be identical to the billing contained in the program for the Play at the time of the Official Press Opening.

>   (c)   No casual or inadvertent failure to comply with the provisions of this SECTION shall be deemed a breach of this Contract unless such failure can, but shall not, be rectified as soon as practicable.

SECTION 8.13 **Approval of Use of Producers' Names**. Producer shall not use the name of any other person, firm or corporation as a producer of the Play unless Author has consented in writing.

SECTION 8.14 **House Seat Records**. If Author receives an alloca-tion of house seats pursuant to ARTICLE XXII herein, Author agrees to maintain a true, complete and accurate record, in accordance with the requirements of the Arts and Cultural Affairs Law of the State of New York and the regulations promulgated thereunder, of Author's disposi-tion of such house seats. Author agrees not to dispose of such house seats at a price above the regular box-office prices for such tickets.

SECTION 8.15 **Debt by Author**. If Author is indebted to the Guild or to Producer, the Guild my file with the Negotiator (as described in ARTICLE XII herein) a memorandum to that effect, and the Negotiator shall thereupon withhold from Author's share of income held by the Negotiator, the amount of such indebtedness and shall pay the same over to the Guild and/or Pro-ducer as their interests may appear. The foregoing shall not limit Producer's rights to pursue other remedies in connection with the collection of any indebtedness.

SECTION 8.16 **Revue Sketches**. (a) Any sketch or number of a revue and any song or musical number in the Play which shall not have been used on the Official Press Opening in New York or within 3 weeks thereafter, or having been so used shall be omitted from the Play for 3 successive consecutive Performance Weeks, may be withdrawn by Author and used by him for any purpose, free of any claim by Producer, subject only to such financial interest in additional uses as Producer may theretofore have acquired.

(b) If a sketch, song or other contribution of one or more persons constituting Author is omitted from a condensed or tabloid version of the Play, then such person whose work is so omitted shall nevertheless share in the proceeds from such version, provided his contribution shall have been included in at least one-half of the then prior performances of the Play. In such case, each such person shall share in the proceeds of the condensed or tabloid version in the same proportion that his original compensation hereunder bears to the total compensation due hereunder to all persons constituting Author.

Section 8.17 **Cast Albums**. (a) Producer and Author may agree, in ARTICLE XXII herein, on the terms regarding the creation of Cast Albums. For the purposes of this Contract, the term "**Cast Albums**" shall mean all audio recordings of the Play (or any portion thereof) performed by the cast of any production that is presented by or under lease or license from Producer. Author and Producer shall calculate and share, in perpetuity, the proceeds (other than amounts advanced by record companies for the creation of the album or for investment in the Play) received from the worldwide exploitation of such Cast Albums in the manner set forth in ARTICLE XXII herein, but in no event shall Author receive less than 60% and Producer less than 40% of such proceeds and in no event shall Producer's share of such proceeds be included in the calculation of Recoupment hereunder.

(b) If Producer in *ARTICLE XXII* acquires the rights to create Cast Albums but does not produce or license a production of the Play in the British Isles, Australia or New Zealand pursuant to the provisions of *ARTICLE IX* herein, then Author, without any financial obligation to Producer, shall be free to authorize a record company, other than the record company designated for the original cast album, to record the cast album in such area except that prior to entering into such an agreement, Author will give the record company that records the original cast album, written notice of the terms of the proposed agreement and such record company shall have 30 days within which to match the monetary terms of such other offer.

Section 8.18 **Music Publishing Rights**. Author and Producer may agree, in ARTICLE XXII herein, on certain terms regarding the disposition of the various music publishing rights in the music and lyrics of the Play.

Section 8.19 **Musical Scores**. Producer shall in the first instance furnish all necessary orchestral scores, conductor's scores, orchestra parts and vocal parts ("**Scores**") at Producer's own expense. Subject to the provisions of the following sentence, Producer shall be the sole and exclusive owner of the physical Scores (as distinguished from the copyrights therein) and Producer may, subject to Author's copyrights in such Scores, sell, license, assign, rent or otherwise dispose of such Scores and retain any sums received therefrom, which sums shall not be counted in the calculation of Recoupment. Notwithstanding the foregoing, if Author elects to own the Scores, then such election shall be set forth in ARTICLE XXII herein and the following provisions shall apply:

(a) The Scores shall belong jointly to the Lyricist and Composer of the Play immediately upon delivery thereof to Producer. Such Scores may be used by the Lyricist and Composer at any time after the close of the First-Class Performances in the Territory, whether or not the deductions or payments referred to in this SECTION have been completed.

(b) The Composer and Lyricist alone shall have the right to contract for the publication of the music and lyrics of the Play or any part thereof, without prejudice to the right of Producer to arrange for separate payment to Producer by the music publisher. The Composer and Lyricist alone may permit the reproduction of the music and lyrics or any part thereof by discs or any other means or devices.

(c) Producer shall, at the request of the Composer and Lyricist, or the Guild, make available to the Guild as soon as feasible after the Official Press Opening in New York City, said Scores for the purpose of making a copy thereof. Upon the close of the run of each Company, Producer shall deliver to the Composer and Lyricist the complete Scores and prompt book; *provided, however,* that the Producer may make and retain a copy of such Scores and prompt book but not for use or sale.

(d) Producer may deduct from the Royalties otherwise payable to each of the Composer and Lyricist $500 in the aggregate in each Performance Week in which such deduction would not reduce the Royalties payable to Author to less than $4,500 for Out-of-Town and Preview Performances or less than $3,000 for all other performances hereunder, until a sum equal to 50% of the Producer's actual expenditure for the Scores shall have been recovered by Producer. Producer shall pay to the Guild the monies so deducted until there shall have been presented to the Guild evidence of Producer's actual expenditures for such Scores, whereupon the Guild shall pay Producer the monies held by it to the extent of 50% of such actual expenditures. The deductions so made, unless otherwise agreed upon, shall be borne by the Composer and Lyricist according to their respective percentages of compensation.

(e) The Composer and Lyricist may at their option pay outright to the Producer at any time a sum equal to 50% of Producer's expenditures for such Scores or such remaining balance thereof as may then be unpaid.

Section 8.20 **Additional Collaboration**. This SECTION shall apply only in the case of a musical adapted from a book, play, motion picture or other underlying copyrighted work written by someone other than Producer and in which Producer, prior to the engagement of the Bookwriter, Composer and Lyricist, acquires an option on or owns the rights to adapt such underlying work for the musical stage.

(a) **Replacement Before First Rehearsal**—After delivery of any draft of the Play, but prior to the first full cast rehearsal, Producer may reject any component, i.e., book, music or lyrics or, if the author of such component is comprised of more than one person, then all or any part of the component written by such person(s) (the "**rejected component**"). The rejection of any such component is subject to the approval of any remaining authors. Upon such rejection:

    (i)   the author of the rejected component shall be entitled to retain the amount of the Option paid or payable to him hereunder as of the date of rejection, but will not be entitled to any additional Option Payments which might otherwise become payable after the date of rejection. All rights and material contributed by such author shall revert to him, except that he may not use any such material in a manner that would infringe upon or otherwise violate the rights of Producer or of the authors of the underlying work or of the other components of the Play, and he shall not receive billing credit, Royalties or Subsidiary Rights income in connection with any presentation of the Play.

    (ii)   Producer may not use any part of the rejected component but may enter into an APC with a replacement author, acceptable to the remaining authors, if any, to write new material for the component.

    (iii)   Should a dispute arise as to whether Producer is using any part of the rejected component, such dispute shall be submitted for resolution to the Theatrical Conciliation Council whose decision shall be final and binding.

(b) **Replacement During Rehearsal but Before First Paid Public Performance**—From the first day of full cast rehearsal until the day prior to the first paid public First-Class Performance of the Play hereunder, Producer may reject a component and enter into an APC with a replacement author for such rejected component, subject to the approval of all the remaining authors. Such approval will be deemed granted by any remaining author who fails to communicate with Producer regarding such approvals within 3 days after receiving written notice from Producer of the proposed change. If an APC is entered into with a new author, Producer shall retain all rights under this Contract to use any part of the rejected component and the following shall apply:

(i) The replaced author shall retain all Option and Advance Payments paid or owing at the date of rejection but shall not be entitled to any additional Advance Payments which might otherwise become payable after the date of rejection. The replaced author shall also receive 1/2 of such author's share of the Royalties and Subsidiary Rights income and all other sums otherwise payable under this Contract. Such author shall retain his ownership interest in the Play and in all copyrights and other rights therein and thereto, except that he shall not be entitled to exercise any control over, nor to participate in any decisions with respect to, their exploitation.

(ii) Any Royalty, share of Subsidiary Rights income or other sums payable to the new author shall not reduce the amounts payable to the remaining co-authors, if any.

(iii) The new author shall receive billing credit if he chooses to accept it. Any dispute regarding the substance or existence of billing for the replaced author shall be submitted to arbitration as provided in ARTICLE XX herein.

(c) **Replacement From the First Paid Public First-Class Performance Until the Day Prior to the Official Press Opening in New York City** — From and after the first paid public First-Class Performance of the Play hereunder until the day prior to the Official Press Opening in New York City, Producer may reject a component and enter into an APC with a replacement author for such rejected component, subject to the approval of all the remaining authors. Such approval will be deemed granted by any remaining author who fails to communicate with Producer regarding such approvals within one day after receiving written notice from Producer of the proposed change. If an APC is entered into with a new author, Producer shall retain all rights under this Contract to use any part of the rejected component and the following shall apply:

(i) The replaced author shall receive his full share of the Option and Advance Payments, Royalties and Subsidiary Rights income otherwise payable under this Contract, subject to SECTION 8.20(c)(iii) herein. Such author also shall retain his ownership interest in the Play and in all copyrights and other rights therein and thereto, without the restrictions described in SECTION 8.20(b)(i) herein.

(ii) Subject to SECTION 8.20(c)(iii) herein, any Royalty or other sum payable to the new author shall not reduce the amounts payable to the remaining co-authors, if any.

(iii) The new author's share of Subsidiary Rights income, to the extent it does not exceed one-sixth of Author's total Subsidiary Rights compensation, shall be borne by the original Author (including the replaced author) and by Producer in the same ratio as Author and Producer share such compensation hereunder. Any amount by which the new author's share of Subsidiary Rights compensation exceeds one-sixth of the Author's total Subsidiary Rights compensation shall be borne by Producer.

(iv) The replaced author shall receive his contracted-for billing credit if he chooses to accept it. The new author shall be entitled to such billing credit as he and Producer shall agree, subject to the replaced author's contractual rights.

(d) **Author of Multiple Components/Multiple Authors of One Component**.

(i) If the author of a rejected component is also the author of any other non-rejected component, the provisions of this SECTION shall apply to the author as if he were not the author of the non-rejected component, and all Option, Advance, and Royalty Payments, Subsidiary Rights and all other sums otherwise payable to author for all components written by him shall be deemed to be allocated equally between or among such components in making the calculations referred to in this SECTION.

(ii) If there are multiple authors of a component and Producer rejects one such author (with the approval of the other authors), the provisions of this SECTION shall apply only to the rejected author of such part and all of the Option, Advance, and Royalty Payments,

Subsidiary Rights and all other sums payable to the authors of such component, as a whole, shall be deemed to be allocated equally between or among such authors, unless otherwise provided in ARTICLE XXII herein, in making the calculations referred to in this SECTION.

(e) **Royalty Payments to New Author**—The rejection and subsequent addition of any new author shall neither reduce the aggregate Royalties payable pursuant to *ARTICLES IV* and *V* herein nor increase that portion of such Royalties payable to the new author beyond the amount of such Royalties which were payable to the replaced author.

Section 8.21 **Deleted Music and Lyrics**. Unless otherwise specified in ARTICLE XXII herein, all rights in and to any music and lyrics which shall be deleted from the Play prior to the Official Press Opening in New York City shall revert to the Composer and Lyricist, respectively, for their use, free from any claim by the Producer provided, however, that the Composer and Lyricist shall not have any right to use or authorize the use of any such lyrics which (a) refer to any character in the Play by the same name as the Character in the Play if the name is sufficiently distinctive to identify with the Play or (b) depict or portray an important situation which is contained in the Play or (c) contain any of the distinctive dialogue or distinctive phrases from the Play or (d) have as their title the name of any character in, or the title of the Play if such name is sufficiently distinctive to identify with the Play. If any such compositions are included in any agreement for an Audio-Visual Production of the Play, the Composer and Lyricist shall not be entitled to any larger additional compensation by reason thereof and the Producer's share of the income therefrom shall not be diminished.

ARTICLE IX
Additional Production Rights

SECTION 9.01 **Grant of Second-Class Performance Rights**. (a) Author hereby grants Producer the sole and exclusive rights to produce one or more Second-Class Performances of the Play on the speaking stage in the Territory during the time that Producer continues to have rights to present the Play hereunder. For the purposes of this Contract, the term "*Second-Class Performance*" shall mean all performances of the Play other than Stock, Amateur and Ancillary Performances (as those terms are defined in SECTION

11.01 herein), Off-Broadway Performances (as defined in SECTION 9.02 herein), and First-Class Performances and Developmental (i.e., "workshop") Productions.

    (b) Author's Royalties for Second-Class Performances shall be calculated and paid in the manner set forth in SECTION 4.02(d) herein with respect to Touring Performances, unless Author's Royalty is calculated in whole or in part on the basis of a fixed fee payable to Producer, in which case the Royalty shall be calculated and paid in the manner set forth for Fixed-Fee Performances.

    SECTION 9.02 **Grant of Off-Broadway Performance Rights**. (a) Author hereby grants Producer the sole and exclusive rights to produce one or more Off-Broadway Performances of the Play during the time that Producer continues to have rights to present the Play hereunder. The foregoing grant is subject to the conditions precedent that Producer has Vested (as defined in SECTION 11.02 herein) in the Territory and that Producer is not simultaneously presenting any other performances of the Play in New York City. For the purposes of this Contract, the term *"Off-Broadway Performances"* shall mean performances of the Play in theatres which are classified as Off-Broadway pursuant to the Actors' Equity Association Agreement Governing Employment Off-Broadway, as that agreement may be amended from time to time.

    (b) Author's Royalties for Off-Broadway Performances shall be calculated and paid in the manner set forth in *ARTICLES IV* and *V* herein with respect to Touring Performances except that Author's post-Recoupment Royalties shall be such amount as may be agreed upon by Author and Producer and set forth in *ARTICLE XXII* herein, but in no event more than 7% of the Gross Weekly Box Office Receipts.

    SECTION 9.03 **Grant of Rights in the British Isles, Australia and New Zealand**. (a) Author hereby grants to Producer the sole and exclusive rights to produce one or more productions of the Play for a consecutive run, as theatrically understood, in a regular evening bill, in a first-class manner, in a first-class theatre, on the speaking stage in one or more of the following *"Additional Territories"*:

        (i) The United Kingdom of Great Britain (i.e., England, Northern Ireland, Scotland and Wales) and in Ireland (collectively the *"British Isles"*)

(ii) Australia

(iii) New Zealand

(b) The foregoing grant is subject to the conditions precedent that Producer has Vested in the Territory and is not in breach of any provision of this Contract.

(c) Producer's rights to present the Play in the Additional Territories shall include the right to present "tryout" performances prior to the presentation of the Play in the Additional Territory equivalent of first-class theatres.

(d) The terms of this Contract applicable to First-Class Performances in the Territory shall apply to performances of the Play in the British Isles except as may be provided to the contrary herein.

(e) If Producer chooses to produce the Play pursuant to a lease or license to a third party in Australia or New Zealand, Producer's rights shall be subject to the following procedure: Producer shall give Author written notice of the terms of any third party offer for the production of the Play in such Additional Territory. Producer may accept the offer unless Author shall, within 5 business days after receipt of Producer's notice, give Producer written notice, delivered either in person or by wire communication, that the offer is unacceptable, stating Author's reasons therefor, together with a definite offer from a third party, on terms at least as favorable to Producer as those contained in the offer which Producer is willing to accept. If within the prescribed period of time Author submits such an offer, Author may accept such offer. If within the prescribed period of time Author fails to submit such an offer, then Producer may accept the original offer. If the offer presented by Author is from a producer or other entity or person in which Author has any financial or other interest, or if a dispute arises as to whether such offer is at least as favorable to Producer as the offer which Producer obtained, or if any other dispute arises under this SECTION 9.03(e), the parties shall submit the matter to the Theatrical Conciliation Council for the purposes of (i) determining whether or not such offer is the result of good-faith arm's length negotiations, or (ii) determining whether the offer presented by Author is at least as favorable to Producer or (iii) resolving any other dispute, as the case may be. If the Council determines that the offer is the result of good-faith arm's length negotiations or is at least as favorable to Producer, as the case may be, then Author may accept such offer; however, if the Council determines that such offer is not the result of such negotiations, or is not at least as favorable to Producer, as the case may be, the offer presented by Producer shall be accepted. The decision of the Council in connection with any matter presented under this SECTION 9.03(e) shall be final and binding on the parties hereto.

SECTION 9.04 **Payments Required to Extend Rights in the Additional Territories**. The following provisions of this SECTION shall apply separately to each Additional Territory:

(a) Unless Producer presents the first paid public performance of the Play in an Additional Territory within 6 months after the close of First-Class Performances in New York City, Producer's rights to present the Play in such Additional Territory shall automatically terminate unless such rights are extended as provided in this SECTION.

(b) Producer shall be entitled to three consecutive 6-month exten-sions of such rights upon payment of $1,000 for the first extension, $1,500 for the second extension and $2,000 for the third extension, which payment must be made prior to the expiration of the rights period then in effect, *provided, however,* that for the third extension, Producer must give Author, simultaneously with the payment of $2,000, written notice of the intended date of the first paid public performance together with copies of documents representing one of the following:

(i) a commitment for the licensing of the Additional Territory equivalent of a first-class theatre, with occupancy to occur before the end of the third extension period or

(ii) contracts for the engagement of the principal members of the cast or the director, pursuant to which such person(s) agrees to render services before the end of the third extension period.

The extension of Producer's rights and option for the third extension period shall not be prevented or affected by the fact that any of these commitments or contracts may be made subject to conditions, such as the availability of a person or theatre, the attainment of full capitalization of the production, further negotiations regarding material terms, the execution of a formal agreement, or any other condition, or the fact that any of these commitments or contracts may later be breached or unenforceable.

SECTION 9.05 **Royalty Payments in the Additional Territories**. (a) Author's Royalties for performances of the Play in the British Isles shall be calculated and paid in accordance with the provision of ARTICLES IV and V applicable to Touring and Fixed-Fee Performances, except that all references to fixed dollar amounts in such ARTICLES shall be reduced to one-third of the stated amounts. Author's Royalties for performances in Australia and New Zealand shall be 6% of the Gross Weekly Box Office Receipts.

(b) The payments made pursuant to SECTION 9.04 herein for an Additional Territory may be deducted from the Royalties earned by Author from any Company presenting the Play in such Additional Territory at the rate of up to 50% of such Royalties per Performance Week commencing for the Performance Week in which such Company has reached Recoupment. Such deductions shall be permitted only in such amounts as will not cause Author to earn, for any week in which such deductions are made, Royalties of less than the foreign currency equivalent (at the time of payment) of $900 per Full Performance Week.

(c) Sums payable to Author in connection with Performances of the Play in any Additional Territory shall be paid after deduction of all withholding and other taxes due thereon pursuant to the laws of the applicable Additional Territory, all conversion and remittance costs applicable to such payments and all payments required to be made to any author's society or similar organizations. Producer shall not be liable for losses incurred due to fluctuations in the exchange rate.

(d) In addition to the Royalties payable pursuant to this SECTION, if Author earns in any Performance Week Royalties equal to less than 6% of the Gross Weekly Box Office Receipts for such week from productions in Australia or New Zealand, Producer shall, simultaneously with the payment of Author's Royalties for such week, pay to the Guild, on Author's behalf (for the benefit of Author's representatives), a sum equal to 10% of the difference between the amount of Author's

Royalties and a sum equal to 10% of the Gross Weekly Box Office Receipts.

SECTION 9.06 **Transfer of Rights to an Additional Territory Producer**. Provided Producer has complied with the provisions of SECTION 9.03(b) herein, Producer may produce the Play alone or in association with or under lease or license to an Additional Territory producer or manager, subject to Author's written consent. In such case, Producer's obligations to make the payments herein provided shall remain unimpaired. The contract between Producer and the Additional Territory producer or manager shall require the Play to be produced in the manner and on the terms provided herein with respect to productions in the Additional Territory.

SECTION 9.07 **Advances for Performances in the Additional Territories**. If the Play is produced in any Additional Territory in association with or under lease or license to an Additional Territory producer or manager pursuant to the provisions of this ARTICLE, and if, in connection therewith, Producer receives an advance payment applicable against royalties payable to Producer, or a lump sum in lieu of a portion of such royalties, Author shall receive 50% of such advance or lump sum as an advance against Royalties payable for such production. Author's share of the advance or lump sum received by Producer with respect to an Additional Territory may be deducted from the payments due pursuant to SECTION 9.05 herein with respect to such Additional Territory.

SECTION 9.08 **Author's Presence in the Additional Territories**. If the Play is presented in any Additional Territory by or under grant of rights from Producer, Author shall have the right to be present for up to 3 weeks in order to attend rehearsals, tryouts and the opening of the first production of the Play in such Additional Territory. Producer shall reimburse Author for hotel and travel expenses during such period and at any other time when the presence of Author is required by Producer. Unless specific dollar amounts are provided in ARTICLE XXII herein, the amounts reimbursable by Producer under this SECTION shall be the cost of reasonable hotel and travel accommodations. In any event, Author's hotel and travel accommodations shall be of a class equal to the greater of the class charged to the Company by Producer or Director.

SECTION 9.09 **Producer's Financial Participation in Additional Territory Uses**. (a) If the Play is not presented in any Additional Territory by or under grant of rights from Producer within the period set forth in SECTION

9.04 herein, then Author shall thereafter have the sole right to produce or authorize the production of the Play in any such Additional Territory in which Producer's rights have lapsed and, provided that Producer has Vested in the Territory and is not in breach of any provision of this Contract, Author shall pay Producer the following amounts:

    (i)   with respect to the British Isles, 25% of the compensation earned by Author (after deduction of agents' commissions, if any) regardless of when paid, in connection with each contract for the production of the Play (including any contracts for British Isles Subsidiary Rights, other than Media Productions in which Producer will have previously acquired a worldwide interest) entered into on or after the Effective Date of this Contract but prior to the expiration of 7 years from the date on which Producer has Vested in the Territory; provided, however, that with respect to each contract for the presentation of the British Isles equivalents of First or Second-Class Performances, Author shall pay Producer 10% of the compensation earned by Author (after deduction of agents' commissions, if any) regardless of when paid, in connection with each such contract entered into after said 7-year period or after the close of the first First-Class Performance in the British Isles, whichever first occurs, but before the expiration of 40 years from the date on which Producer Vested in the Territory; and

    (ii) with respect to Australia and New Zealand, 35% of the compensation earned by Author (after deduction of agents' commissions, if any) regardless of when paid, in connection with each contract for the production of the Play (including any contracts for Australian or New Zealand Subsidiary Rights, other than Media Productions in which Producer will have previously acquired a worldwide interest) entered into on or after the Effective Date of this Contract but prior to the expiration of 6 years from the date on which Producer has Vested in the Territory;

(b) If the Play has been presented in any Additional Territory by or under a grant of rights from Producer in accordance with the provisions of this ARTICLE and Producer has Vested in such Additional Territory and is not in breach of any provision of this Contract, Producer's financial interest in Author's compensation derived from the disposition of

Subsidiary Rights in such Additional Territory (other than Media Productions in which Producer will have previously acquired a worldwide interest), will be as follows:

(i) with respect to the British Isles, Producer will have the same financial interest in British Isles Subsidiary Rights as Producer has with respect to such Subsidiary Rights in the Territory, and the time periods described in the applicable Producer's Alternative (as defined in SECTION 11.03(c) herein) shall be measured from the last performance of the Play in the British Isles; and

(ii) with respect to Australia and New Zealand, Producer's financial interest in Australian and New Zealand Subsidiary Rights shall be equal to 40% of the compensation earned by Author (after deduction of agents' commissions, if any) regardless of when paid, in connection with each contract for the disposition of such Subsidiary Rights entered into on or after the Effective Date of this Contract but prior to the expiration of 7 years from the date on which Producer Vested in such Additional Territory or 4 years from the last performance of the Play in the Additional Territory, whichever is later.

SECTION 9.10 **Additional Rights to Present Backers' Auditions**. While Producer has the rights to present the Play hereunder, Producer shall also have the rights to present Backers' Auditions of the Play.

ARTICLE X
Reopening Rights

SECTION 10.01 **Reopenings in the Territory**. (a) Provided Producer has Vested in the Territory, Producer may, within 4 months after the last performance of the Play in the Territory, notify Author in writing of Producer's intention to reopen the Play in the Territory. In such case Producer may so reopen the Play within 12 months following such last performance; provided, however, that if the Play is not reopened within four months from such last performance, Producer must, in order to retain his right to reopen the Play, pay Author the following sums (as non-returnable advances against Royalties payable): $500 per month for up to four months, commencing with the fourth month following the last performance, and $1,000 per month for up to an additional four months.

(b) If Producer presents the Play in the Territory but closes the Play prior to having Vested, Producer may reopen the Play provided he gives the Author written notice, within 30 days after such closing, of Producer's intention to reopen the Play, pays Author $500 per month (as non-returnable advances against the Royalties payable), commencing one month following the closing until the Play has reopened, and commences rehearsals for such production no later than 3 months after the closing.

(c) All the provisions of this SECTION shall apply to each reopening in the Territory. Such reopenings may be First-Class, Second-Class or Off-Broadway Performances.

SECTION 10.02 **Reopenings in the Additional Territories.** (a) Provided Producer has Vested in the British Isles, Producer may, within 4 months after the close of the last performance in the British Isles, notify Author in writing of Producer's intention to reopen the Play in the British Isles. In such case Producer may reopen the Play in the British Isles, within 12 months following such last performance, in accordance with the provisions of SECTION 10.01(a) herein.

(b) If Producer presents the Play in the British Isles but closes the Play prior to having Vested in the British Isles, Producer may reopen the Play in the British Isles in accordance with the provisions of SECTION 10.01(b) herein.

(c) Provided Producer has Vested in Australia or New Zealand, Producer may retain the rights to reopen the Play in such Additional Territory upon paying Author (as non-returnable advances against the Royalties payable) $900 per month, for up to 6 months, commencing one month following the last performance in such Additional Territory. In no event may Producer reopen the Play after 7 years from the date on which Producer Vested in such Additional Territory.

(d) If Producer presents the Play in Australia or New Zealand but closes the Play prior to having Vested in such Additional Territory, Producer may reopen the Play in such Additional Territory in accordance with the provisions of SECTION 10.01(b) herein.

(e) All the provisions of this SECTION shall apply to each reopening of the Play in the applicable Additional Territory. Such reopenings must be the Additional Territory equivalent of First-Class Performances.

SECTION 10.03 **Closing**. Producer shall in each instance, immed-iately upon determining to close a run of the Play, give written notice thereof to Author.

ARTICLE XI
Subsidiary Rights

SECTION 11.01 **Definitions Relating to Subsidiary Rights**. For the purposes of this Contract, the term *"Subsidiary Rights"* shall mean those rights in the Play relating to the following methods of exploitation:

(a) *"Media Productions"*—shall mean Audio-Visual Productions (as defined below), and radio uses.

(b) *"Audio-Visual Productions"*— shall mean motion picture, television, video cassette and video disc productions, soundtrack albums, tapes and discs for all of the foregoing; and all other kinds of visual and audio-visual productions in connection with the Play, whether now existing or developed in the future. All of the foregoing shall be considered Audio-Visual Productions, regardless of the method or mode of reproduction, projection, transmission, exhibition, or delivery used, However, Audio-Visual Productions shall not include Foreign Local Television Productions. For the purposes of this Contract, the term *"Foreign Local Television Productions"* shall mean all television productions of the Play in a foreign language produced and distributed exclusively for television exhibition outside the Territory and the Additional Territories.

(c) *"Commercial Use Products"*—shall mean wearing apparel; toys; games; figures; dolls; novelties; books; souvenir programs; and any other physical property representing a character in the Play or using the name, character or the title of the Play or otherwise connected with the Play or its title.

(d) *"Stock Performances"* — shall mean all performances of the Play presented in the English language pursuant to one of the Actors' Equity Association agreements governing employment of actors in productions classified, pursuant to the terms of such agreements, as "stock," "resident theatre," "university resident theatre," "dinner theatre," or "guest artist contract" productions (and the equivalents of such performances outside the United States).

(e) *"Amateur Performances"* — shall mean all performances of the Play presented in the English language and using only non-professional actors (i.e., an actor who is not a member of a performing arts union or guild in the Territory or outside the Territory, as the case may be).

(f) *"Ancillary Performances"* — shall mean all performances of the Play presented in the English language as condensed and tabloid versions, so-called concert tour versions and opera versions based on the Play as well as foreign language performances of all kinds in the Territory or each Additional Territory, as the case may be, and performances of the Play pursuant to one of the Actors' Equity Association agreements governing employment of actors in productions classified pursuant to the terms of such agreements as: "theatre for young audiences," "small professional theatre," and "non-profit theatre code" productions (and their equivalents outside the United States).

(g) *"Revival Performances"* —

(i) In the City of New York — all First-Class, Second-Class and Off-Broadway Performances of the Play in the City of New York and all performances at Lincoln Center (regardless of how classified), presented after the expiration of Producer's rights to present the Play in the Territory; and

(ii) Outside the City of New York — all First and Second-Class Performances of the Play in the Territory, presented after the expiration of Producer's rights to present the Play in the Territory and presented outside the City of New York, provided that, with respect to each contract entered into for such production, the Play is presented in at least 3 cities throughout the Territory. Notwithstanding the foregoing, if any of such cities is the City of New York, the 3-city minimum shall automatically be waived. Until the Play is presented in the third city or in the City of New York, whichever first occurs, Author shall pay all sums due to Producer from such Revival Performances to the Guild, which shall hold such sums until the first presentation of the Play in the third city or the City of New York, whichever first occurs, and then pay such sums to Producer. No interest shall accrue to Producer's benefit on such sums held by the Guild.

(iii) In the Additional Territories—all performances of the Play in any of the Additional Territories (which are the Additional Territory equivalents of First or Second-Class Performances in the Territory), presented after the expiration of Producer's rights to present the Play in such Additional Territory.

(iv) Remakes, Prequels, Sequels and Spin-Offs—Revival Performances shall also include performances of all "remakes," "prequels" (i.e., stories which occur at an earlier point in time than the story in the Play), "sequels" and "spin-offs" of the Play produced in the manner described in SECTIONS 11.01(g)(i), (ii) and (iii) above.

SECTION 11.02 **Definition of Vested**. For the purposes of this Contract, the term "*Vested*" shall mean that Producer has presented the Play in one of the manners described below:

(a) With respect to the Territory, for the following number of consecutive (as customarily defined in the theatre industry) paid public First-Class Performances:

(i) 10 Preview Performances plus the Official Press Opening of the Play in New York City, or

(ii) 5 Preview Performances plus the Official Press Opening in New York City plus 5 Regular Performances, or

(iii) 5 Out-of-Town and 5 Preview Performances plus the Official Press Opening in New York City, provided there are no more than 42 days between the last Out-of-Town Performance and the first Preview Performance, or

(iv) 5 Preview Performances plus the Official Press Opening in New York City if the Play has been presented previously by someone other than Producer and is presented by Producer hereunder with substantially the same cast and scenic designs as existed in the prior presentation.

Each Preview Performance given in New York City within 10 days of the Official Press Opening in New York City (even though not consecutive) shall be considered a "consecutive" performance for the purpose of this paragraph, provided that the scale of box-office prices of each such Preview Performance is at least 65% of the scale of box-office prices announced for the Regular Performances and that each such Preview Performance is publicized in advance in the paid "ABC" listings of The New York Times and a similar listing in any other newspaper, magazine or other periodical of general circulation in the City of New York. Any Preview Performance given more than 10 days before the Official Press Opening shall not be considered a "consecutive" performance for the purpose of this paragraph.

(b) With respect to the Territory, for 64 consecutive paid public Out-of-Town Performances, whether or not the Play has its Official Press Opening in New York City, provided that breaks may be made in performances outside of New York City because of the necessities of travel so long as the 64 performances shall have been given within 80 days of the first performance.

(c) With respect to the Territory, for 64 consecutive Out-of-Town Performances in arenas or auditoriums if, because of the nature of the Play or the size or complexity of its contemplated production, the performance of the Play in a traditional first-class theatre would not be feasible or desirable. The same provisions of SECTION 11.02(b) shall apply in connection with breaks for travel.

(d) With respect to the British Isles, for the following number of first-class performances:

(i) if the Play is first produced in London, then for 21 consecutive performances in London, or

(ii) if the Play is first produced outside of London, for 64 performances within 80 days after the first performance, presented either outside of London, or partly in London and partly outside of London.

(e) With respect to Australia, for 21 consecutive performances, including an Official Press Opening, provided such performances are the Australian equivalent of First-Class Performances in the Territory.

(f) With respect to New Zealand, for 21 consecutive performances, including an Official Press Opening, provided such performances are the New Zealand equivalent of First-Class Performances in the Territory.

SECTION 11.03 **Participation in Subsidiary Rights**. Although Producer is acquiring rights in the Play and Author's services solely in connection with the production of the Play, Author recognizes that by a successful production Producer makes a contribution to the value of other rights in the Play. Therefore, although the relationship between the parties is limited to play production as herein provided, and Author alone owns and controls the Play with respect to all other uses, nevertheless, if Producer has Vested in the Territory and Producer is not in breach of any provision of this Contract, Author hereby agrees that:

(a) *No Outright Sale*—Author will not authorize or permit any outright sale of the right to use said Play for any of the Subsidiary Rights purposes during the period therein specified without Producer's prior consent. In no event shall there be any outright sale of any such rights prior to the first paid public First-Class Performance of the Play, except that an outright sale of rights for Audio-Visual Productions may be permitted if made subject to the provisions of SECTION 13.07 herein.

(b) *Best Efforts*—Author will use best efforts to exploit the Play for Subsidiary Rights purposes.

(c) *"Producer's Alternatives"*—

  (i) Producer shall have the right to choose Alternative I or II of the 3 Producer's Alternatives set forth in this SECTION and shall give Author and the Guild written notice of such choice on or before 12 o'clock midnight on the first day of rehearsal at which Producer requires all cast members of the Principal Company. If Producer fails to give such notice in a timely manner, Author may choose which Producer's Alternative will apply upon giving Producer and the Guild written notice of such choice on or before 12 o'clock midnight on the next business day following said rehearsal date. If both Producer and Author fail to choose a Producer's Alternative in a timely manner, Producer's Alternative III will apply.

  (ii) Participation in Territory—With respect to the exploitation of Subsidiary Rights in the Territory, Author shall promptly pay to Producer, based on the applicable Producer's Alternative, the designated percentage of Author's compensation directly or indirectly earned (after deduction of agents' commissions, if any), from the disposition of the specified Subsidiary Rights anywhere in the Territory, pursuant to each contract entered into on or after the Effective Date of this Contract but prior to the expiration of the periods described in the applicable Producer's Alternative (regardless of when such compensation is paid); provided, however, that with respect to Media Productions, Producer's participation shall be in Author's compensation earned from exploitations anywhere in the world:

Under Producer's Alternative #	If any of the following Subsidiary Rights are disposed of	Author will promptly pay Producer, based on the following percentages of Author's Compensation directly or indirectly earned (after deduction of agent's commissions, if any from such dispositions pursuant to each contract entered into on or after the Effective Date of this Contract but prior to the expiration of the specified periods of time after the last performance of the Play hereunder (regardless of when such compensation is paid):
I	Media Productions	50% in perpetuity
	Stock and Ancillary Performances	50% for the first 5 years then 25% for the next 5 years
	Amateur Performances	25% for five years
	Revival Performances	20% for 40 years
	Commercial Use Products	See SECTION 11.05
II	Media Productions	50% in perpetuity
	Stock and Ancillary Performances	30% for 36 years
	Amateur Performances	0%
	Revival Performances	20% for 40 years
	Commercial Use Products	See SECTION 11.05
III	Media Productions	30% in perpetuity
	Stock, Amateur and Ancillary Performances	30% for the first 20 years then 25% for the next 10 years

	and 20% for the next 10 years
	(total of 40 years)
Revival Performances	20% for 40 years
Commercial Use Products	See SECTION 11.05

(d) ***Revival Participation***—

    (i) In paying Producer's financial participation in Revival Performances, Author shall secure the payment of one-half of such sum (i.e., 10%) from the producer of the Revival Performances.

    (ii) Notwithstanding the provisions of SECTION 11.03(c), Producer's financial participation in remake, prequel, sequel and spin-off Revival Performances shall be 10% rather than 20%.

(e) ***Foreign Participation***—Author shall have the exclusive right to negotiate and contract for all performances of the Play and for other Subsidiary Rights purposes described in this ARTICLE outside the Territory and outside the Additional Territories, and Author shall promptly pay Producer 25% of the compensation earned by Author (after deduction of agents' commissions, if any), regardless of when paid, in connection with each such contract (other than contracts for Media Productions in which Producer will have previously acquired a worldwide interest) entered into on or after the Effective Date of this Contract but prior to 7 years from the date on which Producer Vested in the Territory. With respect to contracts for Foreign Local Television Productions, Author shall pay Producer 50% of such compensation earned by Author (after deduction of agents' commissions, if any) for such contracts entered into on or after the Effective Date of this Contract but prior to 15 years from the date on which Producer Vested in the Territory.

(f) ***Participation in Audio-Visual Sequels***—If the producer of the Audio-Visual Production, in the original contract for Audio-Visual Production rights, is granted the right to make one or more Audio-Visual Production remakes, prequels, sequels or spin-offs upon the payment of additional compensation, then, if and when such additional compensation is paid, Producer's share of such compensation shall be one-half of the Media Productions percentage set forth in the applicable Producer's Alternative.

SECTION 11.04 **Author's Share of Subsidiary Rights**. No person who is not an Author (as specifically defined in SECTION 1.05 herein) may participate in Author's share of any Subsidiary Rights proceeds; provided, however, that for the purposes of this SECTION only, the term "Author" shall include each collaborator, adaptor, novelist and owner of underlying rights whose material is used in the Play.

SECTION 11.05 **Producer's Rights Regarding Commercial Use Products**. (a) Anything to the contrary herein notwithstanding, Author hereby grants to Producer the sole and exclusive rights to create, manufacture and sell (or have created, manufactured and sold) Commercial Use Products, during the time that Producer retains any rights to present the Play hereunder, except that if on the last day of such period, a contract exists with a third party for the creation, manufacture or sale of Commercial Use Products, then such contract will continue in full force and effect until the expiration of its term, but in no event for more than 5 years from the date of such contract (or the last extension thereof). This grant of rights shall be for the Territory and for each Additional Territory in which Producer presents or licenses the rights to present the Play. Producer shall pay Author the following amounts, regardless of when paid, in connection with each contract entered into for the exploitation of Commercial Use Products:

(i) with respect to sales of such products on the premises of theatres in which Producer presents the Play, a sum equal to 10% of the gross retail sales (after deduction of taxes);

(ii) with respect to sales of such products in other locations, a sum equal to 50% of Producer's net receipts from such sales (i.e., the gross amounts paid to Producer less all customary third party costs actually incurred in the creation, manufacture and sale of such Commercial Use Products).

(b) After the expiration of Producer's rights to exploit Commercial Use Products in the Territory or any Additional Territory, Author may exploit or enter into contracts for the exploitation of Commercial Use Products in such locations in which Producer's rights have expired, subject to any contracts which may continue in effect as described in SECTION 11-05(a) herein. Author will pay Producer the following amounts (after deduction of agents' commissions, if any) regardless of when paid, in connection with each such contract entered into before the expiration of 40 years after the last performance of the Play in the

Territory or such Additional Territory, as the case may be, provided Producer has Vested in such location:

(i)   with respect to sales of such products on the premises of theatres in which Author's Play is presented, a sum equal to 10% of the gross retail sales (after deduction of taxes);

(ii) with respect to sales of such products in other locations, a sum equal to 50% of Author's net receipts from such sales (i.e., the gross amounts paid to Author less all customary third party costs actually incurred in the creation, manufacture and sale of such Commercial Use Products).

(c)   In addition to Producer's rights and financial interest described in SECTIONS 11.05(a) and (b) herein, provided Producer has Vested in the Territory, Producer shall also have such rights and financial interest on a worldwide basis in those cases where the rights to exploit Commercial Use Products are disposed of together with Author's dispositions of rights to exploit any or all Media Productions.

(d)   If there are Revival Performances in the Territory or any Additional Territory, Producer's right to share in Commercial Use Products income, from contracts entered into simultaneously with or subsequent to those Performances in such location (other than contracts which are related to the disposition of rights to Media Productions), shall revert to Author; *provided, however,* that Producer shall have the right to make arrangements with the producers of the Revival Performances with respect to the exploitation of Commercial Use Products created or manufactured by Producer, and to retain all sums derived therefrom.

(e)   None of the sums described in this SECTION, paid to or retained by Producer in connection with the exploitation of Commercial Use Products, shall be included in the calculation of Recoupment hereunder.

SECTION 11.06 **Producer's Rights to Consult in Dispositions of Subsidiary Rights**. If Producer shall be entitled to share in Author's Subsidiary Rights income with respect to the Territory, or with respect to any of the Additional Territories, Author will not undertake to grant any Subsidiary

Rights in the Territory and the applicable Additional Territories, during the periods in which Producer is entitled to share in such income, without giving Producer the reasonable opportunity to consult fully with Author in connection with the exploitation of all such rights.

SECTION 11.07 **Restrictions on Dispositions by Author**. (a) In addition to Producer's rights as set forth in SECTION 11.06 herein, Author represents that, except to the extent set forth in ARTICLE XXII herein, Author has not authorized or permitted, and covenants that Author shall not authorize or permit, unless Producer first consents in writing, the exploitation (or publicity regarding future exploitations) of any of the rights hereinbelow described, prior to the dates specified below:

Rights	**Specified Date**
(i) Worldwide Media Productions (other than radio) and Foreign Local Television Productions:	the Effective Date of this Contract, subject to the provisions of ARTICLE XIII herein.
(ii) Separately with respect to the Territory and each Additional Territory: First and Second-Class, Stock, Amateur, Ancillary, Off-Broadway and Revival Performances (and their equivalents outside the Territory); and radio:	the date on which all of Producer's rights to produce the play have expired in the Territory or such Additional Territory, as the case may be, or the date on which Producer has in writing declared that he will not reopen the Play, except that selected songs may be released for radio use at any time.
(iii) Separately with respect to the Territory and each Additional Territory: Commercial Use Products:	the date on which all of Producer's rights to produce the play have expired in the Territory and each Additional Territory, as the case may be, subject to any contracts which may continue in effect as described in SECTION 11.05 herein.
(iv) Worldwide music, publishing and mechanical reproduction rights including, without limitation, cast album rights.	the date of the Official Press Opening of the Play in New York City, subject to SECTION 8.18 herein.

(b) If Author has disposed of any rights in the Play outside the Territory prior to the Effective Date of this Contract then, provided Producer Vests in the Territory, Producer will receive a sum equal to one-half the amount Producer would have been entitled to receive hereunder had Producer Vested in the Territory prior to the disposition of such rights. Except to the extent that such sums have been previously paid by Author, such sums shall be paid to Producer from Author's share of the first monies, if any, received by Author on or after the Effective Date of this Contract from all Subsidiary Rights exploitations.

SECTION 11.08 **Reservation of Audio-Visual Production Rights Outside the Territory**. If Author disposes of any rights outside the Territory, other than Audio-Visual Production rights, Author shall reserve in Author's contract therefor, and for Author's own use, all Audio-Visual Production rights in such foreign area (including the Additional Territories) and such contract shall provide that the exercise of such reserved rights in such foreign area, by Author or any person authorized by Author, shall not be deemed restricted in any way by the terms of such contract or competitive with any rights so disposed of.

ARTICLE XII
The Negotiator

SECTION 12.01 **Choice of Negotiator**. Edward E. Colton is appointed as Negotiator.

SECTION 12.02 **Alternate Negotiator**. Franklin R. Weissberg is appointed as Alternate Negotiator. The Alternate Negotiator shall have all the rights and duties of the Negotiator and shall have the power to act in the Negotiator's absence.

SECTION 12.03 **Disqualification of Negotiator**. If it appears that the Negotiator and/or the Alternate Negotiator by reason of his relations with any Producer who has received motion picture financing, directly or indirectly, or his representation of any Author or Producer of the Play or for any other reason whatsoever, might, in the disposition of the Audio-Visual Production rights in the Play, act in a dual capacity or occupy a position possibly conflicting with complete representation of Author, the Dramatists Guild Council may,

upon the request of Author or Producer involved, replace the Negotiator and/
or the Alternate Negotiator with a Temporary Negotiator, for the purposes of
disposing of the Audio-Visual Production rights in connection with the Play.

SECTION 12.04 **Selection of New Negotiator**. The Negotiator and
Alternate Negotiator shall each serve until he resigns, is removed by action of
the Theatrical Conciliation Council or otherwise becomes unable to perform
his services. Any new Negotiator and any new Alternate Negotiator (other
than a Temporary Negotiator) shall be appointed by action of the Theatrical
Conciliation Council.

SECTION 12.05 **Duties of Negotiator**. (a) The Negotiator shall act as the
representative of the Author in connection with the disposition of Audio-Visual
Production rights in the Play, and shall have the right generally to conduct
negotiations therefor subject to such written instructions as may be issued to
him by the Theatrical Conciliation Council. Whenever Author and Producer
are represented by an agent in connection with the disposition of such rights,
the Negotiator shall cooperate with and work in conjunction with said agent.
The Negotiator shall have the right to consummate such sale or lease after
consultation with Producer and subject to the approval of Author and after
according Producer all the rights to which Producer is entitled pursuant to
the terms of this Contract. The Negotiator shall also receive and distribute the
monies resulting therefrom as provided herein. All contracts shall be signed by
the Negotiator or, in his absence, the Alternate Negotiator and countersigned
by a person designated by the Guild. In order to aid Author and Producer in
obtaining the best possible terms, the Negotiator shall keep Producer apprised
of current practices in the sale of Audio-Visual Production rights.

(b) If such rights are disposed of prior to the production of the Play, the
Audio-Visual Production rights contract must be signed before the
beginning of rehearsals. In such a case the contract shall be on the
basis of a minimum guaranteed payment or an advance, plus or on
account of percentage payments based on the receipts of the Audio-
Visual Production or the box office receipts of the Play, or both, and
shall be subject to the approval of the Guild and Producer.

SECTION 12.06 **Disposition of Proceeds**. All monies received from the
disposition of Audio-Visual Production rights in the Play shall be forthwith

deposited by the Negotiator in a special account entitled "The Dramatists Guild Negotiator's Account" in a bank located in New York City as may be designated from time to time by the Guild. All withdrawals therefrom shall be made by check signed by the Negotiator or, in his absence, the Alternate Negotiator or, if appointed, the Temporary Negotiator, and countersigned by a person designated by the Guild.

SECTION 12.07 **Compensation of Negotiator**. Prior to making any withdrawals from the proceeds deposited in the Dramatists Guild Negotiator Account in connection with the Play, there shall first be deducted 1¼% of such sums so deposited. Said 1¼% shall be deducted from the amounts payable to the agents in respect of the agents' commission or, if there are no agents, then from the total sums on deposit prior to making any payments to Author or Producer. Said 1¼% shall be divided 85% to the Negotiator and 15% to the Guild as full and complete compensation for their services in connection with the disposition of the Audio-Visual Production rights in the Play.

SECTION 12.08 **Instructions to Negotiator**. The Negotiator shall, in connection with the disposition of Audio-Visual Production rights in the Play, follow the procedures set forth in EXHIBIT B attached hereto and made a part of this Contract.

ARTICLE XIII
**General Provisions Regarding
Audio-Visual Productions**

SECTION 13.01 **Cooperation by Author**. Author agrees to co-operate and shall cause his agent to cooperate with the Negotiator and shall promptly transmit to the Negotiator all offers for Audio-Visual Production rights received directly by or on behalf of Author and shall disclose to the Negotiator any arrangements, actual or contemplated, between Author and any third party with whom negotiations may be pending for the disposal of the Audio-Visual Production rights. Moreover, Author agrees that unless Producer shall consent thereto, Author will not insist on any commitment or agreement with any such third party for Author's personal services as author, actor, director, or in any other capacity, as a condition of disposition of the Audio-Visual Production rights to such third party.

SECTION 13.02 **Conflicts**. The release date of the Audio-Visual Production rights production shall not interfere with either the Regular or Touring Performances of the Play. Such release date shall be fixed by Author, and Producer shall be given written notice thereof. If Producer files no objection with the Negotiator within 3 business days after such notice is sent, the release date will be deemed to be satisfactory to Producer. If within such 3-day period, Producer states in writing his reasons for objecting, the Negotiator shall give due consideration to Producer's objections and shall then fix a release date which shall be binding and conclusive on the parties.

SECTION 13.03 **Rights of Producer**. If Producer deems himself aggrieved by any disposition of Audio-Visual Production rights, his sole recourse shall be against Author and then only for fraud or willful misconduct; Author's refusal to grant the right to make a motion picture or other Audio-Visual Production remake, prequel, sequel or spin-off of the Play or of the picture or other Audio-Visual Production made therefrom shall not be a basis for Producer deeming himself aggrieved; and in no event shall Producer have any recourse, in law or in equity, against any purchaser or lessee of such rights, or against anyone claiming thereunder, or against the Negotiator, the Guild, or others who voted for the selection of the Negotiator.

SECTION 13.04 **Revues**. A separate song or sketch from a revue may be disposed of for Audio-Visual Production rights purposes only at the expiration of 18 months after the end of Producer's rights to present the Play hereunder. Author shall give Producer notice of such proposed disposition. If Producer, within 5 days after notice to him thereof, objects thereto, then the approval of the Theatrical Conciliation Council hereof shall first be obtained before such disposition can be made. Unless otherwise agreed among those constituting Author, Author's share of the proceeds (after deduction of Producer's share, if any is owing) shall be participated in only by the authors of the song or sketch so disposed of.

SECTION 13.05 **Rights in Case of New Producer**. (a) If the Audio-Visual Production rights have not been disposed of within 5 years after the date on which Producer has Vested in the Territory, and if a third party presents Revival Performances commencing after said 5-year period, then the compensation which Producer shall be entitled to receive from Author's disposition of rights in Audio-Visual Productions as provided in SECTION 11.03(c) herein shall be reduced in the following manner provided that Author pays the amount of such reduction to the producer of the Revival Performances: if the producer of such Revival Performances presents at least the same number of First-Class Performances and at least the same number of Second-Class Performances (counted separately) as Producer, Producer's share of Audio-Visual Production rights proceeds earned after the date on which such performances are equaled shall be reduced by 25%; if the number of First-Class and the number of Second-Class Performances (counted separately) presented by the producer of the Revival Performances exceeds by more than 150% the number of each such class of Performances presented by Producer, Producer's share of Audio-Visual Production rights proceeds earned after the date on which the number of Producer's Performances (of both classes) are so exceeded, shall be reduced by 50%; if neither of the foregoing occurs, then Producer's share of such proceeds shall remain unchanged.

(b) The foregoing reduction in Producer's share of Audio-Visual Production rights proceeds may occur only once, regardless of the number of producers presenting Revival Performances.

SECTION 13.06 **Defaults by Producer**. (a) If Producer is in default to a member of the Guild in the payment of compensation or other monies accruing from the production of the Play, the Guild may file with Producer and the Negotiator a memorandum to that effect, and the Negotiator shall thereupon withhold from Producer's share of Audio-Visual Production rights proceeds, the amount stated in such memorandum and shall forthwith notify Producer in writing thereof. Unless Producer demands arbitration thereon within 10 days from Producer's receipt of such notice, the Negotiator shall make payment to Author of the amount shown to be due in such memorandum.

(b) If Producer shall have furnished a bond, and the Guild shall have drawn on such bond because of Producer's defaulted obligations on the Play, and Producer shall have failed to replenish the bond after notice and demand according to its terms, the Guild may file with Producer and the Negotiator a memorandum to that effect, stating the amount so to be replenished, and the Negotiator shall thereupon withhold from Producer's share the amount stated in such memorandum, and shall forthwith notify Producer in writing thereof. Unless Producer demands arbitration thereon within 10 days after Producer's receipt of such notice, the Negotiator shall make payment to Author of the amount shown to be due in such memorandum.

(c) In either case, if arbitration is demanded, the Negotiator will hold the amount in question until the arbitration award is rendered and final and shall then pay such amount in accordance with the film award.

SECTION 13.07 **Prior Disposition of Audio-Visual Production Rights**. If Author shall have sold any of the Audio-Visual Production rights in the Play to Producer prior to entering into this Contract, then Author and Producer may not enter into this Contract until one year following the date of the agreement for the disposition of such Audio-Visual Production rights.

ARTICLE XIV
Agents

SECTION 14.01 **Employment of Agent/Commissions**. Author may employ an agent for the disposition of rights in the Play. The commission of such agent shall not exceed 10% of the amounts received from such dispositions except for Amateur Performances, for which the commission shall not exceed 20%. The commissions paid to such agents may be deducted from the proceeds of any disposition in which Producer shares before payment is made to Producer (except for Cast Album proceeds payable hereunder to Producer from which no commission shall be deducted and except in relation to motion picture uses from which the commissions may be deducted only if Producer has consented to the agent's representation of Producer as provided in SECTION 14.02 herein).

SECTION 14.02 **Producer's Consent to Agent for Sale of Motion Picture Rights**. If Producer has not consented to the agent's also representing Producer with respect to motion picture uses, the agent's commission with respect thereto shall not exceed 10% of the proceeds of such disposition to which Author is entitled after payment of Producer's share, and shall be deducted only from Author's share of such proceeds. If Producer shall consent to the agent's also representing him, then the agent's commission shall not exceed 10% of the proceeds of such disposition and shall be deducted from such proceeds before payment is made to Producer. In either case, the agent's commission for motion picture uses shall be reduced in accordance with the provisions of SECTION 12.07 herein.

SECTION 14.03 **Restrictions in Appointments**. In no event shall Author appoint Producer, or any corporation in which Producer has an interest, or any employee of Producer, or the attorney for Producer, or a member of a firm of attorneys representing Producer, as Author's agent or representative. No Author's agent or officer, directing head or employee of an agent shall, with respect to the Play, act in the dual capacity of agent and producer (the word "producer" as used in this SECTION shall include any person having executive direction or any stock interest in Producer, if a corporation, or who is one of the general partners of any partnership, general or limited) in connection with this Contract; and if he does so act, his agency shall be abandoned insofar as the Play is concerned, and he shall not be entitled to collect or receive any monies or commissions in connection with this Contract.

SECTION 14.04 **Payments**. All monies derived from the disposal of rights in the Play shall be paid to Author's agent, but only if the agent is the Dramatists Play Service, Inc., or is a member in good standing of the Society of Author's Representatives, Inc. Otherwise such monies shall be paid to the Guild which shall pay such monies directly to Author, agent and Producer as their respective interests shall appear.

SECTION 14.05 **No Deductions Other Than Agent's Commissions**. Neither Author nor Producer shall make any claim for commissions in connection with any disposition of the Play for any purpose; nor shall Producer be reimbursed by Author for any expenses or disbursements claimed by Producer unless Author, prior to the expenditure thereof, shall have agreed upon the repayment of such disbursements in writing and such agreement has completed the Certification Procedure described in ARTICLE XVI herein.

ARTICLE XV
Theatrical Conciliation Council

SECTION 15.01 **Theatrical Conciliation Council**. The Theatrical Conciliation Council (*"Council"*), an association of professionals in the theatre industry, shall meet for the purposes and at the times set forth in this

Contract and at any other time, at the request of Author or Producer, to consider questions and problems that may arise from time to time during the term of this Contract (including without limitation any issue which may arise under SECTIONS 4.02(d), 5.07, 8.10 and 9.03(e) herein). Each submission to the Council shall be made in a writing describing the matter to be considered with a copy thereof sent to the other party to this Contract.

SECTION 15.02 **Membership of Council**. The Council shall be comprised of two groups of members, i.e. Author Members and Producer Members. Author Members shall consist of playwrights, who have had First-Class Performances of at least one of their plays produced in New York City, and the executive director of the Guild. Producer Members shall consist of theatrical producers and/or theatre owners or operators, who have produced or presented First-Class Performances of at least one play in New York City, or executive directors (or other persons holding similar positions) of theatrical producer/owner-operator organizations.

SECTION 15.03 **Members of Council**. The members of the Council shall be those persons listed in EXHIBIT A attached hereto.

SECTION 15.04 **Replacement of Members**. If a member of either group resigns, is removed in accordance with the by-laws of the Council, or otherwise becomes unable to perform his services, a new member, meeting the qualifications set forth in SECTION 15.02 herein, shall be chosen by a majority of the remaining members of such group.

SECTION 15.05 **Action by Council**. Any decision or other action by the Council, as contemplated by this Contract, shall require a majority vote of all members voting in person at a meeting at which no less than and no more than 5 members of each group are in attendance. If this Contract provides, or if the parties have agreed in writing, that the decision of the Council shall be binding on the parties, then if the 10 members referred to above cannot be assembled within 7 days after the Council has received written notice of the matter to be considered, the matter may be submitted to arbitration by either Author or Producer in accordance with the provisions of ARTICLE XX herein. If the 10 members of the Council are assembled in a timely manner but cannot reach a decision within 7 days after all parties have presented their arguments in support of their positions, then, prior to adjourning the meeting, the Council shall select, by majority vote of those members present, a disinterested third party to resolve the dispute. If a majority of such Council members cannot agree on such third party, then the matter may be submitted to arbitration by either Author or Producer in accordance with the provisions of ARTICLE XX herein.

SECTION 15.06 **Binding Nature of Council Decisions**. If this Contract provides, or if the parties have agreed, in ARTICLE XXII or elsewhere in writing, that the decision or other action of the Council on a particular matter shall be binding on the parties, then once such matter is decided or action taken by the members constituting the Council on the date of such decision or action, neither of the parties hereto may resubmit the same matter to the Council at a later date for any reason including, without limitation, that the membership of the Council has changed.

SECTION 15.07 **Members of Council Held Harmless**. Producer and Author each represents and covenants (a) that neither of them will directly or indirectly undertake or threaten to undertake any claim, action or proceeding of any kind against any Council member in connection with the action or inaction of any such person in his capacity as a member of the Council or the Joint Review Board (as defined in SECTION 16.06 herein) and (b) that Producer and Author will hold each Council member harmless from any liability in connection with such actions or inactions.

ARTICLE XVI
Certification Procedure

SECTION 16.01 **Submission of Contract to the Guild**. For the purposes of this ARTICLE, the term "*Contract*" shall include this Contract and any written amendment thereto. On the first business day following the full execution of this Contract, Author shall commence the "*Certification Procedure*" described in this ARTICLE by submitting two copies of the Contract to the Guild in order to obtain the Guild's opinion as to whether this Contract, as signed, conforms with or is reasonably equivalent (as described below) the form of Approved Production Contract.

SECTION 16.02 **Standards for Certification**. If this Contract, as signed, does not modify any of the provisions of the APC, the Guild shall certify that this Contract conforms therewith. If. however, this Contract, as signed, does modify any of the provisions of the APC, the Guild shall certify that this Contract is reasonably equivalent to the APC only if:

(a) the modifications are reasonably necessary to counterbalance or neutralize special circumstances relating to or arising from the nature of the Play or its contemplated production, which circumstances could reasonably be expected to affect materially Producer's ability to (i) finance the Play, or (ii)   return to investors their capital contributions within a period then prevailing for other productions of similar size and type, or (iii) obtain all the benefits to be accorded to Producer as contemplated by the APC; or

(b) the modifications consist of an increase in the 6% Post-Recoupment Royalty otherwise payable to Author under the APC, in exchange for

(i) a reasonably equivalent reduction or elimination of the Advance otherwise payable to Author under the APC and

(ii) an increase in the Post-Recoupment Royalty adjustment factor from 115% to 120% of Weekly Breakeven.

SECTION 16.03 **Response from Guild**. Within 10 business days following the full execution of this Contract, the Guild shall notify both Author and Producer of its opinion by sending each of them either:

(a) one copy of this Contract bearing the Guild's signature thereby certifying that, in the opinion of the Guild, this Contract conforms with or is reasonably equivalent to the APC; or

(b) a letter advising that it is the Guild's opinion that this Contract neither conforms with nor is reasonably equivalent to the APC. Such letter must specify the reasons for the Guild's opinion and shall contain suggested revisions, which shall be set forth in detail and which would, in the Guild's opinion, make this Contract reasonably equivalent to the APC. This Contract shall automatically terminate 10 business days following the receipt by Producer of the Guild's letter unless, prior to the expiration of such 10-business-day period, one of the following events occurs:

(i) Producer sends the Guild a copy of this Contract to which is affixed a copy of the Guild's letter signed by both Author and Producer, thereby indicating their agreement with the suggested revisions, in which case this Contract as so revised shall thereupon be deemed to have been certified by the Guild as being reasonably equivalent to the APC; or

(ii) Producer submits this Contract and the Guild's letter to the Joint Review Board (as defined in SECTION 16.06 herein) in which case this Contract shall continue in full force and effect, as signed, and the provisions of SECTION 16.05 herein shall be applicable; or

(iii) Producer sends the Guild a letter signed by both Author and Producer amending this Contract to eliminate the automatic termination provisions contained in this SECTION 16.03(b), in which case this Contract shall continue in full force and effect, as signed, notwithstanding the lack of certification. The signing of such letter by Author will be considered by the Guild as the tendering of Author's resignation from the Guild, which the Guild may accept.

If this Contract shall automatically terminate due to the operation of this SECTION 16.03(b), Author shall immediately return all Option Payments received from Producer, less a sum equal to the pro-rata portion of the Option Payment allocable to that portion of the Option Period measured from the Effective Date of this Contract through the date of termination, which sum may be retained by Author.

SECTION 16.04 **Guild's Failure to Respond**. If the Guild fails to send Author and Producer one of the foregoing responses within the applicable 10-business-day period, the Guild shall be deemed to have certified that this Contract is in conformity with or reasonably equivalent to the APC.

SECTION 16.05 **Submission of Contract to Joint Review Board**. If Producer or Author does not agree either with the Guild's suggested revisions or with the Guild's opinion that this Contract neither conforms with nor is reasonably equivalent to the APC, and if Producer and Author do not send the Guild the letter referred to in SECTION 16.03(b)(iii) herein, then, in order to prevent the termination of this Contract pursuant to the terms of SECTION 16.03(b) herein, Producer shall submit this Contract and the Guild's letter to the Joint Review Board (as described in SECTION 16.06 herein) within the applicable 10-business-day period. The Joint Review Board, in making its determination as to whether this Contract conforms with or is reasonably equivalent to the APC, will apply the Standards for Certification set forth in SECTION 16.02 herein. Within 10 business days after its receipt of such documents, the Joint Review Board will send to Author, Producer and the Guild a written decision either:

(a) that this Contract, as signed, conforms with or is reasonably equivalent to the APC in which case this Contract shall be deemed to have been certified by the Guild; or

(b) that specific revisions, which shall be set forth in detail by the Joint Review Board in its decision, are required to make this Contract reasonably equivalent to the APC. This Contract shall automatically terminate 10 business days following the receipt by Producer of such decision unless, prior to the expiration of such 10-business-day period, one of the following events occurs:

(i) Producer sends the Guild a copy of this Contract to which is affixed a copy of the decision of the Joint Review Board signed by both Author and Producer, thereby indicating their agreement with the suggested revisions, in which case this Contract as so revised shall thereupon be deemed to have been certified by the Guild as being reasonably equivalent to the APC; or

(ii) Producer sends the Guild a letter signed by both Author and Producer amending this Contract to eliminate the automatic termination provision of this SECTION 16.05(b), in which case this Contract shall continue in full force and effect as signed, notwithstanding the lack of certification. The signing of such letter by Author will be considered by the Guild as the tendering of Author's resignation from the Guild, which the Guild may accept.

If this Contract shall automatically terminate due to the operation of this SECTION 16.05(b), Author shall immediately return all Option Payments received from Producer, less a sum equal to the pro-rata portion of the Option

Payment allocable to that portion of the Option Period measured from the Effective Date of this Contract through the date of termination, which sum may be retained by Author; or

(c) that the Joint Review Board cannot reach agreement in which case Author shall have 5 business days, following receipt of the decision, to send Producer written notice that Author rescinds this Contract. If Author does not send Producer notice of rescission within said 5-business-day period, this Contract shall continue in full force and effect, as signed, notwithstanding the lack of certification.

SECTION 16.06 **Joint Review Board**. (a) The *"Joint Review Board"* shall consist of two persons (and two alternates) chosen from the then current membership of the Theatrical Conciliation Council. Promptly upon the submission of this Contract to the Joint Review Board, the Author Members shall choose one person and one alternate from their group, and the Producer Members will choose one person and one alternate from their group. The alternates may attend meetings of the Joint Review Board, but shall not cast a vote unless the designated member is unavailable to do so. All decisions of the Joint Review Board shall be made by agreement between the Author Member and Producer Member.

(b) The decision of the Board, pursuant to SECTION 16.05 (a), (b) or (c) herein, shall be final and binding on the Author, Producer and the Guild, subject to the right of Author and Producer to amend this Contract to eliminate the termination provision of SECTION 16.05(b).

SECTION 16.07 **Expedited Review Procedure**. If Producer and Author agree that the review of this Contract contemplated by the foregoing provisions must be accelerated, they may jointly petition the Guild and, if necessary, the Joint Review Board, in writing, to render its opinion as promptly as possible, but in no event later than 5 business days after its receipt of the documents specified above.

SECTION 16.08 **Notices**. All notices and other communications to be given pursuant to the provisions of this ARTICLE XVI shall be in writing, addressed to the party receiving the notice at the address indicated at the beginning of this Contract (or such other address as shall have been designated by written notice), and shall be sent only by (a) personal delivery with receipt acknowledged in writing or (b) registered or certified mail, return receipt requested. Notices shall be deemed given on the day received (at anytime prior to 5 p.m. on such day) at the address specified for the delivery of notices.

ARTICLE XVII
Warranties, Representations and Covenants

SECTION 17.01 **Scope of Warranties, Representations and Covenants**. Author hereby makes the following warranties representations, and covenants with respect to the Play.

    (a) Author is the sole and exclusive Author, owner and the copyright proprietor of the Play and of all rights of every kind or nature therein, and Author has the right and authority to enter into this Contract and to grant the rights granted herein.

    (b) Author makes such additional warranties, representations covenants and indemnities, if any, as may be set forth in *ARTICLE XXII* herein.

ARTICLE XVIII
Claims for Infringement

SECTION 18.01 **Conduct of Defense**. If any infringement or interference with the rights of any third Party is claimed because of the production of the Play, then Producer and Author shall jointly conduct the defense of any action arising therefrom unless either of them choose to engage separate counsel. In no event shall Author be responsible for any material in the Play supplied by Producer. Upon any suit being brought against Author or Producer alone, such person shall promptly inform the other of such fact.

SECTION 18.02 **Expenses of Defense**. If Producer and Author conduct a joint defense of any such third party action, they shall share equally the expenses thereof; however, if Producer or Author engage separate counsel, they shall each bear their own expenses, When Author writes the Play at the request of Producer from material supplied him by Producer and an action is brought on the grounds of plagiarism, then Producer shall defend the action at his own expense and pay all damages that may be found as the result of the plagiarism and pay any judgment rendered against Author on account thereof. If the act or omission upon which any claim is based shall be found to have been caused by either Author or Producer alone, then no part of the expenses shall be paid by the party not at fault, who shall be entitled to all legal remedies that may be available against the party at fault.

ARTICLE XIX
Termination

SECTION 19.01 **Failure to Pay Royalties**. If Producer at any time fails to make any Royalty payment when due (time being of the essence of this Contract) Author may, at Author's option, send Producer written notice to correct such failure or breach within 5 business days after the receipt of such notice. Producer shall either correct such breach within said 5 days or, if Producer disagrees with Author's allegations, Producer shall send Author written notice thereof within said 5 days and either party, or the Guild on behalf of Author, shall immediately submit the dispute to arbitration as provided in ARTICLE XX herein. The award of the arbitrator shall require the party losing such dispute to pay the costs of the arbitration plus the prevailing party's reasonable legal fees, If Producer does not, within said 5-day period, correct such breach or send Author the above mentioned notice, or if Producer does send the notice and the arbitrator determines that all or part of such Royalties should be paid and Producer does not make the payments due as required by the award within 10 business days after Producer's receipt of a copy of such award, then all of Producer's rights granted pursuant to this Contract shall cease, terminate and revert to Author upon the expiration of said 5-day or 10-day period, as the case may be, unless the Guild agrees to extend Producer's time to make such payment. If Producer's office or place of business shall be more than 100 miles from the place from which the notice is sent, then the notices set forth in this SECTION shall be sent by wire communication.

SECTION 19.02 **Failure to Produce Play/Improper Assignment**. All rights granted to Producer under this Contract shall terminate automatically and without notice if Producer: fails to produce the Play within the time and in the manner provided in SECTION 1.03 herein; or fails to Vest prior to the expiration of Producer's production rights hereunder; or fails to make any Option Payment or Advance Payment when it becomes due; or if Producer assigns the rights herein except as permitted in SECTION 21.01.

SECTION 19.03 **Effects of Termination**. If the rights of Producer to present the Play shall cease and terminate in the manner provided in this ARTICLE, Producer shall immediately cease dealing with the Play in any manner and shall forthwith return to Author all literary materials relating to the Play which are in Producer's possession or control, except that Producer may retain one copy of such materials, but not for commercial use or sale. To the extent that termination occurs due to Producer's failure to make any Advance Payments to Author, Author shall return to Producer all Advance Payments theretofore made.

ARTICLE XX
Arbitration

SECTION 20.01 **Obligation to Arbitrate**. (a) Any claim, dispute, or controversy arising between Producer and Author under or in connection with or out of this Contract, or the breach thereof, shall be submitted to arbitration pursuant to the terms of this ARTICLE unless Author selects other remedies as permitted by SECTION 7.01 herein or unless otherwise specifically provided in the APC. The Guild shall receive notice of such arbitration and shall have the right to be party to the same. Failure by Producer to pay any amount claimed to be due by Author or by the Guild is evidence of a dispute entitling the claimant to an arbitration. Judgment upon the award rendered may be entered in the highest Court of the forum, State or Federal, having jurisdiction.

(b) All arbitrations shall be conducted in the City of New York before arbitrators selected from the Theatrical Production Arbitration Board herein created and in accordance with the procedures herein set forth except where Author and Producer agree to hold the arbitration outside New York. In such event, the arbitrators shall be selected from the panel of the American Arbitration Association and the arbitration shall be held in accordance with the rules of said Association.

SECTION 20.02 **Theatrical Production Arbitration Board**. The Theatrical Production Arbitration Board ("*Board*") shall consist of 24 permanent members. 8 shall be chosen by the Guild Council (to be known as the "*Author's Slate*") and 8 by a majority of the Producer Members of the Theatrical Conciliation Council (to be known as the "*Producer's Slate*"). Within 20 days thereafter, a majority of the 16 persons so chosen shall appoint 8 additional persons as public members (to be known as the "*Public Slate*"), provided such persons have never been a member of the Guild or produced a play or owned or operated a theatre. All such persons shall serve until replacement is required as set forth in SECTION 20.03 herein.

SECTION 20.03 **Replacements**. In the event of the death, resigna-tion, illness, incapacity or unavailability of any member, or if a member of the Public State shall produce or have a play produced or become a theatre owner or operator, such member shall be replaced by a temporary or permanent successor to be appointed in the following manner: by the Council of the Guild, if the vacancy is in the Author's Slate; by the Producer Members of the Theatrical Conciliation Council if it is in the Producer's Slate; by a majority of the members of the Author's and Producer's Slates, jointly, if it is in the Public Slate.

SECTION 20.04 **Rules**. The Board, by a majority vote of all members, shall have full power to establish such rules and procedures as it may deem necessary, not inconsistent herewith. In the absence of such rules, the procedure under this ARTICLE shall be in accordance with the commercial arbitration rules then obtaining of the American Arbitration Association, except as hereinbelow otherwise provided.

SECTION 20.05 **The Complaint**. The party aggrieved, whether Author, Producer or Guild (hereinafter referred to as the "*Complainant*") shall file with the American Arbitration Association 5 copies of a written complaint setting forth the claim, dispute, difficulty, misunderstanding, charge or controversy to be arbitrated and the relief which the Complainant requests. A copy of the complaint shall be mailed by the American Arbitration Association to the party complained against (hereinafter referred to as the "*Respondent*") and another to the Guild, if the Guild is not the Complainant.

SECTION 20.06 **The Answer**. The Respondent shall, within 8 days of the mailing to him of the complaint, file 5 copies of a written answer with the American Arbitration Association and the American Arbitration Association shall mail one copy to the Complainant and another to the Guild, if the Guild is not the Complainant. Where the copy or the complaint is mailed to a Respondent at an address more than 500 miles from New York, he shall have 3 additional days to file his answer. If no written answer is filed within such period, the Respondent nevertheless will be deemed to have entered a general denial of the allegations of the complaint.

SECTION 20.07 **Participation by the Guild**. The Guild may file a complaint and demand arbitration, with or without Author's consent; and

Author, in such event, shall be a patty to the arbitration, and shall not discontinue the arbitration without the consent of the Guild.

SECTION 20.08 **Selection of Arbitrators**. (a) Author, or the Guild, if it has initiated the arbitration, shall appoint one arbitrator from the Author's Slate and Producer shall appoint one arbitrator from the Producer's Slate. These two arbitrators shall be appointed within 10 days from the date of the mailing of the complaint to the Respondent.

   (b) If either the Author or the Producer fails to appoint an arbitrator within 10 days after the mailing of the complaint as aforesaid, then such appointment shall be made promptly from the Author's State by the Guild and from the Producer's Slate by the American Arbitration Association. If the Guild initiated the arbitration and fails to appoint an arbitrator within said 10-day period, then such appointment shall be made from the Author's State by the American Arbitration Association.

   (c) Immediately after the appointment of the aforesaid 2 arbitrators, the third arbitrator shall be appointed within 5 days by the 2 arbitrators to be chosen from among the persons on the Public Slate. The American Arbitration Association shall appoint from members of its panels any arbitrator or arbitrators required where for any reason appointment has not been made from the Slates herein provided for.

SECTION 20.09 **Power of Arbitrators**. The arbitrators are empowered to award damages against any party to the controversy in such sums as they shall deem fair and reasonable under the circumstances, to require specific performance of a contract, to grant any other remedy or relief, injunctive or otherwise, which they deem just and equitable. The arbitrators are also empowered to render a partial award before making a final award and grant such relief, injunctive or otherwise, in such partial award as they deem just and equitable. Subject to the provisions of SECTION 19.01 herein, the arbitrators shall determine and indicate in their written award by whom and in what proportion the cost of arbitration shall be borne.

SECTION 20.10 **Special Arbitration**. If the Author or Producer demands an immediate arbitration upon a complaint by either alleging violation of SECTION 1.02(c) or SECTION 8.01(a) or (b) and 5 copies of the complaint are filed with the Guild at any time after 10 days before the date for which rehearsals have been scheduled, the arbitration procedure outlined in this ARTICLE shall be accelerated as follows:

(a) The arbitration hearing shall be held within 3 days after the filing of the complaint.

(b) The complaint shall be delivered or telegraphed to the Respond-ent by the American Arbitration Association. The Respondent must file 5 copies of his answer with the American Arbitration Association within 24 hours thereafter.

(c) The name of the arbitrator appointed by the Complainant shall be set forth in the complaint and the nameof the arbitrator appointed by the Respondent shall be set forth in the answer. If either person so named shall be unavailable, a substitute shall be forthwith named by Author or Producer, as the case may be. The third arbitrator shall be appointed by the persons so selected within 24 hours after the receipt of the answer by the American Arbitration Association. The American Arbitration Association shall appoint from members of its panels any arbitrator or arbitrators required where for any reason appointment has not been made from the Slates herein provided for.

ARTICLE XXI
Miscellaneous Provisions

SECTION 21.01 **Assignability of Rights**. Except as provided below, neither this Contract nor the rights granted herein to Producer shall be licensed or assigned by Producer without his first having obtained the consent in writing of the Author. Notwithstanding the foregoing, Producer may, without Author's consent, license or assign this Contract or any of the rights contained herein to a corporation, partnership or other entity of which any person comprising Producer is a controlling party or controlling shareholder or has a controlling interest, provided that any licensee or assignee shall assume all of the obligations of this Contract and that Producer shall remain personally liable for the fulfillment thereof in the same manner as though no such license or assignment had been made. A copy of any such license or assignment shall be filed with the Guild.

SECTION 21.02 **Obligations to Not-for-Profit Theatre Organiza-tions**. Notwithstanding the provisions of SECTION 11.04 herein, with respect to amounts owed to a not-for-profit theatre organization which has presented the Play prior to Producer's production hereunder, where such amounts are measured as a percentage of Subsidiary Rights income or Gross Weekly Box Office Receipts (or both), Producer and Author shall share such payments in the following manner:

(a) Subsidiary Rights income payments of up to 5% of 100% of such income shall be shared by Producer and Author in the same percentages as they share in such income;

(b) Gross Weekly Box Office Receipts payments of up to 1 1/2% shall be shared equally by Producer and Author.

SECTION 21.03 **Inspection of Contracts**. Author and Producer shall each have the right to inspect contracts entered into by the other if such contracts would affect the inspecting party's financial interest hereunder.

SECTION 21.04 **Equal Employment Opportunity**. Author and Producer agree, that in connection with the presentation of the Play, they will promote equal employment opportunities in consonance with the artistic integrity of the Play.

SECTION 21.05 **Non-Applicability of APC**. The APC shall not apply to any agreement relating to the purchase of rights in the Play made on the basis such that no part of the consideration is contingent upon the production of the Play upon the speaking stage in the Territory.

SECTION 21.06 **Notices**. All notices given pursuant to this Contract shall be in writing and delivered either in person, by wire communication or by registered or certified mail, return receipt requested, to the party being notified, at the address first above written (or such other address as may be designated by written notice). A copy of all notices shall be sent (at the same time and in the same manner as the original notice is sent) to the Guild and to the persons, if any, specified in ARTICLE XXII herein. Unless specified to the contrary herein, notices shall be deemed given on the day received (at any time prior to 5 p.m. on such day) at the address specified for delivery of such notices.

SECTION 21.07 **Proof of Execution**. In making proof of the execution of this Contract or of any of the terms hereof, for any purpose, the use of a copy of this Contract filed with the Guild shall be sufficient provided that at any time after 2 years from the Effective Date, there may be produced from the files of the Guild, in lieu of the copy of this Contract originally deposited therein, a microfilm of said copy.

SECTION 21.08 **Counting of Business Days**. Whenever this Contract provides for the measurement of time by the passage of "*business days*," Saturdays, Sundays and legal holidays in the Territory, and if applicable in any Additional Territory, shall not be counted. If such measurement is made in "*days*," then only such legal holidays shall not be counted.

SECTION 21.09 **Binding Nature of Contract**. This Contract shall be binding upon and inure to the benefit of the respective parties hereto and their respective successors in interest and permitted assigns, but shall be effective only after having completed the Certification Procedure set forth in ARTICLE XVI herein.

SECTION 21.10 **Changes in Writing**. This Contract may not be amended and no amendment will be effective unless and until the amendment is reduced to writing, signed by the panics hereto and has completed the Certification Procedure set forth in ARTICLE XVI herein. This Contract may not be amended orally under any circumstances. Any attempted oral amendment of this Contract shall be null and void and of no legal effect.

SECTION 21.11 **Permissible Variation in Certification Proce-dure**. (a) If the following two conditions exist at the time this Contract is presented to the Guild for Certification, the Guild reserves the right to certify this Contract regardless of the terms contained herein:

(i) this Contract is entered into with a producer who has, after the date of the promulgation of the APCs, entered into a contract (or amendment of such a contract) for the presentation in New York City of First-Class Performances of a play written by an author who, at the date of signing such contract (or amendment) was a member of the Guild, and

(ii) on the date of signing this Contract, such prior contract (or amendment) has not been determined by either the Guild or the Joint Review Board to conform with or to be reasonably equivalent to the APC (other than by reason of the Guild's failure to respond timely, as provided in SECTION 16.04 herein, or the Joint Review Board's inability to reach a decision).

In such case, the Guild's decision to certify under the foregoing circumstances shall be final and unreviewable by the Joint Review Board, and the provisions of SECTION 16.05 herein shall not apply to that certification.

(b) The foregoing provisions of this SECTION shall not apply if the prior contract (or amendment) was not in conformity with or reasonably equivalent to the APC due to, in whole or in part, the existence of provisions which were less favorable to the producer than those contained in the APC.

SECTION 21.12 **Severability**. Should any part, term or provision of this Contract be decided by the courts to be in conflict with any law of the state where made or the United States, the validity of the remaining parts, terms or provisions shall not be affected thereby.

SECTION 21.13 **Applicable Law**. Unless the parties specify to the contrary in ARTICLE XXII herein, this Contract shall be governed by and construed in accordance with the substantive laws of the State of New York without reference to rules regarding the conflict of laws.

SECTION 21.14 **Counterparts**. This Contract may be executed in several counterparts and all counterparts so executed by all the parties hereto and affixed to this Contract shall constitute a valid and binding agreement, even though all of the parties have not signed the same counterpart. The Guild's certification of this Contract, pursuant to the Certification Procedure described in ARTICLE XVI herein, shall be affixed to any one of the counterparts signed by Producer.

SECTION 21.15 **Headings and Captions**. The headings and captions of the ARTICLES and SECTIONS of this Contract are inserted for convenience only and shall not be used to define, limit, extend or describe the scope or intent of any provision herein.

SECTION 21.16 **Pronouns**. Whenever the context may require, any pronoun used herein shall include the corresponding masculine, feminine or neuter forms.

ARTICLE XXII
Additional Production Terms

(Producer and Author may add to this Contract certain additional terms provided that such terms do not conflict with or modify any of the provisions of this APC unless such provisions of the APC expressly permit modification in this ARTICLE. Examples of acceptable additional terms are the following: Rights to Present Developmental Productions; Revised Definition of Completed Play; Author's Billing Credits; Cast Albums; Music Publication Provisions; Orchestral Score Ownership; Choice of Producer's Alternative III; Author's Travel Expenses; House Seats; Special Arrangements Among Persons Comprising Author; Merger of Rights; Royalty Adjustments for Repertoire Performances; Persons to Whom Copies of Notices Should be Sent; and Agency Clause. Modifications in the terms of the APC may also be made in order to counterbalance or neutralize special circumstances as described in SECTION 16.02 herein.)

SECTION 22.01 **Division of Payments**. The division of Payments hereunder among those persons comprising Author shall be as follows:

Author	**Percentage Share**
Bookwriter	%
Composer	%
Lyricist	%
	100%

ACCEPTABLE ADDITIONAL CLAUSES FOR APPROVED PRODUCTION CONTRACT FOR MUSICAL PLAYS

Section 22.02 **Additional Warranties, Representations and Covenants**.

(a) The Play is or will be duly protected by copyright in the United States of America and Bookwriter with respect to the connecting dialogue, Composer with respect to the music and Lyricist with respect to the lyrics have not done or omitted and will not do or omit any act and, to the best of each respective Author's knowledge, no person has done or omitted any act, the result of which could cause the Play to fall into the public domain in the United States or in any country which is a signatory to the Universal Copyright Convention, the Buenos Aires Convention or the Berne Convention. The warranties by Bookwriter, Composer, and Lyricist hereinabove set forth do not extend to the Basic Work. Without limiting the generality of the foregoing, no publication will be authorized by the Bookwriter, Composer, or Lyricist with respect to their respective contributions unless it be made a condition thereof that the Play be duly protected by copyright in all countries that are members of the Universal Copyright Convention, the Buenos Aires Convention and the Berne Convention;

(b) the Play will be written by the author and is based on a story by entitled   ;

(c) the Play does not and will not libel, slander or defame or violate, infringe upon, conflict or interfere with any rights of privacy or publicity or any other rights whatsoever of any third party;

(d) to the best of Author's knowledge there is not now and shall not be outstanding any grant, assignment, encumbrance, claim, contract, license, commitment or other disposition of any right, title, or interest in or to the Play or any of the rights granted hereunder, adverse to or inconsistent with the rights granted hereunder to Producer and the enjoyment and exercise thereof by Producer, or by which such rights, or their exercise by Producer, or any third party pursuant to a grant of rights from Producer, might be diminished, encumbered, impaired or invalidated in any way;

(e) except for material in the public domain, and the story by upon which the Play is based there exists no literary, dramatic or musical material created by Author which is substantially similar to the Play and as to which Producer has not acquired the rights hereunder;

(f) to the best of Author's knowledge there is no claim, action, suit or proceeding relating to the Play pending or threatened before any court, administrative or governmental body;

(g) Bookwriter with respect to the connecting dialogue, Composer with respect to the music and Lyricist with respect to the lyrics will indemnify and hold harmless the Producer and all others claiming by, through or under Producer against any claims, demands, suits, losses, costs, expenses (including reasonable counsel fees), damages or recoveries (including any amounts paid by Producer in settlement, but only if each respective Author consents thereto in writing, which consent shall not be withheld unreasonably) by reason of that Author's breach of any of the representations, warranties or covenants contained herein.

Producer will indemnify and hold harmless each of the parties comprising the Author and all others claiming by, through or under each of the parties comprising the Author against any claims, demands, suits, losses, costs, expenses (including reasonable counsel fees), damages or recoveries (including any amounts paid by each of the parties comprising the Author in settlement, but only if Producer consents thereto in writing, which consent shall not be withheld unreasonably) by reason of Producer's breach of any of the terms contained herein.

Section 22.03 **Cast Album**. Producer, with Author's consent (not to be withheld unreasonably), is hereby granted the exclusive right to contract for the disposition of the rights to make Cast Albums of any and all Companies presenting the Play hereunder. The proceeds received by Producer from the disposition of such Cast Album rights, after deduction of such sums as are required to be paid by Producer (or advance by the record company) such as the cost of services of the cast and orchestra (including, but not limited to, any percentages payable to performers and other elements reasonably required to be furnished by Producer for said album) shall be divided 60% to Author and 40% to Producer. Author shall not be entitled to a share of any investment made by the record company in the production. Author shall have the right to approve any use of Author's name, likeness and biographical resume in connection with said Cast Album. Lyricist and Composer shall arrange with the publisher of the music for a maximum limit for mechanical rights payments of 75% of the statutory rate for the Cast Album; however, the fee for mechanical rights shall be in an amount that is customary for such fees and will be in an amount satisfactory to both the Composer and the Lyricist.

(a) The record company will not in any way restrict the recording and release of an original cast motion picture or television production sound track album.

(b) Producer arranges for payment, accompanied by statements showing clearly and in detail the nature and sources of the royalties, to be sent directly to Author by the record company, and arranges that the contract with the record company shall grant to Author the right, at least semi-annually, to examine and make copies from the books and records of the record company relating to the Cast Album of the Play.

(c) The Composer and Lyricist have approval of the record producer and Author shall sign the Cast Album agreement.

(d) Composer and Lyricist shall own and control all small perform-ing rights and publishing and recording rights in the music and lyrics.

Section 22.04 **Music Publication**. (a) Composer and Lyricist shall jointly have the sole right to select and contract with the music publisher for the score and to retain all proceeds from the publication, mechanical reproduction, synchronization, small performing, and all other rights in the separate musical compositions in the score of the Play. The fore-going shall not be deemed to diminish Producer's interest, if any, in proceeds from dramatic rights in the separate music and compositions. Producer and Bookwriter shall retain their proportionate percentage interests in dramatic productions utilizing the musical compositions regardless of whether the entire Play is used.

(b) The Composer with regard to the music and Lyricist with regard to the lyrics warrant, represent and covenant that the contract with the music publisher who publishes the respective music and the lyrics of the Play does contain or will contain provisions to the following effect:

(i) The music publisher has not made and will not make a contract that would interfere with the disposition of the Audio-Visual Production rights in the Play and that it shall execute, without additional compensation, such instruments and agreements as the Composer and Lyricist or the producer of the Audio-Visual Production may reasonably request consistent with the contract or proposed contract that Author shall make or desire to make with such producer. The music publisher shall abide by any restrictions on music imposed in any agreement of the Composer and Lyricist regarding the disposition of Audio-Visual Production rights in the Play.

(ii) The music publisher shall grant to the cast album record company, video disc and/or video tape company contracted with by Producer of the Play, and/or Author and/or the purchaser of the Audio-

Visual Production rights to the Play, such recording license as is usual and standard for such recordings upon terms and conditions satisfactory to Composer and Lyricist but without additional compensation therefor.

(iii) The music publisher shall make no disposition of the music and lyrics of the Play contrary to the restrictions set forth in the Approved Production Contract between the Composer and Lyricist and Producer.

(c) The Composer with regard to the music and Lyricist with regard to the lyrics agree that if Producer has Vested in the Territory, neither they nor their respective music publisher nor anyone claiming through them shall, without Producer's prior written consent, sell, license or otherwise dispose of the right to use any of the music or lyrics of the separate musical compositions of the Play (except in connection with the sale, license or disposition of rights in the Play as a whole), in connection or for synchronization with any Audio-Visual Production or commercial until the expiration of 5 years from the last performance in the United States or Canada of the Play hereunder, but after the expiration of said 5 years they shall be free to sell and license not more than one musical composition of the Play in connection with any Audio-Visual Production rights, production or commercial, *provided, however*, that no right shall be given to use any such composition as a "production number" or as a "grand use" (as those terms are commonly understood in the entertainment industry) nor shall any right be given to use the title of such composition as or in connection with an Audio-Visual Production, and *provided, further* that if no Audio-Visual Production rights in the Play have been sold, licensed or otherwise disposed of by the end of said 5 year period, then the Composer and Lyricist and their music publisher may deal in the separate musical compositions without limitation, subject to all Producer's rights to share in the proceeds therefrom as Producer is entitled to receive pursuant to this Contract. Anything herein to the contrary notwithstanding, the Composer and Lyricist also agree that they will not, before the end of said 5 year period, make any disposition of musical compositions which contain or involve the title of the Play, the names of the characters of the Play or distinctive incidents, dialogue or phrases from the Play, except in connection with the sale, license or disposition of rights in and to the Play as a whole. Nothing herein contained shall be deemed to restrict rights customarily administered by the American Society of Composers, Authors and Publishers, Broadcast Music, Inc. or any similar organization, to license small performing rights throughout the world in the music and lyrics of the separate musical compositions in the Play. If at any time the Audio-Visual Production rights in the Play are sold, the restrictions on the use of the separate musical compositions and the titles thereof shall be superseded to the extent such restrictions are incon-sistent with the contract between the producer of the Audio-Visual Production and the Composer and Lyricist (or their publisher).

Section 22.05 **Author's Billing**. (a) Author shall receive billing in all advertising and publicity issued by, authorized by, or under the control of Producer, excluding the theatre marquee, but only if no other name except the star's appearing above the title is on the marquee, so-called "ABC" and "teaser" ads and critic's quotations where only the title of the Play, the name of the theatre, and name of any star above the title appears. The name of the Author shall be at least fifty percent (50%) of the size of the type used for the largest letter in the title of the Play. Wherever the name of any person comprising the Author shall appear, all names of such persons will appear. The billing credit referred to herein shall be as follows:

"Book and lyrics by, Music by   ."

(b) Wherever, aside from theatre programs, credits are accorded in connection with the Play in so-called "billing box," and Author is entitled to credit, the size of both Author's and Producer's billing credits shall be determined by the size of the title of the Play.

(c) "Teaser" ads are any advertisements, including without limitation posters and billboards, which mention only the title of the Play, critical quotations and/or names of the theatre and/or any star billed above the title, and which do not mention any credits for Producer, Author, actors, director, designer and the like. It is understood, however, that Author will receive billing in the first run of window cards.

(d) No inadvertent failure to accord the billing credit herein provided shall be deemed a breach hereof, but such failure shall be remedied promptly upon written notice from the Author to Producer or any of the Authors.

(e) Bookwriter, Composer and Lyricist shall have approval of biographical materials issued by Producer as well as of the biography in the playbills.

Section 22.06 **Producer's Acquired Rights to Musical Adaptation**. Producer has acquired the rights to do a musical adaptation of a story pursuant to   . Bookwriter, Composer and Lyricist each acknowledge he has seen and read the aforementioned agreements assigning the rights in the Basic Work ( ) by
and agree to such terms as they affect each of them.

Section 22.07 **Transportation and Living Expenses**. The reasonable hotel and traveling expenses to be paid by Producer to each person comprising the Author while away from their respective homes provided for in SECTION 8.04 and SECTION 9.08 shall be:

    (i) One Hundred Fifty Dollars ($150.00) per day (if in England, the equivalent in English pounds; if in Australia, the equivalent in Australian currency; or if in New Zealand, the equivalent in New Zealand currency) for hotel and other living expenses during the rehearsal period and such other times as each is reasonably available and is required by Producer to be away from his home; and

    (ii) economy-class jet transportation expenses from his home and back and from place to place out of town when he is reasonably available and when such travel is required to attend rehearsals and tryouts. The hotel and traveling expenses hereinabove set forth shall also apply to the San Francisco and Los Angeles productions of the Play.

Section 22.08 **House Seats**. For each performance of the Play under the management of Producer, Producer shall cause two (2) pairs of tickets for adjoining house seats within the first ten (10) rows of the center orchestra section and five additional pairs of good orchestra seats, to be held at the box office for each person comprising the Author, which may be used by a designee of Author, to purchase at the regular box office price. The tickets will be held until twenty-four (24) hours prior to each performance, unless Producer's office or the box office of the theatre is informed prior to that time that Author guarantees payment thereof, in which case the tickets will continue to be held up to the time of performance. In addition, each person comprising the Author shall maintain and deliver to Producer at Producer's request such books and records as are required to enable Producer to comply with the house seat regulation of the Attorney General of the State of New York or other laws or regulation pertaining to allocation and distribution of house seats. Author acknowledges and agrees that the theatre tickets made available hereunder cannot, except in accordance with the regulations promulgated by the Office of the Attorney General, be resold at a premium or otherwise.

Section 22.09 **Developmental Productions**. (a) Producer shall have the sole and exclusive right to present Developmental Productions of the Play in the Territory on the terms provided in Section 4.02(e) above.

(b) Author shall have approval of the locations of such Develop-mental Productions, such approvals not to be unreasonably withheld.

(c) Author's consent to any financial terms that affect him shall be required.

(d) Author shall have the right to be present at the rehearsals and performances of such Developmental Productions, and to be reimbursed for his round-trip transportation and out-of-pocket expenses to said rehearsals and performances.

Section 22.10 **Force Majeure**. If Producer shall be prevented from producing the Play within an applicable Option Period, or if any production hereunder shall be interrupted, due to epidemic, fire, action of the elements, strikes, labor disputes, governmental order, court order, act of God, public enemy, wars, riots, civil commotion, illness of stars or any other cause beyond Producer's control, such as breakdown of the theatre's heating or air-conditioning systems, or any other cause, such prevention or interruption shall not be deemed a breach of this Agreement or a cause for forfeiture of Producer's rights hereunder, and the Option Period shall be extended for the actual number of days of such prevention; provided, however, that if any extension of the Option Period or any interruption of production due to any such cause shall continue for three months, then—Author shall have the right to terminate the applicable Option Period or Producer's right to resume production (as the case may be) by written notice received by Producer not later than 15 days prior to the effective date of the termination of Producer's rights, provided, however, that Producer shall have the right any time before such effective date of termination to extend the term of this Agreement for the Second and Third Option Periods (if it has not already done so), produce the play, or recommence such production, in which case Producer's rights hereunder shall remain in full force and effect pursuant to the terms of this Agreement.

Section 22.11 **Notices**. Copies of all notices hereunder to Producer shall be sent to Tanner, Gilbert, Propp & Sterner, 99 Park Avenue, New York, New York 10016, Attention: Donald C. Farber, Esq.

Section 22.12 **Definition of Vested**. Section 11.02 above shall be deemed amended by the addition of Clause 11.02(a)(v), which shall read as follows: "Any combination of 10 Preview and Regular Performances, plus the Official Press Opening in New York City."

Section 22.13 Agency Clause for Bookwriter and/or Lyricist.

hereby appoints as his sole and exclusive agent with respect to the Play, and authorizes and directs the Producer to make all payments due or to become due to him hereunder, to and in the name of said agent, and to accept the receipt of said agent as full evidence and satisfaction of such payments. In consideration of the services rendered and to be rendered by such agent, said hereby agrees that said agent is entitled to receive and retain as its compensation ten percent (10%) of all proceeds payable to him by the Producer hereunder, and said hereby agrees that his said agent is entitled to receive ten percent (10%) of all other proceeds payable to him with respect to the Play (including but not limited to his share of proceeds derived from any and all subsidiary and additional rights, whether or not the Producer participates therein), except that with respect to proceeds derived from amateur performances said agent's commission shall be twenty percent (20%). Producer hereby retains said agent and agrees that said agent is entitled to receive and retain as its commission ten percent (10%) of the Producer's share of all proceeds payable to the said   from the sale, lease, license or other disposition of subsidiary and additional rights in and to the Play, except that with respect to amateur performances, said agent's commission thereof shall be twenty percent (20%). The foregoing shall not be construed to give the agent any commissions computed upon any share of monies or other proceeds from any first-class production of the Play produced by the Producer in the United States or Canada or produced in the British Isles by the Producer alone or in association with a British producer, or produced by a British producer under a lease or rights from Producer hereunder. Any claim, controversy or difference between any of the persons constituting   and said agent, or the Producer and said agent, arising out of or relevant to this contract, or in connection with the Play, shall be settled by arbitration in New York, New York, in accordance with the rules then obtaining of the American Arbitration Association and any judgment may be entered in any court of any forum having jurisdiction thereof.

Section 22.14 **Agency Clause for Composer**. (See 22.13.)

Section 22.15 **Amendment of Section 4.04**. Section 4.04 of the Contract is hereby amended so as to include the following in the definition of "recoupment":

(f)   In determining whether the production costs have been recouped, there shall be taken into account as income to Producer all sums derived directly or indirectly from the production and presentation of the Play, including not only income from all performances and other activities controlled by Producer (such as souvenir programs and Commercial Use Products) but also, and without limiting the generality of the foregoing, any share of net receipts due to or to become due to Producer in connection with the exploitation or other disposition of any subsidiary rights in the Play in which Producer is entitled to participate pursuant to this Contract.

Section 22.16**Amendment of Section 8.04**. Section 8.04(a) of the Contract is hereby amended so as to include the term "designer" after the term "conductor" on the sixth line.

Section 22.17**Amendment of Section 8.08**. Section 8.08 is hereby amended so as to add the following provision:

The script referred to in Section 8.08 shall be a stage manager's script containing lighting, property plots and all other information usually contained in such scripts, provided that the delivery of such script does not constitute any statement of position by Producer with respect to the use of the script.

Section 22.18**Amendment of Section 8.19**. Section 8.19 is hereby amended so as to add the following provision:

Composer and Lyricist shall also (and they do hereby elect to) own the Scores, as that term is defined in Section 8.19 as well as the copyright therein, in the same manner and to the same extent as the music and lyrics.

Section 22.19**Amendment of Section 11.01**. Section 11.01 is hereby amended so as to include the word "souvenir" prior to the word "books" on the second line.

Section 22.20**Amendment of Section 11.05**. Section 11.05 is hereby amended so as to add the following provision:

No deal will be made for a commercial use that will interfere with the disposition of the motion picture or television rights, and any disposition of the commercial uses will be subject to any motion picture or television deal.

Section 22.21**Amendment of Article XII**. Wherever the phrase "Audio-Visual Production rights" appears in Article XII, the following shall be deemed substituted in its place and stead: "Motion Picture rights."

Section 22.22**Merger**. (a) A "Merger" shall mean that circum-stance in which all contributions of the Author shall combine and become a unified whole for the purpose of performance and disposition of subsidiary rights, and upon merger, no one element may be used or disposed of without all other elements (with the exception of publishing rights to the book, music and lyrics, "small performing rights" in the music and "grand rights." Merger shall occur when Producer has vested pursuant to Section 11.02 of this Contract.

(b) Notwithstanding anything herein to the contrary, it is specifically agreed and understood between the parties that, while it is intended that the provisions of this Contract with respect to merger shall control the exploitation of rights in the Play as herein provided, it is not the intention of the parties that the Play be deemed, nor is the Play a "Joint Work" within the meaning of that term under the United States Copyright Act of 1976, and it is agreed and understood that for the purposes thereof, the book of the Play shall be deemed a separate work, the copyright of which shall be owned by the Bookwriter, and the music and lyrics of the Play shall be deemed a separate work, the copyright of which shall be owned by Composer and Lyricist, as their respective interests may appear.

Section 22.23 **Print Publication**. Notwithstanding anything con-tained in this Contract to the contrary, if the book of the play shall be published in printed form separate and apart from the lyrics and music of the Play, the proceeds therefrom shall be retained solely by the Book-writer. If the book of the Play shall be published in printed form with the lyrics of the Play but not the music of the Play, the proceeds therefrom shall be divided equally between the Bookwriter and Lyricist.

Section 22.24 **Reversion**. If the Play shall not be presented in accordance with the provisions of this Contract, subject to any further agreement among the individual Authors, all rights in the lyrics shall revert to Lyricist, free from any claim by Producer, Bookwriter or Composer; all rights in the music shall revert to Composer, free from any claim by Producer, Bookwriter or Lyricist; and all rights in the book shall revert to Bookwriter, free of any claim by Producer, Lyricist or Composer.

Section 22.25 **Turnaround**. If the Producer's rights terminate or are abandoned prior to their expiration, Author shall have the option to bring a new producer to the project who will pay the underlying rights owner according to the terms of the present agreement with the Producer and the term of the option shall be extended for 12 months.

**Signature Page for Approved Production Contract
for Musical Plays
For the Play Entitled**

IN WITNESS WHEREOF, each of the parties has signed this Contract as of the Effective Date of this Contract.

Producer(s)*	Date of Signing	Author(s)	Date of Signing
_____	_____	_____	_____
		Bookwriter	
_____	_____	_____	_____
		Composer	
_____	_____	_____	_____
		Lyricist	

This Contract is Certified by the Guild in accordance with the provisions of *ARTICLE XVI* herein.

The Dramatists Guild, Inc.

By _____

Date of Signing _____

(If Producer is a corporation, the following must be signed by the person or persons in control thereof, i.e., the person (a) owning or controlling a majority of its stock or a majority of its voting stock; or (b) using their name as part of the corporate title; or (c) rendering services in connection with the Play a Producer; or (d) whose name is included in publicity advertising or programs as Producer or co-Producer of the Play.)

In consideration of the execution of this Contract by Author, the undersigned (if more than one, then the undersigned jointly and severally) hereby agrees to jointly be liable with Producer for the full performance of each and every covenant and provision of this Contract on Producer's part to be performed, including but not limited to the payment of all monies due Author hereunder.

*Where the Contract is signed by a corporate Producer, the officer signing should state his office and the corporate seal should be affixed. Where the officer signing for the corporation is other than the President, a certified copy of a resolution should be furnished showing the authority of said person so to sign.

Where this Contract is signed by a partnership, all the general partners must sign and the partnership names should also be stated.

EXHIBIT A
MEMBERS OF THE
THEATRICAL CONCILIATION COUNCIL

Author Members

James Goldman
Garson Kanin
Arthur Kopit
David E. LeVine
Peter Stone
Stephen Sondheim
Terrence McNally

Producer Members

Richard Barr
Bernard B. Jacobs
Norman Kean
James M. Nederlander
Robert E. Nederlander
Harvey Sabinson
Gerald Schoenfeld

EXHIBIT B
Instructions to the Negotiator

Procedure to Be Followed in the Sale or Lease of Plays for Audio-Visual Production

It is recognized that with regard to the procedure to be followed in the disposition of motion picture rights to plays, theatrical productions are divided into two groups, those completely or substantially financed by motion picture producers and those not so financed (herein referred to as "financed independently of the motion picture industry"). The distinction takes on significance where the disposition of motion picture rights is concerned. The significance lies in the fact that the producer who has motion picture backing (by reason of financial, employment or other contractual relations) occupies a dual position. He is both buyer and seller. As a result of this dual role, it is impossible for him, however strict and unexceptionable his conduct, to escape criticism. This duality does not exist, however, for the producer whose production is financed independently of the motion picture industry. You should bear this distinction in mind in carrying out your duties. It is suggested that you request every producer to make a voluntary disclosure to you of any relationship that he may have which conflicts with the basic relationship of being jointly interested with Author in the proceeds of motion picture monies.

The same possibility of conflict of interests may exist with respect to the disposition of any other Audio-Visual Production rights the proceeds of which are shared by the producer of the stage production. The principles set forth in this Exhibit shall apply as well, to the extent practicable, to the disposition of such rights and all references contained herein to the term "motion pictures" shall also be deemed to refer to Audio-Visual Productions where the context and industry practices appear to the Negotiator to warrant it.

I. Plays Produced by Producers Independently of Motion Picture Backing

You will offer Producer full opportunity to satisfy you that he is certain of his own knowledge that neither all nor any substantial part of his financial backing is directly or indirectly derived from any motion picture producer. You will not, in this connection, be required to exact any onerous legal proof of

Producer, but will rely on your own best judgment, remembering, however, that the burden of proof is on Producer. In the event of Producer's electing to take advantage of this opportunity and of his satisfying you that no substantial part of the financing of the Play was derived from the motion picture industry, it is recognized that his interest in securing the highest price, or the best conditions of sale, or both, is identical with that of Author and that it is to Author's advantage to have the constant benefit of Producer's advice and experience throughout the negotiations of the motion picture rights to the Play.

In the event of Producer's refusal or failure to satisfy you as above, you will decide all questions of his participation in negotiations according to your own best judgment. As provided in SECTION 13.03 of the APC, you are not to be in any way liable for the exercise of discretion.

The Producer having Vested in the Territory, you shall, upon request of either Author (or his agent) or Producer, call a conference between Author (or his agent), Producer and yourself to the end of fixing a price at which the Play may be offered for sale for motion picture purposes; and shall thereafter offer the Play for such sale at the price established.

If at any time during the negotiations for the sale or lease of the Play it is, in your opinion or in the opinion of either Author (or his agent) or Producer, advisable either to reduce or to raise the price at which the Play is to be held for sale, you will again call for a conference for the establishment of a new price. At no time shall the holding price of the Play be changed in either direction without affording Author and Producer full opportunity to confer. Any offer received by you must be forthwith communicated to Author, or his agent, and Producer.

It is desirable that the sales price shall be mutually satisfactory to both Author and Producer. In the event Author decides to accept a definite offer which is unsatisfactory to Producer then, except in the event of the contingency provided for in the second succeeding paragraph, the following procedure shall be followed: You shall forthwith advise Producer by telegram of the price, method of payment and release date. This offer may be accepted by you unless Producer shall, within 2 business days after receipt of the notice, advise you by telegram that the offer is rejected, giving his reasons therefor. If Producer rejects the offer he shall have a period not to exceed 5 business days from the date of the notification from Producer above referred to in which to submit to you a definite "better offer" which shall mean an offer (a) from a party of financial standing capable of making the payments set forth in the offer at the respective times therein provided for, (b) for a price in excess of that contained in the offer which Author is willing to accept and (c) on other terms at least as favorable to Author as those contained in the offer which Author is willing to accept.

If within the prescribed period of time Producer brings in a "better offer" such offer shall be accepted. If, however, the "better offer" is from Producer or an entity in which Producer has any financial or other interest, Producer shall so notify the Author of such offer specifying the price, method of payment and release date. The Author shall then have 10 business days from receipt of Producer's notice to try to obtain a "better offer" by offering the Play in the open market with the Producer's offer as a minimum. If within the prescribed period of time the Author brings in a "better offer," such offer shall be accepted, unless the Producer gives notice within one business day after receipt of Author's notice of an intention to make a higher bid, which shall be made within 2 business days after receipt of Author's notice. This bidding procedure may continue indefinitely until the highest acceptable offer is received. In the event Author and Producer do not agree as to whether or not the offer brought in by Producer is (a) from a party of financial standing capable of making the payments set forth in the offer at the respective times therein provided for, (b) for a price in excess of that contained in the offer which Author is willing to accept, (c) in terms at least as favorable to Author as those contained in the offer which Author is willing to accept and (d) from an entity in which Producer has no financial or other interest, then it is agreed as follows:

You shall have the right in your sole discretion (i) to determine said issue or (ii) to request the American Arbitration Association to appoint two persons who, together with you will constitute the arbitrators to determine said issue. If you, by reason of your relationship with either Author or Producer or for my other reason whatsoever, occupy a position as a result of which you may not be able unbiasedly to determine said issue then, if requested by either Author or Producer or on your own volition, you shall request the American Arbitration Association to appoint three persons who, without you, will constitute the arbitrators to determine said issue, which determination shall hereafter also be referred to as a determination under (ii) hereof. The determination by you under the contingency provided for in (i) or the determination of the majority of the three persons referred to in (ii) shall be binding and conclusive upon Author and Producer. In the event alternative (ii) is adopted, the arbitration shall take place on two days' notice, Sundays and holidays excluded, and the cost of said arbitration shall be borne by Author and Producer in equal proportion. Except as hereinbefore provided for, the rules and regulations of the American Arbitration Association shall apply to any determination made under alternative (ii) but any determination made under (i) shall be made by you without any formal hearing. You shall have the right to make the decision under alternative (i) except in such situations where, in your uncontrolled determination the question involved is a close one.

The exception referred to in the second preceding paragraph is as follows: In the event Producer is associated with or employed by a motion picture producer or has been financed wholly or in substantial part by a motion picture producer or an officer thereof, then you shall not be obligated to offer Producer any period in which to bring in a definite offer in excess of that acceptable to Author, but except as aforesaid, the provisions of the foregoing paragraph shall apply.

If at my time during the negotiations for the sale or even after the consummation of the sale you or Author find any reasonable grounds for doubting the veracity of Producer's statement of his financial backing, you or Author shall forthwith report said doubts to the Council of the Guild and either Author or the Guild may then demand an arbitration under the terms of *ARTICLE XX* of the APC to establish the fact of misrepresentation, if any.

II. Plays Financed by Motion Picture Producers in Whole or in Part

The phrase *"motion picture backer"* as hereinafter employed is construed as describing any film or television producer, subsidiary or affiliate or officer or employee thereof, contributing, in whole or in part, to the financing of the stage production of the Play. The phrase *"motion picture backed producer"* as hereinafter employed is construed as describing any producer whose production is financed in whole or in substantial part by a motion picture backer, or a producer who has had a past or present executive employment relationship or other significant contractual or business relationship with a motion picture backer.

Such productions fall into three classifications, as follows:

(1) That in which Producer has in writing disclosed to Author, upon signing the APC for the Play, the fact that he is, or desires to be, motion picture financed;

(2) That in which Producer does not make such disclosure upon signing the APC, but makes it before the date of the Play's first full cast rehearsal;

(3) That in which Producer has made no such disclosure at any time but is not, at the time of negotiations for the Play's sale to motion pictures, able to satisfy the Negotiator of his complete independence of motion picture financing.

The object of such classification is to protect the interests of all three parties and to avoid the complications which result from motion picture financing of which Author is not aware.

III. Procedure in Case Production Falls
Under Above Classification (1)

It is desirable from all points of view that Producer whose production is to be financed by motion picture capital should, prior to the signing of the APC, disclose in writing to Author either the fact of such financing, or his desire or intention, to obtain such financing. When such disclosure is made and Author signs the APC, it shall be assumed that Author is satisfied with such financing and you will accord the motion picture backers the protection provided in the following procedure.

The Producer having Vested in the Territory, you shall decide when, in your judgment, acting as Author's representative, a holding price at which the motion picture rights to the Play are to be offered for sale or lease should be fixed and after full consultation with both Producer and Author you will arrange with Author to fix that price.

If the fixing of this price gives you any reason to suspect collusion between the motion picture producer and Author which might operate against the spirit and content of the APC or the interest of Producer, or Author's best financial interest, you will forthwith report your suspicions to the Theatrical Conciliation Council as a violation of the APC.

The price being fixed to your satisfaction, however, you will:

(a) Immediately offer the rights at this price to the motion picture backer, with the stipulation that he shallhave 2 days in which to accept or reject the price named.

(b) If at the end of said 2 days the motion picture backer does not accept the Play at the price named, then the Play may be offered in the open market with the rejected price as a minimum, and no further opportunity will be given to, or bids received from, the motion picture producer to meet or better any other bids from any other motion picture corporation in excess of the price rejected by him.

(c) If the Play is not sold in the open market at the price named, or better, you and Author may by agreement reduce the holding price one or more times. If you do so, however, the procedure hereinbefore outlined must be repeated.

If at any time following a rejection by the motion picture backer, Author and Negotiator elect to demand of the motion picture backer an offer as evidence of its interest in the property and the motion picture backer does not submit any such offer within one week after receipt of the Negotiator's request to do so, then the Play shall be considered free and clear of any obligation to the motion picture backer which financed it and shall be offered in the open market and no further opportunity will be given to, or bids received from, the motion picture backer to meet or better any other bids from any other motion picture producer in excess of the price rejected by him.

If the motion picture backer does so manifest its interest by making an offer, this offer must be submitted as a fixed sum, or a fixed sum plus a percentage of receipts, together with a summary of the terms of the proposed contract which shall be acceptable to the Negotiator. Author shall by the terms of such offer have one week after receipt in which to give notice as to whether Author accepts or rejects it. If Author rejects it, however, he may still use it as a minimum holding price at which to offer the property on the open market but no bid will be received from the motion picture backer in excess of such holding price. If, however, no offers are received in excess of this holding price, Author may, if he wishes, offer the Play in the open market at a sum at or below the price set by the motion picture backer and rejected by Author. In this instance, however, the motion picture backer will be free to file offers with you in competition with any other motion picture company and no bid from such backer shall be received in such competition in excess of such minimum holding price. But if Author receives a bid from any other motion picture company at the same price as that offered by the backer, the backer's bid (if kept open) shall receive preference, provided that the other terms of the contract offered by the backer are as favorable as those offered by the other motion picture company.

In all cases of such motion picture financed productions, you will at all times keep Author fully informed of all facts relating to sale or lease, including (but not by way of limitation) offers received, steps in negotiation, execution of the contract and consummation of the sale, but you will not reveal any such facts to anyone other than Author, and the Guild; and you will particularly caution Author against disclosing any such information to the motion picture backed producer,

IV. Procedure Under Classification (2)

When Producer has made no written disclosure of motion picture financing upon signing the APC, but has made it between that date and the date of the first rehearsal of the Play, then Author shall have the right to choose between instructing the Negotiator either to follow the above procedure or instructing him to proceed as in the ensuing paragraph.

V. Procedure Under Classification (3)

Where Producer has not at any time in writing disclosed to Author the fact of any motion picture financing, or cannot, at the time of the negotiations for the Play's sale or lease to pictures, satisfy the Negotiator of his independence of motion picture financing, or has received motion picture backing at some time after the date of the first rehearsal and prior to the offering for sale or lease, whether such backing is disclosed or not, then the Negotiator shall use his utmost efforts to secure a competitive open market for the picture rights to the Play without any of the advantages to the motion picture backer as set forth in the above machinery. In such cases Author, of course, will be doubly cautioned against disclosing any offers to Producer.

EXHIBIT C
Alternative Royalty Formula for Musical Plays

Section 22.02 Notwithstanding anything contained in ARTICLE IV, SECTION 4.02(a), (b) and (c) and the applicable sections of ARTICLE V to the contrary and provided that Author and Producer mutually agree thereto, the following alternate Royalty formula shall be selected and shall become effective commencing with the initial first-class out-of-town performance of the Play:

A. Royalty Adjustment Point "RAP" shall mean:

    (a) Prior to recoupment of Production Expenses, the lower of:

        1. 78% of manifest gross; or
        2. $140,000 above breakeven.

    (b) After recoupment of Production Expenses, the lower of:

        1. 70% of manifest gross; or
        2. $100,000 above breakeven.

B. At "RAP" or above "RAP," Royalties to Bookwriter, Composer and Lyricist will be as follows:

    1. Before Recoupment:

    (a) A combined Royalty of 6% provided that Producer, Director and Choreographer together receive no more than 6% in which case Author's (combined) Royalty will be 6%. The Production entity may receive an additional 1%, without prejudice, provided that the 1% does not go to a General Partner who is *not* a major investor.

    (b) If the Producer's, Director's and Choreographer's combined Royalties exceed 6% or 7% (as the case may be), then the Author's 6% Royalty shall be considered a minimum Royalty.

C. Below "RAP," before and after recoupment, Royalties to Bookwriter, Composer and Lyricist will be as follows: Bookwriter, Composer and Lyricist shall receive a share of the Pool based upon the proportion that 6% bears to the total Royalties to the Author, the Producer, the Director and the Choreographer prior to recoupment but not less than 40% of the Royalty Pool.

D. Below "RAP" and provided that the theatre rental will be derived from a share of weekly operating profits, a Royalty Pool (see Paragraph "C" through "K") will exist to be shared by a Bookwriter, Composer, Lyricist, Producer, Director, Choreographer, Underlying Rights Owner and/or Author of original material, Orchestrator, and Designers.

    1. If the theatre will not join the profit sharing plan, then the original APC musical formula will prevail.

E. The Royalty Pool shall equal:

    1. *Before Recoupment*: The difference between gross weekly box office receipts and weekly operating expense (after the theatre's share and a maximum backers' share of 50% have been deducted), but in no case less than 32%.

    2. *After Recoupment*: At least 40% of the difference between gross weekly box office receipts and weekly operating expenses, but in no case less than the backers' share.

F. Bookwriter, Composer and Lyricist shall receive at least 40% of the Pool; *however*, Author's aggregate share of the Pool will never exceed Author's percentage Royalty.

G. Author of an original book (i.e., one not based upon any previously published, produced or copyrighted work) may negotiate a Royalty for such underlying material of up to 1% of weekly gross receipts, which will be presented in the Royalty Pool as 1 point (but exclusive of the combined compensation of the Bookwriter, Composer and Lyricist referred to in "E" above).

H. At or below "RAP," Author (Bookwriter, Composer and Lyricist) will receive in the aggregate $3,000 per week in addition to their share of the Pool, if any (such $3,000 to be included in the calculation of weekly operating expenses).

I. Weekly operating expenses will be contractually capped not later than the first day of rehearsal, but may be adjusted by mutual approval of Author and Producer not later than two weeks after the Official Press Opening.

This cap can thereafter be raised by:

(a) Changes in industry-wide conditions, such as labor contracts, taxes, or insurance;

(b) Costs incurred in replacing members of the cast;

(c) Additional rehearsals;

(d) Television commercials (not including the initial commercial); and

(e) Costs incurred in moving the production to a different theatre.

J. All weeks will be calculated separately except for the four-week period preceding (and including) Christmas week which may be calculated collectively.

K. If pursuant to SECTION 8.20 Producer enters into an APC with a replacement Author, then the replacement Author will receive from the Pool an amount equal to the replacement Author's share of the Pool computed on a pari passu basis with all of the other Authors.

L. If there is a Developmental production in which contingent compensation is due the Actors for participating in said Developmental production, then such contingent compensation shall be deducted prior to the disbursement of other payments from the Royalty Pool.

APPENDIX F

Collaboration Agreement

AGREEMENT made as of this day of , 19 , by and between John Jones (sometimes hereinafter referred to as "Jones" or the "Bookwriter-Lyricist") and Bill Boyd (sometimes referred to as "Boyd" or the "Composer").

WITNESSETH:

WHEREAS, the parties to this Agreement are collaborating on a Musical Play for which Jones will write the book and the lyrics and Boyd will compose the music, which Play is at this time entitled "Go! Go! Go!"

NOW, THEREFORE, the parties do agree as follows:

1. The parties agree that Bookwriter-Lyricist will write the book and lyrics and that Composer will write the music for the Play. The parties agree that they will jointly register and own the copyright in the music and lyrics. It is agreed that all receipts from all sources in connection with the Play shall be shared by the parties as follows: two-thirds (2/3) to Jones and one-third (1/3) to Boyd. All rights in the individual musical compositions for the Play shall be held by Jones and Boyd jointly and they (and their publishing companies) shall participate equally in the so-called "small performing rights" in the musical compositions contained in the Play as well as the publishing and recording contracts.

2. Each of the parties represents and warrants that the material written and/or hereafter written by such party for the Play shall be original with such party and shall not violate or infringe the copyright, common law copyright, right of privacy, or any other personal or property right whatsoever of any person or entity or constitute a libel or slander, and that such party fully owns and controls such material and all rights therein and has full right to enter into this Agreement and all production contracts and other contracts and consents to be entered nto hereunder.

3. No contract for the production, presentation or publication of the Play, the music and lyrics, or any part thereof, or the disposition of any right therewith connected, shall be valid without the signature thereto of both of the parties to this Agreement. Both parties shall have approval of the Director of the Play. Bookwriter-Lyricist shall have all authors' approvals, except that Composer shall have approval of the Musical Director and Arranger thereof. Powers of Attorney may, however, be granted by one party to the other, by written instrument, setting forth specific conditions under which said Power of Attorney shall be valid. For services rendered under this Power of Attorney, whether in conducting negotiations or consummating a contract, no agency fee or extra compensation will be demanded.

4. Any contracts concerning the use of the Play for a First-Class Production shall be based on the Approved Production Contract of the Dramatists Guild, Inc., which is current and in use at that time, with any changes approved by Donald C. Farber, Esq.

5. Duplicate contracts concerning the Play, the music and the publishing and recording rights therein, including but not limited to the production thereof or the disposition of any rights in the Play, shall be given to each of the parties to this Agreement. Payments to each of the parties shall be made in accordance with the specific instructions from each such party.

6. In any contract for the production or presentation of the Play or for the disposition of any rights therein, the parties shall use their best efforts to secure the insertion in said contracts of clauses providing that on programs, billings posters, advertisements, or other printed matter used in connection with any production thereof or other use thereof in any manner, the names,

as Bookwriter-Lyricist, and, as Composer, shall be in all billing credits in that order, in equal size, boldness and prominence of type. It is further agreed that in no event shall either name appear as an author without the other name.

7. No change or alteration shall be made in the book or lyrics of the Play without the written consent of Jones. No change or alteration shall be made in the music of the Play without the written consent of Boyd.

8. In the event that either of the parties to this Agreement wishes to sell, pledge, lease, or assign, or otherwise dispose of or encumber his share of royalty interests, or any subsidiary rights interest, of any kind or nature, in any media, anywhere in the world, or any part or portion thereof (other than the small performing rights and publishing rights reserved to each), it is agreed that such party (called the "selling party") shall give to the other (called the "buying party") in a written notice with full particulars, sent by registered mail, an option for a period of fourteen (14) days during which the buying party may purchase such rights in said Play as may be offered, at a price and upon such terms as stated in said written notice. Should the buying party fail, within the said fourteen (14) days, to exercise said option in writing, or if the option is exercised, fail to complete the purchase upon the terms and conditions stated in the said notice, then the selling party may sell such rights to any other person, subject to the conditions set forth in the following paragraph.

Before the consummation of the sale to any other person, the selling party must give the other party to this Agreement written notice containing the name and all conditions of the proposed sale to said third party and must give the other party to this Agreement ten (10) business days within which to match the said offer in all respects, exclusive of any specific terms which would not be expedient for the other party to this Agreement to match, such as the procuring of a particular star, director, etc. If said offer is not matched within the said ten (10) business days, then the selling party may complete said sale to said third party upon such terms and conditions, and a copy of the contract for the sale of such rights shall be sent to the other party hereto forthwith.

9. All expenses which may reasonably be incurred under this Agreement shall be mutually agreed upon in advance and shall be shared one-half (1/2) by Jones and one-half (1/2) by Boyd. This also applies to any tax or assessment made by the Dramatists Guild, Inc., on the Play.

10. It is expressly understood that the parties hereto do not form, nor shall this Agreement be construed to constitute a partnership between them.

11. Anything to the contrary hereinabove notwithstanding, the contributions of the respective parties hereto shall be owned by the contributor thereof, and the written consent of both parties shall be required for any sale, license, or other disposition of the Play in any media, provided, however, that in the event the play becomes "vested" in accordance with the terms of the Dramatists Guild, Inc., Approved Production Contract (the "APC"), the respective contributions of the parties hereunder to the Play shall be deemed merged for all purposes in the sense that no party may deal with the Play or any parts thereof except as herein provided, and the term of this Agreement shall be co-extensive with the life of the copyright in and to the Play. In the event that the Play does not become "vested" in accordance with the terms of the APC, then this Agreement shall be deemed terminated and of no further effect and each of the parties hereto shall continue to own their respective contributions to the Play free and clear of any interest therein of the other party thereto. In the event of death of either of the parties hereto during the existence of this Agreement, then the survivor of the parties shall have the sole right to change the Play, negotiate and contract with regard to the disposition thereof, and act generally with regard thereto as though he were the sole author thereof, except, however, that the name of the decedent shall always appear as provided in Paragraph 6 of this Agreement, and the said survivor further shall cause to be paid to the heirs or legal representatives of the deceased party the agreed upon percent of the net receipts of the said Play, and furnish true copies of all agreements to the personal representatives of the deceased.

12. Any controversy or claim arising out of or relating to this contract, or the breach thereof, shall be settled by arbitration by one arbitrator in accordance with the rules of the American Arbitration Association and judgment upon the award rendered by the arbitrator may be entered in any court having jurisdiction thereof.

13. The terms and conditions of this Agreement shall be binding upon and shall inure to the benefit of the executors, administrators, and assigns of the parties hereto.

IN WITNESS WHEREOF, the parties hereto have hereunto set their hands and seals as of the day and year first above written.

_____

John Jones, Bookwriter/Lyricist

_____

Bill Boyd, Composer

Option Agreement for Other Than a First-Class Production

This AGREEMENT is made and entered into as of the First day of June, 1997, by and between Don Dean, whose address is 123 Fifth Street, New York, New York 10114 ("Producer"), and Milton More, whose address is 456 Seventh Ave., New York, New York 12345 ("Author").

WITNESSETH:

WHEREAS, Author has written a certain play presently entitled "Go for It" (the "Play"); and

WHEREAS, Producer desires to produce the Play and to acquire Author's services in connection therewith; and

NOW, THEREFORE, in consideration of the mutual promises and covenants herein contained, and other good and valuable consideration, it is agreed:

1. Representations and Warranties

Author represents, warrants, and guarantees that:

(a) Author is the sole Author of the Play and that the same is original with such Author except to the extent that it contains material that is in the public domain and was not copied in whole or in part from any other work, nor will the uses contemplated herein violate, conflict with, or infringe upon the copyright, right of publicity, or any other right of any person, firm or corporation; and

(b) Author has not granted, assigned, encumbered, or otherwise disposed of any right, title or interest in or to the Play or any of the rights granted hereunder. Author has the sole and exclusive right to enter into this Agreement and the full warrant and authority to grant the rights granted hereby.

(c) There is not now outstanding and there has not been any grant, assignment, encumbrance, claim, contract, license commitment, or other disposition of any right, title, or interest in or to the Play or any of the rights granted hereunder to Producer or by which the exploitation of the rights granted to Producer and the enjoyment and exercise thereof by Producer might be diminished, encumbered, impaired invalidated or affected in any way.

2. Indemnity

(a) Author will indemnify Producer against any and all losses, costs, expenses including reasonable attorneys fees, damages or recoveries (including payments made in settlement, but only if Author consents thereto in writing) caused by or arising out of the breach of the representations or warranties herein made by Author.

(b) Producer agrees that he shall be solely liable for all costs incurred in connection with any presentation of the Play and he shall indemnify and hold Author harmless from any claims arising therefrom.

3. Grant of Rights and Authors' Services

Author has delivered a complete draft of the Play to Producer and Author hereby agrees:

(a) In consideration of the sum of $1,000.00 as an advance against the royalty payments hereinafter provided, the Author hereby grants to the

Producer the sole and exclusive right and license to produce the Play and to present it as a professional Off-Broadway or middle theatre production in the City of New York to open or before June 1, 1997. If before June 1, 1997, the Producer gives author notice together with payment of $500.00, the right and license herein granted shall be extended for the play to open on or before January 1, 1998.

(b) That he will perform such services as may be reasonably necessary in making revisions;

(c) That he will assist in the selection of the cast and consult with, assist and advise director, scenic, lighting and costume designers in the problems arising out of the production;

(d) That he will attend rehearsals of the Play as well as out of town performances (if any) prior to the New York opening of the Play.

4. Outside Production Date

Although nothing herein shall be deemed to obligate Producer to produce the Play, Producer shall without limitation as to any other rights which may be granted hereunder, have the option to produce the Play as an off-off-Broadway or regional theatre production or a workshop or showcase presentation at any time prior to the Off-Broadway or middle theatre production. Unless on or before June 1, 1997 (or January 1, 1998 if the option is extended) Producer produces and presents the Play on the speaking stage in a regular evening bill as a paid public performance n an Off-Broadway or middle theatre in New York City, Producer's right to produce the Play and to the services of Author shall then terminate.

5. Exclusivity and Continuous Run

The rights granted to the Producer are the sole and exclusive nights to produce the Play (the Producer may acquire an option pursuant to the terms of this agreement as hereinafter set forth to produce the Play in the British Isles and in the U.S. and Canada and on tour), and the author agrees that he will not grant the rights to permit anyone to perform the said Play in any media (exclusive of movies) within the United States of America, Canada or the British Isles, during the term of the option herein granted and the run of the Play, or during the period that the Producer retains any rights or option to produce the Play anywhere in the United States, Canada or the British Isles, and further agrees that he will not grant the right to anyone to do a movie version of the play which would be released during the term of the option or the run of the Play, or during the period that the Producer retains any right or option to produce the Play in the United States, Canada or the British Isles, without the written consent of the Producer, which consent will not be unreasonably withheld.

If the Play is produced within the option period herein granted, the exclusive right to produce the Play in New York City shall continue during its New York City continuous run. The Play shall be deemed closed (that is, the New York City continuous run shall have terminated) if no paid performances have been given in New York City for a period of 4 weeks. After the Play has closed and after all options to produce the Play have expired, the rights to produce the play shall revert to the Author subject to any other terms specifically herein set forth.

If the Play is produced outside the City of New York on tour or otherwise, the exclusive right to produce the Play after the option period herein stated shall continue during its outside New York City continuous run. Outside New York City continuous run as herein defined shall mean that there shall not be a lapse of more than eight (8) weeks between presentations of the Play before a paying audience outside New York City. If the option period has expired and if more than eight (8) weeks elapse between any such paid performances, then all rights shall revert to the author except those that may have been specifically herein vested.

6. Consideration

(a) In consideration of the foregoing, and of Author's services in writing and revising the Play and Author's agreement to perform services in connection with the production of the Play as herein provided, Producer agrees to pay Author such sums as may equal five percent (5%), (going to six and one half percent (6 1/2%) on recoupment of the total production costs), of the gross weekly box office receipts of each production of the Play produced under Producer's management, license or control.

(b) Anything to the contrary herein notwithstanding if all other royalty participants, including the Producer with respect to the Producer's fee, agree to a waiver of one-half of his usual royalty, the Author agrees to waive one-half of his royalty, that is two and one-half percent of the gross weekly box office receipts, until recoupment of the total production costs of the production (less bonds, deposits and other recoverable items) on the express condition that: (1) Each week's operating profits are paid directly to the investors as payment toward recoupment of such total production costs; and (2) After recoupment of such total production costs the Author's royalty shall be in an amount equal to seven percent (7%) of the gross weekly box office receipts. Producer does hereby agree to such waiver of one-half of Producer's fee.

(c) In lieu of the provisions of (a) and (b) above, if the other royalty participants agree to be paid in accordance with a royalty pool formula, then the Author agrees to accept a Royalty Pool Formula structured as follows: the Author will be entitled to six points in the Royalty Pool, which will be at least half of the total points in the Royalty Pool. If the total points in the Royalty Pool exceed twelve (12) points, the Author's points will be accordingly increased so that it is at least half. The Royalty Pool will consist of thirty-five percent (35%) of the Weekly Net Receipts. Such Weekly Net Receipts shall mean all Gross Weekly Box Office Receipts less all customary and reasonable expenses except those variable expenses payable to royalty participants as part of the formula. Each royalty participant will receive a minimum payment of $150 per point.

(d) If the Play is presented for a workshop or showcase production or in a regional or off-Off-Broadway theater, Author will be paid a fee of $25.00 per performance.

The Author shall be entitled to inspect the books and records of the Producer for any production hereunder during regular business hours and upon reasonable notice, but not more often than once every six months.

7. Traveling Expenses and Per Diem

Author shall have the right to be present at any or all out of town performances of the Play up to the official New York Opening. The hotel and traveling expenses to be paid by Producer to Author in connection with such out of town performances of the Play, if any, shall be (i) $125 per day for hotel and/or other living expenses and (ii) economy air transportation expenses to and from Author's places of residence as indicated herein, and from place to place out of town.

8. Tours and Out of Town Productions

Producer's production rights hereunder shall be deemed to include "bus and truck" tours of the Play and other out of town (outside of New York City) production of the Play (whether First-Class or Off-Broadway type productions) provided Producer has presented the Play hereunder for not fewer than twenty-one paid public performances.

For each out of town other than First-Class production, Author will receive notice within three months from the last paid public performance and a fee of seven hundred fifty dollars ($750) to be paid as an advance against royalties in the amount as set forth in paragraph 6(a) above.

In connection with any such engagements, Authors royalties may be computed on the basis of Producer's receipts (including but not limited to fixed fees, guarantees, profits, rentals, and any Producer's share of box office receipts), but only if the following conditions exist in connection with such engagements or productions:

(i) that Producer's gross compensation, whether direct or indirect, for presenting the production is a fixed fee or a combination of a guarantee and a share of the box office receipts, payable to the Producer by a so-called "local promoter" or "local sponsor" or other third party acting in a similar capacity; and

(ii) that all other creative royalty participants, royalties and the Producer's management fee be computed on the same basis.

If the foregoing conditions in subdivisions (i) and (ii) hereof are not met, Author's royalties shall be computed on the gross box office receipts of any such engagements and productions.

It is understood that Producer shall have the right to present or license First-Class out of town productions whether or not Producer has exercised the Broadway option under paragraph 10 and that such performances shall be governed by the terms of the Approved Production Contract ("APC") as herein set forth in paragraph 10 of this Agreement provided, however, that the terms of this paragraph shall also be applicable.

9. **Production in the United Kingdom and Ireland**

If the Producer has produced the Play Off-Broadway or in a middle theater in New York for not less than twenty-one paid public performances, Producer shall have the exclusive right to produce the Play on the speaking stage in the United Kingdom and in Ireland upon all the terms and conditions which apply to a New York production, to open at any time up to and including six (6) months after the close of the production in New York, upon sending Author written notice within two months from the close of the last paid public performance accompanied by a payment of one thousand dollars ($1,000) as a non-returnable advance against the royalties in an amount as set forth in paragraph 6(a) above. Producer may produce the Play in association with or under lease to a British or Irish producer. In such case Producer's obligation to make the royalty payments herein provided shall remain unimpaired. If it is to be produced on the West End in London, such contract between Producer and the British or Irish producer shall require the Play to be produced under the same terms as would apply if the original New York production had been produced under the Approved Production Contract for a First-Class Production.

10. **Broadway Production**

Producer shall have the exclusive option, exercisable by written notice given to Author at any time prior to the later of, (i) the expiration of the Outside Production Date described in paragraph 4 hereof if there is no off-Broadway or middle theater production of the Play, or (ii) sixty (60) days after the last performance of the Play Off-Broadway or in a middle theater, to acquire the right to present the Play as a First-Class Production on Broadway in New York City. The time within which the foregoing option may be exercised shall be automatically extended if Producer acquires or exercises rights to produce and present the Play on tour or in the United Kingdom and Ireland under paragraphs 8 or 9 hereof, and Producer may then exercise such option at any time prior to sixty days (60) after the last performances of a British or Irish production, tour or other out of town performance under paragraphs 8 and 9 hereof.

In the event Producer elects to present the play on Broadway and exercise the option under paragraph 10(a) hereof, the minimum terms of the Approved

Production Contract then in use shall become applicable and shall govern the relationship between Author and Producer with respect to the First-Class Presentation in the United State and/or Canada, and the exploitation of other rights under the Contract.

If prior to the Broadway Opening, Producer has become entitled to a share of subsidiary rights in the Play pursuant to this Agreement, such Broadway production shall not affect, limit or reduce such Producer's share thereof and Producer shall continue to be entitled to receive such share irrespective of the number of Broadway performances of the Play and irrespective of anything contained in the Approved Production Contract to the contrary, provided that if Producer becomes entitled to a greater share of subsidiary rights pursuant to the Approve Production Contract, Producer shall receive such greater share, but not shares from both contracts.

In the event Producer shall elect to exercise the option in accordance with paragraph 10(a) hereof, then Author shall enter into and execute and deliver the Approved Product on Contract within seven (7) days of Producer's submission thereof to Author. Notwithstanding the failure or omission of Author to execute and/or deliver the said Contract, it is agreed that upon exercise of such option, all rights in and to the Play which are granted and transferred to Producer by Author in accordance with the said Contract shall be deemed automatically vested in Producer effective as of the date of the exercise of the option, which rights shall be irrevocable under any and all circumstances except in accordance with the terms of the Approved Production Contract.

11. Force Majeure

If Producer shall be prevented from exercising any option hereunder, or if any production of the Play hereunder shall be prevented or interrupted, due to epidemic, fire, action of the elements, strikes, labor disputes, governmental order, court order, act of God, public enemy, wars, riots, civil commotion, illness or any other similar cause beyond the Producer's control, whether of a similar or dissimilar nature, such prevention or interruption shall not be deemed a breach of this agreement or a cause for forfeiture of Producer's rights hereunder, and the time for exercise of such option and/or the time by which the first paid public performance must take place shall be extended for the number of days during which the exercise of such option or presentation of such production was prevented; provided that if a failure to exercise any option or any prevention or interruption of production due to any such cause shall continue for sixty (60) days, then Author shall have the right to terminate Producer's production rights for the interrupted run or terminate Producer's right to exercise such option (as the case may be) by written notice to Producer.

12. Approvals and Changes

(a) No changes in the text of the Play shall be made without approval of Author. Such changes shall become the property of Author. Cast, director, scenery costume and lighting designers, and permanent replacements thereof of all productions of the Play hereunder shall be subject to Author's approval not to be unreasonably withheld. The Author does hereby specifically approve Don Dean, the Producer, as the director of any productions of the Play in any media.

(b) In any case where Producer requests the approval of Author as provided above and the Producer is unable to obtain Author's response to such request forty-eight hours after having sent him a telegram requesting the same, or personally requesting the same, then Author's consent and/or approval shall be deemed to have been given. Author shall have the right to appoint in writing a representative to respond to requests for approval.

13. Subsidiary Rights

Although the Producer is acquiring the rights and services of the Author solely in connection with the production of the Play, the Author recognizes that by a successful production the Producer makes a contribution to the value of the uses of the Play in other media. Therefore, although the relationship between the parties is limited to play production as herein provided, and the Author owns and controls the Play with respect to all other uses, nevertheless, if the Producer has produced the Play as provided herein the Author agrees that the Producer shall receive an amount equal to the percentage of net receipts (regardless of when paid) specified herein below received by Author if the Play has been produced for the number of consecutive performances set forth and if before the expiration of ten (10) years subsequent to the date of the last paid public performance of the Play in New York City, any of the following rights are disposed of anywhere throughout the world: motion picture, or with respect to the Continental United States and Canada, any of the following rights; radio, television, touring performances, stock performances, Broadway performances, Off-Broadway performances, amateur performances foreign language performances, condensed tabloid versions, so-called concert tour versions, commercial and merchandising uses, and audio and video cassettes and discs: Ten percent (10%) if the Play shall run for at least twenty-one (21) consecutive paid performances; twenty percent (20%) if the Play shall run for at least forty-two consecutive paid performances; thirty percent (30%) if the Play shall run for at least fifty-six (56) consecutive paid performances; forty percent (40%) if the Play shall run for sixty-five (65) consecutive paid performances or more. For the purposes of computing the number of performances, provided the Play officially opens in New York City, the first paid performance shall be deemed to be the first performance; however, only seven paid previews will be counted in this computation.

14. Computation of Royalties

"Gross weekly box office receipts" shall be computed in the manner determined by the League of New York Theatres provided, however, that in making such computation there shall be deducted: (a) any Federal Admission taxes; (b) any commissions paid in connection with theatre parties or benefits; (c) those sums equivalent to the former five (5%) percent New York City Amusement Tax, the net proceeds of which are set aside in Pension and Welfare Funds in the theatrical unions and ultimately paid to said funds; (d) commissions paid in connection with automated ticket distribution or remote box offices, e.g., Ticketron (but not ticket brokers) and any fees paid or discounts allowed in connection with credit card sales; (e) subscription fees; and (f) discounts provided to any discount ticket service (e.g. TDF).

15. Accounting

Within seven (7) days after the end of each calendar week Producer agrees to forward to Author the amounts due as compensation for such week and also, within such time, to furnish office statements of each performance of the Play during such week, signed by the treasurer or treasurers of the theatre in which performances are given, and countersigned by Producer or his duly authorized representative. Box office statements and payments due for productions presented more than 500 miles from New York City may be furnished and paid within fourteen (14) days after the end of each week, and for productions presented in the United Kingdom or Ireland, within forty-five (45) days. In cases where Author's compensation depends on operating profits or losses, weekly operating statements shall be sent to Author with payment.

16. Billing Credits

In all programs; houseboards, painted signs and paid advertising of the Play under the control of Producer (except marquees, ABC and teaser ads and small ads where no credits are given other than to the title of the Play, the names of the star(s) if any, the name of the theatre and/or one or more critics' quotes), credit shall be given to Author.

The name of Author shall be in type at least sixty percent (60%) of the size, boldness and prominence of the title of the Play or the size and prominence of the star(s) whichever shall be larger. No names except the title of the Play star(s) or a director of prominence shall be more prominent than Author's name, and no names other than the star(s) or Producer shall appear above that of the Author.

Wherever credits are accorded in connection with the Play in a so-called "billing box" pursuant to which the Author is entitled to credit, the size of both the Author and Producer's credits shall be determined by the size of the title of the Play in such "billing box" and will appear only in the billing box.

No inadvertent failure to accord the billing herein provided shall be deemed a breach hereof, unless the same shall not be remedied promptly upon written notice from Author to Producer.

17. House Seats

Producer shall hold one (1) pair of adjoining house seats for Author or his designee, for all Off-Broadway or middle theatre performances of the Play in New York City, and two (2) pairs for each Broadway performances located in the first ten (10) rows in the center section of the orchestra. Additionally, Author shall have the right to purchase four (4) additional pairs of seats in good locations for Opening Night. Such house seats shall be held seventy-two hours (72) prior to the scheduled performance and shall be paid for at the regularly established box office prices. Author acknowledges and agrees that the theatre tickets made available hereunder cannot, except in accordance with the regulations promulgated by the office of the Attorney General of the State of New York, be resold at a premium or otherwise, and that complete and accurate records will be maintained by him, which may be inspected at reasonable times by a duly designated representative of Producer and/or the Attorney General of the State of New York, with respect to the disposition of all tickets made available hereunder.

18. Radio and Television Exploitation

Producer shall have the right to authorize one or more radio and/or television presentations of excerpts from Producer's production of the Play (each such presentation not to exceed fifteen (15) minutes) for the sole purpose of exploiting and publicizing the production of the Play, including presentation on the Antoinette Perry Award (Tony) television program and similar award programs, provided Producer receives no compensation or profits (other than reimbursement for out of pocket expenses), directly or indirectly, for authorizing such radio or television presentations.

19. Right of Assignment

Producer shall have the right to assign this Agreement to a partnership in which Producer or an entity controlled by Producer is a general partner; to a joint venture in which the Producer is one of the joint venturers; or to a corporation in which the Producer is one of the joint venturers; or to a corporation in which the Producer is one of the controlling principals. Any other assignments will require the Producer's approval in writing.

20. Ownership of Copyright and Ideas Contributed by Third Parties

The Author shall control the uses and disposition of the Play except as otherwise provided hereunder. All rights in and to the Play not expressly granted to Producer hereunder are hereby reserved to Author and for Author's use and disposition. All ideas with respect to the Play, whether contributed by the director, or a third party, shall belong to Author. Any copyright of the Play, including any extensions or renewals thereof throughout the world, shall be in the name of the Author.

21. Limitation on Use of Costume and Scenery Designs

Pursuant to the rules and regulations of the United Scenic Artists, Designing Artists and Theatrical Costume Designers' Contract, Author undertakes and agrees that he will not sell, lease, license or authorize the use of any of the original designs of scenery and costumes created by the designers under the standard Scenic Designing Artists and Theatrical Costume Designing contracts for the production, without the designer's consent to Producer's consent.

22. Notices

Any notice to be given hereunder shall be sent by registered or certified mail, return receipt requested, or telegraph or cable addressed to the parties at their respective addresses given herein, or by delivering the same personally to the parties at the addresses first set forth herein. Any party may designate a different address by notice so given. Copies of all notices shall be sent to: Donald C. Farber, Esq., 14 East 75th Street, New York, New York 10021.

23. Arbitration

Any dispute or controversy arising under, out of, or in connection with this Agreement or the making or validity thereof, its interpretation or any breach thereof, shall be determined and settled by arbitration by one arbitrator who shall be selected by mutual agreement of the parties hereto, in New York City, pursuant to the Rules of the American Arbitration Association. The arbitrator is directed to award to the prevailing party reasonable attorneys' fees, costs and disbursements, including reimbursement for the cost of witnesses, travel and subsistence during the arbitration hearings. Any award rendered shall be final and conclusive upon the parties and a judgment thereon may be entered by the appropriate court of the forum having jurisdiction

24. Applicable Law, Entire Agreement

This Agreement shall be deemed to have been made in New York, New York, and shall be governed by New York law applicable to agreements duly executed and to be performed wholly within the State of New York. This Agreement shall be the complete and binding agreement between the patties and may not be amended except by an agreement in writing signed by the parties hereto.

25. Successors and Assigns

The terms and conditions of this Agreement shall be binding upon the respective executors, administrators, successors and assigns of the parties hereto; provided, however, that none of the parties hereto shall, except as otherwise herein provided, have the right, without the written consent of the parties, to assign his or her rights or obligations hereunder, except the right to receive the share of the proceeds, if any, from the Play, payable to such party hereunder.

IN WITNESS WHEREOF, the parties hereto have hereunto set their hands the day and year first above written.

Producer_____

Author_____

APPENDIX H

Limited Liability Company Operating Agreement

LIMITED LIABILITY COMPANY

OPERATING AGREEMENT

of

THE LAST CHANCE LIMITED LIABILITY COMPANY

to produce the musical play

LAST CHANCE

(the "Play")

with Book, Music and Lyrics by John Vester
in an Off-Broadway Theatre

of 399 seats

with a capitalization of $1,000,000

Managing Member: Charles Clancy

Dated: January 1, 1997

TABLE OF CONTENTS

OPERATING AGREEMENT
of
THE LAST CHANCE LIMITED LIABILITY COMPANY

Operating Agreement made as of this first day of June, 19__, by and among Charles Clancy, with offices at 1809 North Prospect Ave., Peoria, Ill. 43210, as Organizer and Managing Member (sometimes referred to as "Manager") of the The Last Chance Limited Liability Company, (the "Company"), and such parties who from time to time execute this Agreement as Members.

W I T N E S S E T H :

WHEREAS, the parties hereto desire to become members of a limited liability company under and subject to the laws of the State of New York; and

WHEREAS, the parties desire to enter into this Operating Agreement to express the terms and conditions of such Company and their respective rights and obligations with respect thereto; and

WHEREAS, the parties hereto wish Charles Clancy to act as the Managing Member and to be the only Authorized Person to act on behalf of the Company;

NOW, THEREFORE, in consideration of the foregoing of the mutual covenants and conditions herein contained, and other good and valuable consideration, receipt of which is hereby acknowledged by each party to the others, the parties hereto, for themselves, their respective heirs, executors, administrators, successors and assigns, hereby agree as follows:

1. **Definitions**: The following terms as used herein shall have the following meanings:

(a) "Agreement" shall mean the Operating Agreement as set forth herein and as amended from time to time, as the context requires. Words such as "herein," "hereinafter," "hereof," "hereby," and "hereunder," when used with reference to this Agreement, refer to this Agreement as a whole, unless the context otherwise requires.

(b) "Articles of Organization" means the document filed with the Department of State of the State of New York, for the purpose of forming a limited liability company pursuant to the Laws of the State of New York.

(c) "Author" shall mean John Vester who wrote the musical play *Last Chance*.

(d) "Authorized Person" means Charles Clancy, the Managing Member, the only person authorized by this Agreement to act on behalf of the Company in carrying on the business of this Company.

(e) "Bankruptcy" as to any person shall mean the filing of petition for relief as to any such person as debtor or bankrupt under the Bankruptcy Act of 1898 or the Bankruptcy Code of 1978 or like provision of law (except if such petition is contested by such person and has been dismissed within 90 days); insolvency of such person as finally determined by a court proceeding; filing by such person as finally determined by a court proceeding; filing by such person of a petition of application to accomplish the same or for the appointment of a receiver or a trustee for such person or a substantial part of his assets; or commencement of any proceedings relating to such person under any reorganization, arrangement, insolvency, adjustment of debtor liquidation law of any jurisdiction, whether now in existence or hereinafter in effect, either by such person or by another, provided that if such proceeding is commenced by another, such person indicates his approval of such proceeding, consents thereby or acquiesces therein, or such proceeding is contested by such person and has not been finally dismissed within ninety (90) days.

(f) "Capital Contribution" shall mean the total amount of money contributed to the Company by an Investor Member in return for a share of the Company's Net Profits as more fully described herein.

(g) "Company" shall mean the Limited Liability Company formed pursuant to this Agreement as such Membership may from time to time be constituted.

(h) "Expenses" shall mean contingent expenses and liabilities, as well as unmatured expenses and liabilities, and until the final determination thereof, the Managing Member shall have the absolute right to establish, as the amount thereof, such sums as he, in his sole discretion, shall deem advisable.

(i) "Gross Receipts" shall mean all sums derived by the Company from the exploitation or turning to account of its rights in the Play (which shall be acquired from the Managing Member upon formation of the Company) including all proceeds derived by the Company from the liquidation of the physical production of the Play at the conclusion of the run thereof, and from the return of bonds and other recoverable items included in the Production Expenses.

(j) "Interests" shall mean the securities offered hereunder, which in the aggregate shall entitle the Managing Member to fifty percent (50%) of the Net Profits of the Company. An Investor Member purchasing Interests shall be entitled to receive the ratio of fifty percent (50%) of the net profits which his Capital Contribution bears to the Total Capitalization.

(k) "Investor Member" shall mean a member of the Company making Capital Contributions to the Company. The Investor Members do not have any votes, nor do they have authority to act on behalf of the Company. The Managing Member, Charles Clancy, may be an Investor Member as well as the Managing Member if he makes a Capital Contribution to the Company.

(1) "Net Profits of the Company" shall mean the excess of Gross Receipts over all Production Expenses, Running Expenses, and other Expenses. This shall include any Production Expenses incurred or paid out by the Managing Member prior to the inception of the Company, for which the Managing member shall be reimbursed upon Total Capitalization.

(m) "Notice" shall mean a writing, containing the information required by this Agreement to be communicated to any person, personally delivered to such person or sent by registered or certified mail, postage prepaid, to such person at the last known address of such person. The date of personal delivery or the date of mailing thereof, as the case may be, shall be deemed the date of receipt of Notice.

(n) "Option Period" shall mean the term commencing October 1, 1996) ending one (1) year therefrom on October 1, 1997, which may be extended to October 1, 1998, pursuant to the terms of the Production Contract between the Managing Member and the Author dated as of October 1, 1996. A copy of the Production Contract may be examined at the offices of Donald C. Farber, Counsel for the Company, 1370 Avenue of the Americas, New York New York 10019; (212) 245-7777 ("Legal Counsel").

(o) "Other Expenses" shall mean all expenses of whatsoever kind or nature other than Production Expenses and Running expenses actually and reasonably incurred in connection with the operation of the business of the company, including, but without limiting the foregoing, commissions paid to agents, and monies paid or payable in connection with claims for plagiarism, libel, and negligence.

(p) "Person" shall mean any individual, partnership, corporation, company, joint venture, trust, business trust, cooperative, or association and the heirs, executors, administrators, successors and assigns thereof, where the context so admits. All pronouns and any variations thereof used herein shall be deemed to refer to the masculine, feminine, neuter singular or plural, as the identity of the person referred to may require.

(q) "Play" shall mean the musical play written by the Author and presently entitled *Last Chance.*

(r) "Production Contract" shall mean the agreement dated as of October 1, 1996, between the Managing Member as Producer and the Author pursuant to which the Managing Member has acquired and will assign to the company upon its formation certain theatrical stage production rights in and to the Play, and certain other and subsidiary rights therein.

(s) "Production Expenses" shall mean fees of the director, choreographer, designers, orchestrator, cost of sets, curtains, drapes, costumes, properties, furnishings, electrical equipment, premiums for bonds and insurance, cash deposits with Actors' Equity Association or other similar organizations by which, according to custom or usual practices of the theatrical business, such deposits may be required to be made, advances to the Authors, rehearsal charges and expenses, transportation charges, cash office charges, reasonable legal and auditing expenses, advance publicity, theatre costs and expenses, costs of a developmental workshop, and all other expenses and losses of whatever kind (other than expenditures precluded hereunder) actually incurred in connection with the production of the Play preliminary to the official opening of the Play. The Managing Member has heretofore incurred or paid, and, prior to the inception of the Company, may incur or pay further Production Expenses as herein set forth, and the amount thereof, and no more, shall be included in the Production Expenses of the Company, and upon Total Capitalization the Managing Member shall be reimbursed for the expenses so paid by him.

(t) "Running Expenses" shall mean all expenses, charges and disbursements of whatever kind actually incurred in connection with the operation of the Play, including, without limiting the generality of the foregoing, royalties (whether or not paid as a share of a royalty pool) and/or other compensation to or for the Authors, business and general managers, director, choreographer, orchestrator, cast, stage help, transportation, cash office charge, reasonable legal and auditing expenses, theatre operating expenses, and all other expenses and losses of whatever kind actually incurred in connection with the operation of the Play, as well as taxes of whatever kind and nature other than taxes on the income of the respective Investor Members and Managing Member. Such Running Expenses shall include, without limitation, payments made in the form of Gross Receipts as well as participation in Net Profits to or for any of the aforementioned persons, services, or rights.

(u) "Subscriber" shall mean a person or entity who invests in the Company and purchases an interest as an Investor Member.

(v) "Total Capitalization" shall mean receipt by the Company of Capital Contributions totaling $1,000,000.

(w) "Unit" shall mean an Interest equal to a one percent (1%) share of the Net Profits of the Company sold to a Subscriber in return for his Capital Contribution of $20,000. The aggregate number of units sold will entitle the owner or owners thereof to fifty percent (50%) of the Net Profits of the Company.

2. **Formation of Company**:

(a) The parties hereto hereby form a Limited Liability Company pursuant to the provisions of the Laws of the State of New York. The Company shall conduct its business and promote the purposes stated herein under the name The Last Chance Limited Liability Company or such other name or names as the Managing Member from time to time may select. The address of the principal office of the Company shall be c/o Donald C. Farber, 1370 Avenue of the Americas, New York, New York 10019, or such other place or places as the Managing Member may select. Notice of any change in the Company's principal office shall be given to the Investor Members.

(b) Except as otherwise provided herein, the purpose of the Company shall be to produce and present the Play in New York City Off-Broadway to open before the expiration of the Option Period, as same may be extended, and otherwise to exploit and turn to account rights held by the Company in connection with the Play pursuant to the Production Contract.

3. **Date of Commencement; Termination of Company**:

(a) The Company will commence on the date on which, pursuant to the Laws of the State of New York, the Articles of Organization of the Company is duly filed with the Department of State of the State of New York. Amendments to the Articles of Organization, if any, shall be filed at appropriate times.

(b) The Company shall terminate upon January 1, 2050, or the first occurrence of any of the following: (i) the Bankruptcy, death, insanity or resignation of the individual Managing Member and the dissolution, cessation of business or Bankruptcy of the corporate Managing Member, if any; (ii) the expiration of all of the Company's rights, title and interest in the Play; (iii) a date fixed by the Managing Member after abandonment of all further company activities; or (iv) any other event causing the dissolution of the Company under the laws of the State of New York.

(c) Dissolution of the Company shall be effective on the day on which the event occurs giving rise to the dissolution, but the Company shall not terminate until Articles of Dissolution shall be filed in the State of New York, and the assets of the Company shall have been distributed as provided herein. Notwithstanding the dissolution of the Company, prior to the termination of the Company the business of the Company shall continue to be governed by this Agreement.

4. **Capitalization**:

(a) The Total Capitalization of $1,000,000 has been established on the basis of the estimated production requirements for the production of the Play as described above, and is an amount which in the opinion of the Managing Member shall be sufficient to mount an Off-Broadway production in a theatre in New York City with 399 seats. The Company intends and hereby authorizes the Managing Member to sell and issue a total of fifty (50) Units and to admit as Investor Members and Additional Investor Members those persons whose Capital Contributions have been accepted by the Managing Member in accordance with this Agreement. Each Investor Member and Additional Investor Member shall contribute to the Capital of the Company the sum set forth as his contribution opposite his signature affixed to the Subscription Form annexed hereto. The Capital Contribution of each Investor Member shall be payable at the time of his execution and delivery to the Managing Member of the Agreement. Capital Contributions will be used for payment of all expenses incurred in connection with the production and presentation of the Play. All persons whose Capital Contributions and subscription are accepted by the Managing Member shall be deemed to be Investor Members.

(b) If the Total Capitalization is not raised prior to the expiration of the option period as extended, the Managing Member shall terminate the offering hereunder, and all Capital Contributions shall be returned to the Subscribers thereof, with accrued interest (if the funds are held in an interest bearing account), except to the extent utilized by consent of individual Subscribers who have waived their right of refund.

(c) No Investor Member will be required to contribute any additional funds to the Company above his initial Capital Contribution.

(d) If the Expenses actually incurred shall exceed the Total Capitalization, the Managing Member may, by making contributions or loans himself, or by obtaining additional funds or contributions or loans from the Investor Members or others, make available to the Company such sums as shall equal the excess, but such additional contributions or loans shall not have the effect of reducing the share of Net Profits payable to the Investor Members, and any assignment of Net Profits to persons making such contributions or loans shall come from the Managing Member's share of the Net Profits of the Producing Company. If, however, any such loans are made to the Company, such loans shall be entitled to be repaid in full, without interest, prior to the return of any Capital Contributions to the Investor Members.

(e) Unless otherwise provided herein, the Managing Member shall have sole discretion in establishing the conditions of the offering and sale of Units; and the Managing Member is hereby authorized and directed to take whatever action he deems necessary, convenient, appropriate, or desirable in connection therewith, including, but not limited to, the preparation and filing on behalf of the Company of an offering circular, or prospectus with the SEC and the securities commissions (or similar agencies) of those states and jurisdictions which the Managing Member shall deem necessary.

5. **Assignment of Assets by Managing Member**: Subject to any limitations otherwise set forth in this agreement, if any, the Managing Member will, upon completion of Total Capitalization of the Company, assign to the Company all right, title and interest in all assets acquired by him for the presentation of the Play, for which he will be reimbursed by the Company for his actual expenditures in acquiring such assets, and the Company will assume all of the Managing Member's obligations under any agreements respecting such assets.

6. **Distribution of Remaining Cash**: After payment or reason-able provision for payment of all debts, liabilities, taxes and contingent liabilities of the Company, and after provision for a reserve in the amount of $60,000, all remaining cash shall be distributed at least annually to the Investor Members together with the statement of operation herein provided for, pro rata, until

their Capital Contributions to the Company shall have been repaid. Thereafter, all cash in excess of such contingent liabilities shall be paid to the Managing Member and Investor Members in the same proportion in which they shall share in the Net Profits.

7. **Sharing of Net Profits and Losses**: The Net Profits that may accrue from the business of the Company shall be distributed and divided among the Managing Member and Investor Members as follows:

(a) The Capital Contributions of the Investor Members shall first be repaid as provided above.

(b) The Investor Members shall each be entitled to receive that proportion of fifty percent (50%) of the Net Profits which his or her Capital Contribution bears to the Total Capitalization, excluding, however, from such Investor Members all persons who, pursuant to Paragraph 4 hereof, may be entitled to compensation only from the Managing Member's share of such Net Profits, and excluding the contributions so made by such persons.

(c) The Managing Member shall be entitled to receive fifty percent (50%) of the Net Profits.

(d) Until Net Profits shall have been earned, losses suffered and incurred by the Company, up to the Total Capitalization plus additional contributions, if any, shall be borne entirely by the Investor Members in proportion to, and only to the extent of, their respective Capital Contributions. After Net Profits shall have been earned, then, to the extent of such Net Profits, the Managing Member and Investor Members shall share any such losses pro rata in the same proportion as they are entitled to share in Net Profits pursuant to the provisions of this Paragraph 7.

8. **Liability of Members**: No Member shall be personally liable for any debts, obligations, or losses of the Company beyond the amount of his Capital Contribution to the Company and his share of any undistributed Net Profits. An Investor Member shall be liable only to make his Capital Contribution and shall not be required to lend any funds to the Company. If any sum by way of repayment of Capital Contribution or distribution of Net Profits shall have been paid prior or subsequent to the termination date of the Company, and at

any time subsequent to such repayment there shall be any unpaid debts, taxes, liabilities, or obligations of the Company, and the Company shall not have sufficient assets to meet them, then each Investor Member and the Managing Member may be obligated to repay the Company, to the extent of his or her Capital Contribution so returned to him or her or any Net Profits so distributed to him or her, as the Managing Member may need for such purpose and demand. In such event, the Investor Members and Managing Member shall first repay any Net Profits theretofore distributed to them, respectively, and if insufficient, the Investor Members shall return Capital Contributions that may have been repaid to them; such return by the Investor Members respectively to be made in proportion to the amounts of Capital Contributions that may have been so repaid to them, respectively. All such repayments by Investor Members shall be repaid promptly after receipt by each Investor Member from the Managing Member of a written notice requesting such repayment.

9. **Distribution Upon Liquidation**: Upon the termination of the Company, the assets of the Company shall be liquidated as promptly as possible and the cash proceeds shall be applied as follows in the following order of priority:

(a) To the payment of debts, taxes, obligations, and liabilities of the Company and the necessary expenses of liquidation. Where there is a contingent debt, obligation or liability, a reserve shall be set up to meet it, and if and when such contingency shall cease to exist, the monies, if any, in such reserve shall be distributed as provided for in this Paragraph 9.

(b) To the repayment of Capital Contributions of the Investor Members, such Members sharing such repayment proportionately to their respective Capital Contributions.

(c) The surplus, if any, of such assets then remaining shall be divided among the Managing Member and Investor Members in the proportion that they share in the Net Profits.

10. **Death of Member**: If an Investor Member shall die, his or her executors or administrators, or, if the Member shall become insane, or has been dissolved if not a natural person, his or her committee or other representative shall have the same rights that the Investor Member would have had if he or she had not died, become insane, or been dissolved, and the Interest of such Investor Member shall, until the termination of the Company, be subject to all of the

terms, provisions, and conditions of this Agreement as if such Investor Member had not died, become insane or been dissolved.

11. Duties of Managing Member:

(a) The Managing Member shall:

(i) at all times from the inception of financial transactions during the continuance of the Company, keep or cause to be maintained full and faithful books of account in which shall be entered fully and accurately each transaction of the Company. All of such books of account shall be at all times open to the inspection and examination of the Investor Members or their representatives. The Managing Member shall likewise have available for examination and inspection of the Investor Members or their representatives, at any time, box office statements received from the theatre (or theatres, as the case may be) in which the Play is presented by the Company. The Managing Member agrees to furnish financial statements to the Investor Members and the Department of Law of the State of New York pursuant to the provisions of Article 23 of the Arts and Cultural Affairs Law and the regulations issued by the Attorney General thereunder. The Managing Member further agrees to deliver to the Investor Members all information necessary to enable the Investor Members to prepare their respective federal and state income tax returns;

(ii) render in connection with the theatrical productions of the Play such services as are customarily and usually rendered by theatrical producers, and devote as much time thereto as they may deem necessary, and manage and have complete control over all business affairs and decisions of the Company with respect to all productions of the Play;

(iii) have the right to apply for an exemption from any applicable accounting requirements set forth in Article 23 of the Arts and Cultural Affairs Law of the State of New York or in the applicable regulations promulgated thereunder, as such law or regulations may be amended from time to time;

(iv) be entitled to reimbursement by the Company upon Total Capitalization, or if any investors authorize the use of their investment prior to Total Capitalization being raised and they waive the return of their investment, for all out-of-pocket expenses reasonably paid or incurred by the Managing Member in connection with the discharge of his obligations hereunder or otherwise reasonably paid or incurred by the Managing Member on behalf of the Company;

(v) have the right to amend this Agreement from time to time by filing a Certificate of Amendment or a Certificate of Correction, whichever is appropriate, without the consent of any of the Investor Members (A) to add to the duties or obligations of the managing member, or surrender any right or power granted to the Managing Member herein, for the benefit of the Investor Members; (B) to cure any ambiguity, to correct or supplement any provision herein that may be inconsistent with any other provision herein, or to add any other provisions with respect to matters or questions arising under this Agreement that will not be inconsistent with the provision of this Agreement; and (C) to delete or add any provisions of this Agreement required to be so deleted or added by the staff of the SEC or by a State securities commissioner or other government official, whether United States or foreign, which addition or deletion is deemed by such authority to be for the benefit or protection of the Investor Members; and

(vi) have the right to amend this Agreement with the consent of all the Investor Members to add one or more persons, firms or corporations as Managing Member up until the time the financing is completed. In this event, if this occurs prior to Total Capitalization, an offer of rescission will be made to investors who invested before the additional Managing Member is added.

(b) Notwithstanding anything to the contrary contained herein, this Agreement may not be amended without the consent of all the Investor Members who would be adversely affected by an amendment that:

(i) modifies the limited liability of an Investor Member;

(ii) alters the interests of the Investor Members in the allocation of profits or losses or in distributions from the Company; or

(iii) affects the status of the Company for federal income tax purposes.

12. **Additional Services of Managing Member**: In the event that the Managing Member finds it necessary to perform any services of a third person, the Managing Member may receive the reasonable compensation for such services that a third person would have received for the services rendered.

13. **Repayment of Capital Contribution**: The Investor Members shall not have the right to demand and receive property other than cash in return for their Capital Contributions. In the repayment of Capital Contributions, the dividing of profits or otherwise, except as provided in Paragraph 14 hereof, no Investor Member shall have priority over any other Investor Member.

14. **Theatre Guarantee; Union Bonds**: The Managing Member may arrange for the deposit of bonds required by the Actors' Equity Association or any other union or organization or theatre guarantees, without, however, reducing the proportion of Net Profits payable to the Investor Members. Such arrangements may provide for obtaining such bonds or guarantees from persons who may not be Investor Members upon terms which require that prior to the return of Investor Members' Capital Contributions, or the payment of any Net Profits, all funds otherwise available for such purposes shall be set aside and paid over to the Actors' Equity Association, or other such union, organization or theatre, in substitution for and in discharge of the bonds and guarantees furnished by such other persons. In the event such arrangements reduce the estimated production requirements, the Managing Member shall have the right to assign from the proportion of Net Profits allocable to the Investor Members, to the person contributing such guarantee or security, a share not greater than the amount that would otherwise have been allocable to the Capital Contribution required for the respective bonds; provided, however, that in no event shall the shares of Net Profits payable to each Investor Member hereunder be less than the proportion that would otherwise have been payable to such Investor Member had the amount of the respective bonds been contributed by the Investor Members as part of the Total Capitalization.

15. **Payment of Expenses**: Capital Contributions, in the discretion of the Managing Member, may be used to pay Running Expenses, Other Expenses, and Production Expenses.

16. **Additional Members**:

(a) The Managing Member shall have the right to admit Additional Investor Members and/or permit Investor Members to increase their respective interests in the Company without obtaining the consent of any Investor Member, until the Company has investments in the amount of the Total Capitalization. A Member may not assign his or her interest, or any part thereof, in the Company.

(b) All references herein to Investor Members shall refer as well to Additional Investor Members, and all terms and conditions governing Investor Members shall also govern Additional Investor Members.

17. **Co-production**: The Managing Member shall have the unrestricted right, in the Managing Member's sole discretion, to coproduce the Play with any other entity and to enter into any agreement, in connection therewith, including partnership agreements, limited liability company operating agreements, or joint venture agreements; provided, however, that no such co-production or similar arrangement shall decrease or dilute the Interests of the Investor Members.

18. **Abandonment of Play**: In the event that the Managing Member at any time shall determine in good faith that continuation of the production of the Play will not benefit the Company and should be abandoned, he shall have the sole right to make arrangements with any person to continue the run of the Play on such terms as the Managing Member may deem appropriate and beneficial to the Company, or to abandon the same.

19. **Additional Company to Present Play; Licensee**:

(a) In the event the Managing Member shall desire the Company to organize a company or companies in addition to the original one, to present the Play in the British Isles, the United States and Canada, or any other part of the world (if the right to produce the Play in such areas accrues to the Company), then the Managing Member shall have the right to do so and may invite Investor Members to contribute to the capital of such companies, but nothing contained herein shall be construed to obligate the Managing Member to accept the contribution of an Investor Member for such purposes.

(b) The Company may also enter into one or more agreements with respect to the disposition of British production and subsidiary rights of the Play with any partnership, corporation, company, or other firm in which the Managing Member may be in any way interested, provided that such agreement shall be on fair and reasonable terms. The Managing Member shall also have the unrestricted right to employ a producer or manager for such British production, to pay him or her an amount the Managing Member deems appropriate, and to give such person production billing either as a co-producer or associate producer.

(c) In addition, the Managing Member alone or associated in any way with any person, firm, or corporation, may produce or co-produce other productions of the Play in other places and media, and may receive compensation therefore without any obligation whatever to account to the Company or the Investor Members; provided, however, that the Company shall be entitled to receive from any such producing entity the customary fees and royalties payable to it, if any, as producers of the original Play in connection with such other productions.

(d) The Managing Member shall have the right in the Managing Member's sole discretion to make arrangements to license any rights in the Play to any other party or parties they may designate, provided the Company receives reasonable royalties or other reasonable compensation therefor, and, provided further, that the Company shall not be involved in any loss or expenses by reason thereof. In the event of any such license of rights, the Managing Member may render services to the licensee in connection with exploitation by the licensee of the rights so licensed.

20. **Purchase of Production Rights**: If, upon the termination of the Company, any production rights of the Play, with or without the physical production of the Play and with or without the Company's interest in the proceeds

of the subsidiary rights of the Play, are purchased by the Managing Member, the amount paid by such party or parties shall be the fair and reasonable market value thereof, or an amount equal to the best offer obtainable, whichever is higher.

21. **Exclusive Option; Subsidiary Rights Income**: The Managing Member has acquired the exclusive option to produce the Play within the Option Period in an Off-Broadway or Middle Theatre and as a developmental production in the Territory pursuant to the Production Contract. The Company, upon assignment to it of the Production Contract by the Managing Member, and upon the presentation of a designated number of performances produced by the Company, will receive as much as forty percent (40%) of the income derived by the Authors from the disposition of certain of the Authors' subsidiary rights. A copy of the Production Contract is on file at the offices of legal counsel for the Company.

22. **Royalties; Royalty Pool Formula**: The Managing Member represents that the following percentages of the weekly Net Receipts of a production of the Musical as an Off-Broadway production will, in lieu of a percentage of gross weekly box office receipts, be payable by the Company in a Royalty Pool formula as follows:

It is not anticipated that anyone, except the theatre, will be paid a percentage of the gross weekly box office receipts. Instead, subject to the approval of any union having jurisdiction, all royalty participants and the Producer for the producer's fee will share thirty-five percent (35%) (going to forty percent [40%] after recoupment of the total production costs) of the weekly Net Receipts (as defined herein), calculated four every four-week period, and the other sixty-five percent (65%) of the weekly Net Receipts will be paid to the Company. The royalty participants and the Producer for the producer's fee are each allocated a certain number of points for their contributions to the Musical. Each royalty participant's share of the royalty pool will be based on the proportion that his or her number of points bears to the total number of points allocated to all royalty participants.

The minimum guarantee will not be treated as an expense in calculating the Net Receipts but will be treated as an advance against each royalty participant's share of the Net Receipts in the Royalty Pool. The minimum weekly guarantees will be computed and paid on a weekly basis and will be considered profit distributions from the Royalty Pool that will be paid within fourteen (14) days after the end of each four-week cycle. The Royalty Pool for each company presenting the Play shall be computed separately.

Each royalty participant's share of the weekly Net Receipts will be based on the following division:

Author, as Bookwriter, Composer, Lyricist	6.0 points
Charles Clancy, for Producer's fee	2.0 points
Director/Choreographer (Estimated)	2.0 points
Steven M. Levy, General Manager	1.0 point
Donald C. Farber, Attorney	1.0 point
Estimated Total	12.0 points

The Producer reserves the sole right to change, modify, increase, or decrease any of the points allocated to the royalty pool participants and to include other royalty pool participants.

Each royalty participant will receive a minimum weekly royalty in the amount of $150 for each one point allocated to such respective party.

23. **Producer's Fee**: In addition to receiving fifty percent (50%) of the Company Net Profits, the Managing Member shall be entitled to receive a producer's management fee computed as part of the Royalty Pool formula as above set forth. The Managing Member shall also be paid a weekly cash office charge in the sum of $500 for this Off-Broadway production. The aforementioned cash office charge shall be paid to the Managing Member beginning two (2) weeks before the commencement of rehearsals of each company presenting the Play and then two (2) weeks after the close of each such company.

24. **General Manager**: Steven M. Levy has been engaged by the Managing Member to perform the services of General Manager in connection with the Musical. The General Manager shall receive a preproduction fee of $5,000 and a weekly fee of $900 commencing one (1) week prior to the first week of rehearsal and continuing until two (2) weeks after the final performance.

25. **Bank Where Funds Held**: All monies raised from this offer and sale of Interests shall be held in a special bank account in trust at Citibank, Third Avenue and 46th Street, New York, New York 10017, until actually employed

for preproduction or production purposes or until returned to the investors. The Managing Member will have the sole discretion as to whether such funds shall be maintained in an interest-bearing account. Prior to Total Capitalization, the Capital Contribution of a subscriber may only be employed for pre-production or production purposes if specifically authorized by such subscriber.

26. **Immediate Use of Funds**: Any Investor Member who shall sign this Agreement under the category entitled "Investor Members Authorizing Immediate Use of Funds and Waiving Right of Refund" shall not be entitled to reimbursement of his or her Capital Contribution in the event Total Capitalization is not raised. By so signing, Investor Members specifically authorize the Managing Member to utilize their Capital Contribution for Production Expenses incurred prior to Total Capitalization.

27. **Attorney in Fact**: Each of the Investor Members and each of the Additional Investor Members does hereby make, constitute and appoint the Managing Member his true and lawful attorney in fact in his name, place, and stead, to make, execute, sign, acknowledge and file: (1) the Articles of Organization of the Company, including therein all information required by the laws of the State of New York; (2) any amended Articles of Organization, as may be required pursuant to this Agreement; (3) all certificates, documents and papers which may be required to effectuate dissolution of the Company after its termination; and (4) all such other instruments which may be deemed required or permitted by the laws of any state, the United States of America, or any political subdivision or agency thereof, to effectuate, implement, continue, and defend the valid and subsisting existence, rights, and property of the Company as a Limited Liability Company and its power to carry out its purposes as set forth herein.

28. **Counterparts May Be Signed**: This Agreement may be executed in one or more counterparts and each of such counterparts, for all purposes, shall be deemed to be an original, but all of such counterparts together shall constitute but one and the same instrument, binding upon all parties hereto, notwithstanding that all of such parties may not have executed the same counterpart.

29. **Arbitration**: Any dispute arising under, out of, in connection with, or in relation to this Agreement, or the making or validity thereof, or its interpretation of any breach thereof, shall be determined and settled by arbitration in New

York City pursuant to the rules then obtaining of the American Arbitration Association. The arbitrator is directed to award to the prevailing party reasonable attorneys' fees, costs, and disbursements, including reimbursement for the cost of witnesses, travel, and subsistence during the arbitration and hearings. Any award rendered thereon may be entered in the highest court of the forum, state or federal having jurisdiction. The provisions of this Paragraph 29, or any other provisions of this Agreement, shall not, however, operate to deprive the Investor Members of any rights afforded to them under the securities laws of the United States of America.

30. **Documents Filed**: Each of the parties to this Agreement acknowledges and agrees that one original of this Agreement (or set of original counterparts) shall be held at the office of the Company, that the Articles of Organization and such amendments thereto as are required shall be filed in the office of Secretary of State of New York, and that a duplicate original (or set of duplicate original counterparts) of each shall be held at the offices of the Company's Legal Counsel, and that there shall be distributed to each party a conformed copy thereof.

31. **Entire Document**: This Agreement contains the entire agreement between the parties hereto with respect to the matters contained herein and cannot be modified or amended except by written agreement signed by all of the parties.

32. **Waiver**: Except as otherwise expressly provided herein, no purported waiver by any party of any breach by another party of any of his obligations, agreements or covenants hereunder, or any part thereof, shall be effective unless made by written instrument subscribed to by the party or parties sought to be bound thereby, and no failure to pursue or elect any remedy with respect to any default under or breach of any provision of this Agreement, or any part thereof, shall be deemed to be a waiver of any other subsequent, similar or different default or breach, or any election of remedies available in connection therewith, nor shall the acceptance or receipt by any party of any money or other consideration due him under this Agreement, with or without knowledge of any breach hereunder, constitute a waiver of any provision of this Agreement with respect to such or any other breach.

33. **Severability**: Each provision of this Agreement shall be considered to be severable and if, for any reason, any such provision or provisions, or any part thereof, is determined to be invalid and contrary to any existing or

future applicable law, such invalidity shall not impair the operation of or affect those portions of this Agreement which are valid, but this Agreement shall be construed and enforced in all respects as if such invalid or unenforceable provision or provisions had been omitted, provided, however, that the status of this Company, as a Company, shall not be prejudiced.

34. **Agreement Binding**: This Agreement shall be binding upon and inure to the benefit of the parties hereto and their respective executors, administrators, and successors, but shall not be deemed for the benefit of creditors of any other persons, nor shall it be deemed to permit any assignment by the Managing Member or Investor Members of any of their rights or obligations hereunder.

35. **Further Instruments**: Each of the parties hereto hereby agrees that he or she shall hereafter execute and deliver such further instruments and do such further acts and things as may be required or useful to carry out the intent and purpose of this Agreement and as are not inconsistent with the terms hereof.

36. **Governing Law**: This Agreement and all matters pertaining thereto shall be governed by the laws of the State of New York applicable to agreements to be performed entirely within the State of New York.

37. **Offering Material Furnished**: By his signature appended to this Agreement, each Investor Member represents and warrants that together with this Limited Liability Company Operating Agreement, he or she has been furnished with offering material contained in the Private Placement Memorandum, as same may be amended.

38. **Reimbursement of Expenditures Advanced**: Up to the date of this Offering, the Managing Member has expended the sum of $7,500 for payment of legal fees on account and $2,500 for the General Manager for the benefit of the Company.

39. **No Personal Liability of Members**: There is no personal liability of the Managing Member, Charles Clancy, to the Company or to the Members for damages for any breach of duty in his capacity as manager, unless there is a judgment or other final adjudication adverse to him that establishes that his acts or omissions were in bad faith or involved intentional misconduct, or a knowing violation of law or that he personally gained in fact a financial profit or other advantage to which he was not legally entitled or that with respect to any distribution, his acts were not performed in accordance with the applicable laws governing a Limited Liability Company in the State of New York.

40. **Risk Factor**: These securities involve a high degree of risk and prospective purchasers should be prepared to sustain a loss of their entire investment.

41. **Managing Member to Control Business**: The Investor Members signing this Agreement do hereby acknowledge that the Company is to be managed solely by Charles Clancy, the Managing Member, and that the Investor Members do not have any control of the business, except as otherwise herein specifically set forth. The Investor Members will not have authority to conduct any business of the Company and each agrees that he or she will not act on behalf of the Company, nor will he or she represent that they have any authority to act on behalf of the Company, or to bind the Company in any respect.

IN WITNESS WHEREOF, the parties hereto have executed this Operating Agreement on the day and year first above written.

As Managing Member

_____

Charles Clancy

STATE OF NEW YORK)
                   :
COUNTY OF NEW YORK)

On this   day of   , 1997, before me personally appeared Charles Clancy to me known and known to me to be the individual described in and who executed the foregoing instrument, and he duly acknowledged to me that he executed the same.

_____

Notary Public

INVESTOR MEMBERS

INVESTOR MEMBERS WHOSE CASH CONTRIBUTIONS MAY BE USED ONLY UPON FULL CAPITALIZATION

Printed Name: _____

Social Security
No. and/or Employer I.D. No.: _____

Home Address: _____

Home Telephone No.: _____

Business Address: _____

Business Telephone No.: _____

Amount to be Contributed: _____

_____
(Signature)

INVESTOR MEMBERS WHOSE CONTRIBUTIONS
ARE OTHER THAN CASH

THE FOLLOWING SIGN THE FOREGOING AGREEMENT AS INVESTOR MEMBERS, BUT IN LIEU OF A CASH CONTRIBUTION AGREE TO MAKE THEIR CONTRIBUTION BY GIVING, OR CAUSING TO BE GIVEN, THE FOLLOWING DESCRIBED BOND OR SECURITY DEPOSIT OF THE FOLLOWING FACE AMOUNT:

Printed Name: _____

Social Security
No. and/or Employer I.D. No.: _____

Home Address: _____

Home Telephone No.: _____

Business Address: _____

Business Telephone No.: _____

Amount to be Contributed: _____

_____
(Signature)

INVESTOR MEMBERS

INVESTOR MEMBERS AUTHORIZING IMMEDIATE USE OF FUNDS AND WAIVING RIGHT OF REFUND

THE FOLLOWING SIGN THE FOREGOING AGREEMENT AS INVESTOR MEMBERS AND AGREE THAT THEIR CONTRIBUTIONS MAY BE USED FORTHWITH BY THE MANAGING MEMBER FOR PRODUCTION OR PREPRODUCTION PURPOSES. THE UNDERSIGNED WAIVE THEIR RIGHT OF REFUND OF ANY PORTION OF SUCH CONTRIBUTION EXPENDED FOR SUCH PURPOSES IN THE EVENT THE PRODUCTION IS ABANDONED PRIOR TO FULL CAPITALIZATION OF THE COMPANY. THE UNDERSIGNED OBTAIN NO ADVANTAGE BY ENTERING INTO THIS AGREEMENT.

Printed Name: _____

Social Security
No. and/or Employer I.D. No.: _____

Home Address: _____

Home Telephone No.: _____

Business Address: _____

Business Telephone No.: _____

Amount to be Contributed: _____

_____
(Signature)

Articles of Organization

Under Section 203 of the Limited Liability Company Law
of the State on New York.

For the purpose of organizing a Limited Liability Company (the "Company") under the Laws of the State of New York, the undersigned, being over the age of eighteen, does hereby allege as follows:

1. The name of the Company shall be "The Last Chance Limited Liability Company."

2. The office of the Limited Liability Company shall be located in the County of New York, State of New York.

3. The Company will be dissolved upon the sooner of January 1, 2050, the bankruptcy, death, insanity, or resignation of the Managing Member or in accordance with the events set forth in §701 of the Limited Liability Company Law.

4. The Secretary of State of the State of New York is hereby designated agent of the Company upon whom process against it may be served and the post office address to which the Secretary of State shall mail a copy of any process against the Company served upon the Secretary of State is Charles Clancy, c/o Donald C. Farber, 1370 Avenue of the Americas, New York, New York 10019.

5. The Company will not have a registered agent within the State.

6. The company is to be managed by one or more managers.

7. None of the members of the Company are liable in their capa-city as members for any of the obligations or liabilities of the Company.

8. The purpose of the Company shall be to produce and present the Musical Play, *Last Chance* in New York City for an Off-Broadway production, and otherwise to exploit and turn to account rights held by the Company in connection with the play.

9. There is no personal liability of the Manager, Charles Clancy, to the Company or to the Members for damages for any breach of duty in his capacity as Manager, unless there is a judgment or other final adjudication adverse to him that establishes that his acts or omissions were in bad faith or involved intentional misconduct, or a knowing violation of law or that he personally gained in fact a financial profit or other advantage to which he was not legally entitled or that with respect to any distribution, his acts were not performed in accordance with the applicable laws governing a Limited Liability Company in the State of New York.

In witness whereof I have subscribed this certificate and do hereby affirm the foregoing as true under the penalties of perjury, this 1st day of March, 1997

_____

Charles Clancy, Organizer
1809 North Prospect Avenue,
Peoria, Ill. 43210

APPENDIX J

Private Placement Memorandum

Total Capitalization $10,000,000 in
Limited Liability Company Interests in
Bring Them Home LLC

Jackie Robson will be the Managing Member (the "Managing Member" or the "Producer") of Bring Them Home LLC, a limited liability company formed under the laws of the State of New York to produce and present in a Broadway theatre in New York City with approximately 1,933 seats and if successful thereafter elsewhere in the United States and Canada the stage musical play presently entitled:

Bring Them Home ("the Play")

THE UNITED STATES SECURITIES AND EXCHANGE COMMISSION (THE "COMMISSION") DOES NOT PASS UPON THE MERITS OF OR GIVE ITS APPROVAL TO ANY SECURITIES OFFERED OR THE TERMS OF THE OFFERING, NOR DOES IT PASS UPON THE ACCURACY OR COMPLETENESS OF ANY PRIVATE PLACEMENT MEMORANDUM OR OTHER SELLING LITERATURE. THESE SECURITIES ARE OFFERED PURSUANT TO AN EXEMPTION FROM REGISTRATION WITH THE COMMISSION; HOWEVER, THE COMMISSION HAS NOT MADE AN

INDEPENDENT DETERMINATION THAT THE SECURITIES OFFERED HEREUNDER ARE EXEMPT FROM REGISTRATION.

Proceeds to Company $10,000,000
Price to Public $10,000,000

                                    Underwriting
                                    Discount
                                    Or Commission
                                    Per Unit $200,000
                                    Per Unit $200,000

NO DEALER, SALESMAN OR ANY OTHER PERSON HAS BEEN AUTHORIZED TO GIVE ANY INFORMATION OR TO MAKE ANY REPRESENTATIONOTHERTHANTHOSECONTAINEDINTHISPRIVATE PLACEMENT MEMORANDUM (THE "MEMORANDUM"), AND IF GIVEN OR MADE, SUCH INFORMATION OR REPRESENTATIONS MUST NOT BE RELIED UPON AS HAVING BEEN AUTHORIZED BY THE MANAGING MEMBER. THIS MEMORANDUM DOES NOT CONSTITUTE AN OFFER TO SELL OR A SOLICITATION OF AN OFFER TO BUY ANY OF THE SECURITIES OFFERED HEREBY, TO ANY PERSON IN ANY JURISDICTION WHERE SUCH OFFER OR SOLICITATION WOULD BE UNLAWFUL.

THE DATE OF THIS MEMORANDUM IS JUNE 1, 2005.

THESE SECURITIES INVOLVE A HIGH DEGREE OF RISK AND PROSPECTIVE PURCHASERS SHOULD BE PREPARED TO SUSTAIN A LOSS OF THEIR ENTIRE INVESTMENT (SEE "RISK FACTORS"). THIS MEMORANDUM MAY NOT BE USED FOR A PERIOD OF MORE THAN NINE (9) MONTHS AFTER THE DATE OF THIS MEMORANDUM.

THE ATTORNEY GENERAL OF THE STATE OF NEW YORK HAS NOT REVIEWED THIS DOCUMENT OR ANY OTHER DOCUMENT SUBMITTED TO INVESTORS IN CONNECTION WITH THIS OFFERING FOR THE ADEQUACY OF ITS DISCLOSURE AND DOES NOT PASS ON THE MERITS OF THIS OFFERING.

EACHPURCHASEROFLIMITEDLIABILITYCOMPANYINTERESTS ACKNOWLEDGES THAT THE PURCHASE IS AS AN INVESTMENT

AND THE SALE OF SUCH INTERESTS IS SPECIFICALLY LIMITED AS SET FORTH IN THE OPERATING AGREEMENT OF BRING THEM HOME LLC (THE "OPERATING AGREEMENT") AND BY SIGNING THE OPERATING AGREEMENT AGREES TO BE BOUND BY SUCH TERMS.

Limited Liability Company Interests are being offered (the "Offering") by Jackie Robson the Managing Member. The ultimate issuer will be Bring Them Home LLC (the "Company"), a limited liability company formed under the laws of the State of New York. The address of the Company will be c/o Donald C. Farber, 1270 Avenue of the Americas, New York, NY 10020.

Aggregate Limited Liability Company Interests are not actually divided into a specific number of units and monetary amounts. For purposes of convenience, they may be considered to consist of 50 "Units" of $200,000 per Unit with a capitalization of $10,000,000. An investor may purchase fractional Units

All money raised will be held by the Managing Member in a special account at Fleet Bank Madison Avenue at 48th Street, New York, NY 10017 until the total Capital Contributions are raised, at which time the Offering will be closed. The money held in the special account will not be released until the Offering is closed (unless an Investor Member gives permission to the earlier use of his or her investment), and when all funds are released no additional sales will be made. The Offering expires on December 1, 2006. This Memorandum may not be used after nine (9) months from the date of this Memorandum unless it is amended.

TABLE OF CONTENTS

SUMMARY OF THE PRIVATE PLACEMENT MEMORANDUM

The Company has been formed pursuant to the laws of the State of New York for the purpose of producing and presenting the Play and exploiting and turning to account the rights at any time held by the Company in connection therewith. All rights to produce the Play as set forth in the Literary Purchase Agreement and the Option Agreement have been retained by the Company. It is currently anticipated that the Play will open in New York City in a theatre containing approximately 1,933 seats. The Play is a musical adaptation of the novel *Bring Them Home* written by Al Hatley with a book by Abe Manley, music by Jane Ramon and lyrics by Ms. Ramon and Mr. Manley.

All money raised from the Offering shall be held in a special bank account in trust at Fleet Bank until actually employed for pre-production or production purposes of this particular theatrical production or until returned to the Investors Members. The Managing Member shall have sole discretion as to whether such funds are to be maintained in an interest-bearing account. Prior to Total Capitalization, the Capital Contribution of a Subscriber may only be employed for pre-production or production purposes if specifically authorized by such Subscriber. The Investor Members will receive fifty percent (50%) of the Net Profits of the Company and the Managing Member will receive the other fifty percent (50%) of such profits.

The Company shall terminate upon January 1, 2050 or the sooner occurrence of any of the following: (i) the Bankruptcy, death, insanity or resignation of a Managing Member; (ii) the expiration of all of the Company's rights, title and interest in the Play; (iii) a date fixed by the Managing Member after abandonment of all further Company activities; or (iv) any other event causing the dissolution of the Company under the laws of the State of New York. The Managing Members have the right to add one or more persons or corporate entities as Managing Member. In this event, if this occurs prior to Total Capitalization, an offer of rescission will be made to Investor Members who invested before the additional Managing Member are added.

The Company's plan of operation is: (a) to engage in pre-production activities with respect to the Play; (b) upon completion of pre-production activities, to engage in rehearsals of the Play; (c) during the rehearsal period, to begin the promotion and publicity for the Play; and (d) to produce and present the Play.

Since the Company has not yet engaged in its business, there are no income, expense or other financial statements of the Company presently available. The accountants for the Company have not as of yet been engaged. For information with respect to the risks to Subscribers in connection with the Offering, see generally "RISK FACTORS."

THE COMPANY

The Managing Member has organized the Company as a New York limited liability company to raise Capital Contributions totaling for the purpose of producing and presenting the Play and exploiting and turning to account the rights held by the Company therein. The capitalization requirement is, in the opinion of the Managing Member, sufficient to mount a production in a Theatre of 1,933 seats.

If the Total Capitalization has not been raised by the time the option to produce the Play runs out, December 1, 2006, if the option to produce the Play has been extended to that date), the Offering will cease and all Capital Contributions previously received will be returned with accrued interest, if any, (unless the individual Subscriber waives receipt of the accrued interest), except Capital Contributions which have been expended with the consent of individual Subscribers who have waived their right of refund.

The Managing Member will have sole and complete authority over the management and operations of the Company. The Managing Member in her sole discretion may purchase Units of Limited Liability Company Interests in the Company and participate therein as an Investor Member,. c/o Donald C. Farber, 1270 Avenue of the Americas, New York, NY 10020

RISK FACTORS

These securities involve a high degree of risk and prospective purchasers should be prepared to sustain a loss of their entire investment.

1. The vast majority of theatrical productions report losses and unrecovered production costs.

2. Based on a capitalization of $10,000,000 for the production of the Play, and assuming the Play is presented at prevailing box office scale in an approximately 1,933 seats Off-Broadway theatre in New York City with potential gross weekly box office receipts of approximately $1,243,500 and estimated weekly expenses of approximately $727,000 the Play must run for 18.6 weeks (149 performances) to a full capacity house in order to recoup

the total production costs, exclusive of bonds and returnable deposits or for a longer period of time if presented at less than full house capacity.

3. The substantial majority of the plays produced for the stage fail to run long enough to recoup the total production costs. Of those that do, few play to capacity audiences throughout their run.

4. There is no assurance that the Play will be an economic success even if the Play receives critical acclaim.

5. These securities should not be purchased unless the Subscriber is prepared for the possibility of total loss and is able to afford such total loss. The sole business of the Company will be the production of the Play. In such a venture the risk of loss is especially high in contrast with the prospect for the realization of any profits.

6. An individual Subscriber may agree to the use of his or her Capital Contribution prior to full capitalization of the Company, and waive his or her right of refund in the event of abandonment prior to the production of the Play. If the Offering is withdrawn or abandoned for any reason prior to the completion of the Offering, such Subscriber's funds will have been lost without there having been an opening of the production which is the subject of the investment.

7. In the event the Capital Contributions raised through the Offering are insufficient to produce the Play as contemplated, the Managing Member may advance or cause to be advanced, or may borrow on behalf of the Company, additional capital, without interest. Such advances or loans are to be repaid prior to the repayment of the Capital Contribution of any Investor Member. Such advances or loans might result in a considerable delay in the repayment of Capital Contributions, or in a complete loss to Subscribers if such loans or advances equal or exceed the revenues from the production of the Play.

8. If the Company receives an exemption from the requirements of filing certified accounting statements, pursuant to the New York Theatrical Syndication Financing Act, Investor Members may only be furnished with un-audited financial statements. The Managing Member have not, as of the date of this Memorandum, applied for such exemption or determined whether such application will be made. The Managing Member agree to furnish financial statements to the Investor Members and the Department of Law of the State of New York pursuant to the provisions of Article 23 of the Arts and Cultural

Affairs Law and the regulations issued by the Attorney General thereunder. The Managing Member further agree to deliver to the Investor Members information necessary to enable the Investor Member to prepare their respective federal and state income tax returns.

9. Contributions other than cash may be accepted in the form of guarantees or bonds as may be required by Actors' Equity Association, theatres and other unions or organizations, and such contributors will receive the Investor Member's Interest allocable to the amount of bonds or guarantees contributed, and furthermore, shall have the right to be reimbursed in full prior to the return of capital to other Investor Members. The security instruments underlying such bonds or guarantees will be returned to the contributors only after the Investor Members have sufficient money to make payment to such theatre or union of cash in the amount of the bond or guaranty. The first Net Profits will be paid to the theatre or union to release such bond or guaranty prior to the payments to the Investor Members of the return of capital or Net Profits. Such preference may delay the repayment of the Capital Contributions of the Investor Members.

10. The Managing Member have never produced a commercial theatrical stage production in New York City.

11. The Managing Member may have received fees and payments as herein provided. The Managing Member may continue to present the Play regardless of whether the Company realizes any profit. Continuation of the run of the Play may provide additional compensation to the Managing Member in their various capacities, at a time when the show should be closed in the interest of the Investor Members.

12. No market presently exists for resale of the Investor Members' Interests and it is unlikely that one will develop. Investor Members may not assign their interests without the consent of the Managing Member.

13. If the Company has not attained Total Capitalization by the time the option to produce the play runs out (December 1 2005, if the option to produce the Play has been extended to that date), the Capital Contributions of the Investor Members shall be returned promptly, with accrued interest, if any, except there shall be no return of Capital Contributions expended with the

consent of the individual Subscribers who have waived their right of refund. In the event of abandonment, all money not expended for pre-production or production purposes will be returned to Investor Members, including those who have waived their right of refund.

14. Company Net Profits distributed to the Managing Member and to the Investor Members, and Capital Contributions returned to the Investor Members (including accrued interest returned, if any), may be recalled by the Managing Member for the purposes of paying any debts, taxes, liabilities or obligations of the Company.

15. The Managing Member shall have the absolute right to abandon the production of the Play at any time for any reason. If such abandonment occurs after the Offering has closed and before the opening of the Play, the Investor Members may lose all or substantially all of their investment.

16. The Managing Member has not contracted for certain key elements of the production, including the scenic, lighting, sound and costume designers, and the theatre.

17. In any year in which the Company shall report Net Profits, an Investor Member will be taxable for his or his proportionate share of such Net Profits, whether or not such Net Profits have been distributed to such Investor Member.

18. The Managing Member has the right to cause additional persons or any corporate entities to become Managing Member of the Company. In this event, if this occurs prior to Total Capitalization, an offer of rescission will be made to Investor Members who invested before the additional Managing Member are added. In the case of Investor Members authorizing immediate use of their funds who have waived the right of refund, an offer of recission will be made to them, however, they will not receive a return of any contribution to the extent that their funds have been expended for production or pre-production purposes.

19. In addition, a Managing Member alone or associated in any way with any person, firm or corporation, may produce or co-produce other productions of the Play in other places and media, and may receive compensation therefore

without any obligation whatsoever to account to the Company or the Investor Members, provided, however, that the Company shall be entitled to receive from any such producing entity the customary fees and royalties payable to it.

20. The Producer is not obliged to devote his full time and efforts to the Company's activities and may participate in other business activities, including other theatrical ventures.

THE OFFERING

Each of the fifty Units of Limited Liability Company Interests is being offered via this Memorandum at a purchase price of $10,000,000 for a Company capitalization of {**Au: word missing?**}. Fractional Units may, however, be issued by the Managing Member. Subscribers of Units and fractional Units will each be entitled to receive that proportion of 50% of the Company's Net Profits which their respective Capital Contribution bears to the Total Capitalization of the Company. Purchasers of fractional Units will be entitled to the same rights and be subject to the same obligations as purchasers of Units. The Managing Member may purchase Units not exceeding the total amount of $200,000 in the aggregate and will be treated as an Investor Member to the extent of his purchase of such Units. The investment of the Managing Member as an Investor Member may be used to complete the amount of the Offering. In her sole discretion, the Managing Member may permit certain Capital Contributions to be made by the posting of required performance bonds on behalf of the Company. The persons posting such bonds shall participate as Investor Members and shall be entitled to a share of Net Profits of the Company based on the cost of such bonds had they been posted directly by the Company. In addition, Investor Members who post bonds shall have the right to be reimbursed in full prior to the return of capital to other Investor Members.

Offers to subscribe to Limited Liability Company Interests are subject to acceptance by the Managing Member. A Capital Contribution shall be payable at the time of execution and delivery to the Managing Member of the Operating Agreement by the Subscriber. All money raised pursuant to the Offering shall be held in trust by the Managing Member in a special bank account at Fleet Bank until actually employed for pre-production or production expenses or returned to Investor Members. Prior to Total Capitalization, the Capital Contribution of an Investor Member may only be employed for pre-production or production expenses if specifically authorized by such Investor Member. If $10,000,000 in Capital Contributions has not been raised by December 1, 2006 (or at the time the option to produce the play runs out, if the option has not been extended until that time) the Offering will cease and Capital Contributions will be promptly returned to the Investor Members, with accrued interest, if any (unless receipt of such accrued interest has been waived by the Investor Member), except to the extent used pursuant to specific instructions permitting the use of a Subscriber's funds and waiving right of refund.

The Managing Member shall decide whether such Capital Contributions are to be held in an interest-bearing account.

A copy of this Memorandum and the Operating Agreement shall be presented to each potential Subscriber. A potential Subscriber desiring to become an Investor Member in the Company must sign the Operating Agreement and indicate the amount and category of the Capital Contribution being made, as well as the Subscriber's actual residence address (or principal place of business if a corporation, company, association or other entity) and social security or employer identification number. The executed signature page of the Operating Agreement should be forwarded to the Managing Member at the Company address and must be accompanied by a check or money order made payable to for the full amount of the Investor Member's Capital Contribution.

With respect to the Capital Contributions of Investor Members, any one of the following may also apply:

(1) The individual Subscriber may agree in writing to the use of his or her Capital Contribution prior to Total Capitalization and waive the right of refund of such contribution on abandonment prior to the production of the Play;

(2) The Managing Member may accept as an investment in lieu of cash, a cash deposit for Actors' Equity Association or other union bonds, the theater deposit or property, services rendered, or a promissory note or other obligation to contribute cash or property or to render services; and

(3) An individual Subscriber may also invest in the Company by purchasing an assignment from an Investor Member, provided the Managing Member consents to such assignment in writing. An assignment purchased pursuant to this procedure may not be further assigned by such Subscriber and the Managing Member may not waive or modify this restriction.

The Managing Member reserves the right to give to any Subscriber an additional participation in Net Profits for any reason whatsoever, provided such participation is payable solely from the Managing Member's share of such profits, and does not affect the proportion of Net Profits payable to the Investor Members.

As of the date of this Memorandum, the Managing Member has not yet determined a date for the production of the Play.

There is no involuntary overcall provided for in the Operating Agreement, and if additional money is needed above the Capital Contributions raised, the Managing Member may make funds available and must do so in a manner that will not reduce the interest of the Investor Members in the Net Profits of the Company. Any additional funds advanced or loaned to the Company are to be repaid prior to the return of contributions of Investor Members.

USE OF PROCEEDS

The Managing Member anticipates that the Play can be produced in a theatre of approximately 1,933 seats for the Total Capitalization. The present estimates of pre-production and production expenses, and the allocation of Capital Contributions made to the Company are set forth in Exhibit A annexed hereto and made a part hereof.

Nothing contained in the budget set forth in Exhibit A shall limit the right of the Managing Member to make such changes in the above allocations as she may deem necessary or advisable. There is no assurance that the total actual production requirements will not exceed the Total Capitalization. The aggregate limited contributions may, in the Managing Member's discretion, be used to pay Running Expenses and Other Expenses, as well as Production Expenses. The money allocated in the production budget under the reserve category are contingency funds. The payments to be made from this reserve fund are most likely to include: (1) additional expenses for items which constitute Production Expenses due to artistic changes made in the Play prior to the official New York City opening of the Play and (2) additional advertising expenses, as needed.

Based on a capitalization of $10,000,000 for the production of the Play, and assuming the Play is presented at prevailing box office scale in an approximately 1,933 seat Theatre in New York City with potential gross weekly box office receipts of approximately $1,243,500 and estimated weekly expenses of approximately $727,000 the Play must run for 18.6 weeks (149 performances) to a full capacity house in order to recoup the total production costs, exclusive of bonds and returnable deposits, in order to return to the Investor Members their initial Capital Contributions, or for a longer period of time if presented at less than full house capacity.

Of course, there can be no assurance that the Play will run for that length of time or that it will have audiences of any specified size. Furthermore, additional Production Expenses, Running Expenses and Other Expenses may be incurred which would increase the budget, and consequently, the period of time required to recover invested capital.

Persons authorizing the use of their funds prior to the completion of the Offering should take particular note that the funds may be used to repay a Managing Member for his pre-production expenditures, and their funds will have been lost if the Play is abandoned before opening.

Up to the date of this Memorandum, the Managing Member has expended approximately $70,000 consisting of payments Describe expenditures here.

THE PLAY

Insert description of Play here.

COMPENSATION OF THE AUTHOR

The Author will be paid, prior to recoupment of the total production costs of the Play, a royalty of 4.5% of the Gross Weekly Box Office Receipts. After recoupment of the total production costs of the Play, (exclusive of returnable bonds and security deposits), Author will be paid a royalty of 6% of the Gross Weekly Box Office Receipts. In lieu of receiving a percentage of the gross weekly box office receipts, if all the royalty participants agree to share in a pool, the Author has agreed to also share in a royalty pool formula and will share such pool with the other royalty participants in the same proportion that they would have shared in the Gross Weekly Box Office Receipts.

THE PRODUCER

The Managing Member will be entitled to a weekly fee in the amount of 3% of the Gross Weekly Box Office Receipts or if all royalty participants agree to be paid by a royalty pool she will share a 35% pool (going to 40% after recoupment) with the other royalty participants in the same proportion that they would share in the Gross Weekly Box Office Receipts. Ms. Robson has never produced a Broadway play.

Prior to recoupment of the total production costs of the Play ("Recoupment"), the royalty pool participants shall share in 35% of the Net Receipts (as defined in the Option Agreement) of the Company. It is anticipated that as a producers' fee, the Managing Member shall receive 3% of the Gross Weekly Box Office Receipts. After Recoupment, the royalty pool participants shall share in 40% of the Net Receipts of the Company and it is anticipated that the Managing Member shall receive an amount equal to the same proportion that the Managing Member would receive if royalty payments were based on a percentage of the Gross Weekly Box Office Receipts. Prior to Recoupment, all of the Net Profits of the Company shall be paid to the Investor Members. After Recoupment, the Net Profits of the Company shall be divided equally with 50% to the Investor Members and 50% to the Managing Member. The number of participants in the pool may increase or decrease, in which event the share of the Producers in the pool will be accordingly adjusted.

In the event that the Managing Member finds it necessary to perform any other services usually performed by a third person, the Managing Member may, if they so desires, receive the compensation for such services which the third party would have received had such third party directly performed the required services. The Managing Member have not made any plans, arrangements, commitments or undertakings to perform services for the Company which would otherwise be provided by a third person. If such services do become necessary, the compensation would be what is reasonable and proper and would be in the amount actually set forth in the production budget. The Managing Member will receive no compensation, other than that stated above, for any services, equipment or facilities customarily rendered or furnished by a theatrical stage producer; nor will the Managing Member receive concessions of cash, property or anything of value from persons rendering services or supplying goods to the Company.

THE CAST

As of this date of this Memorandum, none of the cast for the Play has been selected. It is anticipated that the cast will be paid the prevailing rates for actors at the time the Play is produced.

THE THEATRE

As of this date of this Memorandum, a license agreement has not been entered into for a theater in which to present the Play. It is anticipated that the theatre will contain approximately 1933 seats.

PRODUCTION RIGHTS

Pursuant to the Option Agreement, the Company has the sole and exclusive right to produce the Play in an Off-Broadway or Middle Theatre in New York City, to open on or before December 1, 2006, unless the option is extended to open the Play on or before December 1, 2007.

SUBSIDIARY RIGHTS

If the Play is produced during the option period, the Producers will have an option to produce the Play in the United States, Canada, Ireland, and the United Kingdom and on tour in accordance with the terms and conditions as set forth in the Option Agreement.

Although the Producer is acquiring the rights and services of the Author solely in connection with the production of the Play, the Author recognizes that by orchestrating a successful production of the Play, the Producer makes a contribution to the value of the uses of the Play in other media. Therefore, although the relationship between the parties is limited to play production as provided herein, and the Author owns and controls the Play with respect to all other uses, nevertheless, if the Producer has produced the Play as provided herein and the Play is Vested, as provided in the terms of the Production Contract entered into with the Author, the Company will be entitled to certain other production rights and to share in the subsidiary rights income from the disposition of rights in the Play all as specifically provided in the Production Contract a copy of which is on file in the offices of Jacob Medinger and Finnegan LLP, the Attorneys for the production company.

RETURN OF CAPITAL CONTRIBUTIONS - SHARE OF COMPANY NET PROFITS

The Investor Members as a group will be entitled to receive fifty percent (50%) of any Net Profits of the Company, each in the proportion to which his or her Capital Contribution bears to the Total Capitalization of the Company. The Managing Member will also receive fifty percent (50%) of such profits. Any Net Profits will be distributed only after all Capital Contributions have been returned to the Investor Members and the Company maintains a reserve fund in the amount of {**Au: missing number**}.

LIABILITY OF MEMBERS

No Investor Member shall be personally liable for any debts, obligations, or losses of the Company beyond the amount of his or her Capital Contribution to the Company and his or her share of any undistributed Net Profits. An Investor Member shall be liable only to make his or her Capital Contribution and shall not be required to lend any funds to the Company. If any sum by way of repayment of Capital Contribution or distribution of Net Profits shall have been paid prior or subsequent to the termination date of the Company, and at any time subsequent to such repayment there shall be any unpaid debts, taxes, liabilities, or obligations of the Company, and the Company shall not have sufficient assets to meet them, then each Investor Member and the Managing Member may be obligated to repay the Company, to the extent of his or her Capital Contribution so returned to him or her or any Net Profits so distributed to him or her, as the Managing Member may need for such purpose and demand. In such event, the Investor Members and the Managing Member shall first repay any Net Profits previously distributed to him or her, respectively, and if insufficient, the Investor Members shall return Capital Contributions which may have been repaid to them, such return by the Investor Members respectively, to be made in proportion to the amount of Capital Contributions which may have been so repaid to them, respectively. All such repayments by the Investor Members shall be repaid promptly after receipt by each Investor Member from the Managing Member of a written notice requesting such repayment. The Investor Members and the Producers will bear the losses of the theatrical production company only to the extent of their actual investment in the Company.

Upon the termination of the Company the assets of the Company shall be liquidated as promptly as possible and the cash proceeds shall be applied in the following order of priority:

(a) To the payment of debts, taxes, obligations and liabilities of the Company and the necessary expenses of liquidation. Where there is a contingent debt, obligation or liability, a reserve shall be set up to meet it, and if and when such contingency shall cease to exist, the money, if any, in such reserve shall be distributed as provided for in the Operating Agreement;

(b) To the repayment of Capital Contributions of the Investor Members, such Investor Members sharing such repayment proportionately to their respective Capital Contributions; and

(c) The surplus, if any, of such assets then remaining shall be divided among the Managing Member and Investor Members in the proportion that they share in the Net Profits of the Company.

OTHER FINANCING

Except as described herein, no person or entity has advanced anything of value toward the production of the Play.

FINANCIAL STATEMENTS

The Company will be the ultimate issuer of these securities. Since the Company has not heretofore been engaged in business, there are no financial statements. The Investor Members will be furnished with all financial statements required by the New York Theatrical Syndication Financing Act and Regulations promulgated in accordance with New York law and will include annual statements of operations.

If the Company receives an exemption from the requirements of filing certified accounting statements and the Managing Member are permitted to furnish an unaudited statement, Investor Members will not have the benefit of a certified accounting and will rely wholly upon the Managing Member' statement for the determination of their share in any Net Profits.

EFFECT OF FEDERAL INCOME TAXES

It is the belief of the Managing Member that for purposes of federal income tax, the Company should be treated as a partnership. A tax ruling from the Internal Revenue Service as to the Company's status as a partnership for federal income tax purposes has not, however, been applied for, nor do the Managing Member intend to apply for such a ruling. If the Company is treated as a partnership for federal income tax purposes, then: (a) the Company will be required to file an annual information tax return but will not itself be subject to federal income tax; and (b) each Investor Member and the

Managing Member, regardless of whether he or she receives any distribution from the Company, will be required to report his or her proportionate share of each item of Company income and will be entitled to deduct (to the extent of his or her basis in his or her Limited Liability Company Interests in the Company) such proportionate share of each item of Company expense on the appropriate tax return of such Investor Member and each Managing Member for each relevant tax period, subject to the limitations set forth in the Internal Revenue Service ("IRS") Code, relating to losses from passive activities. If the Company is so required under IRS provisions or regulations, it shall select a Managing Member to act as its "tax matters partner" in accordance with the applicable IRS provisions and regulations, who will fulfill this role by being the spokesperson for the Company in dealings with the IRS as required under the IRS Code and Regulations.

INDEMNIFICATION

There is no personal liability of the Managing Member, to the Company, or to the Investor Members for damages for any breach of duty in their capacity as Managing Member, unless there is a judgment or other final adjudication adverse to his that establishes that his acts or omissions were in bad faith or involved intentional misconduct, or a knowing violation of law or that she personally gained in fact a financial profit or other advantage to which she was not legally entitled or that with respect to any distribution, his acts were not performed in accordance with the applicable laws governing a limited liability company in the State of New York.

FEDERAL SECURITIES LAW

This Offering of securities has been organized with the intent of qualifying for an exemption from the registration requirements of the Securities Act of 1933, as amended pursuant to Regulation D, promulgated by the Commission under the Act. Limited Liability Company Interests are not registered under the Act. Whether these securities are exempt from registration pursuant to Regulation D or otherwise has not been passed upon by the Commission, the Attorney General of the State of New York or any other regulatory agency, nor has any such agency passed upon the merits of the Offering.

LEGAL COUNSEL

Jacob Medinger & Finnegan LLP; Donald C. Farber and Peter A. Cross, of Counsel, 1270 Avenue of the Americas, New York, NY 10020 are the Attorneys for the production.

Preliminary Offering Circular $1,000,000 in Limited Liability Company Interests

Charles Clancy will be the Managing Member of a Limited Liability Company formed to produce and present Off-Broadway in New York City in a theatre with approximately 399 seats (and thereafter, if successful, elsewhere in the U.S. and Canada) the musical play entitled:

LAST CHANCE (The "Musical")

THE UNITED STATES SECURITIES AND EXCHANGE COMMISSION DOES NOT PASS UPON THE MERITS OF OR GIVE ITS APPROVAL TO ANY SECURITIES OFFERED OR THE TERMS OF THE OFFERING, NOR DOES IT PASS UPON THE ACCURACY OR COMPLETENESS OF ANY OFFERING CIRCULAR OR OTHER SELLING LITERATURE. THESE SECURITIES ARE OFFERED PURSUANT TO AN EXEMPTION FROM REGISTRATION WITH THE COMMISSION; HOWEVER, THE COMMISSION HAS NOT MADE AN INDEPENDENT DETERMINATION THAT THE SECURITIES OFFERED HEREUNDER ARE EXEMPT FROM REGISTRATION.

CLAUSE	COMMENT

Exempt from Registration.

	Underwriting
Price to	Discounts or
Public	Commissions[1]
Per Unit	
$20,000	-0-
Capitalization	
$1,000,000	-0-

NO DEALER, SALESMAN OR ANY OTHER PERSON HAS BEEN AUTHORIZED TO GIVE ANY INFORMATION OR TO MAKE ANY REPRESENTATION OTHER THAN THOSE CONTAINED IN THIS OFFERING CIRCULAR, AND IF GIVEN OR MADE, SUCH INFORMATION OR REPRESENTA-TIONS MUST NOT BE RELIED UPON AS HAVING BEEN AUTHORIZED BY THE MANAGING MEMBER. THIS OFFERING CIRCULAR DOES NOT CONSTITUTE AN OFFER TO SELL OR A SOLICITATION OF AN OFFER TO BUY ANY OF THE SECURITIES OFFERED HEREBY TO ANY PERSON IN ANY JURISDICTION WHERE SUCH OFFER OR SOLICITATION WOULD BE UNLAWFUL.

THIS OFFERING CIRCULAR MAY NOT BE USED FOR A PERIOD OF MORE THAN NINE (9) MONTHS AFTER THE DATE OF THIS OFFERING CIRCULAR. THE ATTORNEY GENERAL OF THE STATE OF NEW YORK DOES NOT PASS ON THE MERITS OF THIS OFFERING.

THESE SECURITIES INVOLVE A HIGH DEGREE OF RISK AND PROSPECTIVE PURCHASERS SHOULD BE PREPARED TO SUSTAIN A LOSS OF THEIR ENTIRE INVESTMENT (SEE "RISK FACTORS").

---

[1] This particular offering has no underwriters.

THE DATE OF THIS OFFERING CIRCULAR IS

_____.

Limited Liability Company Interests are being offered by Charles Clancy of 1809 North Prospect Avenue, Peoria, Ill. 43210 (the "Managing Member" or the "Producer"). The ultimate issuer will be "The Last Chance Limited Liability Company" (the "Company") a limited liability company to be formed under the laws of the State of New York. The address of the Company, will be c/o Donald C. Farber, Esq., 1370 Avenue of the Americas, New York, New York 10019.

Aggregate Limited Liability Company interests are not actually divided into a specific number of units and monetary amounts. For purposes of convenience, they may be considered to consist of fifty (50) "Units" of $20,000 per Unit, with a capitalization of $1,000,000. An investor may purchase fractional Units of not less than one-quarter a unit or $5,000.

All investments will be in cash except if an investment is made in the form of a guaranty or bond to a theatre or union as referred to in Risk Factor (8) hereinafter set forth. Only such instruments acceptable to such union or theatre will be suitable. It is customary for Actors' Equity Association to insist upon a negotiable document with an assignment to the union so that the security is secure.

All monies raised will be held by the Managing Member in a special account at Chemical Bank, 1411 Broadway, New York, New York 10018, until the total capital contributions are raised. The monies held in the special account at Chemical will not be released until the Offering is closed (unless an investor gives permission to the earlier use of his or her investment), and when the funds are released no additional sales will be made. The offering expires on March 1, 1995, unless extended up to September 1, 1995.

The offering statement (including Exhibits) can be reviewed in the office of the Securities and Exchange Commission.

TABLE OF CONTENTS

SUMMARY OF THE OFFERING CIRCULAR

The Company will be formed pursuant to the laws of the State of New York for the purpose of producing and presenting the Musical and exploiting and turning to account the rights at any time held by the Company in connection therewith (see "THE COMPANY"). All rights to produce the Musical as set forth in the Production Agreement (as defined in "THE COMPANY") will be assigned by Charles Clancy to the Company when formed. Within one month after the Articles of Organization have been filed, a written Assignment Agreement will be prepared by the attorney for the Company, assigning the rights contained in the Production Agreement to the Company, which document Charles Clancy agrees to execute. The Assignment Agreement has not been prepared, but it will be a valid assignment and will conform in all respects with New York State Law. It is currently anticipated that the Musical will open Off-Broadway in a theatre in New York City containing approximately 399 seats.

The Managing Member will hold the capital contributions in a special account until not less than $1,000,000 has been raised. The Investor Members will receive fifty percent (50%) of the net profits of the Company, and the Managing Member will receive the other fifty percent (50%) of such profits.

The Company shall terminate upon January 1, 2050, or the first occurrence of any of the following: (i) the Bankruptcy, death, insanity, or resignation of a Managing Member or the dissolution, cessation of business, or Bankruptcy of a corporate Managing Member; (ii) the expiration of all of the Company's rights, title, and interest in the Musical; (iii) a date fixed by the Managing Member after abandonment of all further Company activities; or (iv) any other event causing the dissolution of the Company under the laws of the State of New York. Notwithstanding the foregoing, the Company shall not be dissolved upon the occurrence of the Bankruptcy, death, dissolution, or withdrawal or adjudication of incompetence of a Managing Member if any of the remaining persons constituting a managing member elects with in thirty (30) days after such an event to continue the business of the Company. Currently it is contemplated that the Managing Member will be Charles Clancy. No additional Managing Member to the Company may be accepted unless all Investor Members so consent.

The Company's plan of operation is: (a) to engage in preproduction activities with respect to the Musical; (b) upon completion of pre-production activities, to engage in rehearsals of the Musical; (c) during the rehearsal period, to begin the promotion and publicity for the Musical; and (d) to produce and present the Musical. For further information with respect to these matters, see "USE OF PROCEEDS."

THE COMPANY

The Managing Member will organize the Company as a New York Limited Liability Company to raise capital contributions totaling $1,000,000 for the purpose of producing and presenting the musical and exploiting and turning to account the rights held by the Company therein. The capitalization requirement is, in the opinion of the Managing Member, sufficient to mount a production of the Musical in an Off-Broadway theatre in New York City containing approximately 399 seats. See "THE THEATRE" in this Offering Circular.

If the capitalization has not been raised by October 1, 1997, or October 1, 1998, if the option is extended, the date on which the stage production rights expire pursuant to the Production Contract ("Production Agreement"), the offering will cease and all capital contributions theretofore received will be returned with accrued interest, if any, except capital contributions which have been expended by consent of individual subscribers who have waived their right of refund [see "RISK FACTORS" (5)].

The Managing Member will have sole and complete authority over the management and operations of the Company. The Managing Member in his sole discretion may purchase Units of Limited Liability Company Interests in the Company and participate therein as an Investor Member, but not in excess of $50,000. Purchases of Limited Liability Company Units by the Managing Member may be for the purpose of closing the Offering. If the Managing Member purchases Units of Limited Liability Company interests, he shall do so for investment purposes only and not with an intent to resell the Units. However, at present, the Managing Member has not determined whether he will so participate as an Investor Member or the extent of any such participation. The Managing Member will assign to the Company all rights in the Musical which he has acquired. The Company will assume all obligations and liabilities incurred by the Managing Member in acquiring such rights assigned to the Company. For additional information on the rights acquired by the Managing

Member and the division of proceeds therefrom, see "PRODUCTION RIGHTS" and "SUBSIDIARY RIGHTS."

RISK FACTORS

(1) The vast majority of theatrical productions report losses and unrecovered production costs.

(2) Based on a Company maximum capitalization of $1,000,000 and the estimated weekly expenses for the production of the Musical, and assuming the Musical is presented at prevailing box office scale in a 399-seat theatre Off-Broadway in New York City with potential gross weekly box office receipts of $160,000 and estimated weekly expenses of approximately $109,000, the Musical must run for approximately twenty-four (24) weeks (192 performances) to a full-capacity house in order to return to the Investor Members their initial capital contributions, or for a longer period of time if presented at less than full house capacity. The substantial majority of the plays produced for the stage fail to run long enough to recoup the total production costs. Of those that do, few play to capacity audiences throughout their run. The Author will be paid six percent (6%) of the gross weekly box office receipts until recoupment and seven percent (7%) thereafter unless all persons entitled to a royalty agree to participate in a Royalty Pool Formula as hereinafter described.

(3) There is no assurance that the Musical will be an economic success even if the Musical receives critical acclaim.

(4) These securities should not be purchased unless the subscriber is prepared for the possibility of total loss and is able to afford such total loss. The sole business of the Company will be to produce the Musical Off-Broadway in New York City in a theatre with approximately 399 seats. In such a venture the risk of loss is especially high in contrast with the prospect for the realization of any profits.

(5) An individual subscriber may agree to the use of his capital contribution prior to full capitalization of the Company, and waive his right of refund in the event of abandonment prior to the production of the Musical. Such contribution may be used for any properly budgeted pre-production or production purposes. Investors who authorize the use of their investment in such a fashion should take particular note that their funds may be used immediately to repay the

Managing Member for his expenditures of funds in connection with the production even if the Musical is abandoned or not produced. Subscribers waiving refund may lose all or part of their respective investments, without a production of the Musical having been presented, if insufficient funds are raised to complete the offering, or if the offering is not completed for any other reason. There is no advantage whatsoever to such a waiver unless compensation is separately contracted for from the Managing Member's share of the profits of the producing company.

(6) In the event the capital contributions raised through this offering are insufficient to produce the Musical in an Off-Broadway theatre with approximately 399 seats, the Managing Member may advance or cause to be advanced, or may borrow on behalf of the Company, additional capital. Such advances or loans are to be repaid prior to the repayment of the capital contribution of any Investor Member. Such advances or loans might result in a considerable delay in the repayment of capital contributions, or in a complete loss to subscribers if such loans or advances equal or exceed the revenues from the production of the Musical.

(7) If the Company receives an exemption from the requirements of filing certified accounting statements, pursuant to the New York Theatrical Syndication Financing Act, Investor Members may be furnished with unaudited financial statements. The Managing Member has not, as of the date of this Offering Circular, applied for such exemption or determined whether such application will be made. The Managing Member agrees, as set forth in the Operating Agreement, to furnish financial statements to the Investor Members and the Department of Law of the State of New York pursuant to the provisions of Article 23 of the Arts and Cultural Affairs Law and the Regulations issued by the Attorney General thereunder. The Managing Member further agrees to deliver to the Investor Members information necessary to enable the Investor Members to prepare their respective federal and state income tax returns. See "FINANCIAL STATEMENTS" hereinafter set forth.

(8) Contributions other than cash may be accepted in the form of guarantees or bonds as may be required by Actors' Equity Association, theatres, and other unions or organizations, and such contributors will receive the Limited Liability Company Interest allocable to the amount of bonds or guarantees contributed, and furthermore, shall have the right to be reimbursed in full prior

to the return of capital to other Investor Members. The security instruments underlying such bonds or guarantees will be returned to the contributors only after the Limited Liability Company has sufficient monies to make payment to such theatre or union of cash in the amount of the bond or guaranty. The first net profits will be paid to the theatre or union to release such bond or guaranty prior to the payments to the Investor Members for the return of capital or net profits. Such preference may delay the repayment of the capital contributions of the Investor Members.

(9) The Managing Member has never produced a commercial theatrical stage production.

(10) The Managing Member will participate in the Royalty Pool Formula for each week during the run of the Musical, as well as other remuneration [see "COMPENSATION OF THE MANAGING MEMBER (PRODUCER)"], and he may continue to present the Musical regardless of whether the Company realizes any profit. Continuation of the run of the Musical may provide additional compensation to the Managing Member at a time when the show should be closed in the interest of the investors. See "COMPENSATION OF THE MANAGING MEMBER (PRODUCER)" hereinafter set forth.

(11) No market presently exists for resale of the Limited Liability Company Interests, and it is unlikely that one will develop. Investor Members may not assign their interests without the consent of the Managing Member, which consent will be granted at the sole discretion of the Managing Member.

(12) If $1,000,000 has not been raised on or before the expiration of the initial option period (October 1, 1997), or by such date as the Managing Member has extended the option period (October 1, 1998) (see "PRODUCTION RIGHTS"), the capital contributions of the Investor Members shall be returned promptly, with accrued interest, if any, except there shall be no return of capital contributions expended with the consent of the individual subscribers who have waived their right of refund. All monies not expended for pre-production or production purposes will be returned to investors, including those who have waived their right of refund in the event of abandonment. It should be noted that an investor's funds can be held in a separate bank account for an extended period of time up to October 1, 1998. Such account will be under the control of the Managing Member, who warrants and represents that the funds will not

be used unless and until the total production budget has been raised unless investors have specifically authorized the use of such funds prior to the full capitalization.

(13) Company net profits distributed to the Managing Member and to the Investor Members, and capital contributions returned to the Investor Members (including accrued interest returned, if any), may be recalled by the Managing Member for the purposes of paying any debts, taxes, liabilities, or obligations of the Company.

(14) The Managing Member shall have the absolute right to abandon the production of the Musical at any time for any reason. If such abandonment occurs after this offering has closed and before the opening of the Musical, the investors may lose all or substantially all of their investment.

(15) The Managing Member has not contracted for certain key elements of the production, including the performers; director; scenic, lighting, sound) and costume designers; and the theatre. There are theatres in the city that are the size that would be appropriate for presenting this Musical; however, it is impossible to know in advance what will be the availability of a theatre at the time the production is ready to proceed. See "THE THEATRE" in this Offering Circular.

(16) In any year in which the company shall report net profits, an Investor Member will be taxable for his proportionate share of such net profits, whether or not such net profits have been distributed to such Investor Member.

(17) The Managing Member has the right to cause additional persons, firms, or corporations to become Managing Members of the Company at any time prior to the formation of the Company. In this event, an offer of rescission will be made to those investors (other than those investors who have waived the right of refund) who invested before the additional managing members are added. In the case of investors who have waived the right of refund, an offer of recision will be made to them. However, they will not receive a return of any contribution to the extent that their funds have been expended for production or pre-production purposes.

(18) In addition, the Managing Member alone or associated in any way with any person, firm, or corporation, may produce or coproduce other productions of the Musical in other places and media, and may receive compensation therefor without any obligation whatever to account to the Company or the

Investor Members; provided, however, that the Company shall be entitled to receive from any such producing entity the customary fees and royalties payable to it.

(19) The Managing Member is under no obligation to devote his full time and efforts to the Company's activities (see "THE MANAGING MEMBER"). This fact may affect his ability to successfully manage the production of the Musical. The Managing Member intends to devote as much time as is required to properly attend to the Company activities and will make himself available as required for the proper functioning of the business.

THE OFFERING

Each of the fifty (50) Units of Limited Liability Company Interests is being offered to the public at a purchase price of twenty thousand dollars ($20,000), for a Company capitalization of $1,000,000. Fractional Units may, however, be issued by the Managing Member, but not for less than one-quarter units. Subscribers of Units and fractional Units will each receive that proportion of fifty percent (50%) of the Company's net profits which their respective capital contribution bears to the total capitalization of the Company. Purchasers of fractional Units will be entitled to the same rights and be subject to the same obligations as purchasers of Units. The Managing Member may purchase Units not exceeding the total amount of $50,000 and will be treated as an Investor Member to the extent of his purchase of such Units. The investment of the Managing Member as Investor Member may be used to complete the amount of the Offering. The Managing Member may not resell any Units he purchases. In his sole discretion, the Managing Member may permit certain capital contributions to be made by the posting of required performance bonds on behalf of the Company. The persons posting such bonds shall participate as Investor Members and shall be entitled to a share of net profits of the Company based on the cost of such bonds had they been posted directly by the Company. They may be entitled to preferential treatment in the release of the bond prior to the return of capital to the other Investor Members.

Offers to subscribe to Limited Liability Company Interests are subject to acceptance by the Managing Member. The offering expires on October 1, 1997, unless extended up to October 1, 1998. A capital contribution shall be payable at the time of execution and delivery to the Managing Member of the Operating Agreement by the subscriber. All monies raised pursuant to this offering shall be held in trust by the Managing Member in a special bank account at Citibank, 46th Street and Third Avenue, New York, New York 10017, until actually employed for pre-production or production expenses or returned to investors. Prior to the completion of this Offering, the capital contribution of an Investor Member may only be employed for pre-production or production expenses if specifically authorized by such subscriber. If the capitalization has not been raised prior to the expiration of the option period as extended, October 1, 1998, as provided in the Production Agreement, all capital contributions will be promptly returned to the Investor Members, with accrued interest, if any, except to the extent used pursuant to specific instructions permitting the use of a subscriber's funds and waiving right of refund. Limited Liability Company Interests will be offered to the public by the Managing Member on behalf of the Company, through the use of the mails, by telephone and by personal solicitation.

A copy of this Offering Circular and of the Operating Agreement for The Last Chance Limited Liability Company shall be presented to each potential subscriber. A potential subscriber desiring to become an Investor Member in the Company must sign the Operating Agreement and indicate the amount and category of the capital contribution being made, as well as the subscriber's actual residence address (or principal place of business of a corporation, company, association, or other entity) and social security or employer identification number. Each executed Operating Agreement should be forwarded to the Managing Member at the Company address and must be accompanied by a check or money order made payable to The Last Chance Limited Liability Company in the full amount of the capital contribution indicated on the subscription form in the Operating Agreement.

With respect to the capital contributions of Investor Members, any one of the following may also apply:

(1) The individual subscriber may agree in writing to the use of his capital contribution prior to the sale of fifty (50) Units and waive the right of refund of such contribution on abandonment prior to the production of the Musical.

(2) The Managing Member may accept as an investment in lieu of cash, a cash deposit for Actors' Equity Association, or other union bonds, or the theatre deposit.

(3) An individual subscriber may also invest in the Company by purchasing an assignment from an Investor Member, provided the Managing Member consents in writing to such assignment. An assignment purchased pursuant to this procedure may not be further assigned by the subscriber and the Managing Member may not waive or modify this restriction.

The Managing Member reserves the right to give to any subscriber an additional participation in net profits for any reason whatever, provided such participation is payable solely from the Managing Member's share of such profits, and does not affect the proportion of net profits payable to the Investor Members.

OVERCALL

There is no involuntary overcall provided for in the Operating Agreement, and if additional money is needed above the capital contributions raised, the Managing Member may make funds available and must do so in a manner that will not reduce the interest of the Investor Members in the net profits of the Limited Liability Company. Any additional funds advanced or loaned to the Company are to be repaid prior to the return of contributions of Investor Members.

USE OF PROCEEDS

The present estimates of pre-production and production expenses, and the allocation of capital contributions made to the Company are as follows:

Estimated Production Budget for a 399-seat Off-Broadway Theatre

PHYSICAL PRODUCTION:
Scenery - Build, Paint, Masking, Automation	$125,000.00	
Costumes - Construction, Shoes, Accessories, Millinery, Wigs	50,000.00	
Props and Furniture	20,000.00	
Electric Preparation and Rental	15,000.00	
Sound Preparation and Rental	10,000.00	$220,000.00

FEES:
Director	$ 10,000.00
Choreographer	5,000.00
Scenic Designer	7,500.00
Costume Designer	5,000.00
Lighting Designer	5,000.00
Sound Designer	3,000.00

Music Supervisor	1,500.00	
Technical Supervisor	5,000.00	
Legal Fee	20,000.00	
Accounting Fee	3,000.00	
Hair and Wig Designer	3,000.00	
Assistant to the Choreographer	7,000.00	
Designer Assistants	8,000.00	
Music Contractor	1,500.00	
Casting Director	5,000.00	
General Manager	10,000.00	
Payroll TaxesæDesigner	6,500.00	
Pension & Welfare Director,		
Choreographer, and Designers	8,700.00	114,700.00
REHEARSAL SALARIES:		
Cast	$ 38,415.00	
Stage Manager	8,480.00	
General Manager	6,250.00	
Company Manager	4,140.00	
Press Agent	4,140.00	
Music Director	5,000.00	
Rehearsal Pianists	7,500.00	
Crew	10,000.00	
Wardrobe, Dressers, Hair	1,500.00	
Assistant to Director	1,000.00	
Production Assistant	1,000.00	
Pension & Welfare	7,700.00	
Payroll Taxes	12,000.00	107,125.00
ADVERTISING, PUBLICITY		
AND PROMOTION:		
Press Agent Expenses	$ 1,000.00	
Artwork and Printing	10,000.00	
Photos, Signs, Marquee	6,000.00	
Print Media Advertising	100,000.00	
Group Sales Expenses	10,000.00	127,000.00

OTHER EXPENSES:

Casting and Auditions	$ 2,500.00	
Rehearsal Hall Rental	12,000.00	
Scripts and Taxes	1,500.00	
Orchestration and Copying	65,000.00	
Departmental Expenses	5,000.00	
Musician Rehearsals	7,000.00	
Insurance Deposit	10,000.00	
Trucking and Hauling	7,500.00	
Transportation	7,878.00	
Office Expenses	5,000.00	
Take in, Set up, Work Calls	25,000.00	
Per Diems	10,000.00	
Preliminary Theatre Expenses	6,000.00	
Legal Disbursements	2,000.00	
Local Taxes	2,000.00	
Opening Night Expenses	5,000.00	
Administrative and Phone	2,000.00	
Producer Pre-production Expenses	20,000.00	
Miscellaneous	3,249.00	195,749.00

BONDS AND DEPOSITS:

Author's Option Payment & Advance	$ 2,000.00	
Director's Advance	10,000.00	
Choreographer's Advance	8,000.00	
Actors' Equity Bond	25,000.00	
Company Manager and Press Agent Bond	2,700.00	
Theatre Deposit	31,000.00	78,700.00

RESERVES:

For contingencies, Post Opening, Promotion, Losses during Preview Weeks, and Closing Expenses	$153,848.00

TOTAL CAPITALIZATION $1,000,000.00

It is anticipated that eight performances per week in a 399-seat theatre at capacity will gross $160,000 per week. It is anticipated that the weekly operating expenses at capacity will total approximately $109,000. At capacity with a capitalization of $1,000,000, the total investment would be recouped in approximately twenty-four (24) weeks, that is, in 192 performances.

Persons authorizing the use of their funds prior to the completion of the Offering should take particular note that the funds may be used to repay the Managing Member for the above expenditures, and their funds will have been lost if the Musical is abandoned before opening.

All sums which have heretofore been, or shall hereafter be, advanced by the Managing Member for the benefit and on behalf of the Company will be repaid to the Managing Member from the proceeds of this offering upon completion of financing, or sooner if any investors authorize the use of their investment prior to the total budget being raised and they waive the return of their investment. Up to the date of this Offering Circular, the Producer has expended the sum of $12,000 for the benefit of the Company, which consists of legal fees ($5,000), general management fees ($1,500), option payment ($1,000), and miscellaneous expenses ($4,500).

THE MUSICAL

The Musical takes place on a ship. It involves the interaction of the persons who are taking a pleasure cruise. Ironically, the past lives of some of the passengers contain long-forgotten secrets, which exposes some of the passengers not only to discomfort, but also to danger. Whether the deaths on board are purely coincidental, accidental, or premeditated is only discovered in the final suspenseful moments of the Musical.

BOOKWRITER, COMPOSER, LYRICIST

The Bookwriter, Composer, Lyricist of the Musical is John Vester. Mr. Vester has been composing since the age of seven. This is his first musical that has been optioned for production in New York City. At present, Mr. Vester divides his time between teaching English at Bard College and working on this play.

COMPENSATION OF THE AUTHOR

The Author will receive, pursuant to the terms of the Option Agreement, an advance of $1,000 for the option to present the Musical on or before October 1, 1997, which may be extended until October 1, 1998, by making payment to the Author of an additional advance in the amount of $1,000.

The Author jointly will receive six percent (6%) of the gross weekly box office receipts. In lieu of receiving a percentage of the weekly gross box office receipts, if all the royalty participants agree to share in a Royalty Pool, the Author has agreed to also share in such a Royalty Pool Formula, in which he will collectively be entitled to receive approximately forty-three percent (43%) of the Royalty Pool. See also "ROYALTY POOL ALTERNATIVE" and "THE MANAGING MEMBER (PRODUCER)" herein.

THE DIRECTOR

The Director has as yet not been engaged. It is anticipated that the Director will be paid a fee of approximately $10,000 and will share in a royalty pool in an amount to be negotiated.

THE PRODUCER

The Managing Member will be Charles Clancy. Mr. Clancy resides at 1809 North Prospect Avenue, Peoria, Ill. 43210. Mr. Clancy has not previously produced any commercial theatrical productions.

All sums which have heretofore been, or shall hereafter be, advanced by the Managing Member for the benefit and on behalf of the Company will be repaid to the Managing Member from the proceeds of this Offering upon the sale of fifty (50) Units, or sooner if any investors authorize the use of their investment prior to the total capitalization being raised and they waive the return of their investment. Up to the date of this Offering Circular, the Managing Member has expended the sum of $1,500 for General Management fees, $5,000 for legal fees, $1,000 for the Option and $4,500 for Miscellaneous expenses. See "USE OF PROCEEDS" above.

THE GENERAL MANAGER

The General Manager of the Musical will be Larry Lawrence. The Broadway productions he has managed in the past five years are: GOING, GOING, GONE; RUNNING, RUNNING, NOW; AND HURRY, HURRY, HURRY.

The General Manager shall receive a production fee of $10,000 and a weekly fee of $1,250. The General Manager shall also be entitled to receive an Executive Producer's fee computed as part of the royalty pool, as set forth in "ROYALTY POOL ALTERNATIVE" herein.

THE CAST

As of the date of this Offering Circular, none of the cast has been selected for the Musical. It is anticipated that the cast will be paid the prevailing rates for actors at the time the Musical is produced.

THE THEATRE

As of the date of this Offering Circular, a license agreement has not been entered into for a theatre in which to present the Musical. It is anticipated that the theatre will contain approximately 399 seats and will have a potential of approximately $160,000 at capacity. It is anticipated that the theatre will be paid a weekly fee of approximately $15,000 plus five percent (5%) of the gross weekly box office receipts.

PRODUCTION RIGHTS

The Managing Member has acquired and will assign to the Company the sole and exclusive option to produce the Musical Off- Broadway or in a Middle Theatre in New York City with approximately 399 seats.

The Production Agreement was entered into as of the first day of October 1996 between John Vester, as Author, and Charles Clancy, as Producer. The Production Agreement provides for the exclusive rights to produce the Musical to open on or before October 1, 1997, in consideration of the sum of $1,000 as an advance against royalties, and provides for an extension of the option for an additional one year, that is, until October 1, 1998, in consideration of an additional advance of $1,000.

The Production Agreement provides that if the musical is produced pursuant to the Agreement and runs for twenty-one (21) consecutive paid public performances [computing no more than seven (7) paid previews] that the Producer will have options to produce the Musical on tour for out-of-town productions, for productions in the United Kingdom, and the right to produce the Musical or move it to Broadway in New York City. It is anticipated that the Play will be produced to open Off Broadway in New York City during the Spring, 1997 season.

SUBSIDIARY RIGHTS

If the Musical is produced during the option period, the Producer will have an option to produce the Musical in the United States, Canada, and the United Kingdom and on tour in accordance with the terms and conditions as set forth in the Production Agreement heretofore referred to, entered into as of the first day of October 1996.

The Production Agreement also provides that if the Musical opens Off Broadway or in a Middle Theatre and runs for the number of performances shown below, the Company will receive an amount equal to the percentage of net receipts (regardless of when paid) specified herein below from the Author's receipts from any contracts entered into before the expiration of ten years after the date of the last paid public performance of the Musical in New York City from motion pictures throughout the world or from the following rights in the United States and Canada: radio, television, touring performances, stock perform-ances, amateur performances, foreign language performances, condensed tabloid versions, so-called concert-tour versions, commercial and merchandising uses, and video cassettes of stage productions: ten percent (10%) if the Musical shall run for at least twenty-one (21) consecutive paid performances; twenty percent (20%) if the Musical shall run for at least forty-two (42) consecutive paid performances; thirty percent (30%) if the Musical shall run for at least fifty-six (56) consecutive paid performances; forty percent (40%) if the Musical shall run for sixty-five (65) consecutive paid performances or more. For the purposes of computing the number of performances, provided the Musical officially opens in New York City, the first paid performance shall be deemed to be the first performance, however only seven paid previews will be counted in this computation.

COMPENSATION OF THE MANAGING MEMBER (PRODUCER)

In addition to his share of any net profits of the Company in the aggregate of fifty percent (50%), for which the Managing Member will make no capital contribution, the Managing Member will receive the following compensation and advantages whether or not the Company earns net profits:

(1) Producer will participate in the Royalty Pool for the Producer's fee.

It is not anticipated that anyone, except the theatre, will be paid a percentage of the gross weekly box office receipts. Instead, subject to the approval of any union having jurisdiction, all royalty participants and the Producer for the producer's fee will share forty percent (40%) of the weekly Net Receipts (as defined herein), calculated over every four-week period, and the other sixty percent (60%) of the weekly Net Receipts will be paid to the Company. The royalty participants and the Producer for the producer's fee are each allocated a certain number of points for their contributions to the Musical. Each royalty participant's share of the royalty pool will be based on the proportion that his or her number of points bears to the total number of points allocated to all royalty participants.

Each royalty participant's share of the weekly Net Receipts will be based on the following division:

Author as Bookwriter, Composer, Lyricist	6.0 points
Charles Clancy, for Producer's fee	2.0 points
Larry Lawrence as Executive Producer	1.5 points
Donald C. Farber as Attorney	1.5 points
Director (estimated)	2.5 points
Choreographer (estimated)	.5 points
Estimated Total	14.0 points

The Producer reserves the sole right to change, modify, increase, or decrease any of the points allocated to the royalty pool participants and to include other royalty pool participants.

Each royalty pool participant will receive a minimum weekly royalty in the amount of $150 for each one point allocated to such respective party.

(2) For furnishing office space and secretarial services for the benefit of each production of the Musical, the Managing Member will receive one thousand dollars ($1,000) per week for the Off-Broadway production and $1,500 per week for each First-Class production under his control. This cash office charge shall commence two (2) weeks before the commencement of rehearsals and end two (2) weeks after the close of each company presenting the Musical under the authority or control of the Company. The Managing Member may utilize the office space of the General Manager, and, to the extent that he does, may share part of the cash office charge with the General Manager.

In the event that the Managing Member finds it necessary to perform any other services usually performed by a third person, the Managing Member (Producer) may, if he so desires, receive the compensation for such services which the third party would have received had such third party directly performed the required services. The Managing Member has not made any plans, arrangements, commitments, or undertakings to perform services for the Company that would otherwise be provided by a third person. If such services do become necessary, the compensation would be what is reasonable and proper and would be in the amount actually set forth in the production budget, a copy of which is available for examination at the office of the attorney for the Company and at the office of Charles Clancy.

The Managing Member will receive no compensation, other than that stated above, for any services, equipment, or facilities customarily rendered or furnished by a theatrical stage producer; nor will the Managing Member receive concessions of cash, property, or anything of value from persons rendering services or supplying goods to the Company.

Larry Lawrence, the General Manager, and Donald C. Farber, the Attorney, will advise the Producer and others associated with the production of the Musical in connection with the financing, producing, marketing, and staging of the Musical.

See THE GENERAL MANAGER above concerning Larry Lawrence.

Donald C. Farber is the author of *"Producing Theatre: A Comprehensive Legal and Business Guide";* the General Editor of the five volumes of *"Entertainment Industry Contracts"* published by Matthew Bender, and the author of the theatre volume. He has also authored six other books on theatre and films and has taught Producing Theatre at the New School for Social Research for thirteen sessions twice a year for twenty-two years.

NET PROFITS AND CERTAIN EXPENSES DEFINED

The following terms are defined in the Operating Agreement in the following manner:

"Company Net Profits" shall mean the excess of Gross Receipts over all Production Expenses, Running Expenses, and other Expenses. This shall include any Production Expenses incurred or paid out by the Managing Member prior to the inception of the Company, for which the Managing Member shall be reimbursed upon Total Capitalization.

"Net Profits" for the purpose of the Royalty Pool shall mean Net Receipts less the amount of the Royalty Pool.

"Net Receipts" for the purpose of the Royalty Pool shall mean all Gross Receipts less all Running Expenses except those variable expenses payable to royalty participants as part of the Royalty Pool.

"Production Expenses" shall mean fees of the director, choreographer, designers, orchestrator, cost of sets, curtains, drapes, costumes, properties, furnishings, electrical equipment, premiums for bonds and insurance, cash deposits with Actors' Equity Association, or other similar organizations by which, according to custom or usual practices of the theatrical business, such deposits may be required to be made, advances to the Author, rehearsal charges and expenses, transportation charges, cash office charges, reasonable legal and auditing expenses, advance publicity, theatre costs and expenses, and all other expenses and losses of whatever kind (other than expenditures precluded hereunder) actually incurred in connection with the production of the musical preliminary to the official opening of the Musical. The Managing Member has heretofore incurred or paid, and, prior to the inception of the Company, may incur or pay further Production Expenses as herein set forth, and the amount thereof, and no more, shall be included in the Production Expenses of the Company, and upon Total Capitalization the Managing Member shall be reimbursed for the expenses so paid by them.

"Running Expenses" shall mean all expenses, charges, and disbursements of whatever kind actually incurred in connection with the operation of the Musical, including, without limiting the generality of the foregoing, royalties and/or other compensation to or for the Author, business and general managers, director, choreographer, orchestrator, cast, stage help, transportation, cash office charge, reasonable legal and auditing expenses, theatre operating expenses, and all other expenses and losses of whatever kind actually incurred in connection with the operation of the Musical, as well as taxes of whatever kind and nature other than taxes on the income of the respective Investor Members and Managing Member. Such Running Expenses shall include, without limitation, payments made in the form of Gross Receipts as well as participation in Net Profits to or for any of the aforementioned Persons, services or rights.

"Other Expenses" shall mean all expenses of whatsoever kind or nature other than Production Expenses and Running Expenses actually and reasonably incurred in connection with the operation of the business of the Company, including, but without limiting the foregoing, commissions paid to agents, and monies paid or payable in connection with claims for plagiarism, libel, and negligence.

RETURN OF CAPITAL CONTRIBUTIONS - SHARE OF NET PROFITS

The Investor Members as a group will be entitled to receive fifty percent (50%) of any net profits of the Company, each in the proportion which his capital contribution bears to the total capitalization of the Company. The Managing Member will also receive fifty percent (50%) of such profits. Any net profits will be distributed only after all capital contributions have been returned to the Investor Members and the Company maintains a reserve fund in the amount of $70,000. It is not anticipated that anyone will receive a percentage of the net profits from the Investor Members' share of net profits. The Managing Member may assign some share of his net profits to creative persons or for the purpose of financing the musical; however, this will not affect the share of the net profits to which the Investor Members are entitled. For this reason, the net profits of the Investor Members will not be reduced by payments to any individuals and/or entities providing services to the production.

Before net profits are earned, all losses will be borne by the Investor Member to the extent of his capital contributions. After net profits are earned, the Managing Member and Investor Members will bear losses to the extent of the net profits in proportion to their respective interests. If the Company liabilities exceed its assets, all Members, both Managing and Regular, will be required to return pro-rata any net profits distributed to them, and if a shortage remains, any repaid capital contributions as well. Even if the Musical is successful, the Investor Members may not have their capital contributions returned to them because the Operating Agreement provides that the Managing Member may withhold net profits for investment in other productions of the Musical without notice.

If repayment of capital contributions or distribution of Company net profits shall have been made prior or subsequent to the termination of the Company and, at any time thereafter, there shall be any unpaid debts, taxes, liabilities, or obligations of the Company and the Company shall not have sufficient assets to meet the same, then the Managing Member shall be entitled to recall all or part of the returned capital contributions and distributed Company net profits, in such aggregate amounts and under such circumstances as the Managing Member deems necessary or advisable. Returned capital contributions will not be recalled until all Company net profits distributed to the Managing Member and to the Investor Members have been recalled. If returned capital contributions are recalled, such recall shall be made ratably from all Investor Members based upon their respective capital contributions to the Company, or in the case of Investor Members who have posted bonds in lieu of making cash contributions, withdrawn ratably from the special bank accounts in which amounts equivalent to the repayment of capital contributions are to be deposited on their behalf. If distributed net profits are to be recalled, such recall shall be made from the Managing Member and the Investor Members in the same proportions as they shared in the distribution of such net profits.

Payments by the Investor Members of recalled amounts are to be made within ten (10) days after receipt by each Investor Member of the Managing Member's written request therefor. If an Investor Member does not return his share of distributed net profits or returned capital contributions when due, the remaining Investor Members shall be liable (on a ratable basis dependent upon their respective capital contributions to the Company) for any defaulted amounts, but in no event shall such obligation of any nondefaulting Investor Member exceed the amount of Company net profits theretofore distributed to the Investor Member and capital contributions theretofore returned to the Investor Member and not recalled from the Investor Member. Any residual liabilities of the Company must be borne by the Managing Member or any other persons who may agree to bear such liabilities.

Upon the termination of the Company, the assets of the Company shall be liquidated as promptly as possible and the cash proceeds shall be applied as follows in the following order of priority:

(a) To the payment of debts, taxes, obligations and liabilities of the Company and the necessary expenses of liquidation. Where there is a contingent debt, obligation, or liability, a reserve shall be set up to meet it, and if and when such contingency shall cease to exist, the monies, if any, in such reserve shall be distributed as provided for in the Operating Agreement.

(b) To the repayment of Capital Contributions of the Investor Members, such Partners sharing such repayment proportionately to their respective Capital Contributions.

(c) The surplus, if any, of such assets then remaining shall be divided among the Managing Member and Investor Members in the proportion that they share in the Net Profits.

OTHER FINANCING

Except as described above, no person or entity has advanced anything of value toward the production of the Musical.

FINANCIAL STATEMENTS

The ultimate issuer of these securities is The Last Chance Limited Liability Company, which will be formed. Since the Company has not been formed and has not engaged in business, there are no financial statements. Investor Members will be furnished with all financial statements required by the New York Theatrical Syndication Financing Act and Regulations promulgated in accordance with New York law and will include annual statements of operations.

If the Company receives an exemption from the requirements of filing certified accounting statements and the Managing Member is permitted to furnish an unaudited statement, Investor Members will not have the benefit of an accountant and will rely wholly upon the Managing Member's statement for the determination of their share in any net profits.

EFFECT OF FEDERAL INCOME TAXES

It is the belief of the Managing Member that for purposes of federal income tax, the Company should be treated as a partnership. A tax ruling from the Internal Revenue Service as to the Company's status for federal income tax purposes has not, however, been applied for, nor does the Managing Member intend to apply for such a ruling. If the Company is treated as a partnership for federal income tax purposes, then (a) the Company will be required to file an annual information tax return but will not itself be subject to federal income tax, and (b) each Investor Member, regardless of whether he receives any distribution from the Company, will be required to report his proportionate share of each item of Company income and will be entitled to deduct (to the extent of his basis in his Limited Liability Company Interest in the Company) such proportionate share of each item of Company expense on the appropriate tax return of such Investor Member for each relevant tax period. The disclosure hereunder with respect to tax considerations is based solely on the belief of the Managing Member and not on an opinion by a tax expert or tax counsel and an investor should seek the advice of an independent tax advisor or counsel regarding such matters.

LEGAL COUNSEL

Donald C. Farber, Esq., whose offices are located at 1370 Avenue of the Americas, New York, New York 10019, will act as counsel for the Company.

INDEMNIFICATION

There is no provision in the Operating Agreement or any contract, arrangement, or statute under which the Managing Member is insured or indemnified in any manner against any liability which they may incur in his capacity as such.

There is no personal liability of the Manager, Charles Clancy, to the Company or to the Members for damages for any breach of duty in his capacity as Manager, unless there is a judgment or other final adjudication adverse to him that establishes that his acts or omissions were in bad faith or involved intentional misconduct, or a knowing violation of law, or that he personally gained in fact a financial profit or other advantage to which he or she was not legally entitled or that with respect to any distribution, his acts were not performed in accordance with the applicable laws governing a Limited Liability Company in the State of New York.

FEDERAL SECURITIES LAW

This offering of securities has been organized with the intent of qualifying for an exemption from the registration requirements of the Securities Act of 1933 (the "Act"), as amended, pursuant to Regulation A promulgated by the Securities and Exchange Commission under the Act. Limited Liability Company Interests are not registered under the Act. Whether these securities are exempt from registration pursuant to Regulation A or otherwise has not been passed upon by the Securities and Exchange Commission, the Attorney General of the State of New York, or any other regulatory agency, nor has any such agency passed upon the merits of this offering.

Theatre License Agreement

THEATRE LICENSE AGREEMENT

AGREEMENT made this 28th day of January, 1996, by and between White Way Productions, Inc., a New York corporation having its offices at 165 West 46th Street, New York, NY 10036 (the "Licensor") and Caryn Horowitz, 1331 Havenhurst Drive, #106, West Hollywood, CA 90046 (the "Licensee").

WITNESSETH: Licensor hereby grants to the Licensee and Licensee accepts from the Licensor the right to the use of the Actors' Playhouse (the "Theatre"), located at 100 Seventh Avenue South, New York, NY 10014 for the presentation of the stage play entitled Making Time (the "Play"), for the term upon payment of the licensee fees, overage, guaranty, expenses and other charges and upon the mutual covenants hereinafter set forth.

THE PARTIES DO HEREBY AGREE AS FOLLOWS:

1. **Grant of License**: Licensor hereby grants to Licensee and Licensee hereby accepts from Licensor a license (the "License") for the use of the Theatre for the term of this Agreement (the "Term"), subject to the provisions and terms of this Agreement. The Term shall commence on _____ _____ and continue until the License is terminated in accordance with the Agreement.

2. Expenses To Be Borne By Licensee:

(a) **Basic License Fee**: The Basic License Fee shall be Three Thousand Dollars ($3,000.00) per week. Upon the week following the first anniversary of the Play, the Basic License Fee shall increase to Thirty-Five Hundred Dollars ($3,500.00) per week, and increase by Five Hundred Dollars ($500.00) per week on each anniversary thereafter.

(b) **Overage**: The Overage shall be Five Percent (5%) of 100% of the gross weekly box office receipts.

(c) **Service Package/Payment of Bills**: Licensee shall pay to Licensor on Tuesday of each week the sum of Eight Hundred Dollars ($800.00), in payment of services of the box office treasurer, electric, local telephone, supply bills, trash removal and Holmes Protection. Directory assistance and long distance telephone charges, if any, shall be billed separately, and payable upon proper invoicing. In the event that air conditioning is used, there shall be an additional charge of $25.00 per performance.

(d) **Taxes on Theatre**: Licensee shall pay any taxes imposed on its use of the Theatre by any governmental authority by reason of the engagement, including taxes on rent or occupancy. All other taxes, if any, shall be deducted from the gross box office receipts. Licensee shall not be responsible for real estate taxes on the Theatre. Each party shall pay its own income taxes.

(e) **Box Office Expenses**: Licensee shall pay $25.00 per week to cover miscellaneous box office expenses, including supplies, postage, envelopes, rental of credit card processing equipment, etc. The foregoing does not include a "per ticket" charge for every computer-generated ticket (currently $0.20 per ticket), which will also be deducted from gross box office receipts, at the Weekly Settlement. Licensee understands and acknowledges that such charges may be increased, and/or new charges imposed, by Telecharge, or its successor at the Theatre; Licensee agrees that all such charges shall be borne by Licensee.

(f) **Preliminary Expenses**: Licensee shall pay all preliminary box office expenses, including treasurer and assistant treasurer, box office and mail order personnel, if required, the printing of all ticket envelopes and tickets (if required), and any other out-of-pocket expenses for which Licensor may be obligated by reason of union agreements, or otherwise, during the period prior to the Performance Date, and prior to the commencement of the Term in the case of box-office related expenses incurred at Licensee's request during said period. Preliminary expenses shall be billed and paid on a weekly basis.

(g) **Expenses Subsequent to Closing**: Any expense incurred subsequent to the closing of the Play which is related to the presentation of the Play at the Theatre shall be borne exclusively by Licensee. Without limiting the foregoing, Licensee shall pay, following the last week in which the full Service Fee is paid, one week's box office treasurer's salary, including payroll taxes and fringes assuming a normal amount of post-closing work, it being understood that such obligations may be increased in the event of extraordinary amounts of work.

3. **Definitions**: The term "WEEK" shall mean the period from Monday of a given calendar week to the following Sunday, both days inclusive. The term "PLAY" shall mean the theatrical production specifically referred to in Paragraph 2 of this Agreement. The term "THEATRE" shall include the following: (a) seating capacity of 170 seats, performance area, lobby, two dressing rooms, office space, adequate toilet and shower facilities, stage manager's booth and box office; (b) theatre license, which licensor shall properly maintain (Landlord maintains a valid Certificate of Occupancy reflecting usage of space); (c) adequate equipment for heating of the premises, when necessary; (d) air conditioning in good working order, available when necessary; (e) availability of box office telephone system for use by Licensee. Cost for telephone shall be the responsibility of Licensee and shall be deducted from the Licensee's weekly settlement, in accordance with the section entitled "payment of bills" above. Licensor represents. that the premises and Licensor's equipment are and will be maintained in good working order, except for damages incurred or inflicted by the Licensee, which shall be repaired at Licensee's expense.

4. **Use of Theatre**: The Theatre shall be used by Licensee for the New York Off-Broadway production and presentation of a play presently entitled:

Making Time

during the term aforesaid, noting reservation of use by Licensor in Paragraph 11. The Theatre shall be available for use on Mondays for the following purposes only and subject to the following conditions: load-in and load-out and technical and dress rehearsals. The theatre shall be available to Licensee from two hours prior to performance time to one hour after the conclusion of the performance. Licensee hereby agrees that it shall give to Licensor a schedule of its forthcoming performances at least two (2) weeks prior to the first performance of Licensee's presentation.

5. **Payments by Licensee**: All payments due from Licensee to Licensor will be taken from the prior week's box office receipts when such receipts are there to cover costs. When not sufficient, the Licensee must be prepared at the Tuesday settlement to pay whatever is due from her own account.

6. **Defaults by Licensee**: In the event that Licensee defaults on payments, as described above, Licensor will give written notice to Licensee. The Licensee will have three days to cure default. If payment is not made by Thursday at 6 p.m. the Licensor may terminate the License.

7. **Rehearsal Period and Load-in**: Licensee agrees to give Licensor notice in writing of its rehearsal, load-in, technical, and dress rehearsal schedule at least one week prior to the commencement of such week. Licensee will cooperate in keeping the house clean, especially by not allowing food in the theatre. Smoking in the theatre, of course, is forbidden by law.

8. **Production**: Licensee warrants that it will not violate any copyright laws or infringe upon the literary or other rights of any person, firm, or entity, including, but not limited to, rights of privacy, etc., and agrees to indemnify Licensor for any claims, demands or judgments against or costs sustained by Licensor (including reasonable attorney's fees) arising in connection with the said warranty herein. In the event that the Licensee discontinues the presentation, purpose, or use of the Theatre as contracted for and stated herein, Licensor in its sole discretion, may require Licensee to remove the production and any and all equipment brought into the premises at Licensee's own cost and expense, within 72 hours after notice is given. In such event, payments made heretofore by Licensee to the Licensor shall be retained by Licensor as liquidated damages, and not as penalty, to compensate it for breach of this Agreement by the Licensee without prejudice to Licensor's right to demand any additional monies due it.

9. **Termination; Stop Clause**: This Agreement shall be automatically renewed from week to week unless terminated pursuant to the terms hereof.

(a) **Termination by Licensee**. Licensee may terminate this Agreement on four weeks' prior written notice to Licensor.

(b) **Stop Clause**. Licensor may terminate this Agreement in the event that Licensee's gross weekly box office receipts shall fall below $10,000 (the "Stop Clause Sum") for each of two (2) consecutive weeks commencing with the third week of paid public performances (full or partial). In the event Licensee presents only seven performances in any week relevant to the Stop Clause, the Stop Clause Sum shall be deemed reduced by one-eighth. Licensor may exercise its option within ten days following the end of the second consecutive week that the gross weekly box office receipts have fallen below the Stop Clause Sum for each of two consecutive weeks, by giving it at least one week's written notice of its intention to Licensee. Notice shall be deemed given at the end of the performance week in which it was delivered. In the event Licensor fails to give notice as aforesaid, Licensor's right to terminate and give notice as aforesaid is suspended, subject to revival if the gross weekly box office receipts falls below the Stop Clause Sum again for at least two consecutive weeks (which may include the second week from an immediately preceding consecutive two-week period), exercisable within ten days following the end of any two consecutive weeks that the gross weekly box office receipts have fallen below the Stop Clause Sum.

The following weeks shall not be considered in connection with the operation of the Stop Clause: the two-week periods immediately preceding Christmas and Easter; the two-week period following the week containing New Year's Eve; and the week containing July 4, Labor Day, Rosh Hashonah, and Yom Kippur.

In the event the ticket prices in effect as of the official opening performance are adjusted upward, the Stop Clause Sum will be adjusted upward in an amount proportionate to the increase in the capacity gross proceeds.

Licensee and Licensor covenant and agree that neither they nor their agents, servants, or employees nor anyone acting on behalf of either of them during the run of the Play with the purpose and intent of causing the GWBOR of the Play to exceed the Stop Clause Sum.

(c) **Breach by Licensee; Infringement of Rights**. In addition to any other remedies which Licensor may have pursuant to this Agreement, at law or in equity, Licensor shall have the right, upon Five (5) days written notice (except if a shorter period is specified elsewhere in this Agreement) to terminate the License in the event that (i) Licensee breaches any of the material terms, provisions, covenants or conditions of this Agreement; or (ii) Licensor, in its reasonable discretion, determines that the showing of the Play may subject Licensor to actions for damages, fines, penalties, revocations of license(s) or any other legal action or proceeding by reason of copyright infringement, proceeding under Article 235 of the Penal Law, or otherwise. If the alleged breach is cured or if Licensor is indemnified in a manner satisfactory to Licensor during said five-day period of notice, the License shall not be so terminated.

(d) **Demolition or Sale of the Theatre; Termination of Licensor's Lease**. In the event Licensor loses its rights to license the Theatre pursuant to the term of its lease with the Licensor's Landlord, Licensor may terminate the License on 200 days' notice.

(e) **Other Provisions of this Agreement**. Either party shall have the right to terminate the License at such time and in such manner as is elsewhere specifically provided for herein.

10. **Security Deposit; Notice of Termination.**

(a) Licensee shall pay to Licensor the sum of Twelve Thousand Dollars ($12,000.00) upon the execution of this Agreement as a Security Deposit. At such time as the Basic License Fee increases above $3,000 per week, Licensee shall pay to Licensor an amount equal to the increase multiplied by four weeks, and such larger amount shall be deemed the Security Deposit. Provided Licensee has complied with all the terms and conditions hereof and shall not be in default hereunder and shall have given Licensor at least four (4) weeks' notice of termination of the License (subject to the last sentence of this sub-paragraph), then one-quarter of the Security Deposit shall be applied to the Basic License Fee for each of the last four weeks of the Term. A notice given by noon on Tuesday may be deemed to have been given as of the last day (i.e., Sunday) of the previous week, if so specified in the notice. If not so specified, it shall be deemed to have been given as of the last day (i.e., Sunday) of the week in which it was delivered. Notwithstanding anything to the contrary contained herein, if Licensee gives notice prior to official opening performance, Licensor shall retain the full Security Deposit as liquidated damages.

(b) If Licensee fails to give Licensor four weeks' notice, Licensor shall retain the Security Deposit as liquidated damages, without prejudice to Licensor's additional rights and remedies hereunder. In the event at least one, but less than four weeks' notice is given, Licensor may retain as liquidated damages an amount equal to one-quarter of the Security Deposit times the number by which four weeks exceeds the weeks of notice. By way of example, if two weeks' notice was given, half of the Security Deposit shall be retained as liquidated damages; if one week's notice was given, three-quarters of the Security Deposit shall be retained as liquidated damages, in every case without prejudice to Licensor's rights and remedies hereunder.

(c) Notwithstanding anything to the contrary herein contained, at the election of Licensor and after notification to Licensee of any default in payment of any charges hereunder, Licensor may apply the Security Deposit to any payment due from Licensee for the performance of any obligation of Licensee, whereupon Licensee shall within 24 hours restore to Licensor the amount so applied, and if Licensee shall fail to do so, Licensor may restore such amounts by deducting an equal amount from Licensee's share of the gross receipts, or may at Licensor's election terminate the License.

(d) In addition to the Security Deposit referred to in sub-paragraph (a) above, Licensor shall have the right to retain a maximum of One Thousand Dollars as a reserve for credit card chargebacks following the close of the Play. The difference between this amount and actual amount of chargebacks, if any, shall be remitted to Licensee within ninety (90) days following the close of the Play.

(e) If, upon termination of the License, Licensee fails to terminate the run of the Play and surrender the premises pursuant to this Agreement, Licensor may enforce its rights by injunction and/or any other type of legal and/or equitable relief, and Licensee will be liable for Licensor's attorneys' fees and costs and disbursements in connection therewith.

It is specifically understood that Licensee is not entitled to arbitrate Licensor's termination of the License prior to surrendering the premises, notwithstanding any other provision of this Agreement.

11. **Box Office**: Box Office shall be open at hours to be determined by Licensee. If Box Office will be open for more than 32 hours per week, Licensee agrees to hire a box office assistant. Licensee acknowledges that the Box Office shall be staffed and operated by the Licensor, the holder of the Theatre License, as required by the Department of Licenses of the City of New York, and that the Box Office Bank Accounts are registered in the name of the Licensor, such account to be used solely for box office sales, and not for operational activities of Licensor. Those of the Licensor's Box Office Accounts which shall be utilized by the Licensee's production shall be audited as required, at the Licensee's sole expense, and all monthly and other bank charges on such accounts shall be borne by Licensee. All costs of operating the Box Office incurred by the Licensor, including, but not limited to the purchase of tickets, supplies, postage, envelopes, etc., shall be charged weekly against the Licensee's settlement. Licensee shall pay for all tickets used by Licensee's production, including the cost of any tickets ordered for any period subsequent to the closing of the Play or prior to the date of the actual opening or for any canceled, delayed or changed performances. Licensor shall approve all Box Office ticket price sales prior to the printing of any ticket, such approval not to be unreasonably withheld. The Box Office Treasurer(s) shall be authorized to accept credit card orders, personal checks (mail order only), bank money orders, postal savings orders, or other conventional types of payment as payment for tickets to the Play. All losses in the event of non-payment or non-collection or otherwise in connection with any such orders for the payment of funds shall become the liability of Licensee, and may be deducted from Licensee's box office receipts by the Licensor. Licensor shall provide Licensee with a duplicate copy of the daily and weekly Box Office statements, verified by representatives of the Licensor and the Licensee and the Box Office Treasurer on each Tuesday following the reported week. The Box Office treasurer shall be employed at least one week before the first public performance. The Licensor will select a ticket vendor such as Telecharge or Ticketmaster which the Licensee will use in all advertising, as well as the name of the theatre. Licensee acknowledges that in the event that the outside ticket vendor permits the theatre box office to accept telephone credit card orders, a service charge of $2.00 shall be added to each ticket charged by telephone to a

credit card in consideration for the cost of this operation. This service charge shall be retained solely by Licensor. All losses in the event of non-payment or non-collection or otherwise in connection with any such orders for the payment of funds shall become the liability of the Licensee and may be deducted from the Licensee's box office receipts by the Licensor.

12. **Stage Equipment**: Licensee shall, at its own cost and expense, provide all stage electrical equipment it may require, provided, however, that Licensee first secures approval of the proper governmental authorities having jurisdiction therefor, in all cases where such approval is required by law and complies with ordinances, statutes and laws of the City of New York, and any and all rules and regulations and directives issued by every governmental bureau, department or agency exercising jurisdiction thereof Licensor shall notify Licensee of any violation respecting Licensee's equipment, and upon failure of Licensee, within seven (7) days of such notice to correct or to take appropriate measures to assure the correction of such violation, Licensor shall have the right to terminate this Agreement. Any and all fees for inspection of said equipment by any of the aforementioned agencies shall be paid for by Licensee or reimbursed by Licensee. At the end of the term, Licensee shall remove all such electrical equipment and shall, at its own cost and expense, restore the premises to its condition at the commencement of the term, subject to the provisions herein regarding normal wear and tear.

13. **Concessions**: Licensee reserves to itself the exclusive right, but not the obligation, to operate or contract with concessionaires for the selling of refreshments, beverages, cookies, candy, etc., and any and all revenue therefrom shall belong to Licensee. Licensor agrees that Licensee shall have the right, but not the obligation, to sell copies of sheet music, original cast albums, souvenir books, and/or published texts of the Play or other of the author's published works, on the premises. Licensor shall have approval over all selling personnel, and Licensee shall hold the Licensor harness, and indemnify Licensor from any claims, demands, and judgments arising out of Licensee's selling of such items on the premises. Licensee shall be given notice of any such claim and will have the right to defend and settle such claim.

14. **Licensor's Reservation of Use**: Licensor reserves for itself the exclusive use of Theatre at any and all times not herein licensed to the Licensee. After the Play has opened, Licensee may use the Theatre for understudy or

brush-up rehearsals or auditions at no additional charge, and such granting of rehearsal or audition time in the Theatre shall be restricted to rehearsals or auditions for the original Off-Broadway production of the Play only, and shall not apply to rehearsals or auditions for any subsequent production of the Play. Licensee shall request same of Licensor in writing in advance of the day on which it wishes to do so. Licensor's required approval shall be subject to Licensor's prior commitments of the Theatre which shall have precedence over any such request by Licensee. Licensor reserves the right to permit rehearsals of other productions, presentations for children, auditions, filmings, television productions, recordings, or any other use with respect to any other attractions in the premises during the term or any extension thereof without any reduction of the Licensee's weekly payments hereunder, provided that such activities do not interfere with Licensee's use of the premises and its sets, lights, props, etc. In the event of the use of the premises during the Licensee's term by any other production, Licensor agrees that it shall be responsible to see that the Licensee's setting shall be restored. Licensee shall be reimbursed for the use of the Licensee's electricity, if used by any third party during a rehearsal, audition, etc., at an amount to be mutually agreed upon. Licensor will indemnify and hold harmless from and against any claim, action, loss or liability resulting from the use of the Theatre by Licensor or by any other party other than Licensee. Licensor or its representatives shall always have free access to the Theatre for the purpose of inspection and maintenance so long as the same does not interfere with or conflict with Licensee's use of the Theatre and its performances.

15. **Licensee's Personnel**: Licensee shall engage and provide at its own expense cast, director, choreographer, musical director, scenic, lighting and costume designers, stage manager(s), stage hands, company manager, press agent, porter, house manager, ushers and any and all other personnel required for the first-class Off-Broadway production of the Play. Licensee shall provide all advertising, newspaper and otherwise, all posters, flyers, houseboards, the sight for the electric marquee, and all flags and banners at its sole cost and expense. Licensee shall not engage any Union non-performing personnel without the knowledge, participation, and written approval of the Licensor. Licensor reserves the right in its own discretion to reject the use by Licensee on Licensor's premises of any such personnel, if Licensor deems same detrimental to its Theatre. The foregoing shall not apply to the contracting of actors, director, choreographer, dancers or other performing personnel. Licensee shall commit no act which would alter the conditions of union employment at the

Theatre nor shall Licensee in any way represent itself as acting on behalf of Licensor. Licensee warrants that it shall be solely responsible for all sums payable, on behalf of its employees, for Social Security, Unemployment Insurance, Disability Benefits and other like enactments and for all Federal, State, and Local payroll taxes and any other taxes and fees payable, and shall withhold same from all salaries as prescribed by Law. Licensee shall indemnify and hold Licensor harmless from any claims, demands, or judgment brought against Licensor and arising from the warranties and representations herein; and from any mechanics, or other liens arising from any services performed for Licensee on the premises.

16. **Use of Marquee and Posters**: Licensor agrees to provide Licensee with the exclusive use of the space on the Theatre's marquee and reasonable space within the premises, at no additional cost to Licensee, for pictures, posters, displays advertising the production and houseboards (wherever same is not prohibited to Licensor) and Licensee agrees that such advertising will be executed in a professional manner acceptable to Licensor. Licensor reserves to itself the right to also use additional "billboards" in front of the Theatre or the Theatre lobby to announce the next attraction after this production has given notice of closing.

17. **Programs and Credits**: Licensee agrees that it will use promi-nently the name THE ACTORS' PLAYHOUSE in its address and telephone number in all advertising, throwaways, etc., and on the title page of all programs. Licensee shall include in the programs the Licensor's credits for its staff as supplied by Licensor limited to the amount of space customarily provided for such credits, and include a short history of the theatre, supplied by the Licensor.

18. **Surrender of Premises**: Licensee agrees within 48 hours following the termination of this License all equipment and property brought into the Theatre premises by Licensee will be removed therefrom by Licensee and the Theatre shall be restored by Licensee to a broom clean and proper condition. If Licensee does not remove said equipment and property within this time period, Licensee shall be deemed to have abandoned said equipment and property and title to same shall pass immediately to Licensor. Regardless of title thereto, Licensor may dispose of same as it sees fit, inclusive of the right (but not the obligation) to remove and/or store at the sole expenses of the Licensee. Licensee shall in addition be liable to Licensor for all damages sustained by Licensor caused by Licensee's failure to so vacate, and for all actual costs and

expenses in removing of said equipment and property and disposing of same and for storage charges (if stored). Any improvements, changes, alterations, and/or decoration including, but not limited to painting, refurbishing, altering or improving dressing rooms, seating, stage floor surfaces if required by any contract between Licensee and any Union, shall be made and paid for by Licensee, and Licensor shall have no responsibility with respect thereto nor shall Licensor be called upon to make any contribution thereto. Any improvements or alterations placed in the Theatre, including but not limited to the dressing rooms, lobbies and lighting booth, shall upon installation become the sole property of the Licensor.

19. **Insurance**:

(a) During the engagement Licensee shall carry and pay for Workman's Compensation and Employer's Liability (including New York State Disability Benefits). Public Liability (Personal Injury and Property Damage) Insurance (with bodily injury limits of not less than $1,000,000 and property damage limit of $100,000), and Fire Insurance for full replacement value (with the New York standard extended coverage clause) of all scenery, costumes, electrical and sound equipment, literary and musical material, and all other properties and materials owned, rented or brought into theatre by Licensee. Licensee hereby releases Licensor from any and all liability for any loss or damage caused by fire or other peril including, without limitation, burglary, water damage, etc., other than events caused by culpable negligence or willful acts of Licensor, its agents or invitees. To the extent permitted by law only, such release shall include fires or other casualties resulting from Licensor's negligence. Licensee's Fire Insurance Policy or Policies shall include a waiver(s) of subrogation against Licensor and any corporation or entity affiliated with Licensor. All such insurance shall be in such form and shall be taken in such amounts and with such companies (licensed to do business in New York) as Licensor shall approve. Licensee shall, not later than (3) days prior to the first day of rehearsal, deliver to Licensor certificates of such insurance containing in each case a clause requiring ten (10) days prior notice of cancellation to Licensor. Upon the failure of Licensee to carry and pay for any such insurance, Licensor shall have the right, but not the obligation, to take out and pay for same and charge Licensee for all costs and expenses incurred therefore. Licensee waives all rights of subrogation to the extent permitted by law and will have all of its insurance policies so endorsed.

(b) Licensee shall pay each week to the Licensor the Liability Insurance expense incurred by the admissions of the audience at the rate of $.32 per capita, whether admissions are paid or complimentary. Licensor warrants that this is the current rate and should the current rate change, the Licensee will pay whatever this current rate may be. Licensee shall also pay any premiums over and above the normal premiums paid by Licensor for fire and other insurance coverage, if increased premiums or extended coverage are necessitated by the Licensee's production.

(c) For the purposes of the public liability (personal injury, bodily injury and Property damage) insurance required to be carried by Licensee pursuant to the provisions of subparagraph (a) hereof, the Licensor shall be deemed to be primarily liable for all acts, occurrences or omissions arising out of or relating to the operation of the Theatre premises as distinguished from the presentation in the Theatre, and the Licensee shall be deemed to be primarily liable for all acts, occurrences or omissions arising out of or relating to the presentation in the Theatre as distinguished from the operation of the Theatre premises.

20. **Maintenance**: Licensee shall keep and leave said theatre in good, clean, orderly and sanitary condition at all times, at its own expense. All additional costs or expenses incurred in maintaining the premises resulting from the building or installing of scenery, machinery, props, etc. on the stage or in the Theatre shall be borne solely by the Licensee. Licensee agrees to and does hereby assume responsibility for opening, closing, securely locking and unlocking the licensed premises. It is understood that Licensor assumes no responsibility for any personal property in the licensed premises, whether owned by Licensee, by employees, patrons, or any other persons entering the licensed premises. No part of the Licensee's settings or properties shall be affixed to any surface on the premises without Licensor's prior written consent. Licensee shall not in any way alter the physical appearances and plan of the premises. Licensee acknowledges that no pets or animals are to be brought into the Theatre by it or its personnel or cast.

21. **Labor Relations**: It is a material term of this Agreement that Licensee shall make no negotiations, request any rulings, determinations or decisions

and shall not appear for any purpose before any Agencies, Unions, Societies, Guilds or Organizations which may affect or concern Licensor, the premises and/or Licensee's production without the knowledge, participation, and physical presence of Licensor, and any violation of the provisions of this paragraph by Licensee shall automatically terminate this Agreement and Licensor shall retain any monies held by it as liquidated damages for Licensee's breach thereof.

22. **Exculpation of Licensor**: In the event of the premises being rendered unsuitable or unavailable for presentation of the Play by reason of fire, natural or local calamity or emergency or any unforeseen occurrence or a labor dispute which shall render the fulfillment of this Agreement by Licensor impossible, Licensor shall not be held responsible to Licensee for any damages caused thereby, unless caused by the negligence of the Licensor, its agents or employees. The failure to adjust a labor dispute or settle a fire loss persisted in by Licensor in good faith shall not be deemed negligence.

23. **Compliance with Law Libel Indemnity**: (a) Licensee and Licensor, each for itself, agree to comply in all respects with any and all City, State, and Federal rules, regulations, ordinances, statutes and laws in connection with the use of the premises. Each further agrees to do no act which would in any way jeopardize the Theatre license or reputation of the other and further covenants not to do any act in any way in violation of the rules and regulations of the License Bureaus of the City of New York having jurisdiction of the Theatre. Licensee agrees that all of its scenery, equipment and paraphernalia will be fireproofed in accordance with the laws, ordinances and regulations of the City, State or Federal governments having jurisdiction and proper flameproofing affidavits to that effect shall be submitted to Licensor prior to the first dress rehearsal; (b) Licensee agrees to indemnify and hold harmless Licensor from any and all claims, lawsuits, judgments, damages or costs (including reasonable attorney fees) arising out of Licensee's production and presentation of the Play, and from any breach by Licensee of the covenants, representations and warranties herein. Licensor assumes no responsibility for the Licensee's equipment in the event of theft or destruction, unless caused by the negligence of the Licensor, its agents or employees.

24. **Miscellaneous**: (a) Licensee agrees to take the premises in a broom clean condition "as is" and to exercise reasonable care in the use of the Theatre premises and all of the fixtures and equipment located therein or attached thereto,

and to repair or replace all fixtures and equipment which may be damaged, lost, or destroyed as a result of Licensee's use of said premises, normal wear and tear excepted; (b) no diminution or abatement of any of the payments or other compensation due from Licensee to Licensor hereunder shall be claimed or allowed to Licensee for any inconvenience or discomfort to its business arising from the making of any necessary repairs or alterations to the premises, so long as said premises are not rendered unusable by the Licensee for the presentation of the Play. (c) This agreement shall be assignable to any limited partnership or other business entity organized by the Licensee to produce and present the Play and of which Licensee shall be a general partner or have controlling ownership upon the compliance with the following conditions precedent: (i) Licensee shall be and continue to be primarily liable for all of Licensee's obligations hereunder; (ii) all obligations of Licensee under this Agreement shall be assumed by the assignee; (iii) a written document of assignment meeting such conditions shall be delivered to Licensor. There shall be no right of subletting under this Agreement.

25. **Termination and Liquidated Damages**: The provisions for termination and liquidated damages provided in this paragraph shall be deemed to be in addition and not in limitation of other provisions for similar consequences in preceding portions of this Agreement. This Agreement may be terminated at the option of the Licensor: (a) in the event of any default of Licensee in making any weekly payment or the deficiency due on any weekly statement, this Agreement may, at the option of the Licensor, be terminated as stated in paragraph 4 and Licensor may thereupon retain all advance monies paid to it by Licensee without prejudice to Licensor's right to demand and collect any additional monies due it hereunder; (b) if Licensee fails to present or open the Play due to no fault of Licensor as hereinabove provided or closes the Play prior to the end of the term, any advance payment shall be considered liquidated damages and shall be retained by Licensor as damages for the breach of this Agreement without prejudice to Licensor's right to demand any additional monies due it; (c) Licensor shall have the right to deduct the amount of physical damages so computed (with proper documentation) from any monies therefore paid to Licensor by Licensee or held by Licensor for Licensee's benefit, and shall return to Licensee only the balance thereafter remaining, less any other deductions allowable and due hereunder; and if there shall remain any deficiency, the same shall be payable to Licensor by Licensee on demand.

26. **Arbitration**: Except as herein otherwise expressly provided, any and all disputes, differences or controversies arising between the parties hereto in connection with the interpretation, performance or beach of this Agreement, shall be submitted to arbitration before three arbitrators to be mutually agreed upon. Arbitration shall be held in New York City and under the rules and regulations of the American Arbitration Association and the parties hereby agree to be bound by the determination of the majority of the arbitrators. Judgment on the award may be entered in any state or federal court having jurisdiction.

27. **Relationship Between the Parties**: The Licensor is licensing the Theatre to the Licensee for the run of the Play with the conditions stated in this Agreement, but nothing herein shall be deemed to constitute a joint venture, partnership or trust relationship.

28. **Notices**: All notices provided for herein shall be in writing and shall be effective if sent by registered or certified mail, return receipt requested, to the parties hereto at the addresses set forth below.

29. **General**: This Agreement contains the entire understanding of the parties hereto. There are no representations, warranties, promises, covenants or undertakings other than those expressly set forth. No waiver, change, or modification hereof shall be binding unless the same is in writing, signed by the parties hereto. This Agreement shall be constituted and interpreted pursuant to the Laws of the State of New York. The paragraph headings herein are for convenience of reference only and shall not be construed as part of this agreement.

IN WITNESS WHEREOF this Agreement has been executed by the parties hereto the day and year first written above.

West Way Productions, Inc.   Jared Jones
118 West 56th Street   712 Larchmont Drive
New York, New York 10019   Los Angeles, California 90038

BY: _____   BY: _____
Licensor   Licensee

Notice of Sale of Securities Pursuant to Regulation D

FORM D

FORM D

NOTICE OF SALE OF SECURITIES
PURSUANT TO REGULATION D,
SECTION 4(6), AND/OR
UNIFORM LIMITED OFFERING EXEMPTION

OMB APPROVAL	
OMB Number:	3235-0076
Expires:	**April 30, 2008**
Estimated average burden	
hours per response......16.00	

SEC USE ONLY	
Prefix	Serial
DATE RECEIVED	

Name of Offering   (☐ check if this is an amendment and name has changed, and indicate change.)

Filing Under (Check box(es) that apply):   ☐ Rule 504   ☐ Rule 505   ☐ Rule 506   ☐ Section 4(6)   ☐ ULOE
Type of Filing: ☐ New Filing   ☐ Amendment

A. BASIC IDENTIFICATION DATA

1.   Enter the information requested about the issuer

Name of Issuer   (☐ check if this is an amendment and name has changed, and indicate change.)

Address of Executive Offices	(Number and Street, City, State, Zip Code)	Telephone Number (Including Area Code)
Address of Principal Business Operations (if different from Executive Offices)	(Number and Street, City, State, Zip Code)	Telephone Number (Including Area Code)

Brief Description of Business

Type of Business Organization
☐ corporation   ☐ limited partnership, already formed   ☐ other (please specify):
☐ business trust   ☐ limited partnership, to be formed

                                                  Month   Year
Actual or Estimated Date of Incorporation or Organization: ☐☐   ☐☐   ☐ Actual   ☐ Estimated
Jurisdiction of Incorporation or Organization: (Enter two-letter U.S. Postal Service abbreviation for State:
                                                  CN for Canada; FN for other foreign jurisdiction)   ☐☐

GENERAL INSTRUCTIONS

Federal:

Who Must File: All issuers making an offering of securities in reliance on an exemption under Regulation D or Section 4(6), 17 CFR 230.501 et seq. or 15 U.S.C. 77d(6).

When To File: A notice must be filed no later than 15 days after the first sale of securities in the offering. A notice is deemed filed with the U.S. Securities and Exchange Commission (SEC) on the earlier of the date it is received by the SEC at the address given below or, if received at that address after the date on which it is due, on the date it was mailed by United States registered or certified mail to that address.

Where To File: U.S. Securities and Exchange Commission, 450 Fifth Street, N.W., Washington, D.C. 20549.

Copies Required: Five (5) copies of this notice must be filed with the SEC, one of which must be manually signed. Any copies not manually signed must be photocopies of the manually signed copy or bear typed or printed signatures.

Information Required: A new filing must contain all information requested. Amendments need only report the name of the issuer and offering, any changes thereto, the information requested in Part C, and any material changes from the information previously supplied in Parts A and B. Part E and the Appendix need not be filed with the SEC.

Filing Fee: There is no federal filing fee.

State:

This notice shall be used to indicate reliance on the Uniform Limited Offering Exemption (ULOE) for sales of securities in those states that have adopted ULOE and that have adopted this form. Issuers relying on ULOE must file a separate notice with the Securities Administrator in each state where sales are to be, or have been made. If a state requires the payment of a fee as a precondition to the claim for the exemption, a fee in the proper amount shall accompany this form. This notice shall be filed in the appropriate states in accordance with state law. The Appendix to the notice constitutes a part of this notice and must be completed.

───────── **ATTENTION** ─────────

Failure to file notice in the appropriate states will not result in a loss of the federal exemption. Conversely, failure to file the appropriate federal notice will not result in a loss of an available state exemption unless such exemption is predicated on the filing of a federal notice.

SEC 1972 (6-02)   Persons who respond to the collection of information contained in this form are not
                         required to respond unless the form displays a currently valid OMB control number.   1 of 9

A. BASIC IDENTIFICATION DATA

2. Enter the information requested for the following:

- Each promoter of the issuer, if the issuer has been organized within the past five years;
- Each beneficial owner having the power to vote or dispose, or direct the vote or disposition of, 10% or more of a class of equity securities of the issuer.
- Each executive officer and director of corporate issuers and of corporate general and managing partners of partnership issuers; and
- Each general and managing partner of partnership issuers.

Check Box(es) that Apply: ☐ Promoter ☐ Beneficial Owner ☐ Executive Officer ☐ Director ☐ General and/or Managing Partner

Full Name (Last name first, if individual)

Business or Residence Address　(Number and Street, City, State, Zip Code)

Check Box(es) that Apply: ☐ Promoter ☐ Beneficial Owner ☐ Executive Officer ☐ Director ☐ General and/or Managing Partner

Full Name (Last name first, if individual)

Business or Residence Address　(Number and Street, City, State, Zip Code)

Check Box(es) that Apply: ☐ Promoter ☐ Beneficial Owner ☐ Executive Officer ☐ Director ☐ General and/or Managing Partner

Full Name (Last name first, if individual)

Business or Residence Address　(Number and Street, City, State, Zip Code)

Check Box(es) that Apply: ☐ Promoter ☐ Beneficial Owner ☐ Executive Officer ☐ Director ☐ General and/or Managing Partner

Full Name (Last name first, if individual)

Business or Residence Address　(Number and Street, City, State, Zip Code)

Check Box(es) that Apply: ☐ Promoter ☐ Beneficial Owner ☐ Executive Officer ☐ Director ☐ General and/or Managing Partner

Full Name (Last name first, if individual)

Business or Residence Address　(Number and Street, City, State, Zip Code)

Check Box(es) that Apply: ☐ Promoter ☐ Beneficial Owner ☐ Executive Officer ☐ Director ☐ General and/or Managing Partner

Full Name (Last name first, if individual)

Business or Residence Address　(Number and Street, City, State, Zip Code)

Check Box(es) that Apply: ☐ Promoter ☐ Beneficial Owner ☐ Executive Officer ☐ Director ☐ General and/or Managing Partner

Full Name (Last name first, if individual)

Business or Residence Address　(Number and Street, City, State, Zip Code)

(Use blank sheet, or copy and use additional copies of this sheet, as necessary)

B. INFORMATION ABOUT OFFERING

		Yes	No
1.	Has the issuer sold, or does the issuer intend to sell, to non-accredited investors in this offering?...........................	☐	☐

Answer also in Appendix, Column 2, if filing under ULOE.

2. What is the minimum investment that will be accepted from any individual? .... $_____

		Yes	No
3.	Does the offering permit joint ownership of a single unit?	☐	☐

4. Enter the information requested for each person who has been or will be paid or given, directly or indirectly, any commission or similar remuneration for solicitation of purchasers in connection with sales of securities in the offering. If a person to be listed is an associated person or agent of a broker or dealer registered with the SEC and/or with a state or states, list the name of the broker or dealer. If more than five (5) persons to be listed are associated persons of such a broker or dealer, you may set forth the information for that broker or dealer only.

Full Name (Last name first, if individual)

Business or Residence Address (Number and Street, City, State, Zip Code)

Name of Associated Broker or Dealer

States in Which Person Listed Has Solicited or Intends to Solicit Purchasers

(Check "All States" or check individual States) .... ☐ All States

AL	AK	AZ	AR	CA	CO	CT	DE	DC	FL	GA	HI	ID
IL	IN	IA	KS	KY	LA	ME	MD	MA	MI	MN	MS	MO
MT	NE	NV	NH	NJ	NM	NY	NC	ND	OH	OK	OR	PA
RI	SC	SD	TN	TX	UT	VT	VA	WA	WV	WI	WY	PR

Full Name (Last name first, if individual)

Business or Residence Address (Number and Street, City, State, Zip Code)

Name of Associated Broker or Dealer

States in Which Person Listed Has Solicited or Intends to Solicit Purchasers

(Check "All States" or check individual States) .... ☐ All States

AL	AK	AZ	AR	CA	CO	CT	DE	DC	FL	GA	HI	ID
IL	IN	IA	KS	KY	LA	ME	MD	MA	MI	MN	MS	MO
MT	NE	NV	NH	NJ	NM	NY	NC	ND	OH	OK	OR	PA
RI	SC	SD	TN	TX	UT	VT	VA	WA	WV	WI	WY	PR

Full Name (Last name first, if individual)

Business or Residence Address (Number and Street, City, State, Zip Code)

Name of Associated Broker or Dealer

States in Which Person Listed Has Solicited or Intends to Solicit Purchasers

(Check "All States" or check individual States) .... ☐ All States

AL	AK	AZ	AR	CA	CO	CT	DE	DC	FL	GA	HI	ID
IL	IN	IA	KS	KY	LA	ME	MD	MA	MI	MN	MS	MO
MT	NE	NV	NH	NJ	NM	NY	NC	ND	OH	OK	OR	PA
RI	SC	SD	TN	TX	UT	VT	VA	WA	WV	WI	WY	PR

(Use blank sheet, or copy and use additional copies of this sheet, as necessary.)

C. OFFERING PRICE, NUMBER OF INVESTORS, EXPENSES AND USE OF PROCEEDS

1. Enter the aggregate offering price of securities included in this offering and the total amount already sold. Enter "0" if the answer is "none" or "zero." If the transaction is an exchange offering, check this box ☐ and indicate in the columns below the amounts of the securities offered for exchange and already exchanged.

Type of Security	Aggregate Offering Price	Amount Already Sold
Debt	$	$
Equity	$	$
☐ Common ☐ Preferred		
Convertible Securities (including warrants)	$	$
Partnership Interests	$	$
Other (Specify _____)	$	$
Total	$ 0.00	$ 0.00

Answer also in Appendix, Column 3, if filing under ULOE.

2. Enter the number of accredited and non-accredited investors who have purchased securities in this offering and the aggregate dollar amounts of their purchases. For offerings under Rule 504, indicate the number of persons who have purchased securities and the aggregate dollar amount of their purchases on the total lines. Enter "0" if answer is "none" or "zero."

	Number Investors	Aggregate Dollar Amount of Purchases
Accredited Investors		$
Non-accredited Investors		$
Total (for filings under Rule 504 only)		$

Answer also in Appendix, Column 4, if filing under ULOE.

3. If this filing is for an offering under Rule 504 or 505, enter the information requested for all securities sold by the issuer, to date, in offerings of the types indicated, in the twelve (12) months prior to the first sale of securities in this offering. Classify securities by type listed in Part C — Question 1.

Type of Offering	Type of Security	Dollar Amount Sold
Rule 505		$
Regulation A		$
Rule 504		$
Total		$ 0.00

4. a. Furnish a statement of all expenses in connection with the issuance and distribution of the securities in this offering. Exclude amounts relating solely to organization expenses of the insurer. The information may be given as subject to future contingencies. If the amount of an expenditure is not known, furnish an estimate and check the box to the left of the estimate.

Transfer Agent's Fees	☐	$
Printing and Engraving Costs	☐	$
Legal Fees	☐	$
Accounting Fees	☐	$
Engineering Fees	☐	$
Sales Commissions (specify finders' fees separately)	☐	$
Other Expenses (identify) _____	☐	$
Total	☐	$ 0.00

C. OFFERING PRICE, NUMBER OF INVESTORS, EXPENSES AND USE OF PROCEEDS

b.   Enter the difference between the aggregate offering price given in response to Part C — Question 1 and total expenses furnished in response to Part C — Question 4.a. This difference is the "adjusted gross proceeds to the issuer." .... $ __0.00__

5.   Indicate below the amount of the adjusted gross proceed to the issuer used or proposed to be used for each of the purposes shown. If the amount for any purpose is not known, furnish an estimate and check the box to the left of the estimate. The total of the payments listed must equal the adjusted gross proceeds to the issuer set forth in response to Part C — Question 4.b above.

	Payments to Officers, Directors, & Affiliates	Payments to Others
Salaries and fees	☐ $_____	☐ $_____
Purchase of real estate	☐ $_____	☐ $_____
Purchase, rental or leasing and installation of machinery and equipment	☐ $_____	☐ $_____
Construction or leasing of plant buildings and facilities	☐ $_____	☐ $_____
Acquisition of other businesses (including the value of securities involved in this offering that may be used in exchange for the assets or securities of another issuer pursuant to a merger)	☐ $_____	☐ $_____
Repayment of indebtedness	☐ $_____	☐ $_____
Working capital	☐ $_____	☐ $_____
Other (specify):_____	☐ $_____	☐ $_____
_____	☐ $_____	☐ $_____
Column Totals	☐ $ 0.00	☐ $ 0.00
Total Payments Listed (column totals added)	☐ $ 0.00	

D. FEDERAL SIGNATURE

The issuer has duly caused this notice to be signed by the undersigned duly authorized person. If this notice is filed under Rule 505, the following signature constitutes an undertaking by the issuer to furnish to the U.S. Securities and Exchange Commission, upon written request of its staff, the information furnished by the issuer to any non-accredited investor pursuant to paragraph (b)(2) of Rule 502.

Issuer (Print or Type)	Signature	Date
Name of Signer (Print or Type)	Title of Signer (Print or Type)	

─────── **ATTENTION** ───────
Intentional misstatements or omissions of fact constitute federal criminal violations. (See 18 U.S.C. 1001.)

E. STATE SIGNATURE

1. Is any party described in 17 CFR 230.262 presently subject to any of the disqualification provisions of such rule? ....

       Yes ☐   No ☐

See Appendix, Column 5, for state response.

2. The undersigned issuer hereby undertakes to furnish to any state administrator of any state in which this notice is filed a notice on Form D (17 CFR 239.500) at such times as required by state law.

3. The undersigned issuer hereby undertakes to furnish to the state administrators, upon written request, information furnished by the issuer to offerees.

4. The undersigned issuer represents that the issuer is familiar with the conditions that must be satisfied to be entitled to the Uniform limited Offering Exemption (ULOE) of the state in which this notice is filed and understands that the issuer claiming the availability of this exemption has the burden of establishing that these conditions have been satisfied.

The issuer has read this notification and knows the contents to be true and has duly caused this notice to be signed on its behalf by the undersigned duly authorized person.

Issuer (Print or Type)	Signature	Date
Name (Print or Type)	Title (Print or Type)	

Instruction:
Print the name and title of the signing representative under his signature for the state portion of this form. One copy of every notice on Form D must be manually signed. Any copies not manually signed must be photocopies of the manually signed copy or bear typed or printed signatures.

6 of 9

APPENDIX									
1	2		3	4				5	
	Intend to sell to non-accredited investors in State (Part B-Item 1)		Type of security and aggregate offering price offered in state (Part C-Item 1)	Type of investor and amount purchased in State (Part C-Item 2)				Disqualification under State ULOE (if yes, attach explanation of waiver granted) (Part E-Item 1)	
State	Yes	No		Number of Accredited Investors	Amount	Number of Non-Accredited Investors	Amount	Yes	No
AL									
AK									
AZ									
AR									
CA									
CO									
CT									
DE									
DC									
FL									
GA									
HI									
ID									
IL									
IN									
IA									
KS									
KY									
LA									
ME									
MD									
MA									
MI									
MN									
MS									

APPENDIX								
1	**2** Intend to sell to non-accredited investors in State (Part B-Item 1)		**3** Type of security and aggregate offering price offered in state (Part C-Item 1)	**4** Type of investor and amount purchased in State (Part C-Item 2)				**5** Disqualification under State ULOE (if yes, attach explanation of waiver granted) (Part E-Item 1)	
State	**Yes**	**No**		**Number of Accredited Investors**	**Amount**	**Number of Non-Accredited Investors**	**Amount**	**Yes**	**No**
MO									
MT									
NE									
NV									
NH									
NJ									
NM									
NY									
NC									
ND									
OH									
OK									
OR									
PA									
RI									
SC									
SD									
TN									
TX									
UT									
VT									
VA									
WA									
WV									
WI									

APPENDIX									
1	2		3	4				5	
	Intend to sell to non-accredited investors in State (Part B-Item 1)		Type of security and aggregate offering price offered in state (Part C-Item 1)	Type of investor and amount purchased in State (Part C-Item 2)				Disqualification under State ULOE (if yes, attach explanation of waiver granted) (Part E-Item 1)	
State	Yes	No		Number of Accredited Investors	Amount	Number of Non-Accredited Investors	Amount	Yes	No
WY									
PR									

Appendix N

Form 99: Real Estate Financing Bureau Notification Filing

FORM 99   File # _____

**STATE OF NEW YORK DEPARTMENT OF LAW
BUREAU OF INVESTOR PROTECTION AND SECURITIES
// REAL ESTATE FINANCING BUREAU
NOTIFICATION FILING**

**Pursuant to National Securities Markets Improvement Act of 1996
("NSMIA")**

[   ] Submission to: INVESTOR PROTECTION AND SECURITIES
BUREAU ("IPS")

[   ] Securities
[   ] Theatrical Syndications
[   ] REAL ESTATE FINANCING BUREAU ("REF")

Type of Filing:

[   ] New Filing
[   ] Amendment or Renewal (If name, address or offering has changed,
indicate change):

A. BASIC IDENTIFICATION DATA

Full Name of Issuer (and Theatrical Production company, if applicable):

Address of Executive Offices: Telephone Number (   ) _____ -

(Number and Street)	(City or Town)	(State & ZIP)

Type of Organization:

[   ] business corporation

[   ] not-for-profit corporation

[   ] common fund

[   ] county, city, town or village

[   ] limited liability company

[   ] business trust

[   ] state agency or authority

([   ] agency, authority or instrumentality corporation)

[   ] limited partnership

[   ] political subdivision of state

[   ] other (specify):

Category of "Covered Security" (NSMIA):

[   ] Offering to "Qualified Purchasers" [1933 Act* §18(b)(3)]
[   ] Rule 506 Offering [1933 Act* § 4(2) - per §18(b)(4)(D)]
[   ] Other qualifying offering (specify):
* Securities Act of 1933, as amended

The Securities Will Be Sold By:

[   ] officers or directors of issuer
[   ] officers or directors of an affiliated person

[   ] salespersons employed by issuer
[   ] underwriter, dealer or broker registered in New York

For Theatrical Syndication Offerings, add the following information:
Name of proposed production:
Location of production:
Proposed opening date:

B. INFORMATION ABOUT OFFERING

Total Offering Amount (maximum) $_____Minimum Offering
Amount $_____

Type of Security Offered (brief description):

Enclosures (add additional sheets if necessary):
[   ] Copy of Consent to Service of Process (original to Department of State, Albany NY)
[   ] Offering Documents
[   ] Confidential Attachment to Form 99
[   ] Further information as to [   ] issuer [   ] affiliated persons
[   ] Form D, with Part D (State portion), plus: [   ] copy "as filed" with the S.E.C. " [   ]as filed" copy will follow
[   ] Theatrical Venture Amendment - Required Supplemental Information

C . INFORMATION ABOUT ISSUER, PRINCIPALS AND CONTROLLING PERSONS

As to issuer:

1. Is issuer subject to, or a respondent in any legal action for, any injunction, cease-and-desist order or order or stipulation to desist or refrain from any act or practice relating to the offering of securities in New York or any other jurisdiction?	[ ] Yes [ ] No
2. (a) Has issuer ever been convicted of or pleaded guilty to any crime (i) involving any fraud, or (ii) relating to any financial transaction or handling of funds of another person, or (iii) pertaining to any dealings in any securities?	[ ] Yes [ ] No
2. (b) Is issuer now a defendant in any such criminal proceeding ?	[ ] Yes [ ] No

As to each Principal*, each Controlling Person, and any Sponsoring Entity of issuer:

3. Is any one of the above subject to or a respondent in any legal action for, any injunction, cease-and-desist order or order or stipulation to desist or refrain from any act or practice relating to the offering of securities in New York or any other jurisdiction?	[ ] Yes [ ] No
4. (a) Has any one of the above ever been convicted of or pleaded guilty to any crime (i) involving any fraud, or (ii) relating to any financial transaction or handling of funds of another person, or (iii) pertaining to any dealings in any securities?	[ ] Yes [ ] No
4. (b) Is any one of the above now a defendant in any such criminal proceeding ?	[ ] Yes [ ] No
5. Has any of the above ever been suspended or expelled from membership in any securities or commodities exchange or association or had a securities or commodities license or registration denied, suspended or revoked?	[ ] Yes [ ] No
6. Has any of the above been a controlling person or sponsor with respect to any issuer which engaged in a distribution of securities or any public offering within the past three (3) years?	[ ] Yes [ ] No

If the answer to any of the above is "yes", give material facts on an attached sheet.

* Capitalized terms are defined in Section E of Form 99.

D. CERTIFICATION

The undersigned affirms and certifies, to his or her knowledge and belief after due investigation and inquiry, and under penalty of perjury, that any and all information provided in this Form 99 is true and complete, and that there are no misrepresentations, omissions or untruths contained herein. The undersigned further understands and intends that the information supplied in this Form will be relied upon by the New York State Department of Law and that any false statement made herein is punishable as a Class A misdemeanor under New York Penal Law §175.30, §210.45, or both.

Dated: _____ , 20____

Issuer (name of entity) :

By: _____

Authorized Principal or Controlling Person

_____

Print Name & Title or Affiliation

CONFIDENTIAL ATTACHMENT TO FORM 99

Issuer Name: _____

Form 99 dated: _____ , 20___

ACCESS TO THE FOLLOWING INFORMATION WILL BE WITHHELD PURSUANT TO NEW YORK PUBLIC OFFICERS LAW ("FOIL") §89(2)(b):

Identity of Principals (i) of issuer, (ii) of Controlling Person(s)* and (iii) of Sponsoring Entity:

Name	Date of Birth	Social Security Number

*Capitalized terms are defined in Section E of Form 99.

E. INSTRUCTIONS

1. General Instructions.

Who May File:

All persons engaging in an offering of or transaction in securities within or from New York which are defined as "covered securities" (other than "listed securities" or open-end management type companies registered with the S.E.C. under the Investment Company Act of 1940) under §18 of the 1933 Act as amended by NSMIA. No filing is required for listed securities. Open-end management type companies registered within the S.E.C. under the Investment Company Act of 1940 must file Form NF; other registered investment companies may file Form NF instead of Form 99.

An issuer which may be entitled to submit a Notification Filing for real estate securities may elect instead to submit to REF a filing under New York General Business Law ("GBL") §352-e or an exemption application under GBL §352-g or §359-f(2) pursuant to Policy Statements 100, 101, 102, 103 or 104. An issuer which may be entitled to submit a Notification Filing for other securities may elect instead to file with IPS an M-11 Issuer Statement under GBL §359-e or an application for exemption under §359-f(2), or in the case of theatrical productions, a filing under New York Arts and Cultural Affairs Law ("ACAL") 23.03 et seq. Theatrical ventures must also file, within ten (10) business days of the occurrence, a supplemental statement (in the form of an Amendment to Form 99) advising IPS of the (i) date of the first expenditure of investors' funds and (ii) date of the last public performance, if any, of the original production in New York State.

A request for a "No-Filing Required" letter under Policy Statement 105 (revised 1997) may also be submitted, when the issuer seeks a confirmation by the Department of Law ("DOL") that no Notification Filing is required for the proposed offering or transaction. Such request should be made under the No-Filing Category entitled: "(7) Covered Securities or Transactions Pursuant to NSMIA".

Where To File: Address for both bureaus - 120 Broadway, 23rd Floor, New York, NY 10271

(a) **IPS if:**

    i.   within New York General Business Law ("GBL") §359-e

    ii. exemptible under GBL §359-f(2) and not within clause (v) below

    iii. within ACAL §23.03 <u>etseq</u>

REF if:

    iv. real estate securities or other securities deemed within purview of GBL §352-e or §352-g

    v.   real estate securities exemptible under GBL §359-f(2), including governmental issuers and debt instruments secured by or resting upon revenues, earnings or proceeds of resale or disposition of real estate

When To File: Prior to any sale or offer for sale of securities in or from New York. For theatrical ventures, supplemental statements are required within ten (10) business days of the occurrence, advising DOL (in the form of Amendment to Form 99) of (i) date of the first expenditure of investors' funds and (ii) date of the last public performance, if any, of the original production in New York State.

Copies Required: Two (2) copies of Form 99 must be filed, one of which must be manually signed, along with a photocopy of the manually signed copy. <u>One (1) copy of the Offering Documents must also be filed</u>

Information Required: A new filing must contain all information requested. Amendments require only notification of changes with respect to information given in Form 99.

Form D: In addition to Form 99, submit a copy of Form D as filed. In the event that form D has not yet been filed with the S.E.C., submit a copy of the unfiled Form D (including Part D), and provide information as to when such filing will be effected ("as filed" copy must be submitted when so filed).

Non-Resident Issuers: Consent to Service of Process must be filed with the Department of State, 41 State Street, Albany, NY 12231; a copy must be filed with Form 99.

Effect of Filing: A Notification Filing is deemed made when received at the address given on Form 99. In the event that the information given in the Notification Filing is incomplete, or conflicts with or is otherwise inconsistent with other information in the possession of DOL, the issuer will be notified. Notification Filings shall <u>not</u> be effective for the following offerings or transactions:

a. Any offering wherein the issuer, or its Controlling Person(s) or its Sponsor(s), or one or more of its Principals, or one or more principals of a Controlling Person or a Sponsor (i) are, or during the past six years have been, enjoined from the offer or sale of securities within or from the State of New York, <u>or</u> (ii) have entered into a stipulation or consent, which remains currently in effect, to desist or refrain from making offers of sales of securities within or from the State of New York <u>unless and until</u> the Attorney General makes a determination that these facts or circumstances do not appear to amount to a violation of such prior judgment, order or stipulation, or do not themselves constitute a violation of GBL Article 23-A, or that such action as to the Form 99 filing is not necessary to protect the public interest; and

b. Any offering which involves the purchasers' rights to occupy or utilize real estate or facilities which constitute cooperative interests in realty or a User Syndication requiring a full filing under GBL §352-e.

2. Definitions.

The terms set forth below shall be defined as follows for purposes of completing this Form 99:

a. **Controlling Person** shall mean: Every person who, by or through stock ownership, agency, or otherwise, or who, pursuant to or in connection with an agreement or understanding with one or more other persons by or through stock ownership, agency, or otherwise, controls any person liable under §11 or §12 of the 1933 Act, as amended.

b. **Offering Documents** shall mean: Any printed materials in which is presented, without limitation, the terms of the transaction, a description of the securities offered, the operative documents for the entity which may be formed, any supporting documents and/or the subscription instruments for the investor.

c. **Principal** or **principals**shall mean: One or more (i) general partners of a partnership, (ii) managing members of a limited liability company, (iii) trustees of a trust, (iv) managing directors of an association or other organization, (v) directors of a corporation who hold or control 10% or more of its voting shares or who are also officers, (v) the six highest-ranking officers of a corporation, association or similar entity, including the chief executive officer, the chief operating officer, the chief financial officer, the chief legal officer, and the three highest-ranking vice-presidents (including any previously referred to), (vi) individuals or entities holding 33% or more of the voting equity interest in an entity, **and/or** (vii) individuals who have the status of a person in one or more of the previous clauses with respect to any entity that itself is a principal of the issuer.

d. **Sponsor** or **Sponsoring Entity** shall mean: One or more individuals or entities (i) for whose account or benefit, indirect or otherwise, an issue of securities or an issuer has been created or originated, or (ii) who or which has a proprietary interest in and who directs or takes an active role in the creation, origination or promotion of the issuer or in the acquisition of business activities, business property or investment portfolio items thereof, but excludingattorneys, accountants, engineers, architects, appraisers, real estate brokers, property managers or other contractors or professionals performing services for contractual compensation.

e. **User Syndication** shall mean: Any offering of real estate securities wherein the investors (i) will be entitled to occupy a portion of the issuer's real property, or (ii) will be privileged to utilize the issuer's property or facilities, as members or participants (and not as members of the general public).

3. Filing Fees: Payment should be made by check or money order to "New York State Department of Law" in accordance with GBL §352-e(7)(a) and §359-e(5), or the following schedule may be used:

FEE AMOUNT	OFFERING OR TRANSACTION
$700	• GBL §352-e and §359-e • formerly P.S. *100 or P.S. 101 filing • under Rule 506 of Regulation D • $500 thousand or less offering amount
$1,300	• GBL §352-e and §359-e • formerly P.S. 100 or P.S. 101 filing • under Rule 506 of Regulation D • more than $500 thousand offering amount
$500	• under GBL §352-e or §352-g • formerly P.S. 102 filing • S.E.C. registered as (i) firm commitment underwriting or (ii) distribution to holders of issuer's securities • no GBL §359-e registration
$200	• formerly P.S. 103 or P.S. 104 filing • otherwise eligible per GBL §359-f(2) application for GBL §359-e and/or §352-e exemption
$800	• under GBL §359-e • more than $500 thousand offering amount • not subject to any special filing provision ** • effective for four (4) years
$200	• under GBL §359-e • $500 thousand or less offering amount • not subject to any special filing provision ** • effective for four (4) years
$0	• under ACAL §23.03 etseq.

DOL Policy Statements - available from REF.
** GBL §352-e; GBL §352-g; GBL §359-ff; ACAL §23.03 <u>et</u> <u>seq</u>; New York Business Corporation Law Article 16.